Foundations of Social Entrepreneurship

Foundations of Social Entrepreneurship presents definitions of social entrepreneurship, explains its benefits and challenges, describes the components of an ecosystem of support, and presents practical tools to approach social entrepreneurial projects. It is designed to be easily approachable by anyone without prior in-depth knowledge of the subject. The book is divided into two parts; the first provides readers with theoretical foundations to understand the phenomenon of social entrepreneurship, its different interpretations, the context in which it developed, and its socio-economic function. The second part of the book covers what it takes to create and manage a social entrepreneurial initiative. Pedagogical features are incorporated throughout to aid learning. They include summary tables, international case studies of social entrepreneurs from both developed and emerging economies, as well as suggested exercises and examples of how the tools presented are used in practice. Truly global in its scope, with a strong emphasis on combining theory with practice, this text should be core reading for advanced undergraduate and postgraduate students studying Social Entrepreneurship, Enterprise, and Responsible Business. Online resources include links to resources, chapter-by-chapter PowerPoint slides and instructor's manual.

Tanja Collavo is Senior Teaching Associate at the Cambridge Institute for Sustainability Leadership, where she acts as director of the Master of Studies (MSt) in Sustainability Leadership, flexible route and of the Postgraduate Diploma in Sustainable Business.

Foundations of Social Entrepreneurship

Theory, Practical Tools and Skills

Tanja Collavo

Routledge
Taylor & Francis Group

LONDON AND NEW YORK

Cover image: Getty Images

First published 2023
by Routledge
4 Park Square, Milton Park, Abingdon, Oxon OX14 4RN

and by Routledge
605 Third Avenue, New York, NY 10158

Routledge is an imprint of the Taylor & Francis Group, an informa business

British Library Cataloguing-in-Publication Data
A catalogue record for this book is available from the British Library

Library of Congress Cataloging-in-Publication Data
Names: Collavo, Tanja, 1988– author.
Title: Foundations of social entrepreneurship : theory, practical tools and skills / Tanja Collavo.
Description: Milton Park, Abingdon, Oxon ; New York, NY : Routledge, 2023. | Includes bibliographical references and index. |
Identifiers: LCCN 2022023284 (print) | LCCN 2022023285 (ebook) | ISBN 9780367640217 (hardback) | ISBN 9780367640231 (paperback) | ISBN 9781003121824 (ebook)
Subjects: LCSH: Social entrepreneurship. | Social values—Economic aspects.
Classification: LCC HD60 .C589 2023 (print) | LCC HD60 (ebook) | DDC 658.4/08—dc23/eng/20220531
LC record available at https://lccn.loc.gov/2022023284
LC ebook record available at https://lccn.loc.gov/2022023285

ISBN: 978-0-367-64021-7 (hbk)
ISBN: 978-0-367-64023-1 (pbk)
ISBN: 978-1-003-12182-4 (ebk)

DOI: 10.4324/9781003121824

Typeset in Sabon
by codeMantra

Access the Support Material: www.routledge.com/9780367640231

Contents

Figures

Tables

About the author

Tanja Collavo is Senior Teaching Associate at the Cambridge Institute for Sustainability Leadership, where she acts as director of the Postgraduate Diploma and Master of Studies (MSt) in Sustainability Leadership, Flexible Route. Since 2017, she has been a tutor for the course on Social Entrepreneurship delivered by the University of Oxford, Department of Continuing Education, through which she has tutored over 500 aspiring social entrepreneurs and people of various ages and from various backgrounds interested in learning more about social entrepreneurship. Previously, she has worked as stipendiary lecturer in general management for Jesus College and Exeter College, University of Oxford, and has supported the teaching of various subjects including strategy, leadership, and rethinking business to undergraduate and MBA students at Saïd Business School, University of Oxford.

She has completed a PhD in Management Studies at Saïd Business School in 2018, with a thesis on the brokerage strategies that enabled four organisations to develop the social entrepreneurship sector in England. After her PhD, she continued her research in social entrepreneurship and social innovation as research assistant at the Skoll Centre for Social Entrepreneurship, Saïd Business School, and attempted the co-foundation of a social enterprise. Her research interests include social entrepreneurship, stakeholders' management, and networking strategies to foster multidisciplinary and multi-sector collaborations.

She has published journal articles on social entrepreneurship in the *Journal of Entrepreneurship, Management and Innovation* and in the *New College Collection*, and she co-authored with Prof Alex Nicholls a book chapter on the same topic for the *Atlas of Social Innovation*. She also presented her research at international conferences such as the *Academic of Management Annual Meeting* and the *Annual Conference on Social Entrepreneurship* and she is working on the publication of a journal article and on a book on collaborations.

Acknowledgements

This book would not exist without the precious support and inspiration provided by my students. In my work as tutor and lecturer I have had the privilege to interact with many bright and curious students, whose questions and contributions have kept on refining my understanding of social entrepreneurship and have given me the motivation and determination to write this book. I wish I could thank each of them individually – this book is for them and for those who will come after them.

I also would like to thank Paola Masperi, for the support and access given to build the case study on *Mayamiko*, and Goya Gallagher, for the support and access given to build the case study on *Malaika*.

Finally, I would like to thank my partner, Matt Bilyard, and my close friend, Kate Heathward, for reading significant parts of the book and providing me with feedback from the perspective of someone not familiar with social entrepreneurship, and the several colleagues – Professor Alex Nicholls, Professor Jaideep Prabhu, Fons van der Velden, Dr Deborah Anderson, Dr Heli Helanummi-Cole, and Dr Lilia Giugni – who provided precious expert comments on chapters or sections of this book, and suggested resources and ways to improve them.

Introduction

Tutoring a course on social entrepreneurship for several years has brought to my attention the knowledge needs of very diverse cohorts of students, comprising people from all over the world and aged anything in-between 18 and 80. Some of the students I have had the privilege of tutoring were aspiring social entrepreneurs, keen to learn the tools of the trade and the social business models they could potentially adopt in their organisation. Some others were simply interested in learning more about social entrepreneurship or were looking for inspiration to become social intrapreneurs or support social entrepreneurs. What they were looking for ranged from a basic understanding of social entrepreneurship, to support in setting up their own organisation or specific insights on topics such as fundraising or impact measurement. In each of the countries they came from, which span four continents and various levels of economic development, social entrepreneurship meant something different and was applied and supported in different ways. So how to bring and teach something valuable to all of them, given such diversity?

This book is the result of my answer to that question and of my work as a tutor, as well as of what I learnt through my now almost decade-long research on social entrepreneurship and my interaction with many social entrepreneurs and supporters of social entrepreneurship. It combines all that I learnt in relation to what social entrepreneurship means, theories about what it should achieve and how it should be supported, and best practice in relation to creating and managing social entrepreneurial organisations. As such, I hope it will help many more students become passionate about social entrepreneurship in the years to come and to realise their social entrepreneurial ideas and impact goals.

This book targets students and readers from any country and of any age who are curious and keen to learn more about social entrepreneurship but have relatively little experience or prior knowledge of it. In order to support their learning journey, the book features a mix of theoretical insights, practical examples, and case studies from all over the world, to see how theory relates to practice, as well as exercises to experience first-hand and reflect further on what is presented in the various chapters, practical frameworks and tools to engage in social entrepreneurship (e.g. to spot opportunities, further develop a social entrepreneurial idea, and start the creation of an organisation that will hopefully deliver positive social or environmental impact while achieving financial sustainability), and open-ended questions to verify and challenge their understanding of social entrepreneurship. This makes this book particularly suitable for undergraduate courses on social entrepreneurship and related concepts, such as social impact and social innovation, or for professionals who are approaching social entrepreneurship as part of a career change or life-long learning.

DOI: 10.4324/9781003121824-1

The book is divided into two parts. The first part provides readers with theoretical foundations to understand the phenomenon of social entrepreneurship, its different interpretations, the contexts in which it developed and operates, its socio-economic functions, and its future prospects. Chapter 1 introduces social entrepreneurship both as a concept and as an activity, discusses its historical development and its various definitions, and specifies how social entrepreneurship is conceptualised in the book. Chapter 2 introduces and explains concepts that are related to social entrepreneurship, such as social change, social impact, and social innovation, and activities and organisations that are frequently associated with social entrepreneurship (e.g. traditional entrepreneurship, charities, B Corps, social movements), explaining how social entrepreneurship overlaps with and differs from each of them. Chapter 3 discusses common features attributed to successful social entrepreneurs and the main characteristics of social enterprises, to help students understand how social entrepreneurship might look like in practice. Chapter 4 introduces the concept of "ecosystem" and discusses the various stakeholders that are fundamental for social entrepreneurship to thrive and the roles that they play in relation to it. It also presents the key environmental forces shaping social entrepreneurship ecosystems around the world and the main stages of development that social entrepreneurship ecosystems present. Chapter 5 concludes the first part of the book with some reflections on the achievements and limitations that social entrepreneurship has presented up to date, focusing on recurring challenges that social entrepreneurial organisations have to face and overcome and on ways in which the development of social entrepreneurship can be sustained going forward. The chapter finishes by introducing the concept of systems change, which is increasingly popular in social entrepreneurship ecosystems, and by explaining the basics of systems analysis, systems thinking, and systems leadership, which are approaches thought to support the realisation of systems change.

The second part of the book covers practical tools and insights to spot opportunities for social entrepreneurship, develop a social entrepreneurial idea, and establish a social entrepreneurial organisation. The goal of this second part is to introduce readers to what it takes, in practice, to engage in social entrepreneurship, and to key considerations that aspiring social entrepreneurs need to make to increase their chance of realising positive social and/or environmental impact and to effectively realise something that can be defined as social entrepreneurship. Chapter 6 discusses the importance of gathering knowledge to spot opportunities and presents some tools – codebooks and mind maps – that can help in this regard, as well as tools and frameworks, such as Porter's Five Forces, SWOT analysis, PESTEL analysis, and variations thereof, that can be used for assessing competitors, the landscape of existing solutions, and the environmental forces at play. Chapter 7 introduces Design Thinking as a process that can both support the gathering of knowledge and the development of social entrepreneurial ideas and solutions, providing an overview of how to conduct it and of its main advantages and limitations. Additionally, it explains the importance for any social entrepreneurial organisation to elaborate a mission statement, and how to do so, and to translate its mission into concrete plans, actions, and, eventually, impact. For this purpose, the chapter discusses the concept of Theory of Change and how to build one. Chapter 8 continues the journey began in Chapter 7 by introducing social business models as a way to plan and strategise how to realise a Theory of Change, and by explaining how to build a social business model canvas. It then presents some marketing fundamentals that can help social entrepreneurial organisations to attract resources to implement their social business model and to deliver their value proposition. Chapter 9 discusses the main elements that make up a social entrepreneurial organisation – its legal form, governance structures, organisational structure, leadership style, human resource management, organisational culture, and adherence to ethics – focusing on the challenges and characteristics related to each of them that are specific to organisations wanting to realise social and/or environmental impact adopting an entrepreneurial and innovative approach. Chapter 10 presents the challenges that social entrepreneurial organisations face in securing the necessary funds to operate and the main funding options available to them. It then introduces three elements that successful social entrepreneurial organisations need to learn how to manage – networks, risks, and growth – presenting some tools and insights that can help to manage them. Finally, Chapter 11 discusses impact measurement, reflecting on the challenges it presents, explaining the main approaches used to engage in this activity in social entrepreneurship ecosystems, and providing some tips on how to identify helpful metrics, set up an impact measurement system, and report the impact achieved.

I hope this book will inspire and engage many students and aspiring social entrepreneurs, and support many social entrepreneurial organisations, providing them with the knowledge and tools to increase their understanding of social entrepreneurship and their chances of success in realising social and environmental impact in innovative ways. In a world characterised by global challenges, a climate crisis, and wicked problems, social entrepreneurship is needed more than ever, not only to directly create positive social and environmental impact but also to act as catalysts of attention, resources, and solutions. I hope you will enjoy the journey and find your own special way to contribute to a more just and inclusive society!

Part 1

Theoretical foundations of social entrepreneurship

1 Introduction to social entrepreneurship

Key content

This chapter introduces social entrepreneurship both as a concept and as an activity. It briefly explores its history, before discussing in detail the different meanings it can have and the way it is going to be defined in this book.

1.1 A first glimpse into social entrepreneurship
1.2 Historic and global overview
1.3 The many definitions of social entrepreneurship
1.4 This book's definition of social entrepreneurship

Learning objectives

- Get a broad understanding of the concept of social entrepreneurship.
- Learn how social entrepreneurship developed as a concept and as an activity in different parts of the world.
- Distinguish the main schools of thought on what social entrepreneurship is about.
- Reflect on the factors driving the emergence of social entrepreneurship as a concept.
- Understand how social entrepreneurship and related concepts are defined in this book.

1.1 A first glimpse into social entrepreneurship

Social entrepreneurship has been on the rise as a global phenomenon for the past 30 years. In several countries, there are courses on social entrepreneurship, networks that support social entrepreneurs, legislation regulating social enterprises, and different funders ready to support social entrepreneurial initiatives. A notable example of social entrepreneurship is that of *Grameen Bank*, the first financial intermediary providing micro-credit to those unserved by the traditional financial system. Another one is the *Aravind Eye Hospital*, delivering for the first time essential eye surgery and eye care to those who could not afford it, by standardising procedures and asking those who could afford to pay to cover the costs of operating on poorer patients in exchange for add-on services. Further examples of social entrepreneurship around the world are numerous and increasingly well-known: from bakeries that train and employ women

DOI: 10.4324/9781003121824-3

who suffered from domestic violence to gyms that reinvest their profits into diversity and inclusion programmes; from producers of bottled water that set up clean water systems in Africa to organisations bringing healthcare services to rural villages by leveraging old vehicles and mobile technology. In all likelihood, you are using the products or services of at least one social enterprise in your daily life – but you might not be aware of it. As a concept, social entrepreneurship is still relatively vague and unknown. Many entrepreneurs and organisations do not know that they are engaging in social entrepreneurship and/or they prefer not to label themselves as social entrepreneurs, social enterprises, or other forms of social entrepreneurial organisations, because they fear to confuse their audience.

As the name suggests, social entrepreneurship is a phenomenon that brings together social and community concerns with a business mindset, entrepreneurial innovation, and market considerations. That said, there are many different definitions of what these two words – social and entrepreneurship – mean when they are put together. This is because:

1 Even as standalone words, both "social" and "entrepreneurship" present multiple definitions.
2 The individuals and organisations that pushed for the establishment and growth of social entrepreneurship in the late 1990s had very different views on what it should be about.
3 The variety of socio-economic contexts in which social entrepreneurship exists means that there are different gaps to fill and issues to tackle, different interpretations of how social entrepreneurship could support further socio-economic development, and different approaches to legislating on and regulating this activity.
4 Social entrepreneurship takes place through various organisational forms and social business models, creating a variety of practice that is hard to group under a single definition.
5 The involvement of universities in conceptualising social entrepreneurship created a multitude of definitions and related debate, which spread into the world of practice.

So, in the end, what is social entrepreneurship?

Social entrepreneurship sits in between the private, public, and third sectors (Figure 1.1). It combines the skills, mindset, and tools of business, with the understanding of social problems and closeness to beneficiaries typical of the third sector, and the desire to advance public interests, welfare, and social equality typical of the public sector. Additionally, it operates in collaboration with all three of these sectors, and tries to compensate for their failures. For example, social entrepreneurship aims to help and empower people to solve the social and environmental issues that traditional sectors are unable to address due to a lack of knowledge and/or resources, or that they inadvertently make worse through their behaviours and policies.

Sitting at the intersection of these three traditional sectors means that to engage in social entrepreneurship it is important to speak the language of each, to understand their constraints and resources, to relate to them and to value their contributions to society while trying to make up for their shortcomings. It also requires at least aiming to achieve a double or triple bottom line. A double bottom line is the combination of social impact with financial sustainability (which implies the ability to cover costs through different forms of funding over the medium- to long term, and not profitability). A triple bottom line is the simultaneous pursuit of social impact, financial sustainability,

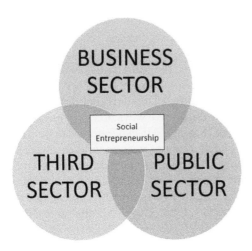

Figure 1 The location of social entrepreneurship in relation to traditional sectors

and the protection of the environment. While there are currently not many examples of triple bottom line in the social entrepreneurship space, climate change and growing concerns for the environment are encouraging an increasing number of social entrepreneurial organisations to minimise their carbon footprint while achieving their social mission. Before exploring the different forms of social entrepreneurship, however, it is important to understand its history both as a concept and as an activity.

1.2 Historic and global overview

When discussing the history of social entrepreneurship, it is important to distinguish between social entrepreneurship as an activity and social entrepreneurship as a concept, since the two have different roots and origins.

1.2.1 Social entrepreneurship as an activity

Social entrepreneurship existed as an activity well before it was formally recognised as a concept. From the Enlightenment, societies have encouraged private initiatives to generate economic and social benefits. Cooperatives and initiatives to entrepreneurially support local communities – such as colonies – have been going on for almost two centuries. For example, in 1844, a group of artisans employed in cotton mills in Rochdale, a town in the north of England, established a cooperative business, the *Rochdale Equitable Pioneers Society*. Written testimonies of what we would now define as social entrepreneurship emerged in Europe and in the Americas already in the 19th century. Robert Owen, a Welsh entrepreneur who operated in the cotton trade, tried in the first half of the 19th century to provide his workers with education opportunities both for themselves and their families. He built "villages of cooperation", where his workers could grow their own food and create their own products as ways to improve the livelihoods of their families. Similarly, The *Fundacion Social*, a foundation aiming to generate revenues to enhance its social impact, was reported as existing in Colombia in 1911.

Significant efforts to foster socio-economic development through private, entrepreneurial initiatives were prompted by the aftermath of World War II. Many countries around the world had suffered innumerable losses, from human, social, and economic points of view. This created a widespread need for poverty alleviation, social solidarity, and reconstruction initiatives. At the same time, the Marshall Plan, the creation of international organisations to sustain peace and human rights, and the technological development triggered by the war, created an unprecedented availability of resources and opportunities to produce social impact in innovative ways. *Oxfam* opened its first charity shop to sustain part of its activities through self-generated income in 1948. Enterprises employing vulnerable people, such as those with mental or physical disabilities, otherwise excluded from the job market, were reported in the United States and in Europe in the 1960s. The *Grameen Bank* – now described as one of the main examples of social entrepreneurship – was founded in Bangladesh in the late 1970s and was established as an official bank in 1983. One of the so-called antecedents of social entrepreneurship, the Fair Trade movement, also emerged between the 1940s, when the first NGOs and religious organisations started to sell raw materials and handicrafts produced in rural communities across the globe, and the early 1990s, when the *Fairtrade Foundation* and related label were created.

The birth and growth of these different entrepreneurial forms of delivering social impact over time attracted the attention of several stakeholders – from governments keen to promote this form of activism and citizen participation through favourable legislation, to philanthropists and businesspeople keen to support ways to help society that they believed had the potential to succeed. This, in turn, triggered both more initiatives of this kind and a growing awareness that bringing them under the same umbrella might help to attract even more resources and support. This is how the concept of social entrepreneurship as a distinct activity ultimately came to be.

1.2.2 Social entrepreneurship as a concept

As a concept, social entrepreneurship was created and brought to the fore in the 1990s and early 2000s. Banks and Drucker were among the first to introduce the words "social entrepreneur" and "social enterprise" in the 1970s, within their work on social movements and corporate social responsibility respectively. However, in their writings those concepts were far from being central and passed relatively unobserved until much later on. Dennis Young, an American scholar, and Bill Drayton, the founder of *Ashoka*, talked about "innovative non-profit entrepreneurs" and "innovators for the public" respectively in the 1980s, in order to define whom we now call social entrepreneurs. Similarly, in 1991, the Italian government promulgated a law regulating "social cooperatives", which are now often considered as a form of social enterprise. However, in all these cases, there was no mention of social entrepreneurship or related concepts as such. "Social" and "entrepreneurship" only started to appear together regularly and frequently in articles and reports published in Europe and in the United States between 1993 and 1998. Key examples in this sense are:

- Harvard Business School creating the *Social Enterprise Initiative* in 1993;
- *Demos*, a UK think tank, publishing a report describing social entrepreneurship as a community-based phenomenon for local regeneration;
- George R. Roberts launching the *Roberts Enterprise Development Fund* to support social enterprises generating employment opportunities in 1997;

- The Inter-American Development Bank replacing its *Small Projects Fund* with the *Social Entrepreneurship Program* in the 1990s;
- Professor Gregory Dees writing a seminal paper titled *The meaning of "social entrepreneurship"* in 1998.

After the first few references to the concept of social entrepreneurship appeared in the United States and the United Kingdom, the idea was picked up by several academics, by the public media, and by a handful of US foundations and UK think tanks. The latter immediately saw the great potential of legitimating entrepreneurial approaches to delivering social impact and tackling the mounting global challenges that existing actors clearly were not able to tackle at sufficient speed and scale. In particular, the concept appealed to Silicon Valley's young millionaires, who perceived entrepreneurship as necessary to solve problems quickly and were sceptical about the ability of governments and NGOs to address complex issues and to manage resources efficiently and effectively.

Among the initial supporters of social entrepreneurship was Bill Drayton, who quickly re-labelled social entrepreneurs as the "innovators for the public" that his organisation – *Ashoka* – supported, and who started to theorise on what their added value was and how to best help them. His work, combined with that of some academics and think tanks, soon inspired other philanthropic organisations, such as the *Schwab Foundation* and the *Skoll Foundation*. In the late 1990s and early 2000s respectively, these started to support individuals, whom they judged to be social entrepreneurs, and to promote their work in elite business and government circles. In the same period, social entrepreneurship became popular in the United Kingdom, where the New Labour government saw in this activity the opportunity to innovate and extend welfare services across the country, and the Coalition government that followed it kept investing in the sector as a way to guarantee welfare during austerity. The government's creation of tailored grants and of a supporting infrastructure for social entrepreneurship eventually attracted several private actors into this new area of activity in the United Kingdom, and prompted the creation of many organisations with the purpose of encouraging social entrepreneurial endeavours, such as *Social Enterprise London*, the *Community Action Network*, and the *School for Social Entrepreneurs*.

Between 2000 and 2005, the concept of social entrepreneurship also gradually picked up in the rest of Western Europe, where the tradition of social business had been supported for decades by the cooperative movement and where the European Union (EU) became a key promoter of this concept. It took instead around five to ten years longer for social entrepreneurship to start emerging in Eastern Europe and China, where the recent communist past or ongoing communist orientation had perpetuated the idea that welfare and social provision were a duty of the state and where a supporting infrastructure started to emerge only as ideas on social entrepreneurship slowly trickled from the West. In both regions, governmental support for and local development of social entrepreneurship markedly increased from around 2010–2015, as signalled by national and local government initiatives, certification programmes, and the rise of organisations defining themselves as social enterprises or adopting forms typical of social entrepreneurship, such as cooperatives or for-profit businesses generating employment opportunities for the marginalised.

Anecdotal evidence and some regional reports and studies suggest that social entrepreneurship also spread in Asia, Africa, and Latin America starting from the early 2000s and in particular after 2010. For example, South Korea introduced the Social

Enterprise Promotion Act in 2007 and Vietnam reported 200 self-identified social enterprises in a survey in 2011. According to a 2016 report on social entrepreneurship published by the Inter-American Development Bank, countries like Chile, Colombia, and Mexico presented flourishing, although still early stage, social entrepreneurship ecosystems. The rise of social entrepreneurship in some of these areas, while obviously varying according to the socio-economic and political context of specific countries, is often attributed to a combination of factors. These include micro-entrepreneurship (sometimes prompted by international and religious organisations), reductions in donations and funds that pushed many local charities to look into revenue-generating opportunities, and the thought-leadership and the ability to attract support at the country level of international organisations such as *Ashoka* or the *British Council*, which wanted to develop social entrepreneurship in many countries of the Global South and, in particular, in Asia and Africa. Similarly, historical connections with the United Kingdom supported the development of social entrepreneurship in countries like Australia and New Zealand, which could tap into UK-based expertise to start developing their own social entrepreneurship ecosystems.

Again though, the history of the concept and of the activity differs. For example, Bangladesh is home to the two most famous social enterprises at a worldwide level – *BRAC* and the *Grameen Bank* – both founded in the 1970s. This is no coincidence since while the concept of social entrepreneurship reached this country only recently, social entrepreneurial practices have been strongly encouraged since the early 1970s, as the country was trying to recover from the devastating Bhola cyclone and from the Bangladesh Liberation War.

The exact extent of the development of social entrepreneurship at a global level is not known, due to a lack of comparative and rigorous studies, and global surveys. As of 2015, when the Global Entrepreneurship Monitor did its latest survey (which was affected by several data and measurement issues) on social entrepreneurship, individuals that defined themselves as engaging in social entrepreneurship existed across all continents, with peaks of activity (10% or more of adult population) in countries as diverse as Peru, Hungary, Burkina Faso, Colombia, Senegal, Poland, Chile, Cameroon, the Philippines, Luxembourg, India, and Israel. In terms of regions, as a percentage of adult population, the highest social entrepreneurship activity (over 10% of adult population) was recorded by the same survey in Australia and the United States and in sub-Saharan Africa, with Middle East and North Africa, Eastern Europe, Western Europe, and Latin America all showing similar levels of overall activity (4–6%).[1]

1.2.3 *The trends behind the rise of social entrepreneurship*

As social entrepreneurship gained traction in the first and second decades of the new millennium, many existing initiatives, including all those mentioned in Section 1.2.1, have been re-labelled as social entrepreneurship and many new entrepreneurial non-profits and businesses interested in delivering social impact rather than (just) profits have emerged. The reason why the creation of this new sector and the re-labelling of some existing initiatives took place in the late 1990s and early 2000s can be explained through the combination of several factors.

1   **The effects of globalisation and new communication channels.** Globalisation, fostered by an unprecedented development of communication and transportation technologies, escalated exponentially from the late 1980s and connected the world

like never before. This generated a new awareness of some exploitative business practices, rising inequalities, of the interconnectedness and interdependency of systems and countries, and of increasingly intense and complex global issues. It also highlighted the failures of governments, businesses, and existing international organisations to tackle social and environmental issues at the necessary speed and scale and their role, in some cases, in exacerbating them. This increased the demand for innovative solutions to global challenges, interest in how to reshape the role of businesses in society, and prompted citizens worldwide to take the matter into their own hands, through means as various as private initiatives (e.g. social entrepreneurship), community initiatives (e.g. cooperatives, associations), online and social media discussions, boycotts, and protests/social movements.

2 **Increasing emphasis on innovation, accountability, and entrepreneurship in the third sector.** Technological development and an increasing belief in the power of innovation and entrepreneurship to spur economic and social development have created pressures for organisations in all sectors to become more innovative and entrepreneurial in order to obtain funds and legitimacy. Similarly, accounting and performance measurement practices have moved from the business to all other sectors, as various stakeholders (i.e. parties that have an interest in the organisation and affect or are affected by it) demand more accountability. This, combined with increasing competition for resources in the third sector due to decreasing productivity, diminishing government funding, and rising number of third-sector organisations, changed the practices of many non-profits. These started to look into revenue-generating options, ways to increase their efficiency and effectiveness, and innovative and entrepreneurial opportunities to address social and environmental issues.

3 **Governments embracing social entrepreneurship as a public policy tool.** As many governments attempted to reform and innovate welfare services, foster development of rural areas, keep up with rapid socio-economic changes, or manage tighter public budgets, they saw the emerging concept of social entrepreneurship as a helpful means to carry out their policies. For this reason, they introduced social entrepreneurship in official documents and policies; created special funds, legislation, and initiatives to support social enterprises; and promoted this new concept as a way to help the transition of countries into market economies and the creation of employment opportunities. This, in turn, pushed many individuals and organisations to join the trend and establish organisations that could be defined as engaging in social entrepreneurship.

4 **Demographic challenges.** Demographic phenomena such as population growth, increasing life expectancy, migrations, urbanisation, women empowerment/entrance in the workforce, or the shift away from traditional family structures have generated new social needs, such as care services for children and the elderly, integration opportunities, and more sustainable cities. Responding to these needs fast and well enough has contributed to the emergence of new businesses delivering social services or promoting sustainability while pursuing revenues and profits.

5 **A new generation of philanthropists.** The explosive growth of the internet made many young entrepreneurs millionaires in a matter of years, enabling them to turn to philanthropy at a very early age. Having made their fortunes through entrepreneurship and being disillusioned about the ability of governments and large international organisations to tackling complex and fast-changing social issues, these new millionaires decided to challenge traditional approaches to charity

and philanthropy and to sustain initiatives combining social impact with a solid entrepreneurial approach. These new philanthropists, in some cases, not only funded social entrepreneurship but catalysed support, legitimacy, and funds from other sectors, thanks to their existing networks, accelerating the creation of narratives and infrastructure sustaining this activity. This, in turn, prompted existing organisations and initiatives to re-label themselves as social entrepreneurs or social enterprises.

6   **Universities developed research and courses on social entrepreneurship.** Ever since the late 1990s, researchers across Europe, the United Kingdom and the United States began to pay attention to social entrepreneurship. This, often with the support and encouragement of new philanthropists, led to the creation of research projects and centres and taught courses on social entrepreneurship. These over time, contributed to the legitimation of this concept. In particular, the teaching of social entrepreneurship created many young graduates willing to engage in social entrepreneurship or to support it through roles in traditional sectors.

Having explored the roots of social entrepreneurship both as an activity and as a concept, it is possible to start understanding its different definitions, which mostly derive from its history and the complex global context in which this concept came to prominence.

1.3   The many definitions of social entrepreneurship

There are still many definitions of social entrepreneurship. Some focus on social enterprises; some on social entrepreneurs and their characteristics; some on social entrepreneurship as a process; some on the operating sectors, missions, and outcomes associated with social entrepreneurship as an activity. Overall, the main definitions of social entrepreneurship can be grouped into three different schools of thought:

a   The Innovation School of Thought
b   The Business School of Thought
c   The Community School of Thought.

Besides these three schools, there are two additional interpretations of social entrepreneurship that were very popular at the beginning of the movement but have now largely been incorporated by one or more of the former three – the Earned Revenues and Shared Ownership schools of thought.

1.3.1   *The Innovation School of Thought*

The **Innovation School of Thought** (IST) is based on the Schumpeterian tradition, which defines traditional entrepreneurs as innovators driving markets and society forward through processes of creative destruction. It focuses on individual social entrepreneurs and sees them as the founders of innovative non-profit organisations, empowering people, and challenging the status quo to end injustice, inequalities, and entrenched social issues, thus ultimately catalysing social transformation. The IST originates from the thinking of US-based organisations such as *Ashoka*, the *Skoll Foundation*, and *Echoing Green*, and of US academics such as Gregory Dees. For example, *Ashoka* defines social entrepreneurs as "individuals with innovative solutions to society's most pressing social, cultural, and environmental challenges. They are ambitious and persistent – tackling major issues and offering new ideas for systems-level change".[2] Similarly, in his foundational paper on social entrepreneurship titled *The Meaning of Social Entrepreneurship*, Gregory Dees defines social entrepreneurs as

> one species in the genus entrepreneur .... They play the role of change agents in the social sector, by:
>> Adopting a mission to create and sustain social value (not just private value),
>> Recognizing and relentlessly pursuing new opportunities to serve that mission,
>> Engaging in a process of continuous innovation, adaptation, and learning,
>> Acting boldly without being limited by resources currently in hand, and
>> Exhibiting a heightened sense of accountability to the constituencies served and
> for the outcomes created.[3]

An example of a social entrepreneur as defined by the IST was Paul Farmer, co-founder of *Partners in Health* (PIH). As a student of Medical Anthropology, he went to Haiti to help people in need of healthcare in rural villages. There, he saw many locals suffering and dying from diseases that in other countries had been cured easily for several decades or even a century. He realised that poverty deprives people of the basic human right to healthcare. That experience changed his life forever. He decided that he wanted to do something more than volunteering to ensure that even the poorest of the poor could access basic healthcare and vaccines. Together with other medics and volunteers – Jim Yong Kim, Ophelia Dahl, Thomas J. White, and Todd McCormack – he co-founded PIH. PIH's mission is to provide a preferential option for the poor in healthcare, doing whatever it takes to make people, who have no other hope or access to health services, get better. The organisation started to operate in Haiti but kept expanding as the co-founders, among whom Paul Farmer has played a leading role, combined work on the field – helping to heal the poor – with lobbying actions and campaigns in the United States. These allowed PIH to obtain global recognition and the funds necessary to grow. Currently, PIH operates in 12 countries, providing over 2 million health visits, either in a clinic or at home, every year. Moreover, following the vision and ambition of its co-founders, it has expanded into providing training programmes for community health workers, research initiatives, mental health support, and to tackle gender inequality in accessing healthcare.

1.3.2 The Business School of Thought

The **Business School of Thought** (BST) focuses on organisations rather than individuals and defines social enterprises as businesses whose main goal is to generate social and/or environmental impact. In other words, it implies that social enterprises are for-profit businesses operating in any sector through market-based mechanisms but pursuing a double or triple bottom line instead of just profits. This view does not exclude the possibility that social enterprises might need to rely on grants or other forms of funding to survive. However, it requires that a significant portion of a social enterprise's funds derives from self-generated revenues obtained by selling products or services in a market. The BST does not have a defined origin, and it is probably the most adopted view of social entrepreneurship worldwide, especially by governments and international organisations. For example, this interpretation of social entrepreneurship underpins the policies for social entrepreneurship in the EU, the United Kingdom, Singapore, Australia, New Zealand, and many other countries.

Additionally, at present, most organisations that define themselves as social enterprises would do so based on this school of thought.

A subset of the social enterprises defined as such by the BST is the Work Integration Social Enterprises (WISEs). These are for-profit businesses that employ vulnerable or marginalised people who would otherwise find it difficult to become integrated or re-integrated into the labour market. Examples of categories of vulnerable/ marginalised people in this sense would be people with physical or mental disabilities, people with certified learning difficulties, ex-convicts, refugees, or people who have been unemployed for a significant amount of time and need re-skilling. WISEs' only difference from traditional enterprises is in whom they employ. Otherwise, they are profit-maximising businesses.

An example of a social enterprise as defined by the BST is the *London Early Years Foundation* (LEYF). LEYF operates 39 nurseries and pre-schools across London. The pedagogy approach that LEYF developed is based on the latest research available on children's learning and aims at building both social and cultural capital. Part of the unique learning experience it offers is enabled precisely by its social mission. LEYF's goal is to have a mix of children from different backgrounds as a way both to boost children's development through diversity and to mitigate the proven impact that poverty and lack of opportunities have on the health and learning of children from the poorest families and communities. To ensure the obtainment of this goal, LEYF reinvests all its profits back into its business. This enables it to offer a free nursery place to 48% of its customers, so that even less affluent families can access high-quality early years' education. Additionally, reinvesting profits in its social mission helps LEYF to routinely train staff, support the local employment of nursery staff, offer apprenticeship programmes, and help mothers and fathers returning to work. As part of its social mission, LEYF also engages in several initiatives to reduce its carbon emissions. At present, it is trying to develop an overarching approach to environmental sustainability that it hopes to translate into an accreditation scheme for other nurseries that want to become environmentally friendly in a more holistic way.

An example of a WISE, instead, is *La Fageda*, a Spanish cooperative founded in 1982 with the aim of improving the social integration of mentally disabled people. It produces dairy products (yoghurts and desserts) using its own cows and a comprehensive quality control in the production line. Thanks to these features, it markets products that are free of additives and that can be branded as "farm-style" throughout Catalonia. These characteristics enable *La Fageda* to differentiate its products from those of multinational dairy producers and to command a premium price of up to 40%. Because of its founding principle of not exploiting disability, *La Fageda* markets itself without making its social impact and social mission public, leveraging its product differentiation instead as a way to compete effectively. Its immediate commercial success enabled it to set up a foundation, which complements the occupational and integration benefits offered by the business by providing occupational therapy, an assisted-living service, and a community integration service to people with mental disability.

1.3.3 The Community School of Thought

The **Community School of Thought** (CST) interprets as social entrepreneurship any activity, whether pursued by an individual or organisation, which aims to benefit the local community and to generate local development. The CST reflects different traditions across Europe related to the solidarity economy and was also initially embraced by the UK government in the late 1990s, when the think tank *Demos* introduced social entrepreneurship as a community-based phenomenon for local regeneration. In their 1997 report *The rise of the social entrepreneur*, *Demos* envisaged the replacement of the existing welfare state with a more entrepreneurial and problem-solving one by means of a wave of social innovation predominantly originating from social entrepreneurs putting underutilised resources at the service of public goods' delivery. This view of social entrepreneurship still represents a significant number of projects that take place across Europe as well as in many African, South American, and Asian nations, where social entrepreneurship is often about helping members of the local community to access new and/or better goods and services. Recently, this typology of social entrepreneurship has been particularly important to sustain communities in refugee camps throughout Europe and the Middle East. According to this view, both businesses and non-profit organisations can be examples of social entrepreneurship, as long as they have as their main aim the generation of social impact in their community.

An example of social entrepreneurship as defined by this school of thought is *Back On Track Syria* (BOTS), which was founded in Germany in 2016 by Petra Becker. She realised how difficult it was for Syrian children to get integrated into German schools, since they did not speak the language and could not prove what they knew already. BOTS started in an emergency shelter in Berlin, where Petra and some volunteers helped refugee children to access the learning materials provided by UNICEF and trained refugee teachers, students, and academics to become mentors for self-organised learning. After the pilot, BOTS team realised that it was difficult to keep helping children when they moved out of the shelter and that the existing resources were not enough to compensate for the missed schooling. As a result, they gathered learning materials from different sources and started to offer self-learning materials and mentoring support for both children and adolescents in Maths, English, Chemistry, and Biology. Children and their families can request these materials online and use them at their own pace, supported by the infrastructure that BOTS developed. BOTS cannot generate revenues because the families whose children it supports cannot afford to pay for its services. As such, it relies on donations from both private citizens and corporate donors. It can be defined as social entrepreneurship based on the CST because it is an innovative initiative making a significant difference for many refugee communities, whose children need to make up for lost school and start their integration process into a new country as quickly as possible.

1.3.4 Additional definitions of social entrepreneurship intersecting multiple schools of thought

Besides the three schools of thought described above, there are two additional conceptions of social entrepreneurship that are now subsets of/intersect at least two of them. They can be defined as the "Earned Revenues" and "Shared Ownership" schools of thought. The **Earned Revenues School of Thought** (ERST) defines as social enterprises the charities, NGOs, and non-profit organisations that start side activities to generate revenues as a way to become less dependent on donations and grants. This conception of social entrepreneurship is a subset of both the BST, since some of these revenue-generating initiatives might be incorporated separately from the non-profit organisation and act as for-profit businesses, and the IST, since revenue-generation might be the result of innovative ways of realising a social or environmental goal.

The **Shared Ownership School of Thought** (SOST) considers instead as social enterprises the organisations, such as cooperatives, that have a distributed ownership, i.e. that provide employees and/or stakeholders with shares, thus involving them in decision-making and enabling them to benefit economically (e.g. by gaining dividends or benefiting from cheaper access to goods and services) from its activities. This conception is a subset of both the BST, since most cooperatives and mutuals operate as for-profit businesses, and of the CST, because, in some cases, setting up a cooperative is a way to contribute to local development and to address a community-relevant issue.

An example of social entrepreneurship as defined by the ERST is *Imbali Visual Literacy Project* (IVLP). IVLP is a South African charity whose mission is to change people's lives through arts' education and training. It trains teachers with no arts background, working in poorly resourced schools, to help them introduce arts in those contexts, and it also trains youth in difficulty to enhance their creative skills useful for income-generating activities such as craft and design. While relying on volunteers and donations to sustain its operations, IVLP generates extra revenues to support itself by selling some of the arts and crafts made through its courses at the museum stores of Museum Africa and the Origins Centre in Johannesburg.

An example of a social enterprise as defined by SOST is the Costa Rican farmer's cooperative *Coonaprosal*. *Coonaprosal* began as a project to make local farmers

Table 1.1 Different schools of thought

School of Thought	Main focus	Key characteristic	Ownership	Social business model
IST	Individual	Views the social entrepreneur as individual innovator and leader, challenging the *status quo* to end injustice and inequality	NA	Non-profit
BST	Organisation	Defines social entrepreneurs as businesses aiming primarily to generate social impact, rather than profit. Probably the most commonly adopted view of social entrepreneurship	Concentrated or shared	For-profit
CST	Either individual or organisation	Considers social entrepreneurship to be any activity aiming to generate benefits for the local community	Concentrated or shared	Either non-profit or for-profit
ERST	Organisation	Defines social entrepreneurship as the revenue-generating activities of non-profit organisations	NA	Non-profit (for-profit if incorporation as separate entity)
SOST	Organisation	Defines social enterprises as businesses having distributed ownership, enabling employees and stakeholders to be involved in decision-making	Shared	For-profit

more competitive in the salt industry. The idea was to buy and pool their produce to offer large international buyers a stronger guarantee in terms of production levels (thus securing more trade) and to increase profit margins by virtue of the opportunity to sell higher volumes. As a result of growing competition in the salt industry, the cooperative began, over time, to diversify its offer, and now sells not only salt but also shrimps and fruits to several countries in Central America. The cooperative ensures, to all participating farmers, training, good prices for their products, support, socialisation, and educational opportunities for them and their families. The values underpinning their strategy are based on those of cooperation and participation and include: mutual aid, responsibility, democracy, equality, and solidarity.

Table 1.1 summarises the different schools of thought presented here.

1.4 This book's definition of social entrepreneurship

A definition of social entrepreneurship that brings together the several interpretations and applications of this concept that exist around the globe can be: *an activity, pursued by an individual or organisation, that has as its main mission the pursuit of a social and/or environmental goal, that takes the interests of all stakeholders into consideration, and that presents entrepreneurial characteristics. These can take the form of a revenue-generating business model, a highly innovative approach, and/or the employment of potential profits to benefit a given community of stakeholders.* This is the definition of social entrepreneurship adopted throughout the book, unless otherwise specified.

This definition tries to encompass as many varieties of social entrepreneurship as possible given the international remit of this book. Additionally, it takes into consideration the most well-known definitions of social entrepreneurship that have emerged from both the worlds of academia and practice (Table 1.2), and includes an important characteristic strongly supported by practice but explicitly mentioned only in a few definitions – stakeholders' engagement. Social entrepreneurship is now recognised as an activity that needs to be characterised by a strong focus on stakeholders, by their active involvement and consultation (in particular of target beneficiaries), and by the attempt to consider ethics and environmental sustainability in all operations and decisions.

Starting from this book's definition and the summary of key characteristics of social entrepreneurship, it is possible to also define three concepts that will recur throughout the book: social entrepreneurs, social entrepreneurial organisations, and social enterprises. **Social entrepreneurs**, following the definition of the IST, are individuals who engage in social entrepreneurship or who found innovative non-profit organisations that aim to challenge the status quo and catalyse social transformation. **Social entrepreneurial organisations** are organisations engaging in social entrepreneurship, i.e. whose main mission is pursuing a social and/or environmental goal, that take the interests of all stakeholders into consideration, and present entrepreneurial characteristics. **Social enterprises** are the most popular and recognised form of social entrepreneurial organisations. Specifically, they are social entrepreneurial organisations operating as businesses pursuing a double or triple bottom line, and therefore whose income is strongly dependent on revenue-generating activities (in many contexts, the expectation would be for a social enterprise to generate at least 30% of its income through revenues).

Table 1.2 Most well-known definitions of social entrepreneurship

Author	Year	Definition
Ashoka[4]	2021	Social entrepreneurs are individuals with innovative solutions to society's most pressing social, cultural, and environmental challenges. They are ambitious and persistent – tackling major issues and offering new ideas for systems-level change. They model changemaking behaviour, and catalyse organisations and movements where everyone can be changemakers.
Austin, Stevenson and Wei-Skillern[5]	2006	Social entrepreneurship is an innovative, social value–creating activity that can occur within or across the non-profit, business, or government sectors.
Choi and Majumdar[6]	2014	Social entrepreneurship is a representation of the combined quality of certain sub-concepts, i.e. social value creation, the social entrepreneur, the SE organisation, market orientation, and social innovation.
Dees[7]	1998	Social entrepreneurs play the role of change agents in the social sector, by: • Adopting a mission to create and sustain social value (not just private value), • Recognising and relentlessly pursuing new opportunities to serve that mission, • Engaging in a process of continuous innovation, adaptation, and learning, • Acting boldly without being limited by resources currently in hand, and • Exhibiting a heightened sense of accountability to the constituencies served and for the outcomes created.
EMES European Research Network[8]	1997	Social enterprises present the following dimensions: • a continuous activity producing goods and/or selling services; • a high degree of autonomy; • a significant level of economic risk; • a minimum amount of paid work. • an explicit aim to benefit the community; • an initiative launched by a group of citizens; • a decision-making power not based on capital ownership; • a participatory nature, which involves various parties affected by the activity; • a limited profit distribution.
Martin and Osberg[9]	2007	Social entrepreneurship has the following three components: (1) identifying a stable but inherently unjust equilibrium that causes the exclusion, marginalisation, or suffering of a segment of humanity that lacks the financial means or political clout to achieve any transformative benefit on its own; (2) identifying an opportunity in this unjust equilibrium, developing a social value proposition, and bringing to bear inspiration, creativity, direct action, courage, and fortitude, thereby challenging the stable state's hegemony; and (3) forging a new, stable equilibrium that releases trapped potential or alleviates the suffering of the targeted group, and through imitation and the creation of a stable ecosystem around the new equilibrium ensuring a better future for the targeted group and even society at large.

NESsT[10]	1997	Social enterprise is the myriad of entrepreneurial or "self-financing" methods used by non-profit organisations to generate some of their own income in support of their mission.
Peredo and McLean[11]	2006	Social entrepreneurship is exercised where some person or group: (1) aim(s) at creating social value, either exclusively or at least in some prominent way; (2) show(s) a capacity to recognise and take advantage of opportunities to create that value ("envision"); (3) employ(s) innovation, ranging from outright invention to adapting someone else's novelty, in creating and/or distributing social value; (4) is/are willing to accept an above-average degree of risk in creating and disseminating social value; and (5) is/are unusually resourceful in being relatively undaunted by scarce assets in pursuing their social venture.
Prabhu[12]	1999	Social entrepreneurs are persons who create or manage innovative entrepreneurial organisations or ventures whose primary mission is the social change and development of their client group.
Roberts Foundation's Homeless Economic Development Fund[13]	1996	Social enterprise is a revenue-generating venture founded to create economic opportunities for very-low-income individuals, while simultaneously operating with reference to the financial bottomline.
Schwab Foundation[14]	2021	Social entrepreneurship is a model that combines the mission, dedication, and compassion to serve the most vulnerable and marginalised populations of society with business principles and the best techniques from the private sector.
Social Enterprise World Forum[15]	2021	Social enterprises have six top-level primary characteristics and features: mission focus, surplus invested in mission, ownership tied to mission, ethically transparent and accountable, trade-generated income, asset locked.
Thompson[16]	2002	Social entrepreneurs are people with the qualities and behaviours we associate with the business entrepreneur but who operate in the community and are more concerned with caring and helping than "making money".
Yunus[17]	2008	Social entrepreneurship is any innovative initiative to help people. The initiative may be economic or non-economic, for-profit or not-for-profit.
Zahra et al.[18]	2009	Social entrepreneurship encompasses the activities and processes undertaken to discover, define, and exploit opportunities in order to enhance social wealth by creating new ventures or managing existing organisations in an innovative manner.

Here below is a set of questions that can help to reflect on whether or not an individual or organisation can be defined as engaging in "social entrepreneurship". For that to be the case, the answer to all of these questions would have to be affirmative.

• Do they try to tackle a social and/or environmental issue leveraging business tools and mindset, or an innovative approach?
• If they manage to become profitable, do they reinvest a significant part of their profits to generate further social and/or environmental impact, reaching more members of their target community or increasing their impact in the same community?

- If they are non-profits and do not present revenue-generating activities or an entrepreneurial orientation, are they so innovative that they have the potential to change the status quo and solve the root cause of a social or environmental issue?
- Are they involving stakeholders, especially beneficiaries, in decision-making and try to treat everyone fairly across their value chain in order to maximise the social impact of their initiative?
- Does their only social impact come from their end result or are their practices and activities also conducted in a sustainable and socially minded way?

While answering these questions is not rocket-science, and it is possible that something can be classified as social entrepreneurship if presenting most of these characteristics but not necessarily all, these questions can be a guidance to distinguish between genuine attempts at social entrepreneurship, other forms of social innovation, and marketing campaigns with very little substance in terms of social innovation that just want to grab the attention of socially and environmentally minded customers.

SUMMARY BOX

- Social entrepreneurship sits at the intersection between the business, public, and third sectors. This means it needs to be in a dialogue with all of them but, also, that it can attract resources and support from each of them and compensate for their "failures".
- Social entrepreneurship as an activity has existed for centuries, while social entrepreneurship as a concept is a recent phenomenon due to specific socio-economic trends that took place between the 1980s and 2000s.
- There are multiple definitions of social entrepreneurship due to the various contexts in which it arose and the different stakeholders that sustain it. The main ones are the IST, the BST, and the CST.
- In this book, social entrepreneurship is defined as

    an activity, pursued by an individual or organisation, that has as its main mission the pursuit of a social and/or environmental goal, that takes the interests of all stakeholders into consideration, and that presents entrepreneurial characteristics. These can take the form of a revenue-generating business model, a highly innovative approach and/or the employment of potential profits to benefit a given community of stakeholders.

- Based on this definition, this book also distinguishes between social entrepreneurs, social entrepreneurial organisations, and social enterprises in the following way:
  - Social entrepreneurs are individuals who engage in social entrepreneurship or found innovative non-profit organisations that aim to challenge the status quo and catalyse social transformation.
  - Social entrepreneurial organisations are organisations engaging in social entrepreneurship, i.e. whose main mission is pursuing a social and/or environmental goal, that take the interests of all stakeholders into consideration, and present entrepreneurial characteristics.

- Social enterprises are social entrepreneurial organisations operating as businesses pursuing a double or triple bottom line, whose income is strongly dependent on revenue-generating activities (in many contexts, the expectation would be for a social enterprise to generate at least 30% of its income through revenues).

Check box – Self-reflection and discussion questions

- Can you think of a historic example (i.e. pre-1990s) that you would consider as an example of social entrepreneurship?
- What are the similarities and differences between the different schools of thought?
- Putting together all that you have learnt so far, what is your view of social entrepreneurship? Do you agree with the one proposed by this book or would you include different characteristics?
- What are the benefits and risks of having multiple definitions of social entrepreneurship?

Check out additional resources related to this chapter to learn more about the definitions presented and the case studies at: www.routledge.com/9780367640231.

Exercises

Exercise 1.1 – Are these social entrepreneurial organisations?

Retrieve information about these organisations through internet search engines, library databases, social media, etc. and explain if you would consider them as social entrepreneurial organisations or not and, if yes, based on which school of thought. In some cases, you can try to be even more specific and explain whether something is a generic social entrepreneurial organisation or a social enterprise.

a   TOMS® Shoes
b   Facebook
c   Blue Ventures
d   Ben & Jerry's
e   Médecins Sans Frontières
f   One Bite Design Studio
g   Metropolitan Museum
h   Vienna State Opera
i   Childline
j   Addiopizzo

Once you are done, compare your answers in small groups or with at least one other student/course participant. How much do they overlap and how much do they differ?

Does it matter if they differ? Discuss similarities and differences and see if the debate helps or not to refine your understanding of social entrepreneurial organisations.

Exercise 1.2 – Find examples of social entrepreneurship

Find at least one example of social entrepreneurship for each of the schools of thought presented in this chapter. Reflect on them to understand which school of thought mostly resonates with you and discuss this with at least one other student/course participant.

Exercise 1.3 – Share your views on the future of social entrepreneurship

Elaborate in a short essay and/or debate in small groups on the following: "Given the current drive for sustainable business and the trends that underpinned the rise of social entrepreneurship, social entrepreneurship will soon cease to exist because all entrepreneurship will need to be social".

Notes

1 Bosma, N., Schøtt, T., Terjesen, S., & Kew, P. (2015). *Special topic report – Social Entrepreneurship*. Global Entrepreneurship Monitor. Lausanne: Global Entrepreneurship Research Association, p.11.
2 Ashoka. (2021). *Social entrepreneurship*. Retrieved from: https://www.ashoka.org/en-us/focus/social-entrepreneurship
3 Dees, J. G. (1998). *The meaning of social entrepreneurship* (unpublished), 4.
4 Ashoka. (2021). *Social entrepreneurship*. Retrieved from: https://www.ashoka.org/en-us/focus/social-entrepreneurship
5 Austin, J., Stevenson, H., & Wei–Skillern, J. (2006). Social and commercial entrepreneurship: Same, different, or both? *Entrepreneurship Theory and Practice*, 30(1), 2.
6 Choi, N., & Majumdar, S. (2014). Social entrepreneurship as an essentially contested concept: Opening a new avenue for systematic future research. *Journal of Business Venturing*, 29(3), 372.
7 Dees, J. G. (1998). *The meaning of social entrepreneurship* (unpublished), 4.
8 Defourny, J.,& Nyssens, M. (2010). Conceptions of social enterprise and social entrepreneurship in Europe and the United States: Convergences and divergences, *Journal of Social Entrepreneurship*, 1(1), 43.
9 Martin, R. L., & Osberg, S. (2007). Social entrepreneurship: The case for definition. *Stanford Social Innovation Review*, 35.
10 Alter, K. (2007). Social enterprise typology. *Virtue Ventures LLC*, 12(1), 11.
11 Peredo, A. M., & McLean, M. (2006). Social entrepreneurship: A critical review of the concept. *Journal of World Business*, 41(1), 64.
12 Prabhu, G. N. (1999). Social entrepreneurship leadership. *Career Development International*, 4(3), 140.
13 Alter, K. (2007). Social enterprise typology. *Virtue Ventures LLC*, 12(1), 11.
14 Schwab Foundation. (2021). *About: Our story*. Retrieved from: https://www.schwab-found.org/about
15 Social Enterprise World Forum. (2021). *What is a social enterprise?* Retrieved from: https://sewfonline.com/about/about-social-enterprise/
16 Thompson, J. L. (2002). The world of the social entrepreneur. *The International Journal of Public Sector Management*, 15, 413.
17 Yunus, M. (2008). *Creating a world without poverty: Social business and the future of capitalism*. New York: Public Affairs Books, 32.
18 Zahra, S. A., Gedajlovic, E., Neubaum, D. O., &Shulman, J. M. (2009). A typology of social entrepreneurs: Motives, search processes and ethical challenges. *Journal of Business Venturing*, 24(5), 522.

2 Social entrepreneurship and social change

Key content

This chapter introduces concepts that are related to social entrepreneurship to continue to narrow down its definition and to explore the role that social entrepreneurship plays in society.

2.1 Social change, social innovation, and social impact
2.2 Distinguishing social entrepreneurship from related activities and organisational forms
2.3 The roles of social entrepreneurship in society

Learning objectives

- Understand the meaning of social change, social innovation, and social impact and how they intersect with social entrepreneurship.
- Identify key elements that help to differentiate social entrepreneurship from entrepreneurship, charitable endeavours, social movements, and other forms of social and sustainable business.
- Become aware of how social entrepreneurship has been contributing to tackling global challenges.

2.1 Social change, social innovation, and social impact

Social entrepreneurship is often associated with social impact, social innovation, and social change. While in some instances there is an overlap between social entrepreneurship and these other concepts and, broadly speaking, social entrepreneurship is one means of achieving social impact, innovation, and change, there are notable differences between these. It is important to acknowledge and appreciate such differences to start understanding social entrepreneurship within the broader context in which it operates.

2.1.1 Social change

Social change is a popular and well-established concept in sociology. The American Sociological Association defines it as "the processes through which individuals, groups and societies alter their structure and culture over both long and short timeframes".[1] Examples of social change are the Reformation, the abolition of slavery, the civil

DOI: 10.4324/9781003121824-4

rights movement, the work-from-home practices rendered possible by digitalisation and accelerated by the COVID-19 pandemic, and the increase in diversity in Western universities and corporations following the denunciations of continued inequality by the #MeToo and Black Lives Matter movements.

There are many different trends, behaviours, or events that can trigger social change: migrations, demographic developments, catastrophic events such as wars, natural disasters and pandemics, technological and social innovations, legislation, social movements, etc. This means that social change has both natural/unintentional and human-led/intentional drivers. In many cases social change is the result of many different processes and outcomes coming together and is not solely attributable to one specific cause.

In 2020, a significant social change was created by a campaign launched on social media by Marcus Rashford, a professional footballer from the English National Team. He had experienced poverty before being lifted from it by his sport talent. When the first COVID-19-related lockdown left many children in the United Kingdom without school meals and their families unable to afford to pay for three meals a day, Rashford launched a campaign challenging the government's decision to not guarantee meals to children during home-schooling. His letter to the government, once posted on his social media, gained so much traction in a matter of hours, collecting over a million signatures, that it effectively led to a change of government policy and to a new country-wide awareness of the difficult economic situation in which many children lived in a rich country like the United Kingdom.

Social entrepreneurship is often described as one of the potential human-led drivers of social change, although not all forms of social entrepreneurship produce social change (Figure 2.1), and the changes generated are not always positive or sustained over time. One of the many instances in which social entrepreneurship has been an important source of positive social change is recorded in a study conducted by Haugh and Talwar (2016).[2] Their research linked the presence of a social enterprise, and its employment and empowerment of women in a village in North India, to important social change in terms of the role, power, and consideration that these women had in their families, as well as in the attitudes of village people towards women's employment. Similarly, many studies and testimonies have attributed the realisation of social

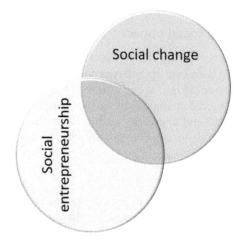

Figure 2.1 Social entrepreneurship in relation to social change

change to famous international social enterprises such as *BRAC*. Obviously, the scale of social change that social entrepreneurship can trigger is strongly dependent on the size of the social entrepreneurial organisation and of the zones in which it operates, and on the number of beneficiaries it reaches. In many cases, change happens because of the contributions of many different actors. Social entrepreneurs and social entrepreneurial organisations can become a force that brings together many of these actors, and that favours dialogue between them to create an even more powerful push for change in the desired direction. This is the case, for example, of *Crisis Action*, which convenes coalitions of individuals and organisations to enhance partners' efforts to protect civilians from armed conflict and its consequences. Its work as catalyst helps its partners to amplify their impact through the creation of a single voice.

2.1.2 Social innovation

Social innovation is a more recent concept compared to social change. As such, it still has many definitions that can be broadly grouped into two core ones: one focused on outcomes, and one focused on processes. The most popular definition based on outcomes was coined by Phills, Deiglmeier and Miller in 2008, and defines social innovation as "a novel solution to a social problem that is more effective, efficient, sustainable, or just than existing solutions and for which the value created accrues primarily to society as a whole rather than private individuals".[3] The most popular definition of social innovation as a process is instead the one provided in 2006 by Mulgan, who described social innovation as "innovative activities and services that are motivated by the goal of meeting a social need".[4] Based on this definition it is the intention that matters and not whether the innovation produces the desired outcome or not, or whether it affects society in a positive way. In either case, what characterises social innovation is the desire to solve an observed social issue and the attempt to do so, in a way that is either original/radical or new, given the context or its application. Examples of social innovation include: the introduction of a National Health Service (NHS) in the United Kingdom in 1984, providing for the first time anywhere in the world free healthcare to all citizens; the introduction of micro-credit by *Grameen Bank* in Bangladesh in the late 1970s; Bottom of the Pyramid initiatives such as the *Health in your hands* campaign, supported by *Hindustan Unilever*, which simultaneously created new markets for the company's products and changed people's habits in a way that was beneficial to their health.

Like social entrepreneurship, social innovation also represents one of many means of generating social change in a purposeful way and it can trigger both positive and negative change as well as no change at all. Similarly, social innovation is also a concept related to opportunity recognition, which gained traction in the early 2000s because of the growing desire by many people to see a more dynamic, flexible, and responsive third sector and a more sustainable approach to growth. While sometimes social entrepreneurs can be the social innovator, there are many examples of social innovation being generated by businesses, charities, regulators, governments, or individuals who would not define themselves as social entrepreneurs. As such, there is only a partial overlap between these two concepts (Figure 2.2). This is evident in the small sample of examples provided in the paragraph above. In this sense, many authors differentiate between social entrepreneurship and innovation by saying that one is portrayed more as an individual activity while the second usually has a more

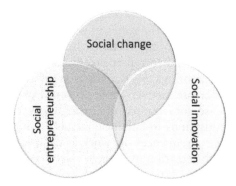

Figure 2.2 Social entrepreneurship in relation to social change and social innovation

collective/collaborative and dynamic origin. While this distinction is forced, since both social innovation and social entrepreneurship can emerge out of individual as well as collective efforts, some studies have shown that a social innovation identified through the outcomes it generates (see definitions above) has a higher potential than social entrepreneurship to be a collective endeavour. Indeed, it is the adoption by different people and groups of an innovation and its production of positive outcomes for a collective that identifies it as a social innovation

Increasingly, social innovation is associated with two socio-economic phenomena: digital innovation and frugal innovation. Sometimes, social entrepreneurs and social entrepreneurial organisations are the actors pursuing these forms of innovation. Other times, individuals and organisations are seen as engaging in social entrepreneurship precisely because they create and deliver social innovations. However, digital and frugal innovation can also be completely independent from social entrepreneurship.

2.1.2.1 Digital innovation

Nambisan et al. (2017) define digital innovation as "the creation of (and consequent change in) market offerings, business processes, or models that result from the use of digital technologies".[5] Digital innovation is a "hot topic" in any sector, but it is especially relevant for social entrepreneurial organisations because it can help them to scale operations and impact at a relatively low cost both for themselves and for their beneficiaries. Digital products and services tend to require lower capital investment than their analogue counterparts, and enable a higher number of beneficiaries to be reached more quickly and across more geographies. Examples of digital innovations range from the usage of mobile networks and phones to perform previously in-person services, such as banking and health checks, to the automation of supply chains and the creation of autonomous vehicles.

Social entrepreneurial organisations in both the Global North and South are increasingly relying on digital solutions to deliver social impact in various sectors. For example, digital innovations have helped increase crop productivity in the agriculture sector, enabled the improvement of water and sanitation in rural villages thanks to the offering of cheap solutions to test and improve water quality, provided access to education and educational content for millions of children, and facilitated the delivery of healthcare in remote villages, e.g. by leveraging mobile technology to connect doctors and patients. Additionally, digital innovation represents an opportunity for social entrepreneurs and social entrepreneurial organisations to connect with peers and supporters all around the world, take part remotely in conferences where they can source ideas and funds, collect analytics that might help them improve their products and services or measure their impact, and reach more customers and beneficiaries. In this sense, the COVID-19 pandemic has played a pivotal role in pushing social entrepreneurial organisations to increase their online presence for marketing purposes and to leverage digital opportunities to generate social or environmental impact.

An example of digital social entrepreneurship is *Reason Digital*. It is a social enterprise based in Manchester, United Kingdom, which partners with other social enterprises, Corporate Social Responsibility (CSR) projects, and charities to help them digitalise their offer. Their services range from building websites and apps and explaining how to best use social media to leading a full-on digital transformation, from strategy to impact measurement. With the support of *Reason Digital*, partners can harness technology to enhance their reach and/or impact, tailoring their digital offering to the specific needs of their beneficiaries.

An example of a digital innovation that can give rise to social entrepreneurial opportunities is the *Enhanced Fish Market Information Service*, launched in Kenya in 2009 for Lake Victoria's fisheries. The service was developed by researchers at the Kenya Marine and Fisheries Research Institute,[6] and consists of an ITC system able to handle data on the key factors that affect fish marketing decisions, such as fish price and quantity in nearby markets, weather, and the availability of logistics support in landing sites. Such data is recorded once or twice a day at landing sites and relevant markets, transmitted to a data centre, re-packaged in a format helpful to fishers and traders, and then sent upon a request. Both phases of data transfer happen in real time through SMS, with additional, summative e-reports sent monthly to interested stakeholders.

While digital innovation is increasingly important for social entrepreneurship and as a trigger of social change, another form of social innovation that is gaining increasing traction and success is frugal innovation.

2.1.2.2 *Frugal innovation*

Frugal innovation is the creation of new products and services that are "good enough" to meet a given need at a lower cost, with fewer resources and, sometimes, in a shorter time frame, than available alternatives. It represents both a way to do more with less, and to provide needed solutions to otherwise inaccessible beneficiaries and customers. In other words, according to Prabhu (2017),[7] frugal innovation is the type of innovation that attempts to maximise the ratio of value to resources. Usually, the products and services created through frugal innovation feature only basic functionalities and appear less advanced than more costly solutions, but precisely for this reason they tend to be affordable even to the poorest segments of the market. Additionally, since frugal innovation usually comes from individuals or organisations who are suffering themselves from resource constraints, it is also often a powerful tool for economic development. While, as a phenomenon, frugal innovation started in the Global South, it is now also expanding in the Global North. Its efficient use of resources fits perfectly with the need to reduce the impact on the planet while still pursuing growth and economic development.

One of the most famous examples of frugal innovation is the one realised by Mansukhbhai Prajapati. When his village in India was hit by an earthquake in 2001, he noticed a photo in a newspaper of a broken clay vase used in the village to collect water and keep it cool. This gave him the inspiration to leverage his knowledge of clay modelling for the construction of sustainable fridges. He knew such fridges would solve many of the issues faced by the people living in his and nearby villages:

- They could help them to preserve fresh dairy products and fruit that could only be bought on certain days.
- They would not be dependent on the unreliable supply of electricity in the area since they would function without it.
- They could be affordable even for the poorest households.

From this intuition, Mansukhbhai Prajapati created *Mitti Cool,* a clay container that could function as a fridge leveraging the combined properties of clay and water, which he could sell for around 2,000 Indian Rupee (just below $30). This innovation proved such a success that Mansukhbhai Prajapati could soon expand his operations and train and hire local women to produce more fridges and other items such as cookware, pots, and tableware. Now his company, called *Mitti Cool* to honour the original invention, is well-known in India and has received several awards, improved the livelihoods of thousands of people, and is ready to expand even beyond its national borders.

As the example of *Mitti Cool* shows, frugal innovation can be a fundamental tool for social entrepreneurs and social entrepreneurial organisations in any country to realise or grow their social impact, and its production and distribution can be the reason why a social enterprise is founded. Like digital innovation, frugal innovation helps to do more with less and to reach more people more rapidly and at lower costs.

2.1.3 Social impact

Like social entrepreneurship and social innovation, social impact is also a contested concept with multiple definitions. Rawhauser et al. (2019), attempting to bring together all the different nuances attributed to the meaning of social impact, defined it as: "beneficial outcomes resulting from prosocial behaviour that are enjoyed by the intended targets of that behaviour and/or by the broader community of individuals, organizations, and/or environments".[8] In other words, social impact can be seen as the improvement of the livelihoods and prospects of individuals, organisations, or entire communities through purposeful action. This means that, while social impact might emerge unintentionally and might be negative, when people mention social impact, they normally refer to that which is purposefully created and is positive for its intended beneficiaries. In many ways, social impact can be seen as the antecedent of social change, although this is not always the case; social impact does not always necessarily lead to social change and it is not always necessary to have social impact in order to generate social change.

Examples of social impact as defined in the paragraph above are as many as the social issues to be solved, including: helping farmers in the poorest regions to increase crop yields through individual support, better quality seeds and information on best practices; saving children from repeated abuse through the creation of a helpline;

helping people cope with mental health issues through effective counselling; creating shelters and training opportunities for the homeless. Common sources of social impact are policies, regulations, certifications, new laws, initiatives related to business sustainability and CSR, the activities of charities and NGOs, the programmes of international organisations (e.g. United Nations (UN), WHO), social innovations, volunteering, and, "obviously", social entrepreneurship. The "obvious" inclusion of social entrepreneurship in this list is clearly linked to the fact that this book defines social entrepreneurship as an activity aiming to realise social and/or environmental impact (see Chapter 1).

An example of a social enterprise that has generated significant social impact is that of *Liberty & Justice*. It is a leading Fair Trade Certified™ apparel company, founded in 2010, that has helped hundreds of women in Liberia to lift their families out of poverty by employing them to produce ethical and sustainable apparel for American clothing brands. The foundation of *Liberty & Justice* was inspired by the *Liberian Women's Peace Movement* and, from the beginning, its mission was to support women in their efforts to bring back stability and peace by leveraging what they know best – sewing. Ninety per cent of the company's employees are women in their 30s, 40s, and 50s, which is very unusual in the garment industry. *Liberty & Justice* pays them wages that are 20% higher than the industry average in the country and gives them the opportunity to partake in the company's shares. Thanks to their employment at *Liberty & Justice*, women have taken a leading role in providing for their families. This and the fact they are involved in key strategic decisions, such as how to react to the Ebola crisis, enable them to feel empowered and valuable and also allow them to send their children to school in a country where children are often sent to work instead, in order to ensure the survival of their siblings.

Despite best intentions, the social impact that social entrepreneurship or social innovation creates could be positive, negative, or non-existent as well as both intended and unintended. This brings up the question of whether it is possible to consider as a social innovation or as social entrepreneurship something that, over time, has evidently not produced its intended impact. This is not an easy question to answer and, as seen with the definition of social innovation, such an answer depends on the point of view adopted – whether that privileges intentions or effects. It is helpful, however, to start reflecting on the importance of assessing the impact generated fairly and of taking a step back when things do not go to plan.

An interesting example in terms of the complex relationship between social entrepreneurship and social impact is that of *TOMS®* Shoes. *TOMS* Shoes was founded in 2006 and became one of the most well-known social enterprises across the world for its creation and adoption of the One for One® model. Their proposition was to donate a pair of shoes to a child in need for every pair of shoes purchased by their customers. The success of this model soon allowed *TOMS* to expand its One for One® approach to the provision of eye care services and safe water through the sale of eyewear and coffee. Between 2006 and 2019, *TOMS* donated over 95 million shoes, 780,000 sight restorations, and committed $6.5 million to impact grants. While these donations undoubtedly generated positive social impact for many people and communities, they also created unexpected negative consequences, which started to be noted in 2015. First, the donation of shoes meant that local shoemakers and cobblers had less business. Second, the One for One® model served more the purpose of making rich customers feel good about themselves than that of tackling the root causes of poverty/lack of shoes. On top

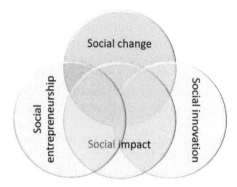

Figure 2.3 Social entrepreneurship in relation to social change, social innovation, and
social impact

of this, *TOMS'* business model began to be imitated by several competitors, thus
putting the company in difficulty even from a business point of view. Ever since,
TOMS has slightly re-targeted its approach, e.g. sourcing the shoes it donates from
local producers in deprived regions and investing significantly in other product
lines and forms of donation. Nonetheless, their story remains a testimony of the
importance of measuring social impact across several indicators and for a prolonged period of time, as well as of having a clear understanding of the problems
affecting the people whom the organisation wants to help. These topics will be
discussed in more detail in Chapters 6, 7, and 11.

To conclude, while social entrepreneurship, innovation, change, and impact might
overlap and are strongly connected, this overlap and connection is only partial, as
shown in Figure 2.3. Social entrepreneurship and social innovation are only two of
the many ways to generate social impact and social change. Social impact, in turn,
can also be a way to generate social change and, while frequently generated by social
entrepreneurship and social innovation, it is not something they automatically trigger.

To fully understand and define social entrepreneurship, it is important to not only
acknowledge its relationship to social innovation, impact, and change, but also to
unpack how it relates to other organisational forms and activities with which it might
partially overlap.

2.2 Distinguishing social entrepreneurship from related activities and organisational forms

Social entrepreneurship is strongly connected to other organisational forms and
activities potentially generating social impact and change, and shares with them some
characteristics (Figure 2.4). These are:

- Traditional entrepreneurship
- Charities
- Social movements
- Other forms of social or sustainable business: Fair Trade Organisations (FTOs),
  B Corps, and Corporate Social Responsibility/Sustainability.

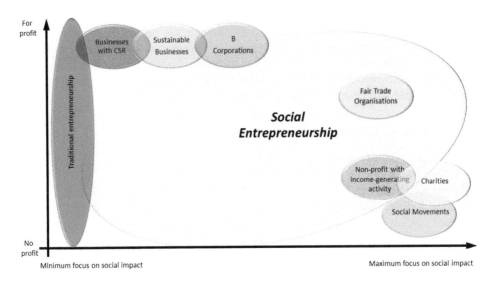

Figure 2.4 Social entrepreneurship and related activities

Distinguishing between these different organisational forms and activities is not always easy, especially since the definition of social entrepreneurship is in constant flux and depends on a country-by-country or even interest group-by-interest group basis. A good starting point to embark on this task, however, is to understand what these other concepts mean and include.

2.2.1 Social entrepreneurship and traditional entrepreneurship

Currently, in the field of management there are two different definitions of entrepreneurship. The first is based on the writings of Joseph Schumpeter and defines entrepreneurship as the "identification, evaluation and exploitation of opportunities".[9] Schumpeter saw entrepreneurship as the ability to spot an opportunity in a market and to take advantage of it through creative destruction, i.e. through coming up with something completely new that has a clear practical application, either through imagination and intuition or through the original re-combination of existing practices and elements. The second definition is based on the practice of entrepreneurship and defines it as the creation of a new firm in a (for-profit) market.

The definition of entrepreneurship based on Schumpeter's writings clearly resonates with the definition of social entrepreneurship of the Innovation School of Thought and, in general, with the reality of many social entrepreneurs that disrupt markets and ways of doing things by re-combining existing elements in novel ways. Similarly, if we define entrepreneurship not as Schumpeter did but as the creation of a new firm, this definition can be compared to the one of social entrepreneurship established by the Business and Community schools of thought. Therefore, by bringing together all possible definitions of entrepreneurship and social entrepreneurship and extracting common features, both types of activity can be seen to involve the identification of an opportunity, the setting up of an organisation to exploit it, and the mobilisation of resources to make the organisation happen. What distinguishes them is only their main goal. Social entrepreneurship aims to tackle a social and/or environmental need or to challenge an unjust status quo, and not to generate profits or disrupt markets. On the contrary, profit generation and market disruption are key motivations behind traditional entrepreneurship. Even when a for-profit business clearly delivers social impact and needs to do so to be profitable, if the prevailing intention is to generate profits, it would still be considered as a traditional enterprise.

2.2.2 Social entrepreneurship and charities

An organisational form that social entrepreneurship is connected to is that of charities. The UN defines a charity as any "non-profit, voluntary citizens' group which is organized on a local, national or international level"[10] that is task-oriented and performs one of the following functions:

- Bringing citizens' concerns to governments;
- Monitoring policies;
- Encouraging political participation at the community level;
- Providing analysis and expertise;
- Delivering services around specific issues, such as the UN pillars of peace and security, human rights, and development.

The definition is very broad, in common with those reported in various dictionaries and legal documents with international value. For example, the Cambridge Dictionary defines charity as "an organisation whose purpose is to give money, food, or help for free to those who need it or to carry out activities such as medical research that will help people in need, and not to make a profit".[11]

Charities come in many shapes and forms and display various degrees of entrepreneurialism and innovation. Distinguishing between charities and social entrepreneurial organisations that operate as non-profit organisations is therefore extremely difficult in many cases, much more so than distinguishing between social entrepreneurship and traditional entrepreneurship. More frequently than not, any definition of charity, NGO, or third-sector organisation easily includes characteristics contained in definitions of social entrepreneurship. How, then, to make a distinction?

If adopting the Innovation School of Thought perspective, the differentiating factor between organisations founded by social entrepreneurs and charities is the innovativeness of the idea, the empowerment rather than help of beneficiaries (e.g. the founder of *Ashoka*, Bill Drayton, often repeated that a charity gives you a fish, while a social entrepreneur would teach you how to fish), and their potential to transform the way a social benefit is delivered. If adopting the Business School of Thought, the differentiating factor between social enterprises and charities is the pursuit of a for-profit versus a non-profit activity or the trading in a market versus the simple delivery of services to people and communities in need. Broadly speaking, charities are less likely than social enterprises to generate a significant amount of income through market-based revenues and to experience mission drift because of the pursuit of a double or triple bottom line. Finally, if adopting the Community School of Thought, any charitable endeavour potentially qualifies as social entrepreneurship as long as it targets a local community and has some business-like element in the way it operates (e.g. revenue-generating activities, innovative approach, usage of business tools for managing the workforce, and the like).

2.2.3 *Social entrepreneurship and social movements*

Social entrepreneurship is also frequently associated with social movements. Mario Diani, one of the most prominent scholars of social movements, defined them as "a network of informal interactions between a plurality of individuals, groups and/or organizations, engaged in a political or cultural conflict, on the basis of a shared collective identity".[12] Together with his colleague Della Porta, Diani (2006)[13] described social movements as "complex phenomena comprising ideas, individuals, events, organisations, and their links that, together, generate collective action". In our digital era, social movements can be both physical – e.g. social movements that bring people to the street to protest against something – and virtual – e.g. multiple people across countries encouraging each other to change habits and perceptions over time without ever being in the same place. Examples of what we call physical social movements could be the women's suffrage movement, the civil rights movement, or the Arab Spring. Examples of virtual movements might be the groups of people that only shop for ethical and Fair Trade products in order to contribute to a more just society or those that follow a religion or culture in a fundamentalist way because they believe society has been corrupted to an excessive degree.

Both social entrepreneurship and social movements aim to change the status quo by giving better opportunities and voice to marginalised people and groups, by reducing inequalities and injustice, or by defending the environment. They also both must mobilise resources to deal with resistance to change, and generate impact that is hard to measure, since it tends to be long term and, sometimes, intangible. Even the instruments and skills used to generate social impact and change might overlap. For example, both social entrepreneurs and leaders of social movements rely on their ability to produce effective communication, and on their identification of a pressing issue to target, for their success.

According to Simms and Robinson (2008)[14] and to Bornstein and Davis (2010),[15] social movements and social activism are different from social entrepreneurship because they attempt to influence and change existing institutions by openly opposing them and by pressuring them into altering their decisions and decision-making processes. For example, the Black Lives Matter movement encouraged companies, public bodies, and local and national authorities to denounce and reject their past ties with, and celebration of, colonialists, and to change their hiring practices and attitudes to become more inclusive. On the contrary, social entrepreneurs and social entrepreneurial organisations set up something new to solve an existing problem by offering an alternative to the way "things are done". By doing so, they tend to operate from within the system they want to change, rather than opposing it from the outside, sometimes directly engaging with organisations they believe are failing or outright damaging society. Additionally, social entrepreneurship can be both an individual and collective endeavour, while social movements, by definition, are collective. That said, it is possible to combine social activism with social entrepreneurship, leveraging a social entrepreneurial organisation and its success as a platform to denounce injustice and to advocate for change in existing institutions, markets, and organisations.

2.2.4 *Social entrepreneurship and its close relatives: Fair Trade Organisations, B Corps, and Corporate Social Responsibility*

Social entrepreneurship is often associated with three business practices that combine market operations with the realisation of social impact. The first of these is Fair Trade Organisations. FTOs are defined as organisations that

> have a clear commitment to Fair Trade as the principal core of their mission. They, backed by consumers, are engaged actively in supporting producers, awareness raising and in campaigning for changes in the rules and practice of conventional international trade.[16]

These are enterprises that sell artisanal goods or produce, generally produced in the Global South. They treat small farmers and artisans as partners, with transparency and respect, and make sure they get a fair pay for their work, while also often providing them with training and resources to make them more competitive, and fighting to secure their rights. Based on this definition, which is the official one provided by the World Fair Trade Organisation (WFTO), FTOs can be interpreted as a form of social enterprises, even if historically they have very different origins. This is because they have a specific type of impact (commitment to Fair Trade) that takes primacy over profits at the core of their mission, engage stakeholders, and pursue a double bottom line.

The second typology of organisation that has a strong connection with social entrepreneurship is the Certified B Corporation (or B Corp). B Corps are for-profit businesses interested in balancing purpose and profit. Famous B Corps would include companies like *Patagonia*, *Ella's Kitchen*, *The Guardian*, and some of *Danone*'s and *Unilever*'s subsidiaries, such as *Ben & Jerry's*. Overall, as of 2020, the B Corp group counted 3,500 members in 150 industries and 74 countries. In order to become B Corps, businesses go through a certification process that involves an auditing of their practices, the publication of their impact assessment on bcorporation.net, and the inclusion of legal provisions for the board of directors to balance profit and purpose.

If we represent social entrepreneurship, as many authors have done, as a continuum of organisational forms ranging from purely non-profit organisations with revenue-generating models or innovative practices, to businesses that have social or environmental impact at the core of their mission, B Corps would sit either at the for-profit extreme of this spectrum or right next to it. What distinguishes B Corps from social enterprises (i.e. businesses with a social or environmental mission) is that they would still be profit-maximisers rather than impact-focused but, in the search for profits, they would try to act fairly towards stakeholders, find as many ways as possible to generate positive social and environmental impact, and minimise harm. An increasing number of social enterprises have recently decided to become a B Corp. Being a Certified B Corp, because of the existence of a standard and widely-recognised certification process, is a more effective way of proving the pursuit of a double or triple bottom line to external stakeholders as compared to self-declaration that the business is a social enterprise.

Finally, social entrepreneurship is often related to CSR or business sustainability. Social entrepreneurial organisations and, especially, social enterprises can be the means through which for-profit businesses can enact CSR or become more sustainable. For example, social enterprises can be used as suppliers, and help companies explore

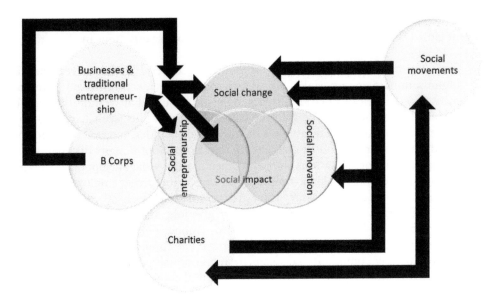

Figure 2.5 Social entrepreneurship and all related concepts discussed in the chapter

new business opportunities that would also generate a positive impact. Various types of social entrepreneurial organisations can be the recipients of volunteering initiatives or of CSR donations. However, even if a business is adopting widespread CSR or is transforming its operations to be more sustainable, this does not mean it becomes a social enterprise.

Unilever, Danone, Mars, Telenor, Procter & Gamble are just some of the many multinational corporations that have realised the business benefits of developing tailored initiatives to provide products and services to underserved populations or to collaborate with NGOs, governments, social enterprises, and other companies to deliver a positive social and/or environmental impact for a community. However, the initiatives that they create – generally through business deals, charitable donations, or volunteering opportunities for their employees – are not at the core of what they do and do not represent their main objective, being the result of cost-benefit calculations. On the contrary, social enterprises have a social and/or environmental impact ingrained in their mission and would pursue it even if that meant giving up potential profits.

Figure 2.5 summarises the interconnections between social entrepreneurship and all the other key concepts, activities and organisations introduced in this chapter.

2.3 The roles of social entrepreneurship in society

Having analysed the different meanings of social entrepreneurship and how social entrepreneurship relates to other concepts that are frequently associated with it, it is important to conclude the definitional journey by looking at the roles that social entrepreneurship can and is expected to perform in society. The roles attributed to social entrepreneurship can be divided into four different categories, here listed from micro- to macro-level. These roles also help to establish how social entrepreneurship can relate to the 17 Sustainable Development Goals (SDGs), agreed by the UN in 2015 to tackle urgent global challenges and subscribed by thousands of organisations in all sectors.

1   *Empowerment of people and communities* – Several social entrepreneurial organisations and, especially, social enterprises provide training and employment opportunities to marginalised people and groups that would otherwise be excluded from the job market. In the Global North, WISEs (see Chapter 1) train and employ people with disabilities or learning difficulties, migrants, youth from disadvantaged areas, and ex-convicts. In the Global South, many different social entrepreneurial organisations employ women in rural villages, support farmers in improving their crop yields so they, in turn, can create further employment opportunities, or create the necessary infrastructure that allows local entrepreneurs to start and thrive. These initiatives not only give jobs and wages to marginalised groups but also help them to feel included, empowered, and to become aware of their value and talents. Additionally, social entrepreneurship is very valuable for heightening community engagement and addressing issues at the local level. Energy cooperatives in Germany and agricultural cooperatives in rural India and China are excellent examples of the power of social entrepreneurship to bring together multiple members of the same community for a productive endeavour, bringing in turn additional benefits to their families, e.g. in the form of more affordable, cleaner energy or better market power. And it doesn't end there. As seen in Chapter 1, many social entrepreneurial organisations consist of community-level projects, which address the most pressing needs given the local situation and provide opportunities for volunteering and inclusion as well as needed social services and impact. By empowering people and communities, social entrepreneurship can contribute to the achievement of SDG 1 (No poverty), 2 (Zero hunger), 7 (Affordable and clean energy), 8 (Decent work and economic growth), 10 (Reduced inequalities), and 11 (Sustainable cities and communities).

2   *Compensation for market and public sector failures* – Social entrepreneurship often meets needs that are not met by traditional sectors and tackles the negative externalities that these sectors produce, i.e. the negative effects on third parties that get inadvertently created through their activities. Examples of these externalities are inequality of opportunities, environmental damage, or impoverishment due to exploitation. What enables social entrepreneurship to do so is its unique balance of creating value and appropriating the value created. Businesses need to capture as much as possible of the value they create in order to be profitable. For this reason, they discard opportunities that make value-capture difficult and have the incentive to appropriate value at the expense of others. The public sector does not aim to appropriate value but, at the same time, does not have any incentive to maximise its creation, since re-election and performance are hardly ever connected to value-creation. Social entrepreneurs and social entrepreneurial organisations, on the contrary, have both the incentive to create value, because they need support and funds from other stakeholders, and to share the value they create, because of their mission. They are willing to accept lower profit margins compared to traditional businesses, tend to have more innovative and stakeholder-empowering approaches compared to public services and traditional NGOs, and are embedded in underprivileged and marginalised communities. This means that they can take business opportunities that businesses discard and supplement the government where it lacks

the resources, knowledge, or willingness to provide a needed product or service. As a consequence, social entrepreneurship can contribute to increase the market inclusion of the poorest of the poor and of marginalised groups, to give them a voice, new skills and opportunities, and to provide them with access to healthcare, water and sanitation, basic financial services and increased agricultural productivity and employment. To summarise, by compensating for market and public sector failures, social entrepreneurship can contribute to the achievement of most SDGs (1–16).

3 *Contribution to economic development and poverty alleviation* – Whatever the context, social entrepreneurship has shown repeatedly its potential to foster inclusive economic development and to tackle poverty. Compared to other third-sector organisations, social entrepreneurial organisations more frequently create employment opportunities and involve their beneficiaries in the creation and development of solutions tailored to them. As said previously, this empowers beneficiaries rather than making them feel passive recipients of charitable support, and is more likely to deliver opportunities for beneficiaries to earn, or to earn more on a stable basis, thus supporting poverty reduction in the communities served. Additionally, by attracting funds and support from different sectors, social entrepreneurial organisations re-direct resources from these sectors to tackle neglected social issues. This supports a fairer redistribution of resources both at a local and global level and opens up additional opportunities for economic development. Finally, social entrepreneurial organisations pursuing a double bottom line have a higher likelihood than charities to survive even in periods of crisis, given their diversified sources of income, and, thus, to have the resilience needed to generate lasting social change over time. By supporting economic development and poverty alleviation, social entrepreneurship can contribute to the achievement of SDGs 1 (No poverty), 8 (Decent work and economic growth), and 10 (Reduced inequalities).

4 *Transformation of systems and institutions* – Finally, one of the key roles attributed to social entrepreneurship, especially by the Innovation School of Thought, is the generation of systems change. Systems change is the intentional process of changing the elements (e.g. networks, dependencies, beliefs) of a system that perpetrate injustices. Social entrepreneurs and social entrepreneurial organisations have characteristics that enable them to catalyse systems change in several ways (see Chapter 5). First, because of their location at the intersection between multiple sectors and their need to attract support, resources, and legitimacy from all of them, they act as a catalyst of attention, funds, and networks. By bringing people and organisations together to solve a specific social or environmental issue, they harness a community of intent and an exchange of ideas that has the potential to significantly alter the way a problem is tackled and the malfunctioning system perpetuating it. Second, by challenging the rules of the game in traditional sectors, social entrepreneurship can be the source of institutional change, which is the change to norms, habits, understandings, and ways of operating. For example, it contributed to bringing entrepreneurial spirit and solutions to the third sector, and new business models and sustainable solutions, plus an attention to all stakeholders, in the business sector. Bringing change normally creates the need to overcome resistance and to legitimate the new way of doing things. Succeeding in these endeavours normally implies managing to alter people's perceptions of how things are and should be, aka institutions. By transforming systems and institutions, social entrepreneurship can contribute to the achievement of SDGs 13 (Climate action), 16 (Peace, justice, and strong institutions), and 17 (Partnerships for the goals).

Not all forms of social entrepreneurship perform all of these roles, and not all of them succeed in generating the change that they desire. However, there are plenty of examples of social entrepreneurship that show its potential to act as force of empowerment, to tackle negative externalities and unmet needs, to be an engine for sustainable economic development, and to become a source of transformation of unjust systems. All these roles support the realisation of the UN SDGs but only in collaboration with other actors. Therefore, the following chapters discuss the many shapes that social entrepreneurship can take and other actors whose input and support it needs to fulfil its potential.

SUMMARY BOX

- Social entrepreneurship is often associated with the concepts of social change, social innovation, and social impact. While social entrepreneurship has a partial overlap with social innovation and is one of the many means to generate social impact and social change, these are all different concepts that should not be used interchangeably.
- Social entrepreneurship is also related to traditional entrepreneurship, charities, social movements, and organisations such as FTOs, B Corps, and sustainable businesses, with which it shares some characteristics. Distinguishing between social entrepreneurship and these other organisational forms and activities is not always easy and requires an in-depth understanding of their motives and ways of operating.
- Social entrepreneurial organisations can be distinguished from charities because of their innovativeness, empowerment of beneficiaries, and approaches to financial sustainability, and can contribute to social movements while operating from an opposite logic (changing the system from within rather than opposing it). Additionally, social enterprises partially overlap with FTOs and B Corps but can be easily separated from traditional entrepreneurship and sustainable businesses or CSR initiatives because of their different mission.
- Social entrepreneurship fulfils four key roles in relation to the UN SDGs: it acts as force of empowerment, it compensates for markets and public sector failures and for their externalities, it is an engine for sustainable economic development, and it is a source of transformation of unjust systems.

Check box – Self-reflection and discussion questions

- How would you define social change, social innovation, and social impact?
- What is the difference between social change and social impact? And between social innovation and social entrepreneurship?
- Why do you think it is important to distinguish between social entrepreneurship and related concepts?
- What are digital and frugal innovation and why are they important for social entrepreneurship?

- What do you think are the most powerful ways to generate social change?
- What are the advantages and disadvantages of social entrepreneurship and related organisational forms compared to traditional entrepreneurship, charities, and social movements when it comes to generating social impact and attracting the necessary resources to do so?
- How can you distinguish, if at all, social enterprises from FTOs, B Corps, and sustainable businesses?
- Does social entrepreneurship really perform the four roles described in this chapter? Or are they just potential roles? Can you find examples to support your view either way?

Check out additional resources related to this chapter to learn more about the concepts, organisational forms, activities, and case studies presented at: www.routledge.com/9780367640231

Exercises

Exercise 2.1 – From social innovation to social entrepreneurship

Read again the example of the *Enhanced Fish Market Information Service* in Section 2.1.2.1 (and or find additional information about this project online) and answer the following questions:

- Does this social/digital innovation have the potential to generate social change?
- How can this service be translated into a social entrepreneurial organisation?
- What are the challenges of implementing such a service?
- What might be the social impact of this innovation and how would you measure it?

Exercise 2.2 – Is this social entrepreneurship?

Case study 2.2.1 – Frontier Market

The founders of *Frontier Markets* realised that people living in the most remote areas in India lacked access to existing solar lighting products that they desperately needed for improving their living conditions and productivity. To address this issue, in 2011, they set up a for-profit enterprise to create a connection between producers and distributors of solar lighting products and local shopkeepers.

As *Frontier Markets* became operative, its founders noticed that their distribution strategy could become even more effective if they were employing local women as door-to-door salespeople. This would increase their reach of families in very remote areas, enhancing the success of their business, while providing a living to women who would otherwise remain excluded from the job market. Therefore, they launched a women entrepreneurship model where they recruited and trained "Saral Jeevan Sahelis" (or "Easy Life Friends") to go door-to-door in their villages to market, sell, and deliver solar lighting products.

Thanks to the knowledge acquired through their extensive network of women vendors, eventually *Frontier Markets* spotted flaws in the products it was selling and decided to expand its activities by starting to produce its own solar torch. Ever since, the business of *Frontier Markets* has been expanding year on year, with the company including in its offer different electric appliances, smartphones, and even financial and educational services.

According to *Frontier Markets*, their commercial success and social impact go hand-in-hand because their service is based on constant communication and proximity with customers, they offer support in the different villages across the life cycle of a product, and they train and support women entrepreneurs.

Case study questions

1   Would you consider *Frontier Markets* as a social entrepreneurial organisation? Why or why not?
    a   If you answered yes to question 1, would you consider *Frontier Markets* as a social enterprise or not?
    b   If you answered no to question 1, how would you define *Frontier Markets* based on the organisational forms discussed in Section 2.2?
2   How could you possibly establish if the main objective of *Frontier Markets* is social impact or profitability, apart from talking to the founding team?
3   Would you affirm or disconfirm that *Frontier Markets* differs from multinational corporations which adopted similar marketing and sales approaches and created new tailored packaging and products to reach customers in remote villages in Africa and Asia?

Case study 2.2.2 – Riders for Health International

Riders for Health International is a non-profit organisation operating in several African countries, such as Lesotho, Kenya, Nigeria, Zimbabwe, The Gambia, and Liberia. It creates and manages vehicle fleets and related maintenance and logistics services to make healthcare and medicines accessible in rural areas when they are needed.

The founders of the organisation, Andrea and Barry Coleman, had the opportunity to travel to Africa as part of their involvement in the racing world. There they discovered that in rural areas many people were dying of diseases that would be curable with access to the appropriate drugs and timely healthcare support. Such access was impeded by the vehicles transporting doctors and medicines often breaking down on their way to villages and/or people having to walk several miles to reach the nearest doctor, pharmacy, or hospital. At that time, Andrea and Barry also noticed several vehicles – motorbikes, cars, and pickups – abandoned on the road, which could have been brought back to service with minimal repairs and maintenance.

They decided to create a locally-based Transport Resource Management system with preventive maintenance service stations that would ensure existing vehicle fleets would not break down. The underlying belief was that establishing a stable logistics link between distribution hubs and villages and enabling health workers to reach anyone in need, no matter where they lived, would, on its own, have an impact on improving the health outcomes and survival of many people. Additionally, Andrea and Barry Coleman spent significant time and effort to raise awareness around the globe about the need to strengthen healthcare-related logistics in African countries, rather than just donating drugs or vehicles.

Riders for Health has provided technical support, spare parts, and regular checks to many health workers relying on vehicles to reach their patients. This has almost eliminated breakdowns, making the most of the vehicles donated by international NGOs, and reducing the costs for anyone involved. The costs of *Riders for Health*'s operations and training programmes for local technicians are covered through contracts with (prevalently) national Ministries of Health, private organisations, and international NGOs. In the last few years, the organisation has also added to its core services a one-off consulting service for other organisations that want to plan and set up transport-based projects. As of 2020, *Riders for Health* had served around 14 million people across Africa and was directly contributing to ensuring that women could deliver their babies in a clinic rather than at home, children could receive immunisation on time with available vaccines, and that a constantly-rising number of rural villages could access primary care.

Case study questions

1 Would you consider *Riders for Health* as a social entrepreneurial organisation? Why or why not?

   - If you answered yes to question 1, would you consider *Riders for Health* as a social enterprise or not?
   - If you answered no to question 1, how would you define *Riders for Health* based on the organisational forms discussed in Section 2.2?

2 Does *Riders for Health* portray itself as a social entrepreneurship? And does its partners and supporters do so? Why do you think that is the case?

3 What is the potential social change and social impact that *Riders for Health* generates?

Notes

1 American Sociological Association. (2020). *Social change*. Retrieved from: https://www.asanet.org/topics/social-change [Last accessed on: 04 December 2020].
2 Haugh, H. M., & Talwar, A. (2016). Linking social entrepreneurship and social change: The mediating role of empowerment. *Journal of Business Ethics*, 133(4), 643–658.

3 Phills, J. A., et al. (2008). Rediscovering social innovation. *Stanford Social Innovation Review*, Fall, 36.
4 Mulgan, G. (2006). The process of social innovation. *Innovations: Technology, Governance, Globalization*, 1(2), 146.
5 Nambisan, S., Lyytinen, K., Majchrzak, A., & Song, M. (2017). Digital innovation management: Reinventing innovation management research in a digital world. *MIS Quarterly*, 41(1), 224.
6 Abila, R. O., Ojwang, W., Othina, A., Lwenya, C., Oketch, R., & Okeyo, R. (2013). Using ICT for fish marketing: The EFMIS model in Kenya. *Food Chain*, 3(1–2), 48–63.
7 Prabhu, J. (2017). Frugal innovation: Doing more with less for more. *Philosophical Transactions of the Royal Society A*, 375(2095), 1–22
8 Rawhouser, H., Cummings, M., & Newbert, S. L. (2019). Social impact measurement: Current approaches and future directions for social entrepreneurship research. *Entrepreneurship Theory and Practice*, 43(1), 83.
9 Shane, S., & Venkataraman, S. (2000). The promise of entrepreneurship as a field of research. *Academy of Management Review*, 25, 217–226.
10 United Nations – Civil Society. (2021). *Who we are*. Retrieved from: https://www.un.org/en/civil-society/page/about-us
11 Cambridge Dictionary. (2021). *Meaning of charity in English*. Retrieved from: https://dictionary.cambridge.org/dictionary/english/charity
12 Diani, M. (1992). The concept of social movement. *The Sociological Review*, 40(1), 1–25, 13.
13 Della Porta, D., & Diani, M. (2006). *Social movements: An introduction* (2nd ed.). Malden, MA: Blackwell, 5.
14 Simms, S. V. K., & Robinson, J. A. (2008). Activist or entrepreneur? An identity-based model of social entrepreneurship. In Robinson, J. A., Mair, J., & Hockerts, K. (Eds), *International perspectives on social entrepreneurship*. Basingstoke & New York, 9–26.
15 Bornstein, D., & Davis, S. (2010). *Social entrepreneurship: What everyone needs to know®*. Oxford: Oxford University Press.
16 World Fair Trade Organisation. (2020). *Definition of Fair Trade*. Retrieved from: https://wfto.com/who-we-are

3 Characteristics of social entrepreneurship

Key content

This chapter explores key characteristics of social entrepreneurs and of the most popular form of social entrepreneurial organisation, i.e. social enterprises, highlighting the variety of forms that social entrepreneurship can take and how this allows its presence in many different sectors.

3.1 Portrait of a social entrepreneur
3.2 Portrait of a social enterprise
3.3 Social entrepreneurship's sectors of operation

Learning objectives

- Become familiar with the motivation, personality, and skills attributed to social entrepreneurs, and with the challenges they face.
- Learn about the key organisational characteristics of a social enterprise.
- Reflect on which combinations of organisational characteristics of social enterprises might work best in different contexts.
- Appreciate the variety of sectors in which social entrepreneurship operates and how this relates to the broader socio-economic contexts in which it exists.

3.1 Portrait of a social entrepreneur

Social entrepreneurs come from many backgrounds and operate in different ways. Yet there are personality traits, skills, and challenges that tend to be common in all (or at least most) of the successful ones. Learning about them can help aspiring social entrepreneurs to understand if they have what it takes and/or what skills they might need to develop. Additionally, it can help people interested in social entrepreneurship to understand what might trigger it and how best to support it. The next sections create an ideal portrait of a social entrepreneur looking at four key areas: motivation, personality, skills, and challenges.

3.1.1 Motivation of social entrepreneurs

The single most important prerequisite of social entrepreneurship is undoubtedly motivation. There is a consensus around three key factors that might push a person to become a social rather than traditional entrepreneur:

DOI: 10.4324/9781003121824-5

1   They have witnessed or experienced a social issue first-hand.
2   They have a background (e.g. role models from family, voluntary activities, teachers, peer groups) that helped them to develop a strong sense of justice, and the desire to fight for what they believe to be "the right thing".
3   They want to make a political statement and demonstrate that social and environmental issues can be tackled through different/novel/more powerful approaches than existing ones.

For example, studies of social entrepreneurship in the African continent showed that a key component of social entrepreneurial motivation is the adherence to the Ubuntu philosophy – which stresses the importance of interdependence and reciprocity – and attention to the needs of the local tribe or community.

Having direct experience of an issue or seeing how it impacts the life of others is fundamental for two reasons. It spurs the motivation to work hard to address that issue and to prioritise helping others over becoming richer, and it favours the development of empathy, a key skill for social entrepreneurs. Too often, organisations in the third sector adopt a top-down approach and just make assumptions about what people need. Understanding the pain and struggles of potential beneficiaries and customers significantly increases the likelihood of coming up with an idea that works while reducing the risk of making damaging assumptions (see Chapters 6 and 7 for additional details on this topic).

Similarly, only a strong desire to help others, an aversion to injustices and inequality, and established beliefs about what is acceptable and fair and what is not, can drive the motivation to embark on an arduous journey such as that of social entrepreneurship. While traditional entrepreneurs start a new venture because they want to leverage a market opportunity, social entrepreneurs often do so because they feel there is a moral obligation to rectify a situation or to drive change. These beliefs can be innate, due to direct or indirect experience of social and environmental issues or, in some cases, can emerge from having been raised or exposed at a young age to role models and influencers fighting for social justice or environmental protection. These role models can be found anywhere – among family members, peers, leaders of religious or charitable groups, idols, and so on.

But why would a person, who is motivated to make the world a better place, opt for social entrepreneurship rather than for joining a social movement, volunteering, or working for a charity? Personality and skills, combined with the desire for occupational independence, self-fulfilment, and achievement, help to explain the entrepreneurial side of motivation.

3.1.2 Personality of social entrepreneurs

The personality of a social entrepreneur tends to resemble that of traditional entrepreneurs because they perform the same key activities. Any type of entrepreneur needs to be able to translate an idea into something practical, attract resources to make it happen, and legitimise what they are creating. According to an extensive amount of existing literature, performing these activities requires:

*   determination;
*   passion and dedication;

- confidence and self-belief;
- comfort with uncertainty and risk;
- independence;
- proactivity/doers attitude.

Probably, one of the fundamental characteristics for succeeding as a (social) entrepreneur is determination. Starting something new is likely to trigger resistance from incumbents and many refusals of requests for support. A long time might pass before initial efforts lead to something tangible and usually a 24/7 commitment to work is necessary to keep an entrepreneurial venture or project going. In most cases, success does not even come – around 90% of start-ups do not make it past their first five years – and many attempts are required before developing something that works. Only the determination to succeed (and a certain degree of patience and resilience) can ensure that an entrepreneur gets to the finish line, finding the strength to overcome indifference and issues, and deploying the energy, time, and effort necessary to keep the project alive and evolving.

Determination, in turn, is usually sustained by passion for a cause or by the dedication to solve a problem that is deeply felt and considered extremely interesting or important. Entrepreneurs and social entrepreneurs usually start from an idea triggered by their personal experience and by their search for, or finding of, a solution to a problem. Having confidence in that idea and believing that it has the potential to target an unmet need also felt by others is a key ingredient for building commitment and sustaining efforts. Similarly, a strong self-belief, particularly in their personal ability to overcome obstacles and to succeed no matter what, is fundamental for entrepreneurs to remain determined even in the face of difficulties or limited resources.

Successful entrepreneurs and social entrepreneurs also need to be comfortable with uncertainty and risk. As discussed above, entrepreneurial start-ups are likely to fail. Often, (social) entrepreneurs risk their own income and job security to push forward their idea, with no guarantee that the risk will pay off. Any entrepreneurial endeavour is subject to external influences, from devastating events such as wars, crises, and pandemics, to small but frequent changes in technology and customer preferences, etc. Additionally, any project has specific risks that depend on the ability of the entrepreneur to attract the right type and amount of support, on competition, on finding the right team, strategy, and the like. Only people who are comfortable with not knowing what happens next and who can manage the stress that might arise from potential failure or unexpected circumstances can build the resilience necessary to be a successful (social) entrepreneur, without damaging irreparably their own well-being.

Finally, successful (social) entrepreneurship requires independence and proactivity. Entrepreneurs have to be the ones solving problems on a daily basis, making the necessary decisions, taking risks, and scouting the right opportunity. They need to have a "can-do" and makers' attitude. People that wait for instructions or reassurances are not likely to make things happen. Skills then do the rest to translate ideas into successful and lasting organisations.

3.1.3 Skills of social entrepreneurs

Translating ideas into something practical benefits from the ability to learn from negative feedback or failure and to develop competencies on an ongoing basis, and from managerial skills. These include the good management of budgets and resources, attention to strategy and external relations, planning, organisational skills, and competence in monitoring outcomes and in managing people. Additionally, starting something new requires the ability to recognise opportunities in unmet needs and to realise these opportunities through an innovative approach and bricolage – i.e. through the assembling of existing resources in new ways and combinations.

Attracting resources and, in particular, raising the necessary financial resources to operate, requires the ability to persuade others and solicit tangible support. These, in turn, depend on effective communication and storytelling, accountability through impact measurement and reporting, trust-building, and extensive networking. Finally, providing legitimacy to a new idea or organisation requires the development of a vision that can inspire and guide others, the ability to forge alliances of supporters that certify the project as something believable and worthy, and the ability to challenge the status quo in a responsible and effective way. Going against existing habits tends to generate resistance, and only those that articulate well why what they propose is helpful can succeed at establishing something new.

Personality tends to go hand in hand with skills. A person with certain characteristics and attitudes is likely to develop skills related to those characteristics and attitudes.

Table 3.1 Roles, personality traits, and skills of successful social entrepreneurs

Roles	Personality traits	Skills
Translating ideas into something concrete	• Determination • Passion and dedication • Confidence and self-belief • Comfort with uncertainty and risk • Independence • Proactivity	• Ability to persuade others • Ability to cope with negative feedback and failure • Ability to recognise opportunities in unmet needs • Managerial skills • Adoption of an innovative approach • Bricolage • Fundraising
Attracting resources	• Determination • Patience • Proactivity	• Ability to persuade others • Ability to cope with negative feedback and failure • Ability to attract and mobilise resources • Networking skills • Storytelling and communicating • Trust-building
Legitimising a new idea, activity, or organisation	• Determination • Passion and dedication • Comfort with risk	• Developing a vision • Storytelling and communicating • Alliance-building • Driving change/challenging status quo • Creating additional social impact

Legend: The arrows indicate the presence of a positive feedback between the personality and skills involved.

Exercising these skills, in turn, ends up shaping part of their personality. For example, someone who is an extrovert is likely to spend more time meeting and interacting with people than an introvert would do. This helps them develop good communication skills which, in turn, enhance their success in interacting with others, thus likely increasing their propensity to being extroverted. For social entrepreneurs, it is no different. Personality traits such as those described above are not only helpful per se but are also conducive to skills that support the entrepreneur in further securing the resources and legitimacy they need. For example, confidence and self-belief are likely to enhance persuasiveness, which can help alliance-building. Similarly, independence and proactivity make it more likely that a person will spot opportunities where others do not see them, and that they will engage in bricolage and develop solutions and approaches that are novel.

Table 3.1 summarises the key traits of social entrepreneurs in terms of motivation, personality, and skills and highlights how some traits support success and are connected to one another.

3.1.4 Challenges for social entrepreneurs

So far, the chapter discussed what it takes to be a successful social entrepreneur. However, it is also important to highlight the challenges social entrepreneurs face, which might affect them even when their endeavour is relatively successful. Being a social entrepreneur is frequently a lonely career. While many organisations are the results of a partnership, most tend to be founded by a single individual who, for many months if not years, needs to make all the decisions, take all the risks, face all the uncertainty, and bear all the doubts.

Being a (social) entrepreneur is also stressful. It requires commitment and sometimes sacrifices in terms of both personal and professional life. To make things even worse, social entrepreneurs often feel the anxiety of not doing enough to solve the problem they want to tackle. While no one likes to fail, social entrepreneurs know that if they do, the people they want to help might be left without support, or the situation they want to rectify might remain ignored. This sense of responsibility is something that profoundly affects the mental health of social entrepreneurs, to the point that some of them quit because they cannot handle the pressure and the burden. Support from peers, awards, rewards, and appreciation from others can be powerful ways to mitigate this issue and sustain their resilience.

Successful social entrepreneurs frequently face the tough decision between rewarding themselves for their initiative and hard work and redistributing the additional value created among stakeholders. As seen in the previous chapters, social entrepreneurship is characterised by the separation between value creation and value appropriation, by the reinvestment of profits to generate social impact, and by the desire to fairly share the value created with contributing stakeholders. What is "fair", however, is very difficult to determine. Many social entrepreneurs are criticised if they earn too much or if they keep some of the profits realised for themselves. While unusually high profits might signal the unfair rewarding or even exploitation of some other factor of production, a healthy level of profitability is helpful to keep an organisation afloat. Social entrepreneurs that manage to make their organisation profitable while respecting all stakeholders and reinvesting part of the profits generated to create even more social impact should be rewarded for their effectiveness. Instead, they face the risk of being stigmatised. This adds pressures and can worsen the entrepreneur's mental health and impact their motivation to work hard over time.

Similarly, success might bring with it the challenge of mission drift. This is the risk of increasingly sacrificing the realisation of impact to be more successful financially, due to pressure from investors and other stakeholders. While impact and profits can go hand in hand, in practice this is not always the case and social entrepreneurs often need to deal with difficult trade-offs between serving existing beneficiaries better/ serving more beneficiaries and ensuring they become and remain profitable. If left unchecked, mission drift can represent a reputational risk, affect organisational culture, alienate some stakeholders, and, most importantly, jeopardise the delivery of social and environmental impact. Social entrepreneurs have the difficult job of understanding what to accept and what to refuse.

In contexts with significant institutional voids, i.e. with a lack of intermediaries and institutions that support market transactions such as banks giving access to credit, enforcement of property rights, or information on market participants, social entrepreneurs might also face the challenge of building sufficient trust with the local community to be able to operate, unless their initiative emerged from within that community. In the presence of institutional voids, mutual self-help is the norm, as is the reliance on informal, sometimes illegal means of "making-do". Values and beliefs tend to be anchored in tradition and everyone needs to respect and adhere to them if they want to be part of the community. Only social entrepreneurs who manage to keep building a local presence under those circumstances, showing respect for the local way of life, and remaining in constant dialogue with the rest of the community – ideally activating participatory processes and building on existing initiatives and structures – can hope to succeed. This challenge can be particularly difficult to overcome for social entrepreneurs who are not original members of the community or do not share their problems/life experiences.

Finally, social entrepreneurs often find it hard to detach themselves from their original idea, even when it might not be working as well as it could. Many social entrepreneurial organisations have failed because their founder became too fixated on their way of doing things and did not let others contribute their insights. A certain degree of attachment to an idea or initiative, and a certain rigidity are to be expected from people who invest time, effort, and passion into a project. As said above, determination, commitment, and self-belief are necessary ingredients to succeed. However, there comes a point when learning from others is equally important to ensure the survival of an organisation, and this is where many social entrepreneurs end up failing. They are unwilling to share or modify their idea or to adopt solutions elaborated by others. They do not release control and tasks even when they feel overwhelmed and might have the resources to hire competent managers. They pretend not to see the success of different approaches or what is not working in their approach. This is when all starts to collapse or, even in the best case, to underperform. While there is no recipe for preventing this downside of successful social entrepreneurship, exchanges with peers, empathy, and the conscious effort to detach slightly from the original idea once things start to evolve can help social entrepreneurs to find a good balance between pride and determination on the one hand and humility and development on the other.

Figure 3.1 represents the portrait of social entrepreneurs that the existing literature provides.

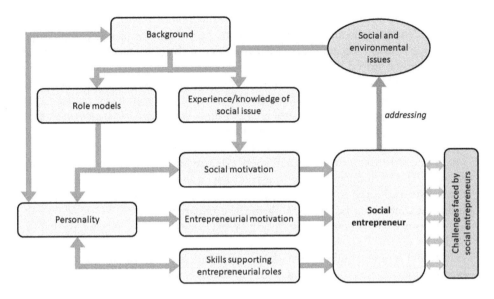

Figure 3.1 Portrait of a social entrepreneur

PORTRAIT OF A SOCIAL ENTREPRENEUR IN PRACTICE – ABHI RAMESH

Abhi Ramesh was born in India but moved to Atlanta with his family at the age of five. In an interview for news outlet Mic, Abhi once affirmed that the start of their life in the United States was not easy. "I used to get yelled at any time I'd throw away even a tiny piece of food left on my plate ... Eating out wasn't really a thing we would do". This made him aware of the problem of food scarcity and waste from a very young age.

As a student of business at the *University of Pennsylvania – Wharton Business School*, he became familiar with entrepreneurship and got engaged with several projects and initiatives that had a strong social impact component. As a result of his studies and the experiences he had while at *Wharton*, Abhi co-founded three different start-ups – *Altair Prep*, *TrendBent*, and *StoreTok* – before accepting a job in the financial sector.

In this new role, he came across many food logistics companies that were struggling to create value for their customers and remain profitable. There he realised that there was a high amount of waste – up to a third of the fresh food produced never reached the final customer. In the same period, he noticed around Philadelphia that many people did not have access to fresh produce because their local grocer would not sell them. Combining the two experiences and the research he had started to do, Abhi realised there was the opportunity to satisfy an unmet demand of affordable and available fresh produce by reducing some of the waste he had witnessed.

Inspired by this insight, he quit his job and rented a van to visit farms in Eastern Pennsylvania and New Jersey. There, he bought any produce that would have gone to waste because it was not suitable for the retail market at a reduced price. He then stored it in his flat, boxed it, and re-sold it to people in Philadelphia, who did not have the resources to buy or easy access to fresh produce. He used most of his savings trying to get this activity going until he realised that there was enough demand to officially set up a venture. *Misfits Market* came to be in 2018. In order to keep the produce affordable for low-income families, Abhi decided to set the business up as an online platform, to avoid the overheads needed to run an in-person shop. Meanwhile, he leveraged his existing network in the financial sector to attract the attention and support of venture capitalists and hired a team that would bring in competences, e.g. in the food industry, that he felt he needed to help the company grow.

Misfits Market is now a subscription box service that buys, checks, packages, and sells directly to consumers products that are perfectly fine to eat but that traditional retailers and supermarkets would not stock and sell, such as vegetables with strange shapes or that look ugly or strange, products that have been mis-labelled or mis-packaged, and items that would be too small or too large for supermarket shelves. Because these are products that otherwise would not reach the final consumer, *Misfits Market* can buy them at discounted prices and offer them to their own customers at a price that is often 30–40% lower than that of mainstream retailers. Customers order boxes of different sizes and can personalise them picking from a list of available products. The boxes are delivered to their homes. Between its launch and 2020, and also thanks to the sudden opportunity created by the COVID-19 pandemic, *Misfits Market* distributed over 5 million pounds of fresh produce that would have otherwise gone to waste, and attracted over $16 million in investment.

In 2020, Abhi was recognised by *Forbes* magazine as one of the top 30 social entrepreneurs under 30, in its yearly classification.

3.2 Portrait of a social enterprise

As there are many ways to be a social entrepreneur, there are also many typologies of social entrepreneurial organisations. Among these, this chapter will focus on social enterprises (see definition in Chapter 1), which are the most popular form of social entrepreneurship worldwide.

The typology of social enterprises depends on the choices that their founder(s) make in terms of social business model, connection between impact and revenues, legal form, and governance structures. These choices are strongly influenced by the mission of the social enterprise, the socio-legal context in which it operates, and the way in which it originated (e.g. set up by an entrepreneur, spin-out, spin-off, community endeavour, charity attempting to generate revenues, etc.). While showcasing the full variety of organisational characteristics and typologies that social enterprises present around the world would go well beyond the scope of this book, the rest of the chapter builds some high-level portraits of the key organisational characteristics defining a social enterprise.

3.2.1 Social business models for social enterprises

A social business model (see Chapter 8 for additional details), essentially, is a description of how social entrepreneurial organisations (and thus also social enterprises) plan to generate value for key customers and/or beneficiaries, and to ensure that their generation of value is going to be financially viable. It involves explaining what the organisation plans to do, how, for whom, through which resources (and related costs) and channels, and how all these elements are going to fit together.

Acceptable social business models for social enterprises vary significantly across geographies. This mostly depends on what combination of sources of income is acceptable and allowed for social enterprises within that specific context. Studies of African social enterprises found that most of them survive through a mix of revenues and subsidies, donations, or grants. This is because they tend to have minimal or negative profit margins due to their frequent choice to pay employees and suppliers well above market rates. Most social enterprises within the European Union (EU) are fully reliant on revenues and investments to cover their costs, since the countries in which they operate in are likely to conceive them as "full-on" businesses. Social enterprises in the United States, instead, are frequently set up as non-profit organisations with significant revenue-generating activities. They are expected to recover some of their costs through revenues, while relying on donations and grants to sustain a significant portion of their value-creation activities.

A social business model can help a social enterprise to survive and adapt as its situation evolves, and to avoid funder-led mission drift, by enabling it to understand what type of funds to rely on (see Chapter 10 for more details on funding options). For example, while a social enterprise may ultimately aim for profitability, it might opt to survive through a mix of revenues, subsidies, awards, or loans in its early stages, as it tries to introduce a significant innovation, or when scaling up. Most importantly, establishing what social business model to adopt is the first step to make strategic and operational decisions in relation to connecting impact and revenues, legal form and governance structures.

3.2.2 Options to connect impact and revenues for social enterprises

Social enterprises have many options to connect their social/environmental impact with their generation of revenues. On one side of the spectrum, they might opt for a full integration and be, according to the definition of Alter (2007),[1] embedded social enterprises. This is the case when social enterprises both earn revenues and realise social/environmental impact through the production or provision of the same product or service. Examples of embedded social enterprises are: microfinance providers; Fair Trade Organisations; social enterprises whose products and services have an embedded social/environmental impact, e.g. selling products that reduce waste by recycling materials. On the other side of the spectrum, the generation of impact and revenues might be completely separate. A social enterprise might generate revenues through the sale of a product or service and use that to subsidise different activities that achieve social/environmental impact. Alter (2007) defined the social enterprises that adopt this organisational form as external social enterprises. Examples of external social enterprises are those adopting the "buy one, donate one" model (see *TOMS* Shoes in Chapter 2) or those like Oxfam that generate revenues through retail sales and then use the money thus collected to fund their activities related to poverty reduction and economic development.

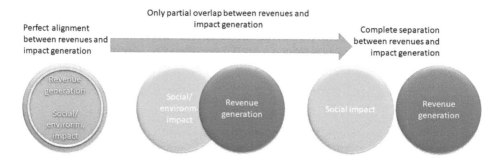

Figure 3.2 Options to connect impact and revenues (adapted from Alter, 2007, p. 18)

Within these extremes, there can be different levels of integration between impact and revenues, as well as different levels of beneficiaries' involvement in the activities that generate impact (e.g. from mere recipients of social impact, to beneficiaries who are also paying customers, and to partners or employees contributing to social impact creation as well as benefiting from it) (Figure 3.2). An example of partial integration between impact and revenues is the *Aravind Eye Hospital*. Its mission is to provide free, high-quality eye surgeries to people who would not be able to afford a surgery or hospitalisation otherwise. To do so, the Institute created a standardised process of surgery delivery inspired by that of *McDonald*'s and offers ad hoc training to surgeons, nurses, and ophthalmologists, in order to maximise efficiency and minimise costs. Meanwhile, it provides high-quality surgeries to those who can afford to pay, offering them extra services in exchange for a fee. Each paying customer covers the cost of two people who cannot afford to pay. This way, in some cases, the surgeries provided are both a source of impact and revenues. In other cases, they are only a source of impact, while revenues are generated through the provision of related services to wealthier customers.

3.2.3 Legal forms for social enterprises

Legal forms are instruments regulated by law that provide organisations with a legal status and, thus, with the opportunity to act as an independent entity with specific rights, obligations, and responsibilities. In most countries, social entrepreneurial organisations can be legally incorporated as limited shares companies, cooperatives, associations, and non-profit organisations. The type of legal form adopted is strongly influenced by the context in which they operate and the related regulations, historical roots of social entrepreneurship, the mission, and the social business model developed.

Social enterprises normally have the same incorporation options as any other social entrepreneurial organisation – although in some contexts they might avoid incorporating as a non-profit due to stringent limitations on revenue-generation or funding options. For example, in Nigeria social enterprises can incorporate as Companies Limited by Guarantee, Incorporated Trustees, or Cooperatives. Incorporated Trustees are exempt from Company Income Tax, provided they do not generate profits through trade and their trustees do not receive any income from the organisation. Companies Limited by Guarantee are taxed normally but can generate revenues through business activities and might benefit from tax deductions if they reinvest some of their profits into activities delivering social impact. They can also have subsidiaries that are set up as Incorporated Trustees for achieving their social or environmental goals.

However, in some countries, there are specific legal forms for incorporating a social enterprise. As of 2020, special legal forms and status for social enterprises existed in 15 countries in the EU, the United Kingdom, Albania, Serbia, South Korea, and in some federal states of the United States and Canada. Seven countries in the EU that created a specific legal status for social enterprises also have slightly adapted existing legal forms for cooperatives or, in a few cases, non-profit organisations, to suit the requirements of social enterprises. Four additional EU countries and the United Kingdom have instead just adapted existing legal forms instead of creating a new legal status ex novo. For example, the United Kingdom adapted the Community Interest Company to enable the incorporation of social enterprises, while Belgium instituted the Social Purpose Company to allow existing companies incorporated as cooperatives or for-profits to gain a special status signalling their being a "social enterprise". Countries like Austria, Finland, France, Greece, Poland, or Switzerland, while not necessarily creating ad hoc acts and forms, officially recognise WISEs (see Chapter 1) and cooperatives as social enterprises.

Having a special legal status and/or official recognition can be very beneficial for a social enterprise. It regulates the funds they can obtain, how they should be governed, and it might help them benefit from favourable taxation (e.g. social cooperatives in Italy and WISEs in Belgium can benefit from a reduced VAT rate, and companies with a social purpose that do not distribute profits can enjoy a privileged tax status in Austria and Germany). It also creates reassurances for external stakeholders that the social enterprise is indeed trying to achieve a double or triple bottom line.

Both in countries where legislators have created specific legal forms for social enterprises and in countries where this is still not the case, traditional incorporation forms tend to be the norm rather than the exception. For example, in the Philippines over 90% of social enterprises are incorporated as cooperatives and associations, in Romania and Hungary the majority of social enterprises are incorporated as non-profit organisations, and in countries like China, Russia, or Kenya, the majority of social enterprises are registered as businesses (based on local forms).

The preference for traditional legal forms is due to reasons as varied as: the availability of information; support and funding options; the self-perceived ability to navigate the legal and fiscal requirements associated with a specific form; the ease of management and understanding of the governance requirements; tax liability and security concerns; the opportunity to tailor the form to the specific needs of the social enterprise; the familiarity of stakeholders with the more established forms. In some extreme cases, where governments do not allow the formation of new non-profit organisations or social enterprises for fear that they might be working towards political destabilisation, incorporating as a for-profit enterprise might even be a forced choice. When a social enterprise is incorporated through an existing and non-specific organisational form, it can either have a special status as a social enterprise, be recognised as such if it respects certain criteria (e.g. through certification programmes), or it can define itself as a social enterprise but without any way of proving it.

One interesting option that many social enterprises choose is to incorporate as multiple legal entities. Guo and Bielefeld (2014)[2] suggest that it is better to incorporate two separate entities when customers are motivated entirely by self-interest, the activities used for revenue-generation are entirely separate from those that allow to realise social or environmental impact, revenue-generating activities are profitable, suppliers charge normal rates, and there is no chance to benefit from volunteers contributing to the programme.

For example, in the United Kingdom, a common way of dealing with potential trade-offs between impact and profit is to set up a social enterprise as two different organisations – a business that maximises revenues and profits, attracts investments without constraints, and operates in traditional markets; and a charity that receives all the profits generated by the business as a donation and employs them to generate social/environmental impact (e.g. see the case study on Mayamiko in Apeendix 1). Alternatively, some social enterprises choose to incorporate through two separate for-profit entities – a core one, and one that supplies it. This allows the latter, which is usually that generating impact, to keep growing its business and impact beyond that of the original company, by selling its products or services to other organisations too (e.g. see the case study on Malaika in this chapter and in Chapter 9). Similarly, a social enterprise may decide, based on its experience and the feedback received, to expand its mission and to realise an additional type of social/environmental impact. In cases like this, providing the new form of impact through a separate entity might be an opportunity to generate both additional impact and revenues, and it thus makes sense to create a spin-off or spin-out with either the same or a different legal form.

Finally, in several countries, the legal form can be an important way to signal the de facto status of an organisation as a social enterprise pursuing a double or triple bottom line, even if this is not explicitly mentioned in the articles of incorporation. For example, in many European countries, as well as in Brazil, the Philippines, the United States, Nigeria, and Japan. WISEs and cooperatives are normally recognised as social enterprises. Similarly, many stakeholders in the United States would consider the trading arms of charities and B Corps as social enterprises.

3.2.4 Governance of social enterprises

Governance is the set of rules, principles, systems, relationships, and processes through which an organisation operates and is controlled, and through which its actions and directions are held to account. It creates the framework within which decisions are taken and goals are set and monitored and it is one of the key ways to integrate the interests and perspectives of different stakeholders, engage them in decision-making, shape leadership, and ensure transparency and accountability. Sometimes, governance structures also contribute to establishing and maintaining reputation and form the basis for networking and fundraising opportunities. Establishing governance structures is one of the key ways to ensure that any social entrepreneurial organisation – and even more so social enterprises that are normally subject to stronger market pressures due to their revenue-generating activities – does not suffer from mission drift (see Section 3.1.4). As such, governance set-up is one of the most delicate decisions to be made.

Frequently, the governance structures and their membership are determined, partially or substantially, by the legal form, as well as by funders, and by the socio-economic and political environment in which the social enterprise operates. For example, in some European countries such as Italy, Greece, or France, multi-stakeholder participation in governance is a requirement for an organisation to be considered as a legitimate social enterprise. In other countries, there are no constraints or expectations and social enterprises have complete freedom in deciding whom to involve in governance and decision-making, and why and how. According to a policy brief published by SEFORÏS in 2017 and based on the study of social enterprises in eight countries (China, Germany, Spain, Hungary, Portugal, Romania, Sweden, and the United Kingdom),

> 22.8% of the organizations indicated to have 3 or more stakeholders represented, while 41.7% of the organizations have only one type of stakeholder on the board... Board inclusiveness, understood as involving beneficiaries in the board, we find, is highest in Sweden (30,8% of social enterprises have at least one beneficiary on the board) and Hungary (30,6%) and lowest in Germany (4,6%). 90% of the boards across countries also include women.[3]

Whatever the legal requirements, there is always some room for manoeuvre to tailor governance structures to the specific needs of the social enterprise. There are three main theories that guide governance choices: stakeholders, stewardship, and institutional theory. The first encourages to establish governance structures in a way that guarantees the representation of the interests of different stakeholders (e.g. beneficiaries, customers, investors and other funders, employees, representatives of the community in which the social enterprise operates, public authorities, and the like). The second encourages instead to establish governance structures in a way that guarantees that the leaders and managers of the social enterprise pursue its mission and best interests. Finally, the third encourages the adoption of governance structures that confer external legitimacy to the social enterprise. What approach gets privileged is often a function of the values of the founder(s) and of the social business model, and it ends up shaping how governance structures operate in practice.

Independently from the approach adopted, there is a consensus that stakeholders' voices need to be heard and considered. However, there are many ways to engage stakeholders and governance structures might not always be the best approach. For example, the research of George and Reed (2016)[4] established that it is more important to recruit, as board members, individuals with the knowledge and expertise that the social enterprise needs, or with management and entrepreneurial skills, rather than individuals who represent stakeholders but lack such skills and knowledge. The ways in which stakeholders are engaged determine who ends up getting involved in what types of decisions and initiatives.

Formal means to involve stakeholders in governance include: making representatives of each stakeholder category members of the Board of Directors (for businesses), Board of Trustees (for non-profit organisations), or membership (for cooperatives); creating a stakeholder committee independent from the board; deciding, if applicable, to which extent decision-making power is connected or not to the ownership of the social enterprise's shares (e.g. one share of capital equals one vote vs. one member equals one vote). Informal means include instead: the organisation of committees and assemblies; the distribution of regular surveys to understand the opinions of different stakeholders; the set-up of advisory boards just to gather advice or feedback. The legal form adopted, combined with the composition of the board, of its membership, and the choice between formal and informal mechanisms to involve stakeholders, determines both how well different stakeholders are represented and if a social enterprise is privately, publicly, or collectively owned.

Many founders of social enterprises do not give enough attention early on to governance, focusing instead on fundraising and operations. Governance structures that are not well aligned with the social enterprise's goals and social business model can create tensions between board members and managers or between different formal bodies. Poorly planned governance structures can render unclear where responsibility and ownership of decisions lie, and, if led by powerful or long-standing members, might hinder change. When investment in appropriate governance structures arrives too late, it is one of the main threats to both growth and a sustainable achievement of a double or triple bottom line.

Figure 3.3 represents the portrait of social enterprises that the existing literature provides.

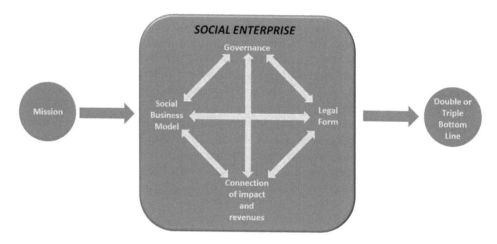

Figure 3.3 Portrait of a social enterprise

PORTRAIT OF A SOCIAL ENTERPRISE IN PRACTICE – MALAIKA

Malaika was founded in Egypt in 2004, by Margarita Andrade and Goya Gallagher, two Ecuadorian women with a passion for this African country. They were looking for a way to earn a living while staying in Egypt and, thanks to their background in design and passion for embroidery and hand-drawn thread work, they spotted an important market opportunity. Egyptian cotton is one of the best cottons in the world and is used for luxury products in several countries. Therefore, Margarita and Goya started to buy bed linens made of Egyptian cotton to sell them in Ecuador. Through this initiative, they became aware that the working conditions in manufacturing factories in Egypt were harsh and, therefore, that providing more of the same jobs was probably doing more harm than good for locals. Similarly, they observed that while Egyptian cotton was very popular abroad for luxury household items, there were no producers of high-end bed linens in Egypt.

Eventually, Margarita and Goya came to the realisation that solving these two issues simultaneously could have been the idea they were looking for. They hired a flat in Cairo and established there a workshop to teach local women how to do embroidery. Once having mastered the trade, the women could take some cotton linens back home and embroider them while taking care of their family. This helped women to earn income for their family and exert their creativity without disrupting social norms and enabled Margarita and Goya to start selling high-quality cotton table and bed linens enriched by handmade embroidery inspired by Egyptian history and culture. In a very short time, the sales picked up and so Margarita and Goya set up *Malaika*, a stand-alone business. In just a few years, both the products sold and the embroidery training provided by *Malaika* enjoyed increased demand and allowed the generation of enough revenues to establish a linen factory, where women (as well as men) could find stable employment under fair conditions. Since 2018, *Malaika* has been able to train 50 women every two months.

Owning a factory rather than just trading bed linens also allowed Margarita and Goya to control the entire production process, thus ensuring that business success and positive social impact would go hand in hand. *Malaika* is now a thriving and growing social enterprise with an increasingly international outlook, employing over 60 workers in its factory, and providing training and self-employment opportunities to an ever-increasing number of Egyptian women and refugees. When women want to work full-time or change their role in the company, Margarita and Goya try to provide them with the training needed and a job opportunity at the factory whenever possible.

The choice of a legal form for *Malaika* was quite straightforward. In Egypt, it is very difficult to start new NGOs and, when they began to develop their business idea, Margarita and Goya had never heard of social entrepreneurship. For these reasons, they set up *Malaika* as a for-profit business, funding it first through personal funds and then through the profits they made selling the linens to rich Egyptian customers. While, initially, the choice to set up what was essentially a training programme as a business seemed risky, since it precluded access to grants and donations, in the end it proved to be the right choice. Having to create a social business model entirely dependent on revenues to sustain operations pushed Margarita and Goya to be bold and proactive and, in the end, favoured the very fast growth of *Malaika*. For example, Margarita and Goya established collaborations with other stakeholders such as magazines specialised in interior design with an international outlook to enhance the business' growth opportunities.

While, formally, the governance of *Malaika* is in the hands of the two co-founders, who managed to avoid requesting external investments by growing organically through the revenues generated, employees are always kept in the loop and the two co-founders request and react to their feedback on an ongoing basis. For example, after realising that childcare was impeding women from joining training or making the most of it, Margarita and Goya started paying for nursery places for the children of their trainees.

In terms of connecting revenues and impact, *Malaika* is set up as an embedded social enterprise (see Section 3.2.2). Its social impact happens through training and employing women in different operational and managerial positions and through providing women with an opportunity to become self-employed and to earn income while looking after their family. The training programme both ensures a competent workforce and empowers women by making them learn new, valuable skills. For example, *Malaika* started to offer literacy classes to make sure all the women it employs can read and write. As such, there is a dual impact realised for Egyptian and migrant women that end up training and working at *Malaika*: the improvement of their economic standing and of that of their families, and the increase in women's pride and self-confidence. Helping and training these women, in turn, stands at the core of *Malaika*'s social business model, since it is the key means to produce the luxury bed and table linens that differentiate *Malaika* from other producers and whose sales fund its entire operations and training programmes. The more *Malaika* expands its business, the more it generates social impact and the more social impact it generates, the more it increases its attractiveness as an employer and its income and, thus, the business opportunities and social impact it can pursue.

Since the requests of training always exceed *Malaika*'s workforce needs and its training capacity, the co-founders have recently incorporated their training arm as a separate business – *Threads of Hope*. This trains women in different types of embroidery and is a supplier of embroidery and talent for various other brands in addition to *Malaika*. This has increased the socio-economic impact realised and the potential to scale it further.

3.3 Social entrepreneurship's sectors of operation

Social entrepreneurs and enterprises operate in many different sectors, mostly based on the context in which they are located. In countries characterised by welfare states, social entrepreneurship tends to be conducted through social enterprises and deployed to provide training and employment, tackle social issues such as homelessness and marginalisation, and to complement the public provision of healthcare, social housing, education, and social care, in the presence of limited resources and budgets or of groups with special needs. For example, in the EU, WISEs are the most common typology of social enterprise and services frequently provided through social entrepreneurship would include care and support for people with disabilities or for the elderly, affordable recreation opportunities in disadvantages communities, and integration projects for stigmatised groups such as ex-convicts or refugees.

In many countries characterised by institutional voids, social entrepreneurial organisations tend to be involved in economic development, poverty alleviation, food security, women empowerment, and the provision of basic services and infrastructure such as water and sanitation, basic healthcare, and primary education. In these contexts, social entrepreneurship is often characterised by frugal innovation (see Chapter 2), by a strong connection with the local community, by the creation of activities helping the poorest of the poor to obtain economic security for their family, and by the leveraging of new technology to provide basic services needed for economic development such as electricity, clean water, or banking. For example, according to the work of Sengupta et al. (2018)[5] social entrepreneurship in India is often "associated with the emancipation of rural women from social and cultural taboos limiting their capabilities ... education, and housing for the underserved". Similarly, in Kenya, social enterprises operate mostly in employment creation, community support, environment, and education and, according to existing studies, in both Kenya and Zambia they have been pivotal to the provision of basic needs and poverty reduction, especially in underprivileged and rural areas.

Both in the Global North and in the Global South, social entrepreneurship is increasingly present in sectors such as agriculture, clean energy, environmental conservation, culture/arts and crafts, microfinance/financial services and eco-tourism, especially through cooperatives and Fair Trade Organisations. Additionally, as seen in the previous chapter, social entrepreneurship contributes in all contexts to reducing inequalities, differences in access to opportunities, and people empowerment, and its contributions are unlikely to end there.

In contexts such as the United Kingdom, which have started to invest in social entrepreneurship at an early stage and where the prevailing narrative on social entrepreneurship focuses on social enterprises as businesses with a social mission, social enterprises now operate in almost any sector (e.g. consulting, creative and digital industries, personal care and beauty, manufacturing, transport, etc.), bringing in new ways of doing things and new ethical considerations concerning how things are done, showing that there is a potential upward trajectory for the usage of social entrepreneurship in any country. Such potential, however, can only become something tangible if there is a local ecosystem supporting social entrepreneurship. Therefore, the next chapter looks at how this might look like.

SUMMARY BOX

- Successful social entrepreneurs present common motivation, personality traits, and skills. They either have witnessed or experienced a social issue first-hand, have a background that gave them the desire to fight for what they believe to be "the right thing", or want to demonstrate that social and environmental issues can be tackled through novel approaches. To succeed they need to overcome resistance, attract and redeploy resources in an innovative way, legitimise their idea and work, deal with frequent failure and negative feedback, and be determined to succeed against all odds.
- Successful social entrepreneurs also run into common challenges, such as high levels of stress, the need to handle risks of mission drift and excessive investment in their own idea, stigmatisation if they benefit financially from their venture, and the need to build and maintain trust to keep operating in local communities.
- Key organisational characteristics that determine the profile of a social enterprise are its social business model, connection between revenues and

impact, legal form, and governance structures. These characteristics help to determine how it pursues its double or triple bottom line, how it is perceived by and involves its stakeholders, the risks it faces, and its prospects of financial sustainability.

- Social entrepreneurship is present in an increasing number of sectors in many countries. It is an established practice both in the Global North and in the Global South in sectors such as employment and job creation, education, healthcare, social care, energy, and agriculture.
- The existing institutions, level of economic development, and history of a country significantly impact the sectors where social entrepreneurship is most present and its characteristics.

Check box – Self-reflection and discussion questions

- What are the top five characteristics that a social entrepreneur needs to succeed? Why?
- Beyond motivation, personality, and skills, what do you think contributes to the success or failure of a social entrepreneur?
- What are the main characteristics of a social enterprise? Why does each of them matter?
- Why is it important for a social enterprise to think strategically and holistically about the integration between its key organisational characteristics?
- What are the benefits and risks of different legal forms and their consequences in terms of other key organisational characteristics of social enterprises?
- What determines the sectors of operation of social entrepreneurship?
- Do you think that there are sectors more suitable for social entrepreneurship or that social entrepreneurship should and will thrive in any kind of sector? Why?

Check out additional resources related to this chapter to learn more about the concepts presented and the case studies at: www.routledge.com/9780367640231

Exercises

Exercise 3.1 – Discover the forms social enterprises have in your country

Do a small research on social enterprises in your country: search information online, from networks that support social enterprises and/or talk to founders and managers of social enterprises you are familiar with. Write a (300–500 words) report on the legal forms that social enterprises can adopt in your country and on other ways (e.g. governance structures, guarantees, common social business models) through which they safeguard their pursuit of a double or triple bottom line, and, if appropriate, distribute ownership or limit their distribution of dividends.

Exercise 3.2 – Create the artistic portrait of a social entrepreneur or social enterprise

Select a social entrepreneur or social enterprise that you find particularly inspiring and create their portrait through either a presentation, video, infographic, poster, or any other visual means, using the characteristics described in this chapter and adding anything not covered that might be interesting and applicable to the case you chose. How do different characteristics go hand in hand together? Are there any clashes or characteristics that hamper success based on your analysis? Share your portrait with peers/ the rest of the class. Together, you will create a mosaic of the many different forms that social entrepreneurship can take. Make sure to reflect on at least a couple of portraits created by others to see how they relate or differ from your own one.

Exercise 3.3 – Handle a challenge typical for a social entrepreneur

Gather in a small group (three to four people) and discuss one of these options:

a   If you are the founder of a social enterprise, should you have the right to have a pay comparable to that of a traditional entrepreneur/CEO of a comparable business and/or to keep for yourself part of the profits? Why or why not? Would your answer change if, instead of the founder of a social enterprise, you were a social entrepreneur/founder of any other type of social entrepreneurial organisation?

b   If your only way to get the necessary income to grow your venture was to accept the investment of an impact investor that asks a place in your board and a profit margin that you can only achieve by changing how your social enterprise operates, what would you choose and why? And what if the pressure was coming from a donor (e.g. venture philanthropist) instead of from an impact investor?

At the end of the group discussion, report back to the class how your group decided to handle the challenge, making sure to mention what you found especially difficult in coming to a decision, and ask for feedback.

Notes

1 Alter, K. (2007). Social enterprise typology. *Virtue ventures LLC*, 12(1), 1–124.
2 Guo, C., & Bielefeld, W. (2014). *Social entrepreneurship: An evidence-based approach to creating social value*. Hoboken: John Wiley & Sons.
3 Mair, J., Wolf, M., Rathert, N., & Ioan, A. (2017). Policy brief on governance of social enterprises. *SEFORÏS European Policy Brief*, 10 April 2017. Retrieved from: https://www.hiig.de/en/publication/policy-brief-on-governance-of-social-enterprises/. [Last accessed on: 04 February 2021]
4 George, C., & Reed, M. G. (2016). Building institutional capacity for environmental governance through social entrepreneurship: Lessons from Canadian biosphere reserves. *Ecology and Society*, 21(1), 18.
5 Sengupta, S., Sahay, A., & Croce, F. (2018). Conceptualizing social entrepreneurship in the context of emerging economies: an integrative review of past research from BRIICS. *International Entrepreneurship and Management Journal*, 14(4), 782.

4 The social entrepreneurship ecosystem

Key content

This chapter introduces the key stakeholders of social entrepreneurship ecosystems and discusses the roles that each of them plays in supporting social entrepreneurship, before introducing the environmental forces that shape stakeholders' roles and interactions, and the different stages of development that social entrepreneurship ecosystems can present.

4.1 Ecosystems – what they are and why they matter
4.2 The stakeholders of social entrepreneurship ecosystems
4.3 Environmental forces affecting social entrepreneurship ecosystems
4.4 Differences in social entrepreneurship ecosystems

Learning objectives

- Understand the importance of the ecosystem for the development and success of social entrepreneurship.
- Become aware of the different stakeholders that constitute a social entrepreneurship ecosystem and of their different, necessary roles.
- Know the key context-level and ecosystem-specific forces that shape stakeholders' roles, interactions, and forms of social entrepreneurship.
- Learn what characteristics distinguish emerging, developing, and mature ecosystems.

4.1 Ecosystems – what they are and why they matter

We often celebrate the achievements of social entrepreneurs and depict them as heroes, leaders, shakers, systems changers, and the like. However, very few social entrepreneurs and social entrepreneurial organisations would succeed without a supportive ecosystem. Social entrepreneurship, like most other things in life, is a joint endeavour. It is frequently inspired by people, innovations, and the work of others. Similarly, to happen it requires providers of funds and advice, workforce, industry experts, lawyers, accountants, volunteers, beneficiaries, etc. No social entrepreneurial idea, no matter how good it is, can survive without the

DOI: 10.4324/9781003121824-6

support of others, and the list of these others keeps growing as the size and impact of an organisation grow.

Stakeholders are fundamental not only to support the development of a specific organisation but also to create a broader supportive environment in which social entrepreneurship can exist and thrive. Before social entrepreneurship was "a thing", pioneers like Bill Drayton had to define it, identify existing examples, and help them stand out, and build, or lobby to build, structures, laws, and funding options that would enable the existence of what they defined as "social entrepreneurship". When they succeeded, additional stakeholders chipped in to further legitimise social entrepreneurship as a concept (e.g. universities and thought leaders), to help its realisation of impact (e.g. consultants, impact investors), to develop rules regulating social enterprises (e.g. policymakers), and to bring social entrepreneurs and social entrepreneurial organisations together for peer support and learning (e.g. intermediaries, foundations). Thanks to them, social entrepreneurship is thriving in many countries, and many ecosystems supporting its development are now in place.

The concept of an ecosystem (a contraction of "ecological system") derives from the natural sciences and was introduced in business studies by researchers of strategy and regional development to highlight the dynamic interplay between the actors and forces operating within the same business environment. Any ecosystem normally consists of a community of interdependent stakeholders – individuals and organisations, their relationships and interactions, the physical environment surrounding them, and the environmental forces that shape their relationships. Ecosystems can exist at the local, regional, national, or international level, depending on the activity considered and the stakeholders involved. While, within an ecosystem, different elements might act independently, it is possible to spot connections, interactions, and shared learning.

A social entrepreneurship ecosystem (Figure 4.1) is likely to include the following elements:

- Social entrepreneurs and social entrepreneurial organisations;
- Customers and beneficiaries – individuals and organisations that derive value from social entrepreneurship;
- Resource providers – funders, suppliers, partners, intermediaries, consultants, providers of physical infrastructure such as shared office space, etc.;
- Competitors – businesses and various non-profit organisations;
- Collaborators – normally businesses and non-profit organisations but also public authorities at various levels;
- Promoters – public authorities, individual and organisational champions, universities;
- Environmental forces – context-level and ecosystem-specific forces (see Section 4.3).

Social entrepreneurs and social entrepreneurial organisations are both constrained and supported by their ecosystem and, through their activities, projects, outputs and outcomes, contribute to shape it. This chapter introduces the key stakeholders and environmental forces that make up a social entrepreneurship ecosystem.

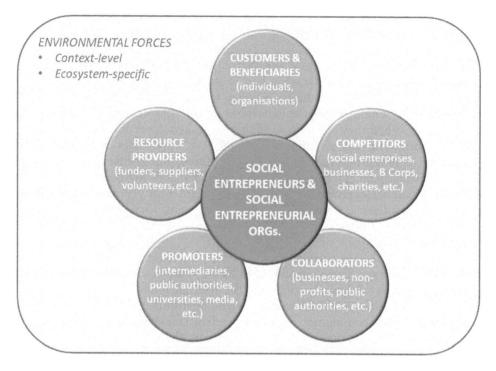

Figure 4.1 The social entrepreneurship ecosystem

4.2 The stakeholders of social entrepreneurship ecosystems

All key stakeholders of social entrepreneurship ecosystems can play multiple roles. For example, public authorities can be resource providers, promoters, and customers. Similarly, businesses can be resource providers, collaborators, and customers (as well as potential competitors). Table 4.1 summarises the main roles that key stakeholders can play.

While Table 4.1 represents key stakeholders, this list is not exhaustive. There are additional stakeholders that also contribute to sustaining social entrepreneurship.

Table 4.1 Key stakeholders of social entrepreneurship ecosystems and their roles

Stakeholder	Customers	Collaborators	Promoters	Resource providers
Intermediaries				
Public authorities				
Funders				
Universities and training centres				
Incubators and accelerators				
Businesses				

For example, media (e.g. newspapers, televisions, cinema) and social media can help to legitimise social entrepreneurship and to spread helpful information about it. Similarly, social consultants and think tanks generate thought leadership, knowledge, and case studies on social entrepreneurship, and can lobby key stakeholders, such as public authorities, to help it thrive. Other important stakeholders are ethically- and socially-aware customers or volunteers that believe in the power of social entrepreneurship, and religious organisations that sustain social entrepreneurship. Different ecosystems also present actors that are specific to the local context. Social entrepreneurs and social entrepreneurial organisations need to be aware of key stakeholders and engage with them to leverage their expertise and contributions to sustain not only their own survival but also that of the ecosystem as a whole. The next section presents key stakeholders and their main roles in supporting social entrepreneurship.

4.2.1 Intermediaries

Social entrepreneurship would probably not exist if it was not for the efforts of intermediaries. These operate at the local, national, or international level, and come in many forms, such as:

- Network organisations, such as *Ashoka, Aspen,* or the various social enterprise networks that have emerged in different countries – e.g. *Social Enterprise Society of Kenya, East Africa Social Enterprise Network,* or *Social Entrepreneurs in Denmark (Sociale Entreprenører i Danmark)*;
- Foundations, such as the *Schwab Foundation* or the *Skoll Foundation*;
- Industry/sector associations such as *Social Enterprise UK,* the *European Federation of Renewable Energy,* or the *French federation of insertion enterprises (la fédération des entreprises d'insertion)*;
- Local chambers of commerce.

Various studies have found that the absence of intermediaries significantly hampers social entrepreneurs' and social entrepreneurial organisations' access to resources, funds, support, and the opportunity to build trust and meaningful exchanges with relevant stakeholders. In many ways, the extent to which intermediaries are present in a social entrepreneurship ecosystem is a strong indicator of how developed that ecosystem is.

Intermediaries normally adopt the role of resource providers. They connect social entrepreneurs and social entrepreneurial organisations with peers (for inspiration and peer support), mentors (for business advice), potential funders, etc. They also provide them with advice, training, and, often, business support and auditing services, share with them relevant funding and networking opportunities, and organise conferences and gatherings to favour knowledge exchange. Some intermediaries also provide financial support, either in the form of fellowships and stipends for individual entrepreneurs or as grants or investments for social entrepreneurial organisations.

Another important role carried out by intermediaries is that of promoters. They represent the interests of social entrepreneurs and social entrepreneurial organisations with businesses and public authorities. Given their networks spanning multiple sectors, they can lobby for policies and regulations, organise consultations to highlight things needing to be done, attract the attention and endorsements of various stakeholders, and foster international cooperation to give social entrepreneurship a stronger voice. When they engage in storytelling and in the creation of positive narratives, intermediaries are also powerful sources of legitimacy for social entrepreneurship. Their words create a common language around this activity and a shared perception of its value.

Sometimes, intermediaries even provide a sense of identity and belonging to social entrepreneurs. A lot of people who begin the journey into social entrepreneurship do not do so consciously but simply start addressing a social or environmental issue close to their heart in a business-led or innovative way. In most cases, they perceive they are creating something different compared to traditional businesses or non-profit organisations but they cannot articulate what makes it special. Some intermediaries do this for them: they label them, e.g. as social entrepreneurs or founders of social enterprises, and, in this way, help them to explain and fully appreciate their uniqueness, and provide them with a community of peers and supporters.

Generally speaking, intermediaries with tougher selection criteria for entering into their networks are more effective in providing fruitful connections and tailored advice, while intermediaries with larger networks are better in terms of signalling a wide range of opportunities and organising public campaigns to legitimise social entrepreneurship.

Portrait of an intermediary – NESsT

NESsT was founded in 1997 with the mission of supporting social enterprises to foster economic development and dignified employment in emerging economies in Eastern Europe and Latin America. The belief was that social enterprises led by visionary leaders had the potential to create sustainable employment opportunities for people in their community, allowing them to overcome poverty. Its initial funds came from donations of innovative philanthropists, businesses, and business leaders, who believed in the value of social enterprises as a new tool for economic development.

Since its foundation, *NESsT* has invested in 1,200+ early stage social enterprises in low-income communities in over 50 countries, through its Incubation programme. This provides three years of tailored business assistance, grants, technical assistance, mentoring, and support with impact measurement. Additionally, *NESsT* has been educating local stakeholders about the value of social enterprises through its research and engagement with policymakers, impact investors, and businesses. According to the OECD publication "*Boosting Social Enterprise Development – Good Practice Compendium*":

> The social enterprise and sustainability programme launched by *NESsT* for non-profit organisations brought new content, defined key concepts (such as social enterprise and sustainability), and often created new terms in the local languages. *NESsT* operates in different geographies (namely, Europe and South America), offering each region a unique opportunity to pilot and adopt initiatives from the other region and devise similar solutions to comparable social problems.[1]

Stakeholders' engagement and education have been fundamental in increasing the resources and support available to social enterprises in various countries. For example, *NESsT* created a Business Advisory Network of business professionals, who act as advisors for social enterprises on a pro bono basis, and leveraged its network to attract new funds and investments for the social enterprises it supports. Thanks to its connections, *NESsT* has also been able to strengthen its own financial position, which is now supported by a mix of donations from private foundations, corporate contributions, public grants, and revenues generated through consulting services.

As its scale and funds grew, *NESsT* added a further goal of supporting ready-to-grow ventures by creating appropriate financial instruments and initiatives. In 2007, it introduced the first "*NESsT-Citi Social Enterprise Competition*", in partnership with *Citibank*, to identify new ventures worthy of support and to further promote the concept of social enterprise. In 2018, it launched the *NESsT Fund*, an investment fund to provide patient capital (i.e. capital provided by an investor for the long term to help the funded organisation combine the efficiency and scale of market approaches with the impact of philanthropy) to social enterprises and small and medium enterprises in Latin America. The fund focuses on ventures that other funders consider too risky or too small, with the potential to employ individuals making less than the minimum wage and working in the informal economy. Between 2018 and 2019, it also launched three multi-stakeholder initiatives to catalyse efforts and resources to tackle two social issues it cares deeply about: women empowerment and biodiversity protection. These are creating further links between existing partners and social enterprises, thus strengthening the social entrepreneurship ecosystems in various Latin American countries.

4.2.2 Public authorities

After intermediaries, public authorities are probably the next most important stakeholder in social entrepreneurship ecosystems, although this is mostly true in democratic contexts where they have resources to invest, play an important role in regulating markets and delivering welfare, and function relatively efficiently. Public authorities, broadly speaking (although different jurisdictions would have different definitions), are all the organisations that carry out activities in the public interest and are publicly funded through taxes at the local, regional, national, or international level. They include governments, ministries and government departments, the army, the police, and local administrations, etc. Public authorities normally play the roles of customers, resource providers, and promoters.

Public authorities hire or support the hiring of social enterprises as suppliers through their inclusion in private–public partnerships, the addition of impact creation as a criterion in public tenders, contracting a service out to them, and encouraging businesses to do likewise through regulations or vouchers. This is the case, e.g. in the Netherlands, where several local municipalities involved social enterprises in their supply chains and offered them advice and support in kind to make sure they could benefit from this opportunity. That said, there are frequently obstacles for public authorities to sustain social enterprises in this way, namely their lack of knowledge of suitable social enterprises, their inability to reach out to them to signal available opportunities, and their need to justify higher costs when hiring a social enterprise instead of a traditional one.

Most importantly, public authorities can support social entrepreneurship through laws, regulations, directives, and other legislative instruments. These can guarantee special tax regimes for social entrepreneurial organisations, establish dedicated and legal forms for social enterprises (see Chapter 3), and determine the development of supportive public infrastructure. For example, the United Kingdom made social entrepreneurship an explicit remit for the Office for Civil Society, within the Department for Digital, Culture, Media & Sport, and several governments within the European Union created nation-wide strategies to support social entrepreneurship. For example, in 2014, Denmark launched the *National Strategy for Social Enterprise*, and, in 2015, Croatia released its *Strategy for Social Entrepreneurship Development*.

Similarly, public authorities can create dedicated funds, subsidies, grants, and in-kind support mechanisms, such as incubators, training, or office space. In 2010, South Korea's government set up through the Social Enterprise Promotion Act the *Korea Social Enterprise Promotion Agency (KoSEA)*. This helps social enterprises with handling commercialisation processes and issues, provides them consulting services, and encourages the development of support networks. In addition, the South Korean government created a Social Enterprise Support Committee and a certification programme led by the Ministry of Labour, encouraged state agencies to buy from social enterprises, and established mechanisms to partially subsidise facilities and site expenses that social enterprises might incur in. In Latvia, several municipalities have provided premises for social entrepreneurs and enterprises to operate in for free or at favourable conditions, supported them with temporary grants, and, in a few cases, also organised sessions to help them identify sources of funding.

In recent years, the European Union has shown how public authorities can not only provide funds to social enterprises but also play an important role in favouring their access to existing private funders. For example, the *EU Employment and Social Innovation Programme* (EaSI) contains the EaSI guarantee – a risk-sharing mechanism that enables selected financial intermediaries to offer social enterprises and micro-enterprises loans at more favourable conditions compared to market ones. Similarly, in South Korea, two public bodies – the Small and Medium Business Corporation and the Korea Inclusive Finance Agency – provide guarantees to loans for businesses tackling social issues.

Finally, public authorities can promote social entrepreneurship by publishing stories, positive narratives, and case studies about it, and explicitly mentioning social entrepreneurship in their policies and initiatives. In Japan, the Ministry of Economy, Trade and Industry created a *Social Business Study Group*. The Group, beyond supporting the rise of new intermediaries in the ecosystem, the development of new ventures, and knowledge sharing, in 2011 published a book with the stories and profiles of leading social enterprises – the *Social Business Case Book*. This proved very helpful to raise awareness about social entrepreneurship among the general public as well as in other parts of the government.

Sometimes, governments even indirectly contributed to the establishment of social entrepreneurship through their choices about welfare provision. In the United Kingdom, Sweden, or Estonia, the attempts to increase the efficiency and innovation of public services by privatising them led to the creation of several social enterprises. In many African and South American countries, where their colonial past left them with little resources and with complex power systems that promote an inefficient use and re-distribution of public resources, social entrepreneurship emerged to provide forgotten communities access to basic healthcare, education, or water and sanitation. Similarly, in the United States, where the predominant political and economic ideology supports minimal public welfare provision compared to other contexts such as Europe or China, social entrepreneurship has been on the rise to cover gaps in education, healthcare, housing, and support of disadvantaged communities.

Despite the key role that public authorities can play in social entrepreneurship ecosystems, many social entrepreneurs and social entrepreneurial organisations prefer to portray themselves in open conflict and rivalry with them, or to ignore their existence and refuse to solicit their help. They blame public authorities for being too slow in reacting to public needs, too bureaucratic and distant from where problems are felt, and too adverse to innovation. This lack of connection and involvement can represent a significant issue and lost potential, and is one of the reasons why some ecosystems never take off or reach scale.

4.2.3 *Funders*

Social entrepreneurship ecosystems are characterised by a variety of funders, matching the variety of social entrepreneurial organisations. The section above discussed how public authorities are often an important funder. Beyond them, there are other public funders that provide financial resources for social entrepreneurship, such as international development organisations (e.g. *World Bank* or the *Inter-American Development Bank*), financial intermediaries set up and managed by public authorities (e.g. *Big Venture Capital* in the United Kingdom or the *European Social Innovation and Impact Fund* in Germany), and international aid organisations distributing grants in the Global South (e.g. *USAID* and *UK Aid Direct*). For the most part, however, funders tend to be private actors. These can be divided into three main categories: family and friends (not discussed in detail in this book); traditional funders (e.g. banks and credit unions, foundations); new funders (e.g. venture philanthropists, impact investors, Social Impact Bonds, microfinance providers).

4.2.3.1 *Traditional funders*

The main traditional funders operating in social entrepreneurship ecosystems are banks, angel investors, donors, philanthropists, foundations, and charities.

Banks and, in particular, cooperative banks provide both loans and investments to social entrepreneurial organisations, frequently with a reduced interest rate or other special conditions. For example, the *Royal Bank of Scotland* and *Barclays* have set up tailored support programmes for social enterprises, while *Triodos Bank* in the Netherlands, founded in 1968 to support sustainable businesses and money management, is now investing in social entrepreneurial organisations through most of its products in the Netherlands, Belgium, Germany, Spain, France, and the United Kingdom. Additionally, existing investment banks, insurance companies, and asset management companies (e.g. *JP Morgan, UBS, LGT Capital Partners, Zurich*) have helped social enterprises access investment through dedicated impact investment funds.

Angel investors are rich individuals willing to bet part of their wealth on supporting entrepreneurs and start-ups through the provision of seed capital and, sometimes, also through mentorship and introductions. Increasingly, there are many angel investors interested in supporting social entrepreneurial organisations. In the United Kingdom, the social investment bank *ClearlySo* even created a repository of high-net-worth individuals interested in being "social angels", also providing them with services such as due diligence, knowledge sharing, and easy access to new networking and investment opportunities.

Private donors and philanthropists (individual and corporate), foundations, and large charities can fund social entrepreneurial organisations through grants, donations (cash or in-kind), fellowships, and collaboration agreements in which they contribute various types of resources and/or funds (see Chapter 10 for additional details). For example, the *Aspire Coronation Trust Foundation (ACT Foundation)* provides grants to non-profit organisations and social enterprises operating in Africa in areas of key interest (i.e. health, entrepreneurship, environment, and leadership) and in 2021 launched the "*Changemakers Innovation Challenge*", a competition for non-profits and social enter-prises using technology and digital tools to create innovative solutions to social issues in Africa. Winners of the competition obtain both an award and access to training to scale their impact. The *Esmée Fairbairn Foundation* in the United Kingdom provides a mix of grants, social investments, training, and support with strategy development, digital tools and communications, and frequently commissions research to enable knowledge sharing about best practices and to provide its grantees and investees with information helpful for their generation of social or environmental impact.

4.2.3.2 New funders

Many new funders, financial instruments, and intermediaries that have emerged in the last few decades are playing an increasingly important role in relation to funding social entrepreneurial organisations. These include venture philanthropists, impact investors, Social Impact Bonds, crowdfunding platforms, and microfinance providers.

Venture philanthropists are either rich individuals, normally from technology-based sectors, or foundations, who want to support only innovative projects or initiatives with a potential to generate social or environmental impact at scale. Examples of well-known venture philanthropists include the *Robin Hood Foundation*, the *Silicon Valley Social Venture Fund*, the *Draper Richards Kaplan Foundation*, Mark Zuckerberg, and Pierre Omidyar. Venture philanthropists frequently expect some return on investment or proof of impact and, in exchange, provide social entrepreneurial organisations with multi-year funding, business advice, training, mentoring, connections to other supporters (e.g. law-yers, consultants, accountants), and encouragement/tools to measure impact on a regular basis. Venture philanthropy originated in the United States and is now expanding both in Europe and in Asia, where the *European Venture Philanthropists Association* and the *Asian Venture Philanthropy Network* respectively connect venture philanthropists, pool resources, and share best practices. For example, in Japan, the *Nippon Foundation* and *Social Investment Partners* created and operate the *Japan Venture Philanthropy Fund* and the US-based *Social Venture Partners* has opened up a chapter in Tokyo.

Impact investors are individuals or organisations that expect both a financial return and a social/environmental return on their investment. This means they fund organi-sations that can generate some additional economic value for themselves and for those investing in them while also creating measurable social or environmental impact. Impact investment can take place through loans, investment in equity/purchase of shares, or through a blend of these two options. Well-known international impact investors are

Bridges Fund Management, Acumen, Bamboo Capital Partners, Root Capital, and *Yunus Social Business.* Besides them, there is a plethora of organisations that are being set up at the national level (e.g. *Impact First Investment* in Israel, *Asha Impact* in India, *Vox Capital* in Brasil), and of impact investments delivered through existing philanthropic organisations and finance intermediaries (e.g. *International Finance Corporation, Africa Enterprise Challenge Fund, Shell Foundation, Tony Elumelu Foundation*). Recently, there has also been the emergence of impact investing platforms. These vet organisations on a set of criteria combining both financial performance and social impact/sustainability and then share their profiles with individual investors, who subscribed for this service, pooling their investments. Individual investors can pick and choose what they want to invest in. An example of an impact investing platform is *Tickr*, which connects individual and/or corporate investors with a set of investment options in B Corps, social enterprises, and sustainable companies. This way people without advanced experience in finance or social impact can still financially support promising social ventures and increase the funding available in social entrepreneurship ecosystems.

Portrait of an impact investor – Acumen

Acumen was founded by Jacqueline Novogratz in 2001, to provide patient capital to new businesses delivering life-changing products and services to the world's poorest and creating for them new job opportunities. At the time, impact investment was still not "a thing" but Novogratz's experience in Wall Street and microfinance had led her to believe that investing in social enterprises and innovative and sustainable start-ups with a long time horizon, a high tolerance for risk and flexibility, and prioritising impact over financial results, while still demanding a financial return, was the best way to generate sustainable economic development.

Acumen provides patient capital both through debt and equity, prevalently to early stage ventures that increase access to healthcare, water, housing, alternative energy, or agricultural inputs to low-income communities in Africa, Asia, and America. In order to become an *Acumen* investee, ventures need to meet its eight criteria, detailed on its website (https://acumen.org/investment-principles/). Ever since its foundation, *Acumen* has already supported over 100 ventures in 14 different countries. Besides funding them, *Acumen* gives them access to its network of experts and supports their growth through management guidance in strategy, governance, fundraising, and customers' insights. Additionally, *Acumen* developed a *Lean Data* approach to help ventures collect data on the impact they are generating in a timely and efficient way. This consists of leveraging mobile technology to regularly survey customers and analyse their data in real time for continuous improvement and growth.

Building on the experience developed through its investments, in 2006 *Acumen* founded the *Acumen Academy*, where social entrepreneurs and social innovators can acquire new skills, learn about management, storytelling, data analytics, marketing, fundraising, business models, etc. either through short courses or through one-year fellowships that give them access to a mix of seminars designed to empower them to drive social change.

Social Impact Bonds are contracts between a service provider (frequently a social enterprise), an outcome payer (normally a government or a private trust/foundation), and investors (see Figure 4.2). They guarantee substantial and long-term funding for the service provider that wins the contract, while allowing outcome payers to save money (either because they do not repay investors due to the failure of the project or because the social service is cheaper or more effective due to the contract in place) and investors to potentially see a return on their investment.

The first Social Impact Bond was trialled in the United Kingdom in 2010. The UK government acted as the outcome payer and worked with *Social Finance*, a social investment advisory firm, to set up a Bond to raise £5 million from 17 charitable foundations – the investors in the Bond. The Bond funded projects of non-profit organisations with the target outcome of reducing the re-offending rate at Peterborough jail by 7.5%. The projects supported by the bond achieved a 9.7% decrease in the number of convictions and allowed investors to earn a 3.1% interest on their initial investment. Another example is the impact bond created in 2017 by the *British Asian Trust* to fund the work of three Indian charities to improve the literacy and numeracy of 300,000 children in Gujarat and Delhi. The bond raised $11 million through a consortium of corporations and charities such as BT, Comic Relief, and the *Tata Trusts*.

Crowdfunding is a system through which a group of independent individuals lends or invests small sums of money to someone who is starting a project or organisation, in exchange for nothing, a token product, or a pre-determined interest rate or share. Most crowdfunding is obtained through platforms such as *Funding Circle, GoFundMe, Indiegogo, Kickstarter, Kiva, Mightycause*, and *SeedInvest*. Crowdfunding platforms connect social entrepreneurs and social entrepreneurial organisations with many individuals who jointly help them to get the funds they need, especially when they are at too early stage to attract other forms of funding. For example, in 2017, ethical fashion company *Thrædable*, which is a social enterprise producing sustainable t-shirts and bags featuring artwork representing people's stories of the issues they faced, raised £11,740 through the contributions of 266 individual funders on the crowdfunding platform *UpEffect*.

Microfinance providers have been crucial in supporting micro-entrepreneurship and social entrepreneurship in the Global South, giving small loans – usually $100 or less – to low-income people wanting to start a business but lacking access to credit or banking. Sometimes, microfinance providers are purposefully built entities, such as *Grameen Bank* or *Microloan Foundation*, and sometimes they are programmes, foundations, or branches of traditional banks, such as *Bank Rakyat Indonesia* or *Citigroup*. Microfinance provider *FINCA* is an excellent example of the role of microfinance providers in sustaining social enterprises. Since its foundation in 1984, *FINCA*

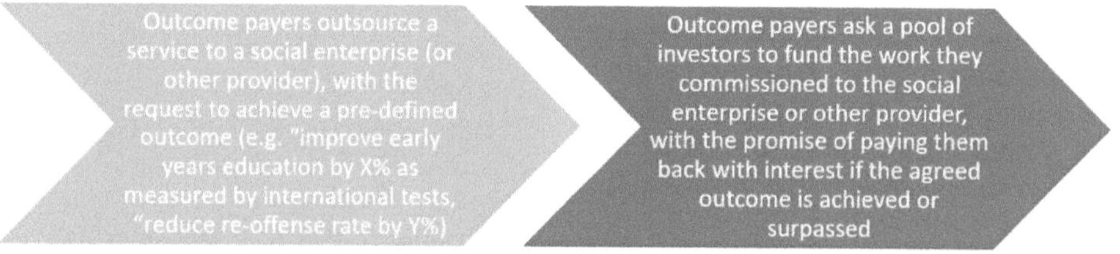

Outcome payers outsource a service to a social enterprise (or other provider), with the request to achieve a pre-defined outcome (e.g. "improve early years education by X% as measured by international tests, "reduce re-offense rate by Y%)

Outcome payers ask a pool of investors to fund the work they commissioned to the social enterprise or other provider, with the promise of paying them back with interest if the agreed outcome is achieved or surpassed

Figure 4.2 The functioning of Social Impact Bonds

has provided loans for over USD 18 million to 7.6 million clients in five continents. Most of these loans have resulted in the formation and growth of new micro-enterprises and social enterprises, generating new employment opportunities and providing essential services to underserved populations. *FINCA* recently started *FINCA Ventures*, which provides patient capital to social enterprises with high growth and impact potential in Africa and helps them realise such potential through business advice and support.

4.2.4 *Universities and other training providers*

Universities act as promoters and resource providers in social entrepreneurship ecosystems by publishing research, teaching, and creating accelerators and incubators that support the development of new social entrepreneurial organisations. Academic researchers generate insights on social entrepreneurship, on its state of development in different contexts, on ways to sustain it, and to measure its impact, etc., thus providing other stakeholders with the necessary information to support it. Research centres on social entrepreneurship, increasingly common across Europe, the United Kingdom and the United States, collect relevant data on social entrepreneurship and foster collaborative research between academics, consultants, and social entrepreneurs at an international level. Notable examples in this sense are the SEFORÏS initiative or the EMES European Research Network.

Universities have also been teaching social entrepreneurship through courses, modules, case studies, and, sometimes, entire programmes. These give students the understanding and skills necessary to engage with social entrepreneurship in different ways, together with inspiration, role models, and opportunities to start building a network of like-minded people. Students' exposure to the concept of social entrepreneurship translates into a pipeline of talent for social entrepreneurship ecosystems, both in terms of social entrepreneurs and in terms of people passionate about social entrepreneurship that can advocate or volunteer for it while working in other sectors, thus generating new precious allies and resource providers.

Finally, universities increasingly set up incubators and accelerators (see Section 4.2.5 for more details) to support the creation and growth of student-led social enterprises. In this way, students can access additional training programmes, mentoring, opportunities for pitching their ideas to potential funders, and support in securing protection for their intellectual property. Examples of university-based incubators and accelerators are *Cambridge Social Ventures* at the *University of Cambridge*, *SOLVE* at the *Massachusetts Institute of Technology*, and *iBizAfrica* at *Strathmore University*.

Several businesses and non-profit organisations also offer educational programmes related to social entrepreneurship, which help to share best practice build a pipeline of talent, and generate networking opportunities. These programmes tend to be more practical and skills-based than university courses and they prevalently target people with professional experience, seeking either a career change or to start and grow their own social entrepreneurial organisation. For example, the *Social Enterprise Academy*, founded in Scotland but now operating in several countries around the world, provides half-day to 12-day courses on various business topics for aspiring social entrepreneurs and managers of social enterprises. Additionally, it delivers programmes to schools to support children and young adults in developing and leading social entrepreneurial organisations in their community.

4.2.5 Incubators and accelerators

Social entrepreneurs and enterprises benefit immensely from the involvement in an incubator/hub or accelerator. Incubators are organisations that support social entrepreneurs and social entrepreneurial organisations for prolonged time periods, until they have acquired the resources and focus to become independent. Incubators are rarely competitive and tend to accept any individual or organisation willing to pay a membership fee and/or give the incubator a stake in the company. They normally provide office space, some networking opportunities, and technical (e.g. legal, accounting, IP protection) support. Incubators can be set up by charities, universities, and businesses but, in some countries such as Kenya, an increasingly important role in this sense is also played by religious organisations, willing to support faith-based social enterprises and/or local communities.

The most famous example of an incubator in social entrepreneurship ecosystems is the *Impact Hub*. Founded in 2005 by a group of young people who had been involved in organising debates and meetings to foster social change, the first *Impact Hub* was based in a run-down loft in London. The idea was to encourage the meeting of social innovators, to help them turn ideas into action and ventures through favouring knowledge exchange, peer support, and co-working. In just a couple of years, the hub became so popular that many people from other locations and countries approached its founders to replicate the concept elsewhere. Now the *Impact Hub* is a network of over 100 hubs in 50 countries all over the world. Recently, the network even established corporate partnerships to help large businesses innovate by connecting them with its community of entrepreneurs.

Accelerators are organisations providing limited, cohort-based programmes that help social entrepreneurs translate their ideas into a start-up or to identify and act on opportunities for growth. Accelerators vary in terms of how selective they are in admitting new participants. They offer substantial mentorship, tailored advice, skills-building seminars, and networking opportunities. Frequently, they also organise pitching events and connections between social entrepreneurs and potential resource providers. An example of accelerator is *Impact Amplifier* in South Africa, which delivers a series of investment-readiness programmes of 3–12 months, involving lectures, sessions with individual coaches, group discussions, and webinars to both individual entrepreneurs and groups. The ultimate goal is for the "accelerated entrepreneurs" to be able to attract new investment for growth at the end of the programme. Based on its decades-long experience, *Impact Amplifier* recently launched an online platform to access its programmes and modules with the help of a virtual coach.

4.2.6 Businesses

As illustrated by the example of the *Impact Hub* above, businesses, and in particular large corporations, are another important stakeholder in social entrepreneurship ecosystems. Many businesses have connected to social entrepreneurial organisations, becoming important customers, collaborators, and resource providers, because of two main drivers: access to new markets and sustainability.

In 2004, C.K. Prahalad published a book titled *The fortune at the bottom of the pyramid* highlighting how people living below or just above the poverty line represented an untapped market for businesses. This prompted many multinational corporations to invest in research and development of new products and in new marketing channels that would enable them to reach Bottom of the Pyramid (BoP) markets effectively and cheaply. It also made them aware of the business opportunity represented by partnering with social entrepreneurial organisations that could offer both an in-depth knowledge of BoP markets and a tool to access them. Similarly, the need to have more sustainable operations and to consider stakeholders beyond shareholders has pushed many businesses to view social entrepreneurial organisations as either suppliers that can help them simultaneously achieve profits and sustainability, or beneficiaries that they can support as part of their Corporate Social Responsibility (CSR) through donations, employees' volunteering programmes, and sponsorships (see Chapter 2).

A fitting example of the multiple ways in which businesses can contribute to social entrepreneurship ecosystems is that of *Unilever*. In 2015, the multinational corporation joined forces with the then UK Department for International Development (now Foreign, Commonwealth & Development Office) to set up TRANSFORM, a programme involving the provision of both funding and business advice to support market-based solutions that meet low-income household needs in sub-Saharan Africa and Asia. Additionally, social enterprises and sustainable businesses can partner with *Unilever* for specific projects through the *Unilever Foundry*, the innovation platform and hub that the corporation uses to spot high-potential innovation and partners that can enhance its sustainability and offer. *Unilever* is also at the centre of several global multi-sector partnerships, often involving social entrepreneurs and enterprises, to achieve the UN Sustainable Development Goals. In these, it leverages its reach, network and customer insights to help the poorest of the poor access new products and services. Finally, *Unilever* is a partner of several intermediaries supporting social entrepreneurship such as *Ashoka*, the *Skoll Foundation*, and *Acumen*.

Businesses are not only key collaborators, customers, and resource providers for social entrepreneurial organisations but, like universities, they also contribute to build a pipeline of talent and key background infrastructure. For example, in many African ecosystems, an important role in terms of training and technology provision has been played by *SAP*, a global corporation specialised in software. *SAP* provides technology training in both schools and universities, and, in partnership with *Acumen*, offers fellowships to CEOs of social enterprises looking to grow their operations and impact. As part of the fellowship, CEOs get to travel to the Silicon Valley to meet technology experts, participate in boot-camps, and access support from *SAP* employees and angel investors. Finally, as a global effort, *SAP* has created an online training course for founders and managers of social enterprises, in collaboration with the *Social Enterprise World Forum*, and allows its employees to volunteer for social enterprises and to work on their own social entrepreneurial idea in the company's incubator.

4.3 Environmental forces affecting social entrepreneurship ecosystems

There are two types of environmental forces (Figure 4.3) that affect social entrepreneurship ecosystems. The first type is the context-level forces that apply to multiple ecosystems (not just social entrepreneurship ones), which normally affect the emergence and speed of development of social entrepreneurship. Context-level forces include: institutions (e.g. laws, regulations, norms, routines, shared beliefs, traditions); level of economic development; existence of a welfare state; type and level of citizens' participation in the third sector; quality of education. The second type is eco-system-specific forces which emerge once the social entrepreneurship ecosystem is in place and affect only the stakeholders involved in it. Ecosystem-specific forces include: standards; prevailing definition of social entrepreneurship; role of public authorities in relation to social entrepreneurship; norms that govern the relationships between stakeholders within that ecosystem. These affect the type of organisations that will survive in the ecosystem, the interactions they set up, and the roles they adopt.

Broadly speaking, context-level forces that encourage the development of social entrepreneurship include:

- Institutions and a culture that encourage private initiatives/entrepreneurship;
- Presence of several networks and funding opportunities;
- Existence of trust between different actors and in the rule of law, i.e. low transaction costs;
- Well-developed public infrastructure;
- Legal protection of intellectual property;
- Thriving and dynamic third sector.

The presence of these context-level forces supports the development of social entrepreneurship ecosystems since it supplies both motivated people who want to engage in or encourage social entrepreneurship, and the tools, skills, and resources they need to do so. Additionally, it enables to sustain social entrepreneurial organisations over time through appropriate funding, easy access to market opportunities, regulations, and initiatives.

Alternatively, social entrepreneurship emerges precisely in contexts characterised by institutional voids, i.e. lacking all of those characteristics (see Chapter 3). However,

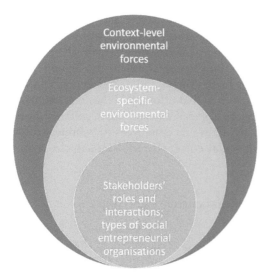

Figure 4.3 The environmental forces shaping social entrepreneurship

in these contexts, social entrepreneurship ecosystems tend to remain fragmented, dependent on support from international/foreign organisations (both multinational corporations and international non-profit organisations), and supporting micro-enterprises rather than a wide spectrum of social entrepreneurial organisations. For example, Mirvis and Googins (2018)[3] explained that the presence of many social entrepreneurship ecosystems only at an early stage in several African countries was due to a mix of policy and regulatory barriers and pre-existing institutional voids, making it very difficult for social enterprises to access funding, networks, training opportunities, and information.

What happens in social entrepreneurship ecosystems, however, depends not only on context-level forces, but also on ecosystem-specific ones. The key ecosystem-specific force that affects stakeholders' roles and interactions is the prevailing definition of social entrepreneurship and the connected presence of certification mechanisms. Since social entrepreneurial organisations exist in many forms, and since these determine what other stakeholders interact with them, why, and how, establishing what social entrepreneurship is about through definitions and certifications has a strong impact on the ecosystem. In most ecosystems, official certifications do not exist and social entrepreneurship labels can be indirectly acquired through awards and fellowships (e.g. becoming an *Ashoka* fellow automatically signals a status of a social entrepreneur), or by becoming a member of an association supporting social entrepreneurship (e.g. *raiSE* in Singapore or the *Estonia Social Enterprise Network*). However, as ecosystems develop, official certifications start to emerge in line with the prevailing definition of social entrepreneurship. Certifications can be delivered either by purposefully founded third-sector organisations – such as the *Social Enterprise Mark* in the United Kingdom and *Sistema B* in Latin America – or by existing organisations such as the *Association for Finnish Work in Finland*. Certification programmes usually list a set of criteria that organisations need to meet, and involve regular audits to check that such criteria are indeed met according to pre-set standards. Sometimes, the certification as a social enterprise can be obtained through a different certified label, such as B Corp, or the certification programmes for WISEs in Austria and the Netherlands.

Pinning down the role of other ecosystem-specific forces such as norms is much more difficult, since they tend to co-evolve with the ecosystem and reflect the power dynamics between its stakeholders. In most cases, stakeholders of the ecosystem might not even be aware of the existence of such forces and might take them for granted. Nonetheless, these forces also contribute to the pace and type of development of the ecosystem and to the forms of social entrepreneurship being encouraged and supported.

4.4 Differences in social entrepreneurship ecosystems

Social entrepreneurship ecosystems around the world can be grouped according to their stage of development: mature, developing, and early stage (Table 4.2).

Mature ecosystems are those found in the United Kingdom, United States, Japan, Singapore, and several countries of the European Union. Social entrepreneurial organisations are plentiful, tackle a large number of social and environmental issues through various approaches, and are sometimes used to privatise welfare provision. Various local, national, and international intermediaries, public authorities, and

Table 4.2 Main characteristics of ecosystems at different stages of development

Type of ecosystem	Prevailing organisations	Roles of social entrepreneurship	Other stakeholders	Support available
Mature	Any typology of social entrepreneurial organisation, high proportion of social enterprises	Presence in many sectors; contribution to privatisation of welfare	All: local, national, and international intermediaries; public authorities; businesses; incubators and accelerators; universities and other training providers; specialised funders and consultants	Support, information, and funds widely available
Developing	Any typology of social entrepreneurial organisation	Presence in many sectors – prevalently education, water and sanitation, agriculture, healthcare, etc.; contribution to socio-economic development	Intermediaries; international NGOs; multinational corporations; universities	Funding from various national and international private organisations available; specialised training; support and networks mostly in main cities
Emerging	Micro-enterprises and necessity-driven enterprises	Poverty alleviation and compensation for an absent welfare state	International intermediaries, microfinance providers, and some corporations with a local presence; few hubs and networks in main cities	Some support in the main cities, mostly from NGOs; funds from international development organisations; little else

incubators support and promote social entrepreneurship; universities offer courses, training, and information to aspiring social entrepreneurs; and there are providers of specialist services such as social impact consulting and impact investment firms. Know-how is widely available to anyone who is interested, and there are several funding options, and multiple ecosystems at different geographical levels. For example, a social enterprise operating in Cambridge in the United Kingdom would be part of a local (Cambridge), regional (greater London area), and national (English) ecosystem of social entrepreneurship, sharing most environmental forces but only some stakeholders. The downside of mature ecosystems is the intense competition between different social entrepreneurial organisations for attention, resources, and customers, and the duplication of efforts and information providers, which might make it difficult to find out what is needed or to reach the right form of support.

In developing ecosystems, such as those of South Africa, Kenya, Ghana, China, India, Brazil, and Vietnam, there is a growing number of social entrepreneurial organisations, mostly engaged in sectors such as education, water and sanitation, agriculture, healthcare, and economic development. There are also several stakeholders supporting them, in particular international NGOs, the CSR programmes of multinational corporations or of large national corporations, and network organisations such as *Ashoka* and *Aspen*. Some universities offer specialised courses, training, and research, and some local intermediaries start to emerge. However, public authorities are not very engaged with social entrepreneurship and access to information, incubators, training, funds, and local networks is limited and mostly concentrated in large cities. Corruption, ideological hostility from the side of the government, and the broader business and legal environment might also represent obstacles to the development of local social entrepreneurial organisations.

In emerging ecosystems such as those of Rwanda, Uganda, Malawi, or Peru there are some examples of social entrepreneurship but they would seldom define themselves as such and would tend to be micro-enterprises (less than five employees) or necessity-driven social enterprises, set up by people looking for self-employment opportunities associated with poverty alleviation or compensation for an absent state. Some international intermediaries, such as *NESsT* and *Ashoka*, and some microfinance providers might have established a small presence and started to support promising initiatives. Similarly, corporations with a local presence might support some forms of social entrepreneurship through their CSR programmes or social enterprise units. Local networks and incubators, promoted by international NGOs, might exist in the main cities, but, beyond them, specific funding, information, or training is almost non-existent, as are funders beyond international aid organisations, and dedicated initiatives of public authorities or universities.

Being aware of the state of development of the ecosystem is important for social entrepreneurs and social entrepreneurial organisations to develop achievable expectations and goals, to forecast risks and issues they might face, and to understand the extent to which they might need to engage in systems change (see Chapter 5) to realise their desired social and/or environmental impact.

SUMMARY BOX

- An ecosystem consists of a community of interdependent stakeholders – individuals and organisations, their relationships and interactions, the physical environment surrounding them, and the environmental forces that shape their relationships.
- The elements of a social entrepreneurship ecosystem are: social entrepreneurs and social entrepreneurial organisations, their customers, beneficiaries, promoters, resource providers, and collaborators, and the context-level and ecosystem-specific forces that shape and govern their relationships.
- The key stakeholders of social entrepreneurship ecosystems consist of intermediaries, public authorities, funders, universities and training centres,

incubators and accelerators, and businesses. Each of these stakeholders performs multiple roles.

- Important context-level forces are the prevailing economic ideology, the
  level of development of the third sector, the presence of legal protections to
  intellectual property and of various funders, and the quality of education.
  Meanwhile, important ecosystem-specific forces are the prevailing definition of social entrepreneurship, certification mechanisms, the way public
  authorities interpret their role in the ecosystem, and norms regulating roles
  and relationships.
- Social entrepreneurship ecosystems around the world can be grouped based
  on their level of development, which can be described as mature, developing, or early stage.

Check box – Self-reflection and discussion questions

- What constitutes a social entrepreneurship ecosystem?
- Why is it important to learn about social entrepreneurship ecosystems?
- Why do social entrepreneurs and social entrepreneurial organisations need
  to be aware of the ecosystem surrounding them?
- Who are the key stakeholders present in social entrepreneurship ecosystems
  and what roles does each of them perform?
- What environmental forces shape the existence and development of social
  entrepreneurship ecosystems?
- What issues are social entrepreneurs and social entrepreneurial organisations likely to encounter because of the social entrepreneurship ecosystem
  in which they operate?
- If contexts characterised by institutional voids make it harder for social
  entrepreneurship ecosystems to develop, will social entrepreneurship ever
  be able to properly support economic development?
- Based on what you know about your country, what level of development of
  social entrepreneurship ecosystems would you expect there? Does reality
  match your expectations or not?

Check out additional resources related to this chapter to learn more about
social entrepreneurship ecosystems and stakeholders at: www.routledge.
com/9780367640231

Exercises

Exercise 4.1 – Explore the local social entrepreneurship ecosystem

Describe in any format your prefer (e.g. short report, map, video, infographic) the
ecosystem of support for social entrepreneurship in your own area or country. How
does it look like? What are the main stakeholders involved? What roles do they perform? What are the main environmental forces at play and how do they affect the
ecosystem?

Once you have completed the description of the ecosystem reflect on:

1   Its stage of development (mature, developing, emerging)
2   Whether or not it is supportive of social entrepreneurship and, if it is, what form(s) of social entrepreneurship it supports the most
3   What is missing and what could be improved

Share your reflections with another student/course participant and compare either the different ecosystems you are describing or the commonalities and differences in your descriptions of the same ecosystem.

Exercise 4.2 – Meet the stakeholders

In groups of four to five members think about stakeholders of the local social entrepreneurship ecosystem that you can reach out to and contact them to conduct a short interview with three or four of them. If you cannot get an interview, ask them to reply to your questions by email, even very briefly, or use existing interviews or blogs you might find online that represent their "voice". The goal is to collect their perspective on what social entrepreneurship is about, why they are supporting it and how, and to reflect on what this might mean for social entrepreneurs and social entrepreneurial organisations. When you are done, collate the information you collected and share it with the rest of the class/course participants.

Exercise 4.3 – Build an ecosystem

Case study – Social Enterprise Coalition

The *Social Enterprise Coalition* (SEC) was founded in 2002 by a group of well-established social enterprises, regional social enterprise intermediaries, multinational corporations, and people interested in engaging with social entrepreneurship. These different stakeholders wanted to create an ecosystem of support for social enterprises in the whole of the United Kingdom. Their idea was to build an organisation bringing together the existing intermediaries at the regional level and representing their views – and those of their members – to the government. When founded, the vision of the SEC was to grow the social enterprise movement, making it mainstream in every area of the economy, by pushing forward the idea of social enterprises as businesses trading for a social purpose, and deserving to be out of business in the absence of profitability.

The government, which aimed to innovate the welfare system through the contribution of social enterprises, immediately supported the initiative, providing the SEC with both funds and access to ministers and to the parliament. Only a few months after its foundation, the SEC received a £450,000 government grant for a period of three years from the Department of Trade and Industry – to be match-funded through other sources. The grant was to be used to represent social enterprises based in the United Kingdom and to create and disseminate information on them. In addition to the grant, the SEC received a yearly membership fee from social enterprises, as well as from individuals and organisations interested in supporting its work. Members could be of four different types; national umbrella bodies of social enterprises, regional networks of social enterprises, national social enterprises, and partner organisations.

In its first years, the SEC began to collect evidence from its members to produce knowledge on social enterprises, their needs, activities, and issues, as a way to start establishing social enterprises as a legitimate organisational form. For example, only a year after its foundation, the SEC wrote a guide on social enterprises, explaining the meaning of the concept, the possible legal structures to incorporate as a social enterprise, and the ways to access relevant funds and information. The knowledge produced helped the Coalition to share best practice with other stakeholders and to start lobbying for favourable legislation and policies. As the SEC and its reports gained attention among Members of Parliament and civil servants, all the political parties created ties with the SEC, engaging with its members and attending its events.

However, as the ecosystem kept developing, many members of the SEC, especially social enterprises, felt that this political attention was more apparent than factual. Many years after the foundation of the SEC, there was still no favourable taxation for social enterprises and despite government's incentives and favourable regulation, most public authorities still privileged businesses when awarding public contracts. Additionally, as the ecosystem was evolving, gathering political attention was not anymore one of the key priorities for social enterprises. What they needed was to attract customers and funds. Their inability to prove the social impact created was limiting their access to public contracts, investments, and to ethical customers. Meanwhile, their pursuit of a double bottom line was preventing them from obtaining the support of charities, foundations, and private donors. Another problem was the general low awareness in the United Kingdom of what "social enterprise" actually meant. Different stakeholders adopted different definitions of this concept and different intermediaries, such as the SEC, had diverging views about the role that social enterprises should play. Consequently, for the general public it was difficult to distinguish social enterprises from traditional charities and enterprises.

As the social entrepreneurship ecosystem entered its developing phase, the SEC found itself in the tough position of having to combine two very different objectives with limited resources:

1 Maintaining strong government links and lobbying activities, in order to guarantee its relevance for policy purposes and thus survival;
2 Helping its members, who also constituted key stakeholders and supporters, solve the issues that were most pressing for them and most critically hampering their success.

Case study questions

1   Is there a way of meeting both goals at the same time or are they incompatible in the presence of limited resources?

2 What activities could the SEC put in place to maintain and strengthen its relationships with the government, parliament, and other public authorities?
3 How could the SEC address the concerns of its members?
4 Do you think the SEC should include other stakeholders in its membership? If so, who and how?
5 If you were the CEO of the SEC, what would you do to ensure the survival of your organisation while also fulfilling your mission of creating an ecosystem supportive of social enterprises in the United Kingdom? What would you privilege and why?
6 How would you evaluate your success in achieving your goals?

Notes

1 OECD, & European Commission: Directorate-General for Employment, Social Affairs and Inclusion. (2017). *Boosting social enterprise development: Good practice compendium*. OECD Publishing, Chapter 21, 236.
2 UpEffect. (2022). *Case study – Threadable*. Retrieved from: https://www.theupeffect.com/ [Last accessed: 24 January 2022].
3 Mirvis, P., & Googins, B. (2018). Catalyzing social entrepreneurship in Africa: Roles for western universities, NGOs and corporations. *Africa Journal of Management*, 4(1), 57–83.

5 The present and future of social entrepreneurship

Key content

This chapter highlights some of the achievements and limitations of social entrepreneurship, leveraging these to reflect on how to best support the development of social entrepreneurship going forward, and it introduces the concept of systems change.

5.1 The achievements of social entrepreneurship
5.2 Limitations of social entrepreneurship and ongoing challenges for social entrepreneurial organisations
5.3 Sustaining the development of social entrepreneurship
5.4 The way forward for social entrepreneurship: systems change

Learning objectives

- Appreciate what social entrepreneurship achieved in the past 30 years.
- Recognise that social entrepreneurship has shown some important limitations.
- Become aware of the challenges that many social entrepreneurial organisations face.
- Learn the basics of systems change and of related concepts – systems analysis, systems thinking, and systems leadership – and why they matter for social entrepreneurship.

5.1 The achievements of social entrepreneurship

Chapter 2 discussed four main roles attributed to social entrepreneurship: the empowerment of people and communities, the compensation for market and public sector failures, the contribution to economic development and poverty alleviation, and the transformation of systems and institutions. While there is not enough data to prove in quantitative terms how well social entrepreneurs and social entrepreneurial organisations are doing in these regards, there is substantial anecdotal evidence confirming that social entrepreneurship successfully fulfils these roles in different parts of the world. Additionally, academic research and various testimonies from stakeholders of social entrepreneurship ecosystems have proven that social entrepreneurship has also:

- contributed to changing some practices in the business, public, and third sectors;
- attracted new resources for the solution of social and environmental issues;

DOI: 10.4324/9781003121824-7

- increased diversity and inclusion among entrepreneurs;
- driven social innovation.

With regard to the first of the above points, while efforts to make business more sustainable have happened well beyond social entrepreneurship, the emergence of social entrepreneurship as a celebrated activity has confirmed that it is possible, at least to some extent, to combine profitability with sustainability. Its appeal among young graduates has helped to show businesses in many sectors the importance of paying attention to their social and environmental impact to keep attracting top talent. Meanwhile, the success of some Fair Trade Organisations has made businesses aware of the need for, and opportunity to, managing their supply chains in a more ethical way, to remain attractive for environmentally and socially aware consumers. As seen in Chapter 4, social enterprises have also represented an opportunity for businesses to source what they need through socially responsible and sustainable suppliers, thus increasing their overall sustainability.

Additionally, the emergence of social entrepreneurship has affected practices in the public sector. It has offered policymakers an opportunity to maintain and innovate some public services despite budget cuts, and to cater to the needs of communities too remote or small for tailored public welfare provision. Besides, as was the case for the business sector, social enterprises have increased the sustainability of the supply chains of public authorities, and have made these chains more aligned with the generation of public benefit, since public money is used to pay suppliers that generate social or environmental impact through their work.

Finally, the existence of social entrepreneurship contributed to spark discussions in the third sector about the opportunity for non-profit organisations to adopt business tools for higher efficiency and effectiveness and to legitimately engage in revenue-generating activities. While business approaches should not be encouraged in all non-profit endeavours and do present risks, e.g. in terms of mission drift, for many third-sector organisations it has been important to consider new alternatives for financial sustainability as resources become scarcer.

Moreover, the hybrid nature of social entrepreneurship has played a role in attracting new resources towards the solution of social and environmental issues. Business leaders, tech entrepreneurs, and corporations not convinced by traditional non-profit approaches have been willing to invest in and support social entrepreneurial organisations, e.g. through venture philanthropy and impact investment. Similarly, public authorities have set up special funds and programmes to encourage social entrepreneurship, seeing in it the opportunity to provide additional or better services, to increase citizens' participation, or to modernise welfare delivery. Finally, by combining social and environmental impact with entrepreneurialism and innovation, social entrepreneurship has also managed to attract new talent to the third sector. The number of training programmes, university courses, hubs, and intermediaries that have been set up to support social entrepreneurship is a testimony to the social, financial, and human capital attracted to the third sector by this activity.

Several studies have also confirmed that, in most countries, social entrepreneurial organisations are proportionally led by more women and members from ethnic minorities than traditional enterprises. This implies that social entrepreneurship is increasing diversity and inclusion among entrepreneurs, encouraging individuals normally not keen or empowered to start up something new to take action. At the same time, researchers have noted that, on average, social entrepreneurs tend to be more educated than traditional entrepreneurs, and there is a general perception that social entrepreneurship has been powerful in attracting young people into entrepreneurship, given that Millennials and Generation Z are keen to do meaningful work, further increasing diversity in this sense.

While social entrepreneurship is not the only driver of social innovation (see Chapter 2), research proved that it encourages the creation and adoption of social innovation. By combining a deep understanding of social issues with business savviness, social entrepreneurship has helped to generate and apply innovations to tackle issues in education, healthcare, agriculture, water and sanitation, and many other sectors. From leveraging mobile technology for healthcare and banking (e.g. *Medic* and *M-Pesa*) to devising innovative knowledge-based ways to enhance the productivity of small farmers (e.g. *One Acre Fund, Vetiver Solutions*); from finding ways to offer quality education at a low cost (e.g. *Teach for All, Fundacion Escuela Nueva*) to creating financially viable social business models that allow training and employing marginalised people (e.g. *Luminary Bakery, Bounce Back*), the solutions created or implemented by social entrepreneurial organisations have positively affected the lives of many people. In some cases, they have also inspired others to replicate successful approaches across different geographies, thus further increasing the number of lives touched by social entrepreneurial and innovative solutions.

Despite these successes and the many more that is not possible to prove, social entrepreneurship has also presented some important intrinsic limitations, and social entrepreneurial organisations still suffer from some ongoing challenges.

5.2 Limitations of social entrepreneurship and ongoing challenges for social entrepreneurial organisations

While a lot has been achieved by social entrepreneurship all over the world in the past three decades, many members of social entrepreneurship ecosystems, researchers, and opinion leaders feel that social entrepreneurship has achieved less than some of its proponents claim. Most of the impact realised never gains enough traction to deliver sustained social change or silver-bullet solutions to complex social issues. This contradicts the claims of many supporters of social entrepreneurs that depict them as revolutionary agents of change or as those succeeding where everyone else has failed. Furthermore, there remains a lack of empirical studies proving that social entrepreneurship produces the desired impact. There are no regulations imposing social entrepreneurs and social entrepreneurial organisations to systematically report on their impact and activities (contrarily to what is the case for public authorities or charities in many countries and, increasingly, for businesses), little is known concerning failures, and methodological difficulties prevent the assessment of the aggregated impact of social entrepreneurship at the national or international level. This creates the perception that the hype around social entrepreneurship might be excessive compared to its actual contribution towards achieving UN Sustainable Development Goals, relative to that of businesses and traditional non-profit organisations.

This hype around social entrepreneurship has enabled some governments to privatise public welfare under lower scrutiny than there would have been otherwise. The more stories exist about social entrepreneurship successfully delivering welfare services, the more people become convinced that such services can be delivered by private instead of public actors, without considering the potential downsides and evaluating whether supporting social entrepreneurship instead of directly delivering welfare services represents the best usage of public money. For example, privatising welfare services might lower their reliability and accessibility, weaken the role of taxation as a redistribution mechanism, and reduce the accountability of public authorities in relation to the citizens they should serve. Even more worryingly, some of the main funders and supporters of social entrepreneurship have purposefully created a narrative around it that tends to reduce or eliminate the role of public authorities in addressing social and environmental issues, positioning social entrepreneurship as a substitute for rather than complementary to public efforts. This contrasts with the reality in many contexts, where government interventions are fundamental to achieve change at scale, and risks to create discrimination between citizens whose needs are addressed because they live in an area where a social entrepreneurial organisation is operating, and those whose needs are not because there is no private organisation compensating for the absence of public providers.

Finally, many observers critique social entrepreneurship for being yet another creation of neoliberalism, which is helping market-related concerns (such as efficiency, competition, and productivity) enter sectors where they should not have a place. This results, for example, in the de-stigmatisation of failure, since the latter is something that happens naturally in free markets. However, when dealing with social and environmental issues, failure can be problematic, because it might leave some fundamental rights and needs unaddressed. Social entrepreneurship's foundation in neoliberalism can also lead to encourage individual and private rather than collective action, potentially "undermining citizens' commitment to political engagement on which democracy is based".[1] Finally, it can result in social entrepreneurship sometimes sustaining instead of challenging the views and power of those actors that have been creating or exacerbating many of the complex challenges it is called to solve, thus helping them escape responsibility and accountability to drive change.

There are also recurring organisation-level challenges that many social entrepreneurial organisations encounter, beyond the intrinsic limitations of social entrepreneurship itself. These challenges are discussed later on in the book and are mostly related to accessing funds (in particular during the very early stages of the organisation), scaling the impact generated (see Chapter 10 for additional details), and measuring impact (see Chapter 11 for additional details). Other common issues are the lack of a financially viable social business model (see Chapter 8 for additional details) and of commercial acumen among managers and employees, combined with little attention to governance structures (see Chapters 3 and 9 for additional details).

On top of these recurring organisational-level challenges, social entrepreneurial organisations have to deal with a persistently poor understanding of what social entrepreneurship actually means among potential customers, supporters, and funders. The multiple schools of thought (see Chapter 1) prevented a common understanding of what social entrepreneurship is about, and stakeholders' grasp of the concept can vary from complete ignorance, to interpretation of social entrepreneurship as some new form of charity, or to confusion between social enterprises and sustainable businesses. Social entrepreneurship is not well-known by the public and this means that social entrepreneurial organisations often need to provide more explanations and reassurances to attract support and generate sales compared to traditional businesses or non-profits. A poor understanding of social entrepreneurship is also at the root of another recurring challenge: the lack of supportive legislative frameworks. The multiplicity of legal forms that social entrepreneurial organisations can adopt (see Chapter

3) makes it difficult for public authorities to design legislation and fiscal measures supportive of social entrepreneurial organisations.

Finally, social entrepreneurs and social entrepreneurial organisations are often affected by challenges connected to the ecosystem in which they operate. For example, research conducted in 54 African countries by the *Africapitalism Institute* and discussed in the *Tony Elumelu Foundation* 2015 report "*Unleashing Africa's entrepreneurs*" found out many context-specific challenges for African social and micro-entrepreneurs, such as taxes, costs of inputs and regulatory compliance, poor public infrastructure, e.g. in terms of connectivity and energy, and intellectual property protection. Similarly, research into India's social entrepreneurship ecosystems revealed issues with corruption, lack of empowerment of people, especially in rural areas, and high costs in terms of land acquisition. Social entrepreneurs and social entrepreneurial organisations are more likely to struggle in countries where there is not a supportive legislative environment, where competition for resources and

CHALLENGES IN PRACTICE – INSIGHTS FROM KENYA AND THE UNITED KINGDOM

Research by the *British Council*[2] and by Smith and Darko (2014)[3] identified some issues hampering the potential of social entrepreneurial organisations in Kenya. Meanwhile, the research I conducted on the social entrepreneurship ecosystem in the United Kingdom[4] and the "*State of Social Enterprise*" report published by *Social Enterprise UK*[5] identified some issues hampering the potential of social entrepreneurial organisations in the United Kingdom. Table 5.1 summarises and compares these findings to illustrate how the challenges described above might be experienced in practice and be strongly context dependent.

Table 5.1 Challenges for social entrepreneurial organisations in Kenya and the United Kingdom

	Kenya	*United Kingdom*
Funding-related challenges (most cited ones)	a insufficient investment in social entrepreneurship, especially for start-ups and not-yet-profitable social enterprises; b lack of networks that connect social entrepreneurial organisations with investors; c lack of information about potential funders; d insufficient capacity for impact measurement to match the requirement of different funders.	a difficult access to and availability of appropriate funds, especially grant funding (although most social enterprises report having enough resources from external funders); b insufficient availability of small investments (up to £50,000); c poor management of cash flows.

Business-related challenges (second most cited barriers in Kenya but not the)	a underdeveloped social business models make it difficult to convince funders; b lack of necessary business skills within the workforce; c unwillingness of charismatic founders to hand over the management of the organisation to professionals with more suitable skills; d over-reliance on customers/beneficiaries not willing/able to pay for the service; e lack of business-related assistance and support services.	a mission drift, especially as both public and private funds have diminished over time; b inability to scale up; c excessive egos hamper collective learning and adoption of best practices; d operational challenges in terms of recruiting staff, finding affordable premises, and managing time pressures; e lack of demand and difficult access to new customers; f high competition.
Context-specific challenges	a low trust for new players in rural communities; b poor infrastructure that makes it hard to implement technology-heavy, energy-based, or mobility-based solutions; c poor understanding of social entrepreneurship among public servants and in the sectors of operation; d absence of legislation specifically aimed at social entrepreneurship.	a London-centrism of the ecosystem and big disparities between the support available in different regions; b difficulties in identifying the right intermediaries given their multiplicity; c excessive fragmentation of the ecosystem, which reduces its lobbying power and favours duplications and dispersion of resources; d poor understanding of social entrepreneurship among customers; e excessive spotlight on white, educated social entrepreneurs who are connected to elite networks; f frustration due to the unsatisfactory impact to date, given the hype around social entrepreneurship.

contracts is high, where it is not easy to access additional markets, and where there is a lack of specialised business support.

To summarise, in its first 30 years of existence as a concept, social entrepreneurship has achieved significant impact but has also seen its potential limited by various internal and external factors. Knowing about achievements, limitations, and challenges (summarised in Table 5.2) is helpful to understand what kind of support will be needed going forward to unleash even more the impact potential of social entrepreneurship.

Table 5.2 Main achievements and challenges of social entrepreneurship

– Empowering people and communities	– Overclaiming impact potential
– Compensating for market and public sector failures	– Affecting public welfare delivery
	– Supporting neoliberal thinking
– Contributing to economic development and poverty alleviation	– Measuring impact
	– Scaling impact
– Transforming systems and institutions	– Accessing funds
– Contributing to changing practices in traditional sectors	– Mission drift
	– Under-developed social business models and management skills
– Attracting new resources	
– Increasing diversity and inclusion among entrepreneurs	– Poor understanding of social entrepreneurship among stakeholders
– Driving social innovation	– Context-related challenges

5.3 Sustaining the development of social entrepreneurship

Based on the limitations and organisational-level challenges described, there is still lots to do to sustain the momentum for social entrepreneurship and to enhance its impact. Addressing key limitations that emerged might require some re-thinking about what social entrepreneurship is meant to achieve and maybe a change in the narrative around it and its current individuals-centric focus, also often described as "hero-preneurship". Increasingly, proponents of social entrepreneurship are realising that this activity need not translate into new efforts and ventures but might sometimes be about what they call "social intrapreneurship", i.e. encouraging change in practices, businesses, public bodies, or third-sector organisations, instead of trying to substitute them or to address their failures from the outside. Different and better communication on social entrepreneurship and on its role in relation to other actors and sectors might also contribute to addressing other challenges, such as its poor understanding, limited scale, or the missing link between funders and initiatives worthy of support.

Intermediaries, incubators, accelerators, and funders will also need to favour even more peer support, collaboration, and exchange between social entrepreneurs and social entrepreneurial organisations and help them to further enhance their business savviness. A lot of the potential of social entrepreneurship is currently being wasted due to poor planning and strategising and to overly reinventing the wheel. Sharing best practices and encouraging replication and knowledge exchange could go a long way in terms of unleashing the generation of impact through social entrepreneurship ecosystems. Better coordination among social entrepreneurial organisations operating in the same context might mean that more needs could be satisfied or that existing interventions are better and more integrated. Similarly, intermediaries and funders could become more effective by joining forces themselves, specialising in different forms of funding and adopting a shared vision to promote social entrepreneurship. For funders, there might also be the need to make less project-specific and more long-term-oriented contributions, to encourage through their money more collective and less individual efforts, and to increase the risk level they are willing to take to ensure that promising innovative and early stage ideas get the support they deserve.

Furthermore, it would be helpful to have more platforms linking talent with social entrepreneurial organisations looking for it. Some platforms, such as *Commongood Careers*, have already started to close the gap between demand and offer of talent and skills but more can and should be done to make people looking for a career change find the right contacts to contribute to the success of social entrepreneurial organisations. Once potential networks are created between recruiters and job seekers, it will be up to social entrepreneurial organisations to attract the right talent focusing on non-financial incentives, such as shared values and the opportunity to make a difference for people in need, or to find the right financial resources to be competitive in the recruitment process.

Generally, it is important for anyone in social entrepreneurship ecosystems to accept that social impact and social change take time; and that joint efforts across sectors and cultural and institutional change are key to preserve the impact and change realised over time. Therefore, increasingly, the future of social entrepreneurship is strongly intertwined with its ability to contribute to systems change.

5.4 The way forward for social entrepreneurship – systems change

Systems change can be defined as "an intentional process designed to alter the status quo by shifting and realigning the form and function of a targeted system".[6] A system is a complex set of interconnected elements operating as a single unit according to specific rules to achieve something. Over the past decade, systems change (see examples at www.routledge.com/9780367640231 on the book) has become a buzzword in many social entrepreneurship ecosystems, as well as in the broader third sector and in some business circles, as a way to approach social change or sustainability challenges. This is due to a recognition that, no matter how good individual social entrepreneurs and social entrepreneurial organisations are, no one alone can be good enough to solve entrenched, long-standing, and complex issues such as climate change, rising inequality, or large disparities in access to education and opportunities, often referred to also as "wicked problems". These exist because there are systems, at multiple levels, creating and perpetuating them, and lasting change is possible only if the elements and forces underpinning those system are altered in a way that ultimately modifies how they work. This is no easy, small, or individual task. This is why many social entrepreneurs and social entrepreneurial organisations are encouraged to adopt systems thinking and to become systems leaders in order to address the social or environmental issues they care about.

5.4.1 *Defining systems*

Within social sciences, a system, a bit like an "ecosystem" (see Chapter 4), can be interpreted as a group of stakeholders that are linked to one another for a given purpose and whose actions and relationships are guided by power dynamics and environmental forces. For example, the education system in any country involves the students and their families, the teachers, the schools and their staff, administrators and funders, the producers of educational resources, the government (in particular the ministry overseeing education), those managing the public infrastructure providing access to the schools, etc. Their activities, relationships, and interests depend, among other things, on the role and importance attributed to education by local culture and traditions, on the number of schools available and on their resources, on the economic development of the country, and whether or not it is conducive of children attending school regularly, etc.

Some of the stakeholders and environmental forces present in a system support its well-functioning and the reaching of its purpose, some actively hinder both, and some others are neutral/passive elements. For example, in an education system, families could be a supporter of its well-functioning because they might fight for its quality in the belief that education is the best way to give their children a better future. Similarly, some NGOs might support its well-functioning by providing wider access to it. On the other hand, the level of economic development might hamper its functioning, since it might force families to ask children to work, in order to support their siblings, or prevent teachers to access the latest and best education materials due to lack of resources. Students might end up being just a neutral element, receiving whatever the system can offer them but without being able to alter it either in a positive or negative way.

In any system there are also stakeholders and forces that are willing and able to drive change, those that resist it, and those that just adjust to anything that happens, without the power, interest, or characteristics to do anything about it. Frequent sources of resistance are traditions, institutions, and humans' tendency to inertia. In an education system, we can imagine the drive for change coming from families being disappointed by the education received or from teachers being overworked or underpaid. We can also imagine that change might be resisted by headmasters afraid of the consequent extra work or by politicians willing to cut public budgets. Finally, by-standers in the face of potential change might be the providers of public transport, who would have no interest in entering the dispute between makers of change and their opponents.

Systems can vary from relatively simple and technical (e.g. a computer, a small organisation) to complex (e.g. large organisations, social systems, natural ecosystems), can be fully isolated or interconnected with multiple other systems, and can exist at multiple scales, e.g. micro (e.g. within an organisation), meso (e.g. within a specific village, city, or region), and macro (e.g. country or international). Normally, complex, interconnected, meso- or macro-level systems are those relevant for social entrepreneurship and this creates complications on two main fronts, the first of which concerns setting boundaries. In complex, interconnected, meso- or macro-level systems boundaries tend to be blurred if not completely non-existent. For this reason, the choice of how to limit the system in order to understand it and analyse it is subjective and depends on the part of the system that is of most interest, the scale at which a social entrepreneur or social entrepreneurial organisation has the power to intervene, the time and resources at disposal, or the intervention they have in mind. Remembering the existence of these subjective evaluations is important as the boundaries might need to change if the situation or focus changes or if the analysis turns out to be incomplete or less meaningful than expected. The second complication is that looking at these types of systems might force the systems thinker to constantly switch from the macro- to the micro-, as they need to simultaneously understand the bigger picture while also thinking about specific interventions that they might realise, targeting a finite and normally small part of the system. This is more difficult than it sounds when enacted in practice and can sometimes reduce the confidence in the analysis made or in the information gathered.

5.4.2 *Analysing a system*

Systems can be analysed, understood, and observed in many ways. A helpful framework to analyse systems that can be used in social entrepreneurship ecosystems consists of three phases: a stakeholders' analysis, the analysis of environmental forces, and the understanding and mapping of feedback loops.

A stakeholders' analysis involves identifying which stakeholders are involved in a system, what role they play, how they relate to each other, and where they stand in terms of supporting versus hindering the functioning of the system and of promoting/resisting change. Table 5.3 represents a potential way to map out stakeholders in a system and suggests strategies to approach them to generate systems change. Alternative ways might include the creation of stakeholders' matrix or the creation of mind maps (see Chapter 6 for additional details).

Once the key stakeholders have been identified, it is important to explore the environmental forces, power dynamics, and vested interests that influence and constrain their thinking and actions. One helpful technique to do so derives from Design Thinking (see Chapter 7 for additional details) and is the construction of a "persona". It entails building a fictional character representing a key stakeholder of the system, exploring and describing how they experience and relate to the system – e.g. their demographics, life standards, needs, hopes, fears, what drives or limits their actions, what influences their perceptions, what affects their power or desire to change. Observations and shadowing are particularly powerful research techniques to bring a "persona" to life, although interviews can be used as a proxy if these are not possible. In general, this is best done as a collective effort, through brainstorming and a frequent review of the assumptions made.

Table 5.3 Stakeholders in a system and how to approach them

Stakeholders' role in the system	Expected resistance to change	Approach to support change
Positive contribution to the functioning of the system	Willing to change due to the perception of things not working	Involve heavily in change efforts
	Fearing change due to vested interests	Keep informed, explaining the benefits of change
Hampering the good functioning of the system	Willing to change due to the perception of things not working	Involve heavily in change efforts, showing how they contribute to issues
	Fearing change due to vested interests	Ignore, while developing tactics to handle resistance
Passive recipient or enactor of the system	Willing to change due to the perception of things not working	Empower and include by showing that actions matter
	Fearing change due to vested interests	Let be, keeping an eye out in case they should be involved in the future

Additionally, it is helpful to represent the forces affecting all the stakeholders in a system through an iceberg model. This consists of four layers:

1   Events (what is visible on the surface/in a system, i.e. the symptoms)
2   Patterns of behaviour (why events are happening in a certain way/trends that are evident over time, i.e. how symptoms develop)
3   System's structure (tangible elements that influence patterns and, thus, events, such as pressures, policies, power dynamics, relationships between the parts, i.e. the causes of the symptoms)
4   Mental models (assumptions, beliefs, values held by people in and about the system, i.e. the causes of the causes)

As for the "persona", building the iceberg model requires observations, interviews, data collection, as well as self-reflection, and is better performed as a collective effort. The *"mapping problem spaces"* framework introduced by Christian Seelos and Johanna Mair (2017) in their book *"Innovation and scaling for impact"*[7] can be a helpful tool to build the most complex layer of the iceberg – the system's structure. Their framework divides structural issues into four categories: Economic, Cognitive, Normative, and Political and, in this way, helps to unpack different influences shaping the system and to identify key ones to target. Once completed, the iceberg model delivers insights on all the forces shaping the system and, therefore, on the root causes of complex issues that should be the target of any intervention or attempts to change the status quo.

Once both stakeholders and environmental forces have been identified, it is important to map out and understand the feedback loops between them. These represent how different elements in the system influence each other – whether in a positive or negative way. In any system, an alteration in one of its elements causes a similar or opposite change in another element, although the time required for this to happen might vary significantly and the change generated might also vary and evolve as time passes. The links among interconnected elements constitute feedback loops, which can be either reinforcing or balancing. Reinforcing feedback loops generate an exponential growth trajectory in either direction, allowing the increasing success of positive initiatives as well as the exacerbation of problems. For example, the growing level of the greenhouse gases in the atmosphere increases global temperature, which, in turn, favours additional releases of greenhouse gases through the melting of polar ice and the desertification of previously fertile areas. These themselves favour the additional release and lower absorption of heat and greenhouse gases, with the ultimate result of exacerbating the problem, generating what we know as the climate change crisis. Balancing feedback loops are, instead, those where the changes triggered by the different variables in the loop counterbalance one another, keeping the system in equilibrium. For example, when inflation rises too much putting at risk the purchasing power of people, governments and central banks activate monetary and fiscal policies that reduce the amount of money available in the economy or increase what people can earn through their investment. This, in turn, supports people's purchasing power limiting the negative effects of inflation. It is the awareness of feedback loops, of their typology, and of the bottlenecks and dynamics they generate that enables to spot opportunities for systems change.

To understand how systems analysis might work in practice, Table 5.4 and Figures 5.1–5.3 provide a high-level analysis, illustrated through the frameworks

Table 5.4 Stakeholders involved in deforestation

Stakeholders' role in the system	Stakeholder	Power in the system	Expected resistance to change	Approach to support change
Protectors of the forest	NGOs – international and local	Medium	Low – if change helps the protection of forests	Involve heavily in change efforts
	Scientists	Low	Low – if change helps the protection of forests	Leverage their insights to bring supporters of change on board
	Forest managers	Medium	Low – if change helps their work	Involve heavily in change efforts
Supporters of deforestation	Gangs/criminal organisations	Medium	High – they benefit from illegal deforestation	Plan how to handle their resistance to minimise risks/harm
	Mining, logging, and farming companies	High	High – they profit highly from expanding business at the expense of the forest	Develop tactics to handle resistance and present alternative business opportunities
	National and local governments	High	Variable – they are influenced by companies lobbying to use forests for profit but might also have the incentive to protect nature	Connect and lobby with them, joining forces with other organisations
	Law enforcers (e.g. army, police)	High	Medium – variable depending on orders they receive	Engage in change so they can keep away criminal organisations and police' illegal activities
Passive recipients or enactors of the system	Local communities	Medium	Variable – some will want to protect the forest, others benefit from deforestation	Empower to take action and involve to discover bottom-up approaches to combat deforestation
	Media and social media	Medium	Variable – depends on who uses them and for what purpose	Engage to leverage their visibility to advocate for change
	Consumers	High	Variable – some just care about getting cheap food and products, others want to push companies towards increased sustainability and ethical behaviours	Engage to support change efforts and to create pressure on governments, mining, logging, and farming industries
	Schools/universities	Low	Low – but they might neglect teaching the importance of protecting forests	Engage to leverage their power to educate the next generations

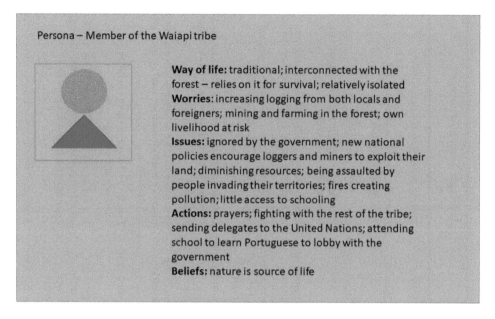

Figure 5.1 Persona involved in the issue of deforestation – member of the Waiapi tribe

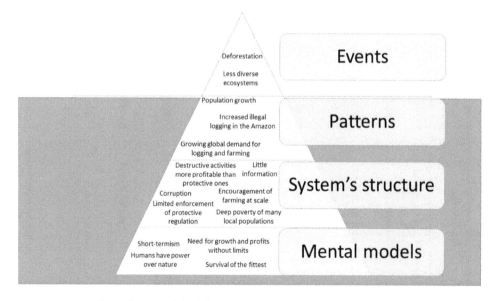

Figure 5.2 The iceberg model of deforestation

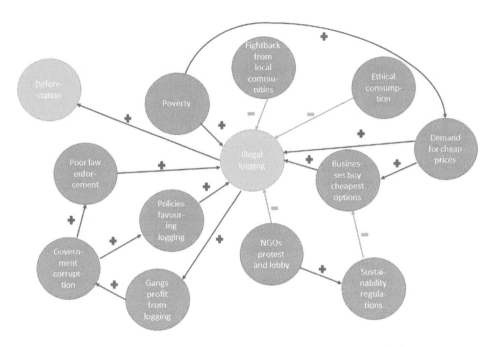

Figure 5.3 Feedback loops impacting illegal logging and, through it, deforestation

described above, of the issue of deforestation (for practical projects, a deeper data-based analysis liked to a specific community or geographical location should be conducted). For practical and visibility purposes, the mapping of feedback loops was limited to explaining one of the main causes of deforestation – illegal logging (Figure 5.3).

Systems analysis, which can be conducted in many ways beyond the one illustrated in this chapter, from fairly intuitive and experience-based ones to very formal ones, is the starting point to adopt one of the two systemic approaches frequently encouraged in social entrepreneurship ecosystems: systems thinking and systems leadership.

5.4.3 Introduction to systems thinking

Systems thinking involves the adoption of a perspective, which focuses on understanding the different elements of a system and the interconnections between them, with the goal of identifying ways to alter the system. It requires combining short-term and long-term perspectives, considering both more and less visible elements and remaining aware of the interrelation between change initiatives and the system itself, whereby initiatives are shaped by the system, can alter it, but then might end up being altered by it in turn.

A key concept in systems thinking is that of leverage points, whose identification is the goal of any systems analysis conducted within this perspective. Donnella Meadows, one of the most famous proponents of systems thinking, defined leverage points as "the places within a complex system where a small shift in one thing can produce big changes in everything".[8] According to her,[9] leverage points can be of 12 different types, which Abson et al. (2015)[10] then grouped into four systems characteristics that interventions can target, each kind of mimicking one of the layers of the iceberg model:

- Parameters – these are mechanistic characteristics that are easy to modify but that become valuable leverage points when they provoke changes in other places within the system. Examples include: the maximum area of forest that can be cut each year; the number of people involved in an initiative; taxes; incentives; standards; the amount of funds given to social projects.
- Feedbacks – these are the characteristics of the interactions between the elements of a system. Examples include: triggers of positive, reinforcing feedback loops; the existence and strength of a balancing loop; the delay between an alteration in the system and the possibility to observe its consequences.
- Design – these are the environmental/institutional/behavioural forces that affect both parameters and feedbacks. Examples include: sources, flows and level of visibility of information; rules and regulations; opportunities for self-organisation and experimentation.
- Intent – these are the underpinning beliefs, values, goals, and understandings that shape the system. Examples include: growth being the core objective for the economy or a given business; the roles attributed to public authorities; the view of what fairness or diversity means.

Once having identified key leverage points, the next step for a systems thinker is to understand what interventions might act on one or more leverage points in the desired way and start a cascade of alterations, which should ultimately result in the desired change. Sustained change is only possible if the intervention and its consequences create value for most stakeholders within the system. For this reason, adopting systems thinking means paying attention to the potential intended and unintended consequences of any intervention on each stakeholder as well as on relationships, sources of formal and informal power, and behaviours, and exploring how different solutions and interventions might fit together.

Systems thinking, on its own, does not lead to specific interventions, but it is a way to start a change project, to create some shared understanding for collective action, or to develop social entrepreneurial ideas starting from specific, desired end results. Go to the book's website (www.routledge.com/9780367640231) and watch the video at link 5.1 to understand how systems change might be prompted by more individuals and organisations adopting systems thinking to understand and tackle social issues. On the contrary, systems leadership is more action-oriented since it is more about mobilising resources and support for change than understanding leverage points, i.e. where to intervene to address an issue of interest.

5.4.4 Introduction to systems leadership

Systems leaders are those that, instead of devising a specific solution to realise social impact themselves, empower others to bring about change, mobilising them and coordinating them to achieve more together than they could do alone. They highlight what is not working and encourage others to share their dissatisfaction and desire for change by creating a sense of urgency. They then create a vision of a better future, in collaboration with key stakeholders, and use it to attract and engage multiple parties and to encourage them to act. Finally, they work to sustain action and engagement, to create safe spaces for collaboration, and to remove potential barriers, until the change they envisaged begins to take shape. Like systems thinking, systems leadership also stems from the belief that it is systems that generate and perpetuate social and environmental issues.

Research from *Bridgespan Group*[11] identified four assets as necessary conditions for an individual or, more likely, an organisation to become a systems leader:

1 A deep understanding of the problem and of the systems producing it
2 A vision for change, developed in coordination with and listening to key stakeholders
3 An organiser mindset
4 Trusted relationships with groups required for change

These assets, in turn, are possible if a person or organisation presents and develops the characteristics and activities summarised in Table 5.5.

Systems leadership is a role that an increasing number of people attribute to social entrepreneurs and social entrepreneurial organisations or hope that they will take on (see Chapter 2), given their experience of the system they want to change and their ability to relate to different actors and sectors. Comparing the list above with the characteristics of social entrepreneurs described in Chapter 3, it is possible to notice a strong overlap between the two. Interestingly, however, something that can help to exercise systems leadership is actually a characteristic that many social entrepreneurs

Table 5.5 Characteristics and activities enabling systems leadership

Characteristic	*Activity*
Flexibility	Favouring imagination as a way to help others envision the better future that they hope to realise
Empathy	Leveraging storytelling through any media to promote a new vision and help others coalesce around it
Awareness of own biases	Fostering conversations and shared reflections
Respect for all opinions and people, and attention for different needs	Undertaking of parallel experiments to see what works best in practice
Deep commitment to a cause that in turn inspires commitment in others	Asking obvious questions to understand the underlying forces driving systems
Openness to feedback and a constant connection with other stakeholders to understand their points of view and to spot solutions	Brokering relationships and coordinating efforts, helping others to also see the full systems in question
	Helping people to understand power dynamics and to feel the power within themselves to change the status quo

find hard to exercise: the ability to understand when a job is done and to hand it over to others, who might be better placed to continue the journey and to enhance the impact created. This, together with the need for systems leaders to bring together many actors and a significant amount of resources, raises questions about the feasibility for social entrepreneurs to act as one.

Moreover, acting as systems leader is no easy task and suffers from the same, compounded, challenges that social entrepreneurship faces, such as difficulties in measuring impact, obtaining funding, raising awareness in others, and making ideas work in practice in the long term. Additionally, like systems thinking, systems leadership can suffer from the high subjectivity in understanding and artificially delimiting a system and from systemic approaches being generally better at explaining than at suggesting specific interventions that will succeed in generating change. Nonetheless, increasingly, social entrepreneurs and others are asked to either lead systems change or contribute to it if they want to make a difference. Thus, understanding how systems work and adopting systems thinking and systems leadership as potential approaches to address issues is going to be increasingly important in the field of social entrepreneurship and might eventually help to generate change delivering lasting impact at scale.

SYSTEMS LEADERSHIP IN PRACTICE: CONSERVATION INTERNATIONAL

Conservation International (CI) was founded in 1987 to protect nature and secure the critical benefits it provides for humanity. Its work currently addresses through a systemic approach three core priorities: protecting nature to halt the climate catastrophe; protecting the ocean to protect humanity; promoting sustainable lands and waters. Each of these areas is characterised by wicked problems, sustained by various negative feedback loops. This is why, over time, *CI* has adopted a systems leadership approach, deploying multiple strategies (i.e. parallel experiments to see what works in practice), and mobilising and empowering multiple stakeholders to generate the impact it desires.

The first pillar of *CI*'s systemic approach is knowledge production, which helps it to gain a deep understanding of the problem it wants to tackle, highlight what is not working, create a sense of urgency, and generate suggestions that can trigger action. *CI* sustains a team of researchers entirely dedicated to conservation science, engages in research collaborations with high education institutions, and supports the work of think tanks, to generate rigorous evidence that it can use for lobbying and mobilisation of other stakeholders. For example, in 2020, the research conducted at *CI* enabled it to identify key ecosystems to target for protection, based on the amount of carbon they can store. This, in turn, informed *CI*'s advocacy and funding efforts.

The second pillar of *CI*'s systemic approach is the attraction and distribution of financial resources, which helps it to act as a coordinator of efforts. *CI* created several innovative financial instruments to support conservation efforts and attract additional funds towards them. For example, it established *CI Ventures*, an organisation investing in start-ups that contribute to sustainability and conservation; it set up a *Carbon Fund* attracting carbon offsetting investments from multinational corporations and redistributing them to conservation projects in Peru, Colombia, and Kenya; and it helped other organisations to set up funds in support of conservation.

The third pillar of *CI*'s systemic approach is partnering, through which it fosters conversations and shared reflections. *CI* engages with both governments and corporations to assist them in understanding the value of preserving nature and in promoting or adopting practices that enhance conservation efforts. Since the Paris Agreement of 2016, *CI* has been partnering with several countries to include nature-based solutions in their Nationally Determined Contributions to combat climate change. Similarly, it engages in many partnerships to increase the impact of conservation projects through multi-disciplinarity and multi-sector support. For example, it founded the *Blue Nature Alliance* with several partners such as the *Pew Charitable Trusts*, the *Rob and Melani Walton Foundation*, the *Minderoo Foundation*, the *Global Environment Facility*, and technology company *Vulcan*, to promote initiatives protecting the oceans.

The fourth pillar of *CI*'s systemic approach is to empower indigenous communities, so they can feel the power they have to change the status quo. *CI* helps indigenous communities to protect their rights and, in this way, the land they look after, by connecting them with policymakers, training them, facilitating their access to critical technology, and promoting their expertise. For example, according to their 2020 Impact report, *CI*

> launched a $25 million public-private partnership with the French government, *Our Future Forests – Amazon Verde*, to empower Indigenous Peoples and local communities to protect the Amazon rainforest they call home in Brazil, Bolivia, Colombia, Ecuador, Guyana, Peru and Suriname and ... supported four Indigenous peoples – the Kayapó, Yawanawa, Ashaninka and Yawalapiti – to implement their community "life plans," holistic strategies to improve territorial governance while honoring traditions and our mission to protect nature for the benefit of all people.[12]

Finally, *CI* is active in storytelling to generate a vision for a better future and help others coalesce around it. It promotes the importance of nature and conservation among the public across the world, aware that only behavioural change and the engagement of many individuals as well as organisations can generate lasting impact. In 2020, it organised a campaign with *TikTok* to promote the importance of protecting oceans and a 15-hour live event on *Instagram* to celebrate Earth Day. To make sure that their various interventions and approaches work and to make adjustments and new plans if needed, *CI* also regularly measures the impact of its work in terms of, e.g. increased amount of conserved areas, number of threatened species that it contributes to protect, or terrestrial and coastal hectares restored.

SUMMARY BOX

- Social entrepreneurship has achieved much in its first 30 years of existence. On top of empowering individuals and communities, compensating for the failures of other sectors, supporting economic development and systems change, it contributed to change in traditional sectors, attracted new resources for the solution of social and environmental issues, increased diversity and inclusion among entrepreneurs, and drove social innovation.
- At the same time, social entrepreneurship has been critiqued for not realising the impact it claims to create, for favouring an uncontrolled privatisation of the welfare sector, and for sustaining neoliberalism, which has contributed to generate some of the world's most pressing issues.
- Social entrepreneurial organisations anywhere in the world still grapple with several recurring challenges: measuring and scaling impact, accessing appropriate funding, handling the risk of mission drift, and developing appropriate social business models and management skills. Additional recurring challenges relate to a poor understanding of social entrepreneurship among stakeholders and to context-specific conditions.
- Potential fixes for some of the limitations and challenges related to social entrepreneurship involve a change in narrative about what social entrepreneurship is about and can achieve; better coordination and less competition between key stakeholders in social entrepreneurship ecosystems; the provision of more business development support to social entrepreneurial organisations; the creation of platforms linking demand and supply of talent.
- Increasingly, social entrepreneurship ecosystems are embracing the concept of systems change as a way to realise sustainable impact at scale. This, in turn, requires the adoption of a systemic perspective, in the form of either systems thinking or systems leadership.

Check box – Self-reflection and discussion questions

- What do you think are the main achievements of social entrepreneurship? Do you agree with those listed in the chapter or are you sceptical about them?
- Are there achievements that were not mentioned that you believe can be claimed by social entrepreneurship?
- What are the main critiques against social entrepreneurship, and do you agree with them? Why or why not?
- What are the main challenges faced by social entrepreneurial organisations?
- What could stakeholders of social entrepreneurship ecosystems do to help social entrepreneurial organisations overcome their main challenges?
- What are systems change, systems thinking, and systems leadership?
- What are the benefits and limitations of systemic approaches (systems thinking and systems leadership)?
- When and how can systems thinking be applied in a social entrepreneurial organisation?

- What are the main characteristics of a systems leader?
- Can you think of an example of a systems leader? Why do you consider them a systems leader?
- If you look back at the past decade, in your own country, what were the greatest changes that took place and provoked a permanent alteration of a system? What or who triggered them?

Check out additional resources related to this chapter to learn more about the concepts and case studies presented, and to explore examples of systemic approaches at: www.routledge.com/9780367640231

Exercises

Exercise 5.1 – The future of social entrepreneurship

Reflect on the current socio-economic changes that you are experiencing and try to imagine how social entrepreneurship and the social entrepreneurship ecosystem might look like in your own country in 10 years' time. Write down your reflections and share them with at least one other student/course participant, specifying what you think the key trends that will affect the development of social entrepreneurship are and in which way they are likely to change it and the ecosystem supporting it.

Exercise 5.2 – The achievements and challenges of social entrepreneurship

Case study – The development of microfinance

When Muhammad Yunus established the *Grameen Bank* in 1983, after trialling, as part of an action research project, the giving of micro-loans to the poor as a way to lift them out of poverty by spurring and sustaining entrepreneurialism, it was a revolution for the third sector. In its first decades of existence, *Grameen Bank* proved that default rates of creditors from poor backgrounds were as low if not even lower than those of traditional banked individuals asking for credit. Similarly, it showed that microfinance had a positive impact on communities and on local development. Following this, *Grameen Bank* became a renowned institution worldwide, many microfinance providers emerged all over the world, and even mainstream banks started to look into how they could reach out to the poorest of the poor.

The rise of microfinance has allowed many micro-entrepreneurs to emerge and generate employment opportunities and economic development for entire communities, to send their children to school and nourish them better, and to improve their own life standards. It also directed many new financial resources to markets previously ignored because they were considered as unviable by existing financial intermediaries, and it enabled poor households to build assets and manage savings and, through these, to deal better with sudden shocks. When working well, microfinance strengthened ties and reciprocal support between communities of borrowers and created opportunities for female empowerment within the household, by giving loans to women and not just to men, as it traditionally was the case in many communities. As microfinance services evolved in the past decades, they became more refined and diversified to better meet the needs of different target customers. As such, they enabled thousands of people to access not only loans but also other financial services and instruments, such as mobile payments or savings accounts.

However, as microfinance practices spread, some of its drawbacks became increasingly apparent. In many contexts, there are not enough productive opportunities to invest in, and contracting debt may put individuals, families, and communities in difficulty, whenever they can not generate enough returns to repay their debt. Not all entrepreneurial ventures are successful and those micro-entrepreneurs whose activity failed to take off found themselves indebted rather than just in poverty. In some cases, in the best-case scenario there were no social benefits reported and in the worst-case scenario the poorest households in a community refused the loans because the minimum amount was considered as too high for their needs or could not receive the loan because the rest of the community would not want to guarantee for them. Microfinance alone cannot solve complex issues that hamper economic development and introducing it in isolation can be risky for vulnerable communities. Additionally, as microfinance providers need to remain profitable to sustain their activities, they can suffer from mission drift and start charging interest rates that are too high to bear for the poorest of the poor, thus limiting their impact to those who already are in a position to afford something. Similarly, many microfinance providers have stayed away from communities considered as too hard or risky to reach, which is where the demand and need for financial services – and thus the potential for positive impact – might be the highest. Finally, in some instances the impact of microfinance providers has been hampered or even prevented by existing regulations and laws or by too unconditional support from funders and stakeholders, which did not push them to improve their efficiency and effectiveness.

Case study questions

Watch the video on Muhammad Yunus and the *Grameen Bank* available at www.routledge.com/9780367640231 webpage on the book in the Additional Resources section to get some inspiration to develop your answers.

1   What can microfinance providers do to make sure they maximise their impact and/or minimise the risk of generating drawbacks?
2   What role can other stakeholders in microfinance ecosystems play to support the generation of positive impact and the solution of existing challenges?
3   What does the development of microfinance suggest about potential challenges and limitations of social entrepreneurial organisations and, in particular, social enterprises?
4   Are the issues connected to microfinance providers something that you expect several social entrepreneurial organisations to grapple with? Why or why not?

Exercise 5.3 – Analysing a system

Starting from the short case on *Conservation International*, and helping yourself with the example of systems analysis provided in this chapter, try to create individually or in small groups a map explaining the negative feedback loops contributing to the deforestation of the Amazon and showing how the work of *CI* helps to change some of those loops (you can create two maps, one excluding and one including *CI's* pillars and projects). Alternatively, pick an issue you care about and try to map the system(s) perpetuating it. Create two maps: one showing the feedback loops in existence without the presence of a social entrepreneurial organisation, and one including the activities and interventions delivered by a social entrepreneurial organisation active in that system. Share your maps with the rest of the group/class and ask for feedback.

Then answer the following questions:

1   Is there anything else that *CI* or the social entrepreneurial organisation you chose could be doing to affect the system?
2   Are there some key feedback loops they are not tackling? If so, why do you think that is the case and what would you suggest?
3   What did you find most difficult in analysing the system?
4   What did you learn from analysing the system?

Notes

1   Spicer, J., Kay, T., & Ganz, M. (2019). Social entrepreneurship as field encroachment: how a neoliberal social movement constructed a new field. *Socio-Economic Review*, 17(1), 222.
2   British Council. (2017). *The state of social enterprise in Kenya*. The British Council report series.
3   Smith, W., & Darko, E. (2014). *Social enterprise: Constraints and opportunities – evidence from Vietnam and Kenya*. ODI.
4   Collavo, T., Nicholls, A., & Ventresca, M. (2018). *Brokerage as an institutional strategy in fragmented fields: The crafting of social entrepreneurship*. University of Oxford web repository, 231–290.
5   Social Enterprise UK. (2019). *Capitalism in crisis? Transforming our Economy for People and Planet -SOSE 2019*, 46–53.
6   Foster-Fishman, P. G., Nowell, B., & Yang, H. (2007). Putting the system back into systems change: A framework for understanding and changing organizational and community systems. *American Journal of Community Psychology*, 39(3–4), 197.
7   Seelos, C., & Mair, J. (2017). *Innovation and scaling for impact: How effective social enterprises do it*. Stanford, CA: Stanford University Press.
8   Meadows, D. (1999). *Leverage points: Places to intervene in a system*. Hartland, VT: The Sustainability Institute.
9   ditto
10 Abson, D. J., Fischer, J., Leventon, J., Newig, J., Schomerus, T., Vilsmaier, U., ..., & Lang, D. J. (2017). Leverage points for sustainability transformation. *Ambio*, 46(1), 32.
11 Farnham, L. (2021, April 2021). *Field catalysts: How system change happens*. Panel discussion at the Skoll World Forum 2021. Retrieved from: https://skoll.org/session/skoll-world-forum-2021/field-catalysts-how-systems-change-happens/ [Last accessed on: 30 April 2021].
12 Conservation International. (2021). *Impact Report 2020*, 10–11.

Part 2

Practical foundations of social entrepreneurship

6 Identifying an opportunity for social entrepreneurship

Key content

This chapter introduces some considerations and practical tools for identifying opportunities for social entrepreneurship and understanding whether a social entrepreneurial idea is worth developing.

6.1 The importance of gathering knowledge
6.2 Understanding the status quo
6.3 Learning about existing competitors, solutions, and the context
6.4 Identifying the right social entrepreneurial idea to develop

Learning objectives

- Understand the importance of knowing a problem before devising a solution
- Appreciate the need to learn about best practice and existing solutions in order to maximise the chances of success
- Build mind maps individually and collectively
- Learn techniques and tools to spot market gaps

6.1 The importance of gathering knowledge

As we saw in Chapter 3, successful social entrepreneurship tends to arise either from personal knowledge or experience of a problem through family members, friends, or one's community. That said, this is not always the case and there are many other reasons why an individual might come up with a social entrepreneurial idea. They might be passionate about something and desire to work in a specific sector or context; they might be looking for ways to innovate their organisation or to make it more sustainable from a financial, social, or environmental point of view; they might be looking for a change in career because they desire to do a more meaningful job; or they might be forced by stakeholders to adopt a social entrepreneurial approach.

Whatever the starting point, it is important to research the social or environmental problem to be tackled. Without knowing the origins of the problem well, and who is affected by it, in which way, and what has been already tried and tested to tackle the issue at hand, the chances to succeed are lower. This seems intuitive but, in reality, most social entrepreneurs start from their own project or gut feeling and then, being action-oriented, get going with their idea without stopping. Sometimes this works, but

DOI: 10.4324/9781003121824-9

sometimes it leads to solutions that are not as good as they could be, if not a duplication of effort and the waste of resources, or to organisations that fail after a few months.

When assessing a social entrepreneurial idea, it is therefore important to double-check the following aspects:

1   Is the idea really addressing a social/environmental issue?
2   If it is, why does this issue exist?
3   How is this idea different or better from what is already happening or has been tried?
4   Is it possible to get support from needed stakeholders?
5   How can the project be sustained financially?

Statistics, while varying significantly across geographies and depending on the parameters used, show that, on average, between 50% and 80% of social enterprises do not make it past their third year of operations. Not much is known about other typologies of social entrepreneurial organisations but based on anecdotal evidence it is possible to assume their statistics might be similar. Many of the issues they encounter, as evidenced by the questions above, can be related to one common factor – a lack of knowledge. This chapter introduces some tools and techniques for gathering this knowledge, to maximise the chances that a social entrepreneur will succeed when developing a social entrepreneurial idea and connected organisation.

6.2 Understanding the status quo

The first step to gathering relevant knowledge for developing a potential social entrepreneurial idea is to learn more about the "who/what" affected by the issue to be tackled, and why they are. As seen in Chapter 5, an ideal way to gather this knowledge would be to perform a system's analysis, involving the key stakeholders and the feedback loops connecting and influencing them. However, very few entrepreneurs, in practice, have the resources, time, and expertise to conduct such an analysis. For this reason, it is helpful to be aware of other ways to quickly and cheaply gather sufficient knowledge to vet an idea.

The easiest option is to do a small research project, leveraging online resources, public libraries, and personal networks to collect primary and secondary data towards understanding more about a problem, whom it affects, how, and why. Primary data is that collected first-hand, from original sources, for a specific purpose. Helpful ways to gather primary data include: informal chats with or shadowing potential beneficiaries, customers, and key stakeholders; formal interviews; attending sector conferences and events; reflecting on someone's own lived experience of an issue; leveraging social media to ask questions to potential beneficiaries and stakeholders; and developing surveys to submit either to a selected group or through online tools that reach many people from various backgrounds (e.g. *Amazon Mechanical Turk, SurveyMonkey, Typeform*). Secondary data is, instead, what has been already collected for other purposes but might contain relevant information. Secondary data can be gathered through: searching online for reports, academic papers available for free (e.g. through *Google Scholar* or *ResearchGate*), blog posts, podcasts, and videos; leveraging public libraries and their databases to find relevant articles in newspapers and magazines or book chapters; scrolling through relevant threads on social media (paying attention, however, to what might represent misinformation and one-sided views), or looking at the studies, statistics, and databases of international organisations such as the *United Nations*, the *World Bank*, the *International Monetary Fund*, large NGOs, etc. In order to make sense of the information obtained through both primary and secondary data there are two potentially complementary tools that can be used: codebooks and mind maps.

6.2.1 Creating a codebook

Codebooks are a way to synthesise and interpret large volumes of information derived from qualitative data. This is accomplished by grouping data into meaningful categories that explain at a glance the key knowledge that the data provides. The development of a codebook normally happens in three steps:

1 *Organising the data*. Data, or key extracts of the data obtained from primary and secondary sources, should be gathered into the same format and stored in the same place, either physical or electronic. This might involve transcribing or summarising notes, videos, and observations in writing, copying, and pasting information from different sources into the same file (while respecting copyright rules) and/or discussing all key insights from different sources in audio or video recordings, based on personal preferences. Whatever names (e.g. beneficiaries' interviews, blogs) help the user to retrieve the data most easily should be the first choice to label the different files.
2 *Analysing the data*. Once data is organised, the second step involves a close reading of the files created and the extraction of key insights that emerge from them. To extract meaningful insights, it is important to always keep in mind what kind of information is needed. Insights can be recorded through writing comments on the side of a text, highlighting relevant sentences, using analytical software such as *NVivo* or *QDA Miner*, or writing key sentences or words down in a separate document/tool. The key goal of this step is to simplify the data at hand and make it become informative on key topics of interest.
3 *Coding the data*. The final step is to group the insights generated through step 2 in broad themes that give them a meaning and help to retrieve the information needed quickly. Each theme created is going to be a code, i.e. a descriptive word, illustration, or short sentence, that summarises the information contained within it. Coding should simultaneously enable the simplification of the data and the spotting of relationships between different notes or themes.

To provide an example of how a codebook might be developed in practice, let's assume that an aspiring social entrepreneur, wanting to know more about "how to become a social entrepreneur", came across the following extract of an interview and decided to incorporate it in a codebook.

"INTERVIEWER: *Why did you decide to create a start-up to teach financial literacy in some Brazilian slums?*
MARIA: *I had been working in the corporate sector for a while, and I did not really aim to become an entrepreneur. However, as I volunteered to bring food to children in some slums, I realised that the lack of food in some families was connected to the inability of mothers and fathers to manage the little that they were earning through various jobs. Through a friend, I was aware of several initiatives of non-profit organisations that were teaching financial literacy to*

women in other countries, and I thought it might be helpful to bring a similar service to the slums. I realised that if I could get some of the existing materials used to teach financial literacy and insert them in an app or deliver them as a text service, we could easily increase awareness about money management and understanding of basic financial concepts. This turned out to be an idea that many considered as valuable. I approached two NGOs active in one of the slums and they decided to support the project right away, connecting me to app developers and to some potential funders in their networks. I wish I had had a clear plan and strategy but, actually, my organisation arose through learning by doing and interacting with different stakeholders. And keeping on asking for more funds and more support to whoever was willing to listen. In just two years, the organisation has kept changing and growing, well beyond my expectations. We accomplished more than I could ever imagine in some areas, but we also had to give up a lot of ideas and do something completely different than we planned. And I am sure the organisation will keep evolving in unexpected ways in the future.

INTERVIEWER: *It is really impressive how an initial intuition turned into an organisation and into many families being impacted in just 2 years.*

MARIA: *Yes, indeed. I think this shows that with some courage and initiative, there are many problems that we can start to solve. What matters is to identify an existing problem or need that has strong negative effects on the people you want to help and to understand why it is not being addressed sufficiently yet and if there is something that could be done about it. In my case, when I decided to figure out why families did not have enough food on the table even when at least one of the parents had a job, I kept asking around what was going wrong. Many volunteers I talked to did not really have a clue about the different issues affecting families, and some NGOs that operated in the slums were more focused on giving food than on understanding why their intervention was needed in the first place. I tried to talk to as many families as possible and, in particular, women from the slums, when I went there to volunteer, and over time I kept hearing the same story over and over again – money tended to finish in just a few days because they overspent as soon as they received some earnings. In these two years I have seen how much my initiative has changed the discourse. Now there are many other non-profits that are trying to figure out what other causes of malnutrition and poverty we are not aware of and to change their approaches to make families in the slums less dependent on charity".*

If, reading this extract, the aspiring entrepreneur thought that the article contained several interesting ideas, step one would be to copy or transcribe the interview (or parts of it) in a separate document, making sure to fully reference the author of the interview and the website from where it was retrieved, and naming the document along the lines of "Interview of social entrepreneur". Once filed, the document may be organised together with other documents also containing first-hand accounts of how social entrepreneurs got their starts. As step two, the aspiring entrepreneur would re-read the document and analyse it with the objective of learning more on "how to become a social entrepreneur" in mind. The analysis could involve the highlighting of key sections of the interview and the creation of notes summarising important information. An example of key sections and related notes is reported here (notes created by the aspiring entrepreneur are in blue):

Note

A   as I volunteered to bring food to children in some slums, I realised that the lack of food in some families was connected to the inability of mothers and fathers to manage the little that they were earning through various jobs. Through a friend, I was aware of several initiatives of non-profit organisations that were teaching financial literacy to women in other countries, and I thought it might be helpful to bring a similar service to the slums.

Spotting a problem and a missed opportunity to tackle it.

B   I realised that if I could get some of the existing materials used to teach financial literacy and insert them in an app or deliver them as a text service, we could easily increase awareness about money management and understanding of basic financial concepts.

Developing a concrete and simple proposal to close the existing solutions gap.

C   "*I approached two NGOs active in one of the slums and they decided to support the project right away, connecting me to app developers and to some potential funders in their networks.*" Asking for help.

D   I wish I had had a clear plan and strategy but, actually, my organisation arose through learning by doing and interacting with different stakeholders. And keeping on asking for more funds and more support to whoever was willing to listen.

Problem solving.

E   "In just two years, the organisation has kept changing and growing, well beyond my expectations. We accomplished more than I could ever imagine in some areas, but we also had to give up a lot of ideas and do something completely different than we planned. And I am sure the organisation will keep evolving in unexpected ways in the future.

Embracing learning and change to respond to what happens.

F   What matters is to identify an existing problem or need that has strong negative effects on the people you want to help and to understand why it is not being addressed sufficiently yet and if there is something that could be done about it. In my case, when I decided to figure out why families did not have enough food on the table even when at least one of the parents had a job, I kept asking around what was going wrong.

Spotting unmet needs and address them with a new approach.

It is important to remember that the notes and parts of the interview considered would have been different if the goal had been different, e.g. if what the aspiring entrepreneur wanted to discover was not "how to become a social entrepreneur" but "solutions to poverty in Brazilian slums" or "causes of malnutrition in Brazilian slums".

In the third and final step for creating the codebook, the aspiring entrepreneur would summarise the notes made by grouping them in three broad themes/codes, signalling key steps of becoming a social entrepreneur, e.g.:

I   Spotting unmet social needs (which could contain extracts A, B, F)
II   Learning by doing (which could contain extracts D, E)
III   Getting support (which could contain extract C)

By generating a list of codes, the aspiring entrepreneur would create a key for interpreting the data, which could then be used to analyse new data that they might collect. If those or other codes kept coming up, then this would signal to the aspiring entrepreneur the key elements/conditions necessary for embarking on a social entrepreneurial journey.

While the example provided here shows a very formal way of building a codebook, this can be done (and is frequently done in practice) more intuitively, noting down key thoughts and bullet points whenever something of interest is found and keeping all those notes in the same place, ready to be retrieved and re-read when the need arises. However done, a codebook is a fundamental step for transforming information into knowledge and distilling key insights that can drive the development of a social entrepreneurial idea, or allow it to be spotted early on if and why it might not work.

6.2.2 Creating a mind map

An alternative and/or complementary way to synthesise key insights about a social or environmental issue to be tackled is to generate a mind map. Mind maps are graphic tools that help visualising thoughts and ideas and exploring the connections and relationships between them, by leveraging "radiant thinking", i.e. the spreading of thoughts out of a single idea. The development of a mind map involves four steps:

1   *Identifying the central idea sustaining the mind map.* When starting a mind map, it is important to decide what it is going to be about, i.e. what the idea that underpins the whole brainstorming or organising exercise will be. In the case of social entrepreneurial endeavours, the central idea is likely to be the issue to be tackled and can be represented either through a word or image. Examples of central ideas include: inequality in country X; water pollution; overfishing in the Atlantic Ocean; and child labour. The central idea should be broad enough to allow for brainstorming, but also specific enough in terms of geography or demographics to make the brainstorming feasible and not overwhelming. The central idea should be positioned at the centre of a page/file/whiteboard.

2   *Writing down concepts related to the central idea.* Once a central idea is chosen, the next step is to pick the most relevant categories or attributes that would allow to reflect on and develop knowledge of that topic. For example, if the central idea chosen is "poverty", key categories to brainstorm could involve "who is affected by it", "causes", "consequences", and "definitions of". Each category or attribute needs to be connected directly to the central idea through a ray/line. In this way, it becomes the next centre of attention to continue the brainstorming and/or knowledge representation process. Each idea that radiates from the central one is called a "basic organising idea" and several additional ideas can get branched out of that.

3   *Brainstorming about each "basic organising idea" identified.* Ideas and insights connected to each "basic organising idea" need to be brainstormed and added to

the mind map, as they emerge. Their addition happens by creating a new line/ray jotting out of the "basic organising idea" and writing text at the other end of it. The shorter and sharper the text included in the map, the better, since mind maps are meant to be visual and intuitive. The goal is to create a hierarchy of ideas and to leverage it to spot quickly the relationships between them, the knowledge gaps, and the clusters of important concepts and connections. The usage of colours and various types of lines can be particularly useful in this sense, as different colours can be used for different categories of ideas (e.g. one colour for stakeholders, one colour for cultural and institutional causes of an issue, one colour for groups of beneficiaries), and different lines can be used to highlight different types of relationships (e.g. causal, correlative, potential, missing).

4   *Checking the mind map and refining it.* It is likely that multiple mind maps will need to be drawn before generating the "final one". This is because, as knowledge is summarised, brainstormed, and visualised, it might become apparent that some things are useless or wrong, or that some of the initial categories were not framed correctly. Different iterations of a mind map are helpful for organising ideas in an increasingly logical way, adding insights that arise while working and observing the mind map, and correcting the mistakes and imprecisions that are likely to emerge during the process.

When used to explore a social entrepreneurial idea, mind maps can be created with four different purposes in mind:

1   Summarising and connecting information retrieved through primary and secondary data in a graphic way rather than a codebook. This might also help identifying knowledge gaps.
2   Brainstorming individually or ideally collectively to generate insights beyond or instead of gathering data through research.
3   Visualising who different stakeholders are and what their role might be in relation to a social or environmental issue. This might also help identifying whether multiple stakeholders might benefit from a potential solution/intervention.
4   Highlighting and uncovering the underlying causes of an issue to spot how to address its causes rather than its symptoms and/or to become aware of the key causes that need to be tackled and considered for a solution to work.

Whatever the purpose, it is helpful to include the following three categories in the mind map: the individuals or groups affected by the issue; the causes of the issue for each of those individuals or groups; the stakeholders or environmental factors impacting those causes. For example, a baseline mind map of the social issue of gender inequality in Italy might look like the one presented in Figure 6.1.

In this map, the starting point is the issue, gender inequality in Italy, as felt by three different categories of women: women, migrant women, and teenage girls, who in this map became the "basic organising ideas". The specification of "women" into these three categories reflects how the causes of the discrimination they experience in their daily lives has (partially or for the most part) different sources. The second layer of this mind map involves brainstormed insights into the principal reasons why gender inequality exists for each of these key categories of women in Italy. The different colours represent the three different orders of causes: personal and family related (green); employers-related (orange); institutions-related (pink). The outermost layer of

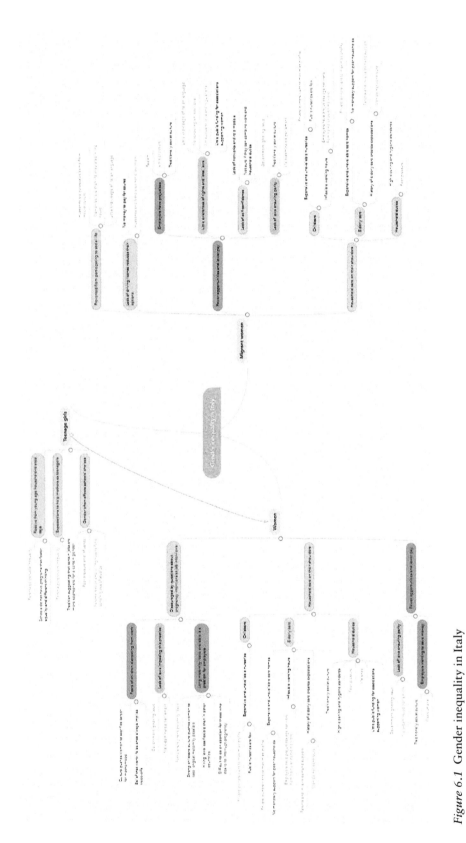

Figure 6.1 Gender inequality in Italy

For a more detailed view of the map, use this link: https://mm.tt/1969841595?t=81xSkOzdth (also available on the book's website – www.routledge.com/9780367640231)

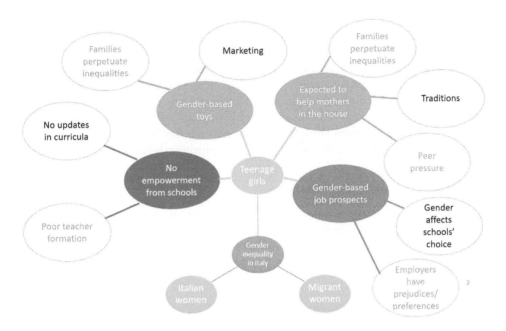

Figure 6.2 Zoom in on the section about teenage girls, within the mind map on Gender Inequality in Italy

the mind map presents the underlying causes of the causes. In this layer, the colour codes only distinguish between environmental factors (black) and stakeholders (light blue) contributing to gender inequality. The list of causes in both the second and third layers is not exhaustive but just a collection of key insights to start exploring potential solutions. Similarly, the colour codes are completely arbitrary and chosen to highlight key information. Figure 6.2 shows in more detail the section of the mind map related to teenage girls.

In general, mind maps can be valuable tools for sharing information with other people and organisations in order to gather their feedback, or to brainstorm collectively on a given issue. Collective rather than individual research is almost guaranteed to deliver more complete insights and might even turn out to be faster since different contributors bring different knowledge, especially if they represent the view of different stakeholders, thus reducing the need to find information through primary and secondary data. Additionally, as seen through the example above, mind maps are very helpful for organising information in an easy and intuitive way, to spot missing knowledge or connections between issues and stakeholders, to surface hidden knowledge through brainstorming, to simplify complex issues in a visual representation that can trigger further insights, and to add information over time, as it is gathered. The "Additional readings and resources" section in the book's website (www.routledge.com/9780367640231) signals various tools that can help to develop a mind map.

6.3 Learning about existing competitors, solutions, and the context

Once sufficient information is gathered about the social or environmental issue, the next knowledge gap to cover relates to existing solutions and potential competitors.

Understanding what is already being done/offered is as important as understanding why that issue exists in the first place. Many social entrepreneurs launch into their idea believing from the get-go that it can be a silver bullet. While in some cases this is true and the original idea works well, in others, much more could be done by learning from existing successes and failures. In some instances, effective solutions are already in place and just need to be adapted to a different context. Knowing and working with this can shorten the time needed to achieve impact. In others, there are so many organisations tackling the same issue that resources to survive and succeed are scarce. Conversely, an analysis of existing solutions could reveal that nothing has been attempted to address a certain issue, in which case it might be worth exploring why this has been the case.

6.3.1 *Running a competitive analysis*

Learning about existing solutions and competitors is not too dissimilar from conducting a competitive analysis in a business setting. The underlying idea in both a competitive analysis and an analysis of a solutions' landscape is that it is important to understand what others are doing in the same space/market/sector in order to spot gaps to fill. The main differences between the two analyses mentioned above are their respective purposes (understanding to learn versus understanding to outperform and differentiate), and the fact that identifying existing solutions is normally more complicated than identifying competitors. This is because solutions of relevance might exist in completely different contexts and could happen at any scale, from individual initiatives to initiatives deployed by multinational corporations and foundations.

Common tools in the business world to conduct a competitive analysis are Michael Porter's Five Forces and the SWOT (Strengths, Weaknesses, Opportunities, and Threats) analysis. Porter's Five Forces analysis involves researching and assessing the pressure on

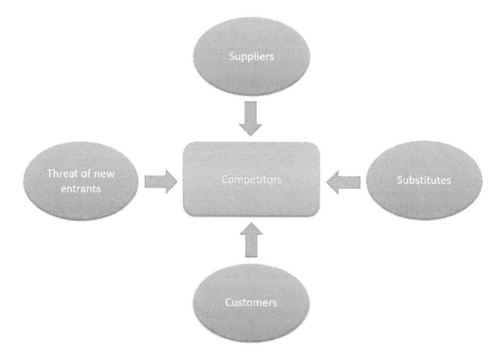

Figure 6.3 Porter's Five Forces (adapted from Porter, 1979, p. 141)[1]

profitability exercised by five key forces affecting competition in any industry: competitors, suppliers, buyers/customers, substitutes, and the threat of new entrants (Figure 6.3). This analysis is useful both for estimating how much each force might threaten the financial survival of the organisation conducting the analysis, highlighting key elements that it needs to strategise on, and for self-reflection on what sector or industry an organisation operates in, since that is not always straightforward to pin down.

A SWOT analysis involves instead the creation of a 2 × 2 matrix matching internal and external factors in a way that enables the spotting of the key strengths and weaknesses of an organisation, as well as upcoming threats and opportunities deriving from the external environment (Figure 6.4). A bit like the mind map, a SWOT matrix is particularly helpful for summarising the knowledge gathered in an intuitive, visual format and to understand at a glance what an organisation should keep investing in and what it should try to change or address.

Another commonly used competitive analysis option is to create a table with a list of the main competitors and a set of key criteria (tailor-made for the sector in question) to rate them against (e.g. with a star system). For example, a company like Mercedes might have a table with BMW, Audi, and Maserati as columns, and characteristics like profits, revenues, international presence, products, prices, key product features, customers, etc. as rows. For a social entrepreneurial organisation, interesting parameters to include in a similar table could be the social mission, partners, beneficiaries, products, or services offered by other organisations. Such an analysis is valuable for displaying all relevant information on competitors in a single place, allowing a quick comparison and fact-checking when making decisions.

Analysing competitors allows the assessment of how successful or not they are, how they decided to approach and target customers, what value they add for customers through their operations, what their next moves might be, and what their key strengths and weaknesses are. This, in turn, is important for providing insights into the potential threats and opportunities the organisation conducting the analysis might encounter, and to help it decide how to differentiate itself from existing offers. This is no different for social entrepreneurial organisations. If anything, for them, conducting a competitive analysis can have a double scope and purpose. On the one

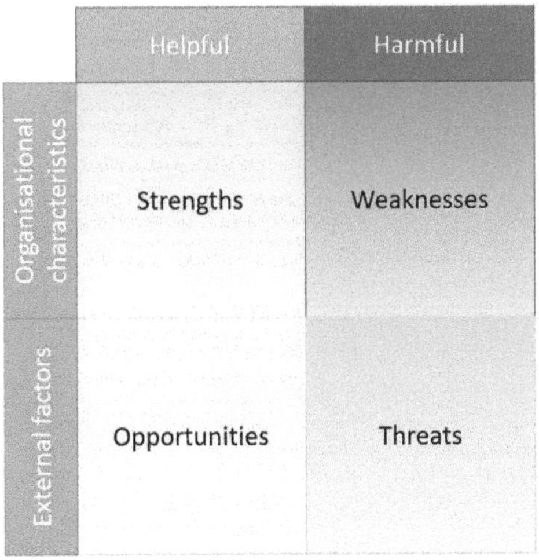

Figure 6.4 SWOT matrix

hand, if they are a for-profit business or pursuing a double or triple bottom line, understanding competitors is fundamental to remaining profitable and making the most of existing business opportunities and, if they are a non-profit, a competitive analysis helps them assess how much competition there might be for key resources (e.g. volunteers, funds). On the other hand, analysing who else is working in the same space can be key, as said before, for learning from others and, in this way, maximising opportunities to generate impact. For example, learning about existing solutions can be helpful for spotting potential allies, or interventions that are particularly effective. Assessing how providers of existing solutions do what they do can support understandings of which approaches to adopt, thus reducing the risk of duplicating effort in a world where resources are extremely scarce in the majority of cases, and enhance the chances of scaling and replicating what works.

6.3.2 Analysing the solutions' landscape

`It is also possible to use the three tools discussed above to assess existing solutions, by just modifying them to reflect the different goal of the analysis (understanding to learn versus understanding to outperform and differentiate). For example, when analysing existing solutions, it is still helpful to think in terms of the key forces that might affect their deployment and success, but the forces of relevance will be those altering the feasibility and effectiveness of a solution rather than profitability. For this reason, a forces-focused framework useful for the analysis of a solutions' landscape should include: the types of existing solutions and their key characteristics (in particular, what they consist of and what social business model makes them possible); the key resource providers and partners; the key barriers faced that reduce the effectiveness or reach of

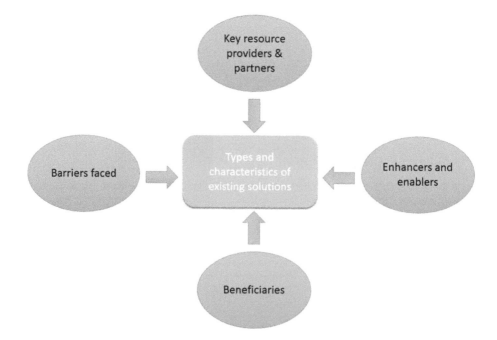

Figure 6.5 Framework for the analysis of a solutions' landscape

Table 6.1 Matrix for a SWOT analysis of a solutions' landscape

	Existing solution 1	*Existing solution 2*	*Existing solution 3*
Brief description of solution	....	....	....
What works well	• A • B • C	• A • B • C	• A • B • C
What does not work well	• A • B • C	• A • B • C	• A • B • C
Relevant insights	....	....	....

solutions; the existing infrastructure and context characteristics enabling or enhancing solutions; the types of beneficiaries served (Figure 6.5). Gathering insights on these forces can help to elaborate a plan for a new solution, to identify key stakeholders to get on board and pending issues or voids to address, and to spot gaps/missed opportunities.

While an analysis using the framework above provides a bird's-eye view of what a landscape of relevance looks like, and what key forces shape the enactment of solutions, a modification of the SWOT analysis (Table 6.1) can help to summarise more in-depth insights on the effectiveness of existing solutions and how these work.

Similarly, whenever helpful, a social entrepreneur or the management of a social entrepreneurial organisation might decide to create ad hoc tables where, instead of broadly summarising information like in the example of Table 6.1, they record detailed information about the most interesting solutions they know about (e.g. type of solution, key resources involved, key activities, target beneficiaries, partners, countries of operation, number of employees).

The insights from the competitive analysis and the analysis of the solutions' landscapes can be combined with those gathered analysing the social or environmental issue of interest. These then provide a broad benchmark against which to assess the validity of the original social entrepreneurial idea, and to decide with more confidence whether (and how) to develop it further.

6.3.3 Analysing the context

The insights gathered through the analysis of competition and of the solutions' landscape can also be complemented by gathering insights on the context in which an aspiring social entrepreneur plans to operate. This is helpful for spotting potential institutional voids or constraints to be addressed, relevant legislation that could shape the operations and the organisational form to adopt, and environmental forces that could either support or hinder the realisation of the social entrepreneurial idea. Again, a helpful framework for finding and synthesising such information can be borrowed from the business context, where it is increasingly used by both traditional businesses and corporations trying to assess opportunities and constraints to become more sustainable – the PESTEL framework. PESTEL is an acronym for: Political, Economic, Social, Technological, Environmental, and Legal. These are categories that, together, include all the key forces that any individual or organisation needs to contend with, and thus to assess context- or environment-led opportunities and risks.

Below is a list of common forces grouped under the PESTEL categories:

- **Political**: type of political regime, strength of political organisations, level of political stability, provision of public services, policies, taxation, bureaucracy
- **Economic**: easiness of starting a business or non-profit organisation, national income, levels of unemployment, inflation, interest rates
- **Social**: demographics, lifestyle, level of education, key trends, culture, working conditions, attitudes
- **Technological**: infrastructure available, adoption of new technologies, changes in digital or mobile technology, research and development activity
- **Environmental**: attention for sustainability, degree of urbanisation, environmental standards, recycling procedures, pollution, natural disasters
- **Legal**: regulatory frameworks, judicial system, level of protection of rights, health and safety regulations, intellectual property, licenses, permits

The PESTEL framework can be helpful for identifying knowledge gaps in relation to the context and as a checklist to ensure that the social entrepreneurial idea is feasible, as well as needed, effective, and an improvement compared with existing solutions. The level of formality of this analysis can vary and it should be interpreted as a living document, constantly updated and revised based on the situation and on the key factors a social entrepreneurial organisation needs to take into consideration.

6.4 Identifying the right idea to develop

The analyses highlighted in the previous sections of this chapter introduce the three key criteria that should be used to evaluate whether there is a valid opportunity to pursue a social entrepreneurial idea:

1 The idea addresses the root causes of a social or environmental issue or plants the seeds for future self-sustained change.
2 The idea addresses an existing gap in the solutions' landscape or leverages existing solutions that have proven to work well to expand the beneficiaries reached.
3 The idea is feasible given the context.

The first criteria is meant to ensure that the idea or project will indeed make a difference. The second is meant to both spot unexploited opportunities that could make a positive difference for target beneficiaries, and to reduce the duplication of effort and repetition of mistakes. The final one is for ensuring that the solution can be enacted to start with.

This said, while knowing more about an issue, the broader context, and the existing solutions to tackle it is generally helpful, it is also important to remember that no research will ever provide all the answers that are needed. A balance between gathering knowledge "theoretically" and just trying out something to learn more about it "by doing" is necessary to really understand the potential of an idea. When an aspiring social entrepreneur feels like they understand enough of an issue and the gaps in addressing it, they should have the courage to try out what they have in mind, even if there are still things they do not know or some doubts about the best approach to take. Only by doing so can they effectively receive feedback from key stakeholders, and spot unexpected opportunities and barriers that research alone would not bring to the surface.

The best way to test an incipient social entrepreneurial idea is to pilot it. Pilots are small-scale projects that test the viability, feasibility, and effectiveness of an idea without investing too much time and resources into it. Setting up a pilot project involves the following steps/answering the following questions:

1   Establishing the goal and designing the pilot – what is the key learning objective to reach through the pilot (e.g. test beneficiaries' reactions, understand what it takes to build a product or service, check causality between two factors)?
2   Setting up the length for the pilot – for how long should the pilot run to reach its conclusions? After how much time will it become too expensive or useless to keep investing in a pilot?
3   Gathering the necessary resources for the pilot – is the pilot a one-person job, or does it require putting together a small team? What are the minimum resources needed for the pilot to deliver its goal?
4   Developing an onboarding plan – who shall be part of the pilot? Who are the beneficiaries and key stakeholders? How can they be convinced to join the pilot?
5   Gathering feedback – What did the pilot achieve? Does the idea work or not? Who will provide feedback and how?

Once answers to these questions are secured, the aspiring social entrepreneur should get going with creating a "minimum viable product or service", i.e. a functioning version of whatever they want to set up that will allow them to see if their idea works or not, and to spot key criticalities before it is too late. The pilot test should never run for too long and should not require significant investments. If, at the end of the established pilot length, no progress has been made or no answer has been obtained, there are three possible options: pursuing the idea at full scale taking a leap of faith based on the research done and the experience accumulated; discarding the idea; setting up a different pilot. Discussing options with other stakeholders, ideally involved in the pilot, is ideal before making a final decision in this sense. Similarly, it is fundamental to check what might change when transforming a pilot into something with bigger scale. The conditions of the pilot might not be the same as those encountered in a full-scale project, e.g. because it might not be possible to find enough support, target beneficiaries might be less receptive than the few ones who engaged in the pilot, the organisational capacity to handle the project might still be lacking. This might reduce the validity of the pilot as a way to gather knowledge and to raise red flags.

Bottom line, a social entrepreneurial idea that is likely to work is one that matches a confirmed, valid, and feasible opportunity to make a difference and address an existing gap, that is able to attract the right people, and that has the potential to obtain the necessary financial resources to survive, while operating under existing environmental forces and related constraints. If, after gathering knowledge, an aspiring social entrepreneur is convinced about the existence of an opportunity, they should go ahead and further develop what they have in mind.

SUMMARY BOX

- It is always difficult to find the necessary resources for launching and sustaining social entrepreneurial projects, and mistakes are often paid dearly. For this reason, it is important to evaluate the context and the potential of a social entrepreneurial idea well before investing in it and asking others to do so.

- Conducting a small research project using both primary and secondary data can be very helpful for learning more about a social or environmental issue. Data can become knowledge when analysed through tools such as codebooks and mind maps. These enable the spotting of recurring causes of an issue, stakeholders, links between these, and existing knowledge gaps.
- Once enough is known about a social or environmental issue, it is also important to know about the competing offers and existing solutions that address it. This is to avoid duplication of effort and the repeat of mistakes, and, most importantly, to spot existing gaps and opportunities. The analysis of existing solutions can take place through tools such as altered Five Forces framework, SWOT matrix, and competitors' comparison tables, normally used for competitive analysis. In addition, it is helpful to use the PESTEL framework to assess the context.
- Gathering knowledge, while important, is usually not enough to assess whether or not to invest in a social entrepreneurial idea. Running a pilot project is an ideal way to complement theoretical insights with practical experience and learning points. Pilots should have a specific object and length and at the end should lead to one of three possible decisions: pursuing the idea, discarding the idea, or planning a different pilot.

Check box – Self-reflection and discussion questions

- Why is it important to do research before developing a social entrepreneurial idea? What key insights do you need to gather?
- Why would you privilege just trying out an idea instead, without doing research prior to committing to it?
- What are codebooks and mind maps and how can you build them?
- What are the comparative benefits and disadvantages of a codebook and a mind map for gathering knowledge on a social or environmental issue?
- What are the similarities and differences between a competitive analysis and an analysis of the solutions' landscape?
- What tools can you use to run a competitive analysis and an analysis of the solutions' landscape? And what is the main purpose of each of them?
- What is a PESTEL analysis and why is it helpful?
- What are the characteristics of a social entrepreneurial idea worth pursuing?

Check out the "Additional resources" related to this chapter to learn more about the tools presented and how they can be used: www.routledge.com/9780367640231

Exercises

Exercise 6.1 – Gathering knowledge

Read/watch the interviews with social entrepreneurs that are available on the book's website (www.routledge.com/9780367640231), in the section "Exercises", and try to analyse them using a codebook based on the process outlined in Section 6.2.1.

You can also watch the TEDx Talks available in the Additional Resources section of the book's website (related to Chapter 6) as further sources of data. Your goal for this exercise is to gather knowledge on what it takes to become a successful social entrepreneur. When you are done, share your analysis with a fellow student/course participant and compare your findings. If you want, also compare your findings with the characteristics of social entrepreneurs mentioned in Chapter 3.

Exercise 6.2 – Developing a mind map

Imagine that you want to develop a start-up to tackle homelessness in the city where you live or that you are familiar with. Do brief research into the problem, its causes, the potential beneficiaries, and the stakeholders involved, and create a mind map.

Exercise 6.3 – Leveraging knowledge to take action

Look at the mind map on gender inequality in Italy (Figure 6.1), and brainstorm individually or in small groups (meeting in person or remotely) about a set of potential solutions you might want to enact based on the information provided. Your suggestions for potential solutions should include considerations of why or why not they would be effective, whom they would target, and an explanation of what solution you would privilege and why. Also reflect on what additional knowledge you would want to gather. Then exchange your ideas with other students/groups and hold a vote in class on the most promising one.

Exercise 6.4 – Conducting a competitive and solutions' landscape analysis

Pick a social entrepreneurial organisation you are familiar with or one you would like to develop. Either alone or in small groups (meeting in person or remotely), try to find information about potential competitors/organisations trying to achieve the same goal or selling similar products and services, alternative solutions, and the context in which it would or does operate, using one or more of the tools and frameworks discussed in this chapter. Write a short memo on what insights you found most valuable, knowledge you could not gather but would have liked to have, and whether the analysis is helpful to assess the validity of the idea.

Note

1 Porter, M. E. (1979). How competitive forces shape strategy. *Harvard Business Review*, 57(2), 137–145.

7 Developing a social entrepreneurial idea

Key content

This chapter presents a process – Design Thinking – and a framework – the Theory of Change – that are increasingly used by social entrepreneurs and social entrepreneurial organisations. They can help the development of a social entrepreneurial idea and its transformation into concrete plans.

7.1 Developing ideas through Design Thinking
7.2 Translating an idea into a narrative – the importance of a mission statement
7.3 Elaborating on the existing opportunity through the Theory of Change

Learning objectives

- Grasp the basics of Design Thinking as a process to develop ideas
- Learn about the main phases that constitute a Design Thinking process
- Appreciate what it takes to translate an idea into action and, in particular, the importance of having a mission statement
- Understand how to read and build a Theory of Change and why it matters

7.1 Developing ideas through Design Thinking

Chapter 6 discussed the importance of gathering knowledge in order to spot opportunities for social entrepreneurship. The tools presented – codebooks, mind maps, and frameworks to analyse the competitors, the solutions' landscape, and the context – are the more traditional way of approaching knowledge gathering. However, in the last few years, there is a process that has gained significant traction in social entrepreneurship ecosystems, which can be very helpful both as an alternative approach for knowledge gathering and as a way to develop and refine social entrepreneurial ideas. This is Design Thinking, a human-centred process (i.e. a process that focuses on end users and their needs and experiences) to support innovation and problem-solving, which involves a mix of rigorous research and creativity. It is based on a combination of techniques from design, social sciences, and creative industries, and requires analysis, visualisation of ideas, observation, rapid ideation, and prototyping. Expected outputs of Design Thinking range from the appreciation of different points of view to fully formed and tested solutions ready to be launched; from the adoption of a curious and learning mindset among key employees and stakeholders to the development of better products and services.

DOI: 10.4324/9781003121824-10

Design Thinking can be a very flexible process, lasting from a few hours to years, and delivering results according to the time, effort, and resources put into it. The type of Design Thinking adopted by social entrepreneurs and social entrepreneurial organisations varies on a case-by-case basis, depending on the reason they undertake it and on the skills and resources available to enact it. In some cases, the process is not even fully formalised, but social entrepreneurs and social entrepreneurial organisations deploy bits of Design Thinking without even realising it, just because they feel it is the right thing to do.

Design Thinking is a process particularly fitting social entrepreneurial endeavours because it stimulates creativity with limited resources, supports the engagement of stakeholders by involving them in the crafting of solutions, and brings to the surface the uncertainty and ambiguity of systems, thus making it acceptable not to have a fully defined plan and to re-tailor solutions based on what is learnt along the way. Broadly speaking, there is a strong overlap between the underlying principles of social entrepreneurship and Design Thinking, and both have the potential to reinforce and support one another. Social entrepreneurship provides opportunities to enact Design Thinking and to leverage this process for the realisation of social and environmental impact. Design Thinking can help social entrepreneurial organisations to develop an organisational culture attuned to stakeholders' engagement and to trial and error, and to find adequate and effective solutions to complex issues/for highly uncertain environments, by providing them with guidance to develop something that is simultaneously desirable, viable, and feasible.

7.1.1 The foundations of Design Thinking

The theoretical foundations of Design Thinking, and of why it can be helpful for social entrepreneurship, have historical origins that date back to the 1950s, when Buckminster Fuller introduced design science as a discipline at MIT, bringing together experts from various fields with the goal of developing new design solutions that would satisfy human needs while respecting the planet. In the 1960s, cooperative design gained traction in Scandinavia and encouraged designers to take on the role of facilitators, while stakeholders, communities, and experts contributed to co-design the products and services that would relate to them and that they would end up using. In the 1970s, Horst Rittel theorised that most problems faced by designers were wicked problems (i.e. problems that seem intractable due to their multiple, interconnected causes) and thus not something that could be solved through a linear process, starting from a determinate problem and clear conditions; and Victor Papanek advocated the need for design to address social challenges instead of evanescent desires. In the same period, Herbert Simon discussed design as a rational set of procedures to solve a well-defined problem and highlighted how good ideas could emerge from simulating and prototyping solutions, and observing what happened. From the 1980s, these different traditions started to come together and paved the way for the current conception of Design Thinking and its usage in social entrepreneurship ecosystems.

One of the first explicit mentions of the concept of "Design Thinking" appeared in 1987, when it featured as the title of Peter Rowe's book on design in architecture and urban planning. In the book, Rowe described the design process and elaborated generalised principles about it with the help of case studies. A few years later, in 1992,

Richard Buchanan published a seminal paper titled *"Wicked Problems in Design Thinking"*, where he theorised how design shaped almost every aspect of contemporary life (communications, material objects, activities, and complex systems) and how design processes might work in practice, given the variety of issues they are called on to tackle. His paper moved Design Thinking from the body of work on how designers approach their profession to a concept that had a potentially much wider application. Ever since, it has been picked up by academics and designers working in different fields and for different purposes, as a process and new paradigm to think creatively about new solutions to complex challenges.

The interpretation of Design Thinking that is of most interest in relation to social entrepreneurship derives from management literature and practice, where there are three related views on the role Design Thinking can play. The first view is the one promoted by innovation firm IDEO, which defines Design Thinking as a set of practices (a constant cycle of creative thinking, prototyping, and testing) that it adopts in three phases (Inspiration, Ideation, Implementation) to help clients innovate, and that anyone – even non-designers – can adopt to enhance their creativity and innovation, with the help of courses and toolkits. In 2011, IDEO even launched IDEO.org, a non-profit organisation that applies IDEO Design Thinking process and tools to improve the lives of people and to encourage others in the third sector to do the same. The second view was promoted by Roger Martin, Dean of the Rotman School of Business at the University of Toronto, who theorised a process inspired by IDEO's Design Thinking as a new way to approach complex, indeterminate managerial and organisational issues and to reconcile tensions that businesses experience between innovating and maximising what they can get out of existing products and services. The third view was promoted by Richard Boland and Frank Collopy, two professors in management information systems, who interpreted Design Thinking as a helpful attitude for managers handling design projects, and who created an academic community focused on theorising on this practice.

In the context of social entrepreneurship, the prevalent conception of Design Thinking is currently the one promoted by IDEO. Partly, this is because it resonates well with some of the core values underpinning social entrepreneurship – human-centricity, cost-effectiveness, innovation, flexibility, and stakeholder engagement – and partly, because IDEO was very proactive in promoting their tools to engage with it, and in making them accessible through various media and partnerships. Design Thinking can be used both in conjunction with other tools for knowledge gathering (see Chapter 6) or in isolation, as a way to test assumptions, develop new ideas, stimulate creativity, proactively involve stakeholders and beneficiaries, and spot opportunities and insights that would not otherwise emerge. The key to Design Thinking approaches is to observe behaviours and understand not only the practical value of the solution proposed, but also how beneficiaries and stakeholders emotionally relate to it.

7.1.2 *The process of Design Thinking*

There are many ways in which the process of Design Thinking is described. They mostly differ in terms of the number of phases involved, which can range from three to seven, but all share the same key underlying principles: empathising with users, ongoing experimentation, stakeholders' engagement, a hands-on approach centred on rapid prototyping and testing, and the encouragement to think out of the box.

For this reason, whatever the process adopted, the effective deployment of Design Thinking requires the presence and exercise of empathy, creativity, collaboration, active listening and critical thinking skills, acceptance of failure, and curiosity for experimentation.

The process outlined in this chapter is the one originally proposed by the *Hasso-Plattner Institute of Design (d.school)* at Stanford University. It involves five phases – Empathise, Define, Ideate, Prototype, and Test. While it is helpful to explain these phases and to think about them in sequential order, Design Thinking is generally conducted as an iterative process, where the sequence of phases might vary and where the same phase recurs at multiple points in time, in a constant cycle of learning and improvement. For example, prototyping might occur throughout the whole process as a way to Empathise and Ideate, and testing might start another sequence of Ideate and Prototype, by providing new insights on users. The different phases can be described as follows:

Empathise. What distinguishes Design Thinking from other approaches for gathering knowledge or developing ideas is the fact that it is human-centred. It is about knowing, understanding, and empathising with the end users/beneficiaries of a proposed product or service to generate solutions that are inspired by and address their needs and wishes. In this phase, observations, interviews, active listening, research, and data triangulation are all helpful ways to learn more about how typical and atypical target users feel and live. Visual representations of insights are then used to summarise and make sense of information. Typical examples in this sense are the building of a persona (see Chapter 5), or the creation of graphic maps showing a day in a user's life/their experience of an issue, including brief notes on the emotions they might feel as their day or experience unfolds. These visual representations can help to touch base with users at multiple points in time, to verify initial insights, explore in depth why and how they think and feel the way they do, and to help them unpack what works and does not work for them.

Define. This phase is about distilling the information gathered from users (and/or other stakeholders) into short, human-centred problem statements, surprising insights, and questions such as "how might we solve issue X?" or "how can we address need Y?". In other words, it is about providing meaning to the information gathered to pave the way for the ideation of solutions, by reframing it into core problems to be tackled, as they are experienced by end users.

Ideate. This phase involves the generation of as many ideas as possible to solve the key problems identified. It aims to maximise creativity and innovation and to make sure that more than one possibility is evaluated before committing to tackle or improve something with just one pre-defined approach. In this phase, it is helpful to brainstorm collectively to explore radical and innovative solutions, involving as many stakeholders as possible and sharing anything that comes up to mind, without judging and censoring ideas, or worrying about how solutions might be implemented. Ideally, in this phase participants should also be encouraged to build upon ideas shared by others, connecting different proposals until interesting solutions emerge.

Prototype. In this phase, multiple low-cost and rapidly generated artefacts, features, experiences, and narratives are created to allow end users to test a basic version of the ideas generated in the previous phase. Prototypes can be anything: drawings, maps, 3D objects realised through any material available, short exercises and role games, videos, pictures, etc. They need to provide end users with the opportunity to get a feeling for the solution being planned, in order to enable the gathering of additional feedback from them. This phase also helps the team involved in the Design Thinking process to think about constraints and issues that might arise when realising a specific solution.

Test. In this phase, the goal is to test prototypes to gather as much information as possible and, through that, to refine or re-create the solutions proposed until they match the needs and wishes of end users as much as possible. Prototypes should be evaluated one by one, modified and discarded based on what emerges. Testing can take place within the team or, ideally, with a small group of end users and other stakeholders. In this phase, it is important to gather all the feedback received on each prototype and iteration in one place and to synthesise it in a way that helps to reconfigure the solution proposed in the way most helpful to users. Prototyping and testing can also be leveraged to confirm insights and to be reassured that the course of action chosen is the right one.

DESIGN THINKING IN PRACTICE

Read the articles and cases in the links on the book's website (www.routledge. com/9780367640231), in the Chapter 7 section, to learn how Design Thinking has been used in practice to tackle a social or environmental issue in an innovative way.

As shown also by the examples on the book's website, the Design Thinking process discussed in this chapter or equivalent ones can be adopted in many ways, depending on the length of time, the skills, and the resources available. Whatever the process adopted, Design Thinking requires storytelling, to help stakeholders understand the process and its outcome and to maximise the chances that the solution generated will succeed once implemented. It also requires managing expectations carefully about what can be achieved through it. For example, if the process is adopted as a one-off exercise to encourage a human-centred mindset in the team, the outcome is more likely to be a stronger consideration of users' needs than an in-depth understanding of end users or a fully functioning, tailored solution for an issue they face, as would be the case if the process was ongoing and conducted through a prolonged engagement with end users and stakeholders. In general, social entrepreneurs and social entrepreneurial organisations deciding to undertake Design Thinking need to keep in mind both its strengths and limitations, be equipped to use it in the way that makes most sense for them, and deal with its shortcomings before they might make the process fail.

7.1.3 The strengths and limitations of Design Thinking

Design Thinking can support social entrepreneurship in many ways. As explained at the start of the chapter, its human-centricity is strongly aligned with the values underpinning social entrepreneurship. It is an inclusive, democratic process that engages stakeholders, encourages and requires empathy, and that should favour the development of ideas that are both impactful and economically viable. In a way, Design Thinking can also help to compensate for one of the issues often faced by social entrepreneurs – their commitment to their vision and ideas. It encourages reflection and the testing of assumptions, and to remain open about being proven wrong, if this is what emerges from the feedback received.

Since it is a process where ideation, creation, testing, and stakeholders' engagement are strongly interlinked, it can also be a way to reduce the risk of the solution proposed failing. Too often, social entrepreneurial endeavours are based on assumptions rather than an actual understanding of target beneficiaries and this can lead to unexpected negative impact, reduced effectiveness or reach, and, in some cases, even to the "failure" of an organisation. Obviously, Design Thinking does not eliminate these risks but, if well enacted, it might raise some red flags early on and provide some understanding into what beneficiaries want and need.

Compared to traditional tools for knowledge gathering (see Chapter 6), Design Thinking has a heightened potential of surfacing implicit needs or hidden motivations and feelings, and of uncovering causal links between problems and both their superficial and more in-depth causes. This can be especially valuable if the social entrepreneur or social entrepreneurial organisation engages in systems thinking (see Chapter 5) or in the development of a Theory of Change (ToC). Additionally, it has a higher potential of being conducive to innovation, because it encourages repeated brainstorming, thinking out of the box, the frequent recombination and generation of multiple ideas and solutions, and their rapid testing and alteration following unexpected inputs and reactions.

At the same time, Design Thinking can be a very chaotic process, requiring an ability to cope well with failure and with the frequent re-thinking and re-building of a solution. This might be an approach that does not fit all and that is not needed for a solution to be developed. For example, a solution to a social or environmental issue might already exist elsewhere and only need some tailoring, or could be inferred from "common sense". In these instances, traditional knowledge gathering and some understanding of the context would probably be enough for the solution to work, and would be a more efficient and cost-effective way to proceed.

Another criticism directed at Design Thinking is that it is generally described as something simple and relatively linear, where following the phases of the process is enough to come up with effective solutions and ideas. The plethora of crash courses on Design Thinking targeted at social entrepreneurs makes it easy for them to feel like they own the process even if they never practise it at length nor received training in design or in the skills needed for it. This risks rendering the process into just a set of motions, not leading to anything really different or productive, and to make Design Thinking be seen as a shortcut to gathering insights from beneficiaries and stakeholders instead of really engaging with them over a prolonged period of time. Design Thinking should never be used in isolation or as a one-off "cool" activity or toolkit but, rather, as a process for keeping an open mind while building meaningful relationships and knowledge in other ways as well. Doing it superficially or as a way to legitimise ideas, without bringing into the "room" diverse voices and dedicating to it sufficient time, skills, and effort, might actually prevent the development of real empathy, human-centricity, and creativity.

Design Thinking also carries the risks of not allowing enough space for strong criticism and of seeing a decrease in the engagement and alignment of different stakeholders as the process goes on, due to its focus on rapid prototyping and testing. This might lead to lost opportunities and sub-optimal results. Relatedly, another potential issue is that most processes of Design Thinking do not involve a phase focused on measuring the impact of the final solution chosen, in terms of both intended and unintended consequences. In the long term, many forms of unexpected impact might emerge and these are not likely to be noted through rapid prototyping and testing. Therefore, social entrepreneurs and social entrepreneurial organisations that do not monitor the outcomes of Design Thinking both in the medium and long term might miss out on key insights and on the need to re-think the solution they developed.

Finally, there might be limits in terms of the operational feasibility of both the Design Thinking process and the ideas that emerge from it. One thing is to generate ideas and prototypes, another is to implement the actual solution. Teams might lack the skills, know-how, and resources to transform prototypes and ideas into solutions that they can sustain over time. Additionally, when enacted by social entrepreneurial organisations, Design Thinking might suffer from power imbalances between the organisation and the stakeholders that it wants to engage. For example, end users might be dependent on an organisation for support and survival and might not feel empowered to have a say or to pinpoint shortcomings of the solutions proposed, for fear of losing their support or of voicing something "stupid". Similarly, if they feel their opinion might not matter or might be overheard, they might not express their thoughts, thus rendering the whole process pointless. Remaining aware of these potential issues is fundamental for taking corrective measures or understanding when it is more helpful to deploy other tools to engage with key stakeholders.

7.2 Translating an idea into a narrative – the importance of a mission statement

Whether social entrepreneurs and social entrepreneurial organisations have identified an opportunity and developed a convincing idea through traditional knowledge-gathering techniques, Design Thinking, or a combination of both, they need to translate that idea into a narrative and concrete plans. This is important for several reasons, among which the key ones are: to communicate it to and gather support from stakeholders, to ensure what they have in mind makes sense for achieving what they want to achieve, and to understand what resources they need to secure.

As discussed in Chapter 4, any social entrepreneurial endeavour requires the support of others – both because solving a social and environmental issue normally requires multiple initiatives and joint efforts and because any initiative or organisation requires different inputs (e.g. ideas, resources, skills, know-how, funds) to take place, thrive, and grow. Convincing others to get on board with a social entrepreneurial idea is undoubtedly affected, as seen in Chapter 3, by the networking and storytelling skills of the social entrepreneur/leaders of social entrepreneurial organisations, and by their personal characteristics. However, no skills or personal ability, on their own, go very far if the idea being promoted is not well articulated and convincing to start with. In general terms, like any good story or news item, a social entrepreneurial idea needs to answer some basic questions: the why, what, how, and who. In particular, when people hear for the first time about a new solution to a social or environmental issue, they want to know and trust in:

- **Why** it matters
- **Who** proposes it
- **What** it is about
- **How** it is going to work

This is why it is important to build a full-on narrative answering all or at least most of these questions, to start attracting interest and support. Putting an idea into writing, and explaining in detail why and how it is going to work can also be extremely helpful for bringing to the surface any weaknesses, elements that had not been considered before, and the resources, infrastructure, and authorisations that might be needed to implement that idea. The mere act of describing an idea is likely to put an aspiring social entrepreneur/leader of social entrepreneurial organisation into difficulty as they might struggle to articulate what they have in mind in a way that is clear, logical, and understandable by others. Answering questions about it as it is shared is then going to surface even more elements that are unclear or only sketched and details that had escaped the initial development, sometimes just because of the excitement of getting started.

There are many ways to translate an idea into a narrative, such as: describing it to others when the occasion arises; creating video interviews about it; pitching it at competitions; writing official documents explaining in standardised formats what the idea is, what it is going to achieve, and the plans to implement it. Whichever option chosen, the narrative needs to start from and be anchored in an explanation of why a social entrepreneurial idea was developed to start with, i.e. what the ultimate goal of an entrepreneur or organisation is. Normally, this is done through the elaboration of a mission statement.

7.2.1 *The mission statement*

A mission statement or statement of purpose is like the Polar Star of any organisation. It describes its fundamental purpose and philosophy and thus provides an anchor and guiding principle for anything that it does – i.e. its strategic planning, operations, structure, the products and services it decides to deliver, and its way of approaching stakeholders. For social entrepreneurial organisations having a mission statement is, if possible, even more important than for other organisations, since mission is one of the defining elements of social entrepreneurship (see Chapter 1). Its goal is to shape the image of an organisation, to guide decision-making, to pinpoint where the organisation should operate and how, and, most importantly, to help define core short-term and long-term objectives.

Mission statements can vary in length from one or a few sentences to entire paragraphs and documents but, whatever the length chosen, they need to contain the following elements:

- **The purpose of the organisation.** Basically, this is the key reason why a social entrepreneurial organisation is set up, and should hint at the social or environmental impact that it aims to realise. Examples of broad goals related to social entrepreneurship could be "Ensuring every person has adequate access to water and sanitation", "Supporting the integration of women in society", "Protecting coral reefs from degradation", or "Helping children to realise their full potential".
- **A clear definition of target beneficiaries and/or customers.** This could be immediately evident from the purpose or might need some additional specification. It needs to ensure that, whatever happens, members of the organisation and stakeholders always remember whom the organisation is there to serve and, as such, whom it should prioritise.

- **The philosophy that underpins the organisation's existence and purpose.** This is the set of beliefs/principles/actions that the organisation considers fundamental for achieving its mission. It should express how the organisation operates and what is not going to be negotiable. For example, the philosophy of a social entrepreneurial organisation might entail "behaving as a good community member", "including sustainability considerations in anything that we do" or "recognising and supporting the unique needs of each beneficiary".

More elaborate mission statements could then also include additional insights such as:

- The geographic scope of the organisation
- The type of image the organisation wants to portray
- The key characteristics of the core product or service they plan to deliver/the solution developed
- The description of the core values of the organisation

MISSION STATEMENTS IN PRACTICE

Here are some examples of mission statements from social entrepreneurial organisations from different parts of the world. For additional details about these organisations and their mission, check the links on the book's website (www.routledge.com/9780367640231), in the Chapter 7 section.

ECOALF,[1] Spain: *We work to ensure a new business model in the fashion industry that can create a balance between our present and future needs and the planet's health. We have a commitment to at least maintain this planet as we found it (if not better...) for the next generations.*

TIWALE,[2] Malawi: *Tiwale is a youth-led community organizing initiative for educational growth opportunities towards marginalized identities. Our approach: Education, Skills Training, Job Creation, Community.*

The Centre for Nutritional Recovery and Education (CREN),[3] Brazil: *To combat undernutrition and obesity for the integral development of the person and the family.*

Hospitals Beyond Boundaries,[4] Malaysia: *We want to improve the health of vulnerable communities through sustainable health care efforts. We believe that poverty forces people to live in environments that make them sick, hence we also look beyond curative measures to include adequate shelter, hygiene, nutrition, and health education.*

Wā Cup,[5] New Zealand: *Solving period poverty with heart, humour, and connection, we are an Aotearoa birthed social enterprise that's sustainable to the womb. We connect people to their bodies and our land in a strive for a more equitable, just and sustainable world. We are period with purpose.*

An effective mission statement is memorable; unique; sets the organisation apart from others; helps to create an organisational identity that attracts the right employees, supporters, and funders; encourages the desired behaviours; acts as a powerful motivator; and is broad enough to leave some freedom to take different courses of action. Research on mission statements in both the business and non-profit sectors has established that effective mission statements enhance employees' commitment, retention, performance, and satisfaction; provide the basis for good external communications and public relations; help to generate attention for the organisation; and help it to build reputation and legitimacy. According to a study by Pandey et al. (2017),[6] linguistic characteristics in the mission statements of non-profit organisations that make them effective and that are associated with a good financial performance tend to: involve references to change; create a sense of commonality; communicate some optimism; use pragmatic language that describes tangible, immediate, and recognisable issues that others can relate to.

7.2.2 *Developing a mission statement*

Because of its strategic importance and the influence it is expected to exert, a mission statement should not be developed in a hurry or without strong commitment, just to satisfy expectations or to have something to put on the organisation's website. It should be the result of lengthy discussions and an iterative process, involving multiple drafts; feedback from stakeholders; in-depth reflections about what represents true, felt, and achievable commitments; and considerations about the knowledge gathered on the social and environmental issue, the context, and existing solutions and competitors (see Chapter 6). In particular, when social entrepreneurial organisations develop their mission statement, they should ensure that it is: clear and understandable for others (e.g. team members, current and future employees, various external stakeholders); aspirational; manageable; something they really believe in and will strive to realise.

Similarly, while mission statements are made to last, since they are expected to provide direction and guide planning and decision-making, as an organisation evolves and adapts to what is around it, they should not be seen as something untouchable or that cannot be improved. Because they are developed at the very early stages of an organisation, they might be the result of the ideas of one or few people, might be strongly influenced by their dreams and aspirations rather than by what would be an effective anchor for plans and operations, and might be outgrown by the success of the organisation over time. For this reason, while it is necessary to put something down in writing at the very start, also as a way to reduce the risk of mission drift, the mission statement should be reviewed, ideally with the support of a broader range of stakeholders, whenever the need arises. This could be due to perceived ineffectiveness, to feedback received, to threats to survival, to new prospects to scale impact, or just to changing context or needs.

Once the fundamental purpose of a social entrepreneurial organisation is well articulated, the second step is to build a narrative around how that purpose is going to be achieved, specifying the set of concrete objectives that will be pursued and how they are going to be met. This requires the elaboration of a ToC.

7.3 Elaborating on the existing opportunity through the Theory of Change

The concept of the ToC originates from the literature on and practice of programmes evaluation, which identifies logic models as helpful tools for understanding causal chains between inputs, outputs, outcomes, and long-term goals and thus to evaluate if and how programmes' targets might be achieved. In particular, it derives from the *Aspen Institute*'s 1995 Roundtable on *"Community Initiatives for Children and Families"* and how to best evaluate them. The Roundtable led to a publication in which Carol Weiss defined theories of change as theories of how and why an initiative works.[7] In her work, Weiss explained how the complexity of community initiatives made it very difficult to both evaluate them and understand if the right elements were in place for the desired change to happen, before it was too late to take corrective action. For this reason, she argued that building theories of change could be a useful approach to highlight how single elements and mid-steps would eventually contribute to the reaching of long-term goals, to bring to the surface related assumptions and, thus, to both plan what to do and what to keep track of along the way. Ever since, an increasing number of organisations in the third sector and government agencies have used theories of change to plan their interventions and to monitor them.

In the context of social entrepreneurship, the ToC is seen as the explanation of how an individual, organisation, project, investment, or intervention aims to generate (intended) social and/or environmental impact. Its usage is increasingly recommended not only as a tool for planning and monitoring, but also to encourage learning and gather support from external stakeholders.

7.3.1 The components of a Theory of Change

A ToC is generally represented through a logic model framework (Figure 7.1), which openly and visually shows the pathway to change through unpacking the logical connections between inputs, activities, outputs, outcomes, and impact. What enters in each box/category tends to be based on a mix of knowledge, experience, evidence, and assumptions, and the framework should be read from left to right. Alternatively, a ToC can be presented as a (short or long) narrative, through written documents, videos, drawings, strips, and other visual tools. However, a logic model is more likely to guarantee rigour in developing the ToC and clarity in explaining it, since it forces the adoption of a logic-based structure. According to Connell and Kubisch (1998)[8] a good ToC should be plausible, doable, and testable.

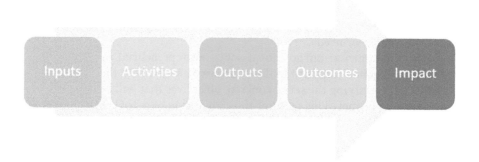

Figure 7.1 The Theory of Change represented as a logic model

The key components of a ToC as illustrated by a logic model framework are:

- **Inputs:** all the human, technological, natural, physical and financial resources, information, contributions, and support that an organisation needs to realise impact. Examples of inputs are funds, people and their skills, collaborators and partners, tangible resources/equipment, spaces, and digital resources.
- **Activities:** what a social entrepreneurial organisation does or will do to realise the impact they aim for. This includes processes, actions, events, projects, and methods. Examples of activities are delivery of a service, design and production of a product, realisation of a media or social media campaign, mobilisation of stakeholders, and employment of beneficiaries.
- **Outputs:** the direct/tangible results of activities. Whenever possible, they should be expressed in quantifiable terms, since they are the first opportunities to understand what should be measured to check if the activities are indeed producing the expected added value/are on track to ultimately deliver the desired impact. For similar reasons, they should also be expressed through specific targets (e.g. "vaccination of at least 2,000 people after three months", rather than "2,000 vaccines delivered"), with such targets being the minimum result believed possible to enable the realisation of impact of the desired scale, depth, and scope. Examples of outputs are the number of beneficiaries reached, the number of hours of training provided, the number or types of connections created, and the amount of donations collected.
- **Outcomes:** changes in individuals, groups, or systems, as expressed by the altered functioning, opportunities, behaviours, knowledge, skills or capabilities, relationships, beliefs, attitudes, etc. that result from activities and related outputs. They are the various benefits that a social entrepreneurial organisation hopes to bring about for its beneficiaries. The same activity or output may be able to trigger multiple outcomes or, conversely, it might be necessary to deliver multiple activities and outputs to generate one single outcome. When establishing key outcomes, it is important to specify the timeframe in which they are expected to happen. This could be the same for all, some, or different for each. Similarly, it is important to describe them with as much precision as possible, reflecting not only on the scale of the desired change, but also on its depth and duration. Scale is the number of target beneficiaries experiencing the change, depth is the extent to which change occurs in or for them, and duration is the length of time during which the change is felt. For example, if a social entrepreneurial organisation is delivering medicines to prevent malaria to a rural village in South America, it is not enough to describe one of the outcomes it generates as "improved healthcare". Better outcome definitions would be, e.g. "reduction by 10% of children that contract malaria on a yearly basis, or 10% reduction in hospitalisations for the whole duration of the programme". These target percentages can be estimated based on existing scientific data, similar projects run elsewhere, or conversations with stakeholders who are familiar with the context and problem. In general, outcomes should be changes that can be measured, that are relevant to ultimately realising the desired impact, and whose achievement is tracked and re-evaluated at different points in time, at regular intervals, in order to make sure the ToC holds true. Examples of outcomes are increased self-confidence or the empowerment of beneficiaries, new employment opportunities, improved access to water and sanitation or to banking services, and generation of awareness about an issue.

- **Impact:** the long-term goal of an organisation as stated in its mission statement. It results from all or most of the outcomes (intended and unintended) that the activities and outputs of that organisation trigger, as well as from those triggered by other organisations, individuals, and events. As such, it is only partially under the control of a social entrepreneurial organisation, and it normally happens and is evaluated after a long time horizon. This does not mean that an organisation should feel powerless or consider its contributions trivial. It should still believe in the necessity of its contribution and establish what it wants to achieve, independently of other factors, through a SMART approach. A SMART approach is one aiming for an impact that is Specific, Measurable, Achievable, Realistic, and Time-bound. Examples of impact are the generation of economic development and multipliers; the alleviation of a social or environmental issue; and the mobilisation of communities. Increasingly, social entrepreneurial organisations tend to express their desired impact in a ToC in relation to the UN Sustainable Development goals (see Chapter 2).

A more detailed illustration of what constitutes a ToC is presented in Figure 7.2.

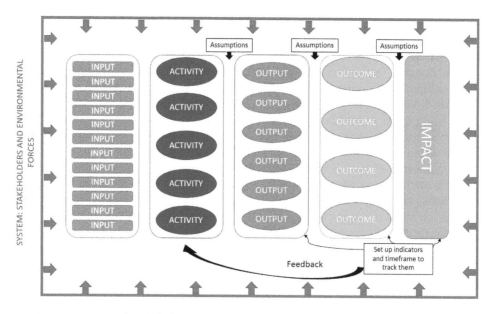

Figure 7.2 More detailed illustration of a Theory of Change as represented by a logic model

---

THEORY OF CHANGE IN PRACTICE

Check four practical examples of how social entrepreneurial organisations have expressed their ToC in the links on the book's website (www.routledge.com/9780367640231), in the Chapter 7 section.

7.3.2 *How to build a Theory of Change*

In order to build a ToC it is necessary to reverse-engineer – i.e. to start from a long-term goal and figure out, working backwards, what will be necessary and sufficient for that result to be achieved, elaborating and testing all the causal links between the different underpinning elements in the process. Specifically, it means starting from the desired social and/or environmental impact and then working out what intermediate outcomes will make it possible and, in turn, what outputs will generate the needed outcomes and what activities and resources are necessary to deliver such outputs (Figure 7.3). Building a ToC requires a well-developed awareness of the context in which the organisation will operate, of the other stakeholders that are or will be involved directly or indirectly, and of the world-views, beliefs, and, therefore, assumptions that underpin it. For this reason, it is best realised as a group exercise with multiple contributions and the encouragement of critical thinking and the challenging of assumptions.

The first step when creating a ToC is to pinpoint what is the long-term impact that the social entrepreneurial organisation aims to achieve, why it matters, and what is the timeframe in which it should be achieved. Ideally, as said above, this information should be derived from the mission statement and should be expressed as a SMART goal. Being as specific and realistic as possible, both in terms of the goal and the timeframe, is important because impact is what the organisation will be held accountable for by external stakeholders and, in particular, by funders. The timeframe might be especially key when approaching funders, since it might determine the length for which financial support will be sought or obtained. For this reason, it needs to be based on careful thinking and on as much knowledge as possible about what it is realistic to achieve given the issue tackled, the number of target beneficiaries that can be reached, and the relevance of the social entrepreneurial organisation in relation to other stakeholders. Knowing what other contributions will be needed for the desired change to happen can be extremely helpful for building the rest of the ToC,

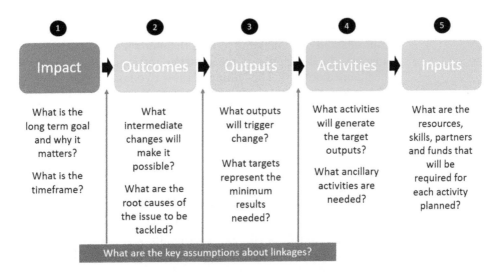

Figure 7.3 Illustration of how to build a Theory of Change

in particular with regard to knowing if some of the key activities that will need to be set up include the onboarding of other stakeholders or the brokering of coalitions of change makers.

Once the long-term impact is set, the most difficult part begins. This is the second step and it consists of mapping the intermediate outcomes that will lead to the desired impact. Establishing causality between outcomes and impact, and therefore the key outcomes to include in a ToC, is often very difficult and requires an in-depth knowledge of the root causes of a social issue; of existing interventions to address it and of their results; and of what the behaviours, needs, and constraints of target beneficiaries are. This is why Chapters 6 and 7 discuss various tools to gather knowledge and an introduction to Design Thinking approaches. Without in-depth knowledge, it is difficult to develop a credible ToC based on valid and ideally tested assumptions that will withstand external scrutiny. In addition to a foundation of existing knowledge, it is likely that this part of the development of a ToC will require significant time, various iterations, and the involvement of as many points of view as possible and thus the organisation of workshops, interviews, and brainstorming sessions with different stakeholders. A key component of this phase is making the assumptions about the connection between each outcome and the desired impact explicit, and noting them down in a separate box/below the ToC logic model (see Figure 7.2). This is to ensure that the logic flow remains clear and convincing. To defend the assumptions made, it can be useful to draw on existing research in psychology, sociology, international development, economics, policy, and on any study that has verified their existence "in the field"/in real settings and interventions.

The third step involves the specification of the outputs that will deliver the planned outcomes. While this phase might be a bit easier than the previous one, it will still require an in-depth knowledge about what produces outcomes of interest, according to existing interventions and research, and the ability to develop outputs that are quantifiable and specific. As said above, in the absence of specific targets, which can be seen as the pre-conditions necessary to generate change, it might become difficult to make others believe in the possibility that the social entrepreneurial initiative described will deliver tangible change at the scale, depth, and of the duration it desires. Additionally, even in this stage, it will be important to reflect on the assumptions made to link outputs and outcomes and to note them down in a separate box.

The fourth step involves the description of the activities and inputs that will enable the generation of the planned outputs. The "filling of these two boxes" normally goes hand in hand because it is easier to think about necessary inputs activity by activity rather than compiling a list for all the activities described. When describing activities, it is important to evaluate their feasibility and acceptability given the context, and to include ancillary/support activities that might be required alongside core ones to generate the right conditions for change. For example, if a social entrepreneurial organisation aims to deliver mental health support to teenagers, its core activities would include the set-up of clinics and of appointments or the creation and delivery of courses on mental health in schools, while ancillary activities would include creating partnerships with schools or promoting the service on the right social media in order to make teenagers aware of its existence. Before finalising the set of activities, as seen in Chapter 6, it is important to involve stakeholders and, especially, beneficiaries. They should have the opportunity to provide feedback on what is being planned, to assess if that might address the issue they are facing or if there might still be obstacles for them to be able to benefit from it. At this stage, it might be even worth thinking if beneficiaries could or should be involved in the delivery of the activities, e.g. being employed by the organisation, volunteering, serving as board members. When looking at inputs, these should include all the resources, skills, partners, and funds an organisation will be dependent upon. Even if this will not necessarily feature in the ToC, in this stage, it is also helpful to start thinking about how these will be obtained, for as much and as long as needed.

The final step in building a ToC is to reflect on the risks that might alter its effectiveness or how it works in the first place. These could or could not be explicitly mentioned in the ToC and include, mainly, the risk that some of the assumptions might not hold true, the impossibility to produce some of the planned outputs or outcomes due to external factors or sudden changes and disruptions, and the risk of losing access to some key input. The more key risks can be identified, the easier it will be both to develop contingency plans and to keep track of whether they are actually happening and thus to take necessary action.

To illustrate how the elaboration of a ToC might work in practice (Figure 7.4), let's pretend to be a social enterprise whose mission is *"make sure that every member of our community has a place to call home"*. Starting from this mission statement, a potential long-term impact that could underpin the social enterprise's ToC could be "to eliminate homelessness in community X in fifteen years' time" (with the time-frame dependent on the number of homeless people and the success of existing initiatives). In order to understand what outcomes the social enterprise should aim for, the members of the social enterprise would need to gather knowledge on what proved to be the best interventions to tackle homeless in similar contexts, what conditions reduce the possibility that people will become homeless again, what others are doing to reach a similar impact, and what is generally known about causes of homelessness. This research would deliver many insights but, for the sake of the example, let's assume that the main finding is that homelessness is more likely to be reduced if there are employment opportunities for homeless people. Based on this, the scale of the organisation and the number of homeless people in the community, the social enterprise could establish as core outcomes the creation of at least X new job opportunities in five years' time, the increase in self-confidence in and upskilling of at least Y homeless people in three years' time, and the creation of a network of support for homeless people looking for a job in one year's time. At this point, the social enterprise would need to reflect on why it believes these outcomes would lead to its desired impact. Key assumptions it could include in its ToC are the fact that homeless people who find employment will then be able to find and pay for accommodation, that homeless people feel comfortable living in an enclosed space after being in the open for many years, that unemployment is one of the root causes of homelessness in its town, and that skills, self-confidence, and lack of networks are the main barriers preventing employment. If these do not hold true, its ultimate impact might never be reached.

Once the outcomes are established, it is necessary to determine the outputs that would enable these to happen. Potential target outputs, in this case, could be: the release of a certificate of completion for all the homeless people that go through the training, specifying the skills they gained; the creation of X number of partnerships with businesses that would employ trainees; having helped all trainees with the development of their CV; having matched all trainees with a mentor who can support them in the search for jobs; having provided a weekly counselling session for each trainee. In this phase, key assumptions that the social enterprise might include are that completing the training actually means having gained new skills; that the support of mentors and CV development are enough to secure job interviews; that weekly counselling sessions, combined with mentorship, are enough to enhance and sustain the mental health and self-confidence of trainees; that each business partnership will deliver placement opportunities for trainees; and that there are no other skills needed beyond those provided by the training such as, e.g. language proficiency.

The following step involves establishing what activities and resources will be needed to generate target outputs. The delivery of certificates is likely to require the provision of training. The social enterprise would need to specify what type of courses it will provide, for how long and involving how many trainees, and for how many hours of learning and practice each. This, in turn, might require a location to hold the training, the hiring of trainers, and the purchase of equipment. The creation of partnerships is likely to require the identification of businesses in need of the skillset the training is providing, the initiation of discussions, and the elaboration of attractive proposals. In terms of inputs, this might require the hiring of a partnership development professional, research into businesses in the community, and information about grants and other forms of financial support that might be available to businesses hiring homeless people. This exercise would continue until the creation of all necessary outputs is explained by a matching set of activities and resources. At the end of this phase, the social enterprise would also need to think about potential ancillary activities – and the related inputs – it might need to achieve its outputs. In this example, ancillary activities might be the promotion of the existence of the training among the homeless, the creation of a library of training and CV-related resources, and maybe the creation of in-house employment opportunities for trainees.

As a final step, it would be helpful to develop some considerations about key risks. Potential risks for the effectiveness of this specific ToC might be the emergence of a sudden economic crisis that would significantly reduce the job vacancies in the community, the provision of skills that are not well aligned with jobs actually available on the market, homeless people not accepting job offers for reasons other than skills and

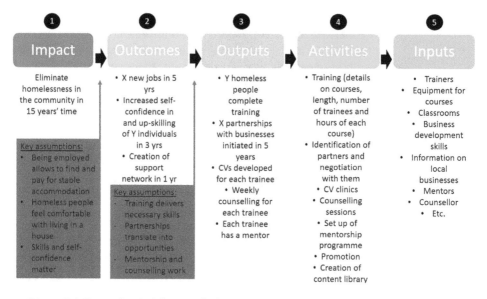

Figure 7.4 Example of a Theory of Change

self-confidence (e.g. not being used to regular working hours), training and mental health support not delivering expected outputs and outcomes due to a misunderstanding of target beneficiaries, or new jobs not translating into reduction of homelessness due to the excessive cost of accommodation in that community.

Like any other tool presented so far, the ToC should also be a constant work in progress, to be adjusted and refined as the social entrepreneurial organisation learns by doing what works and what does not, faces unexpected challenges, develops new ideas, finds collaborators and supporters, and validates or invalidates initial assumptions through monitoring impact. Additionally, it might be helpful to elaborate the ToC as a narrative as well as a logic model, to provide in a single place information on the context, solution proposed, planned impact, and considerations regarding assumptions and risks.

7.3.3 The benefits and risks of the Theory of Change

A ToC is a powerful tool for many purposes and, as said at the start of this section, in particular for planning, evaluating, learning, and engaging with stakeholders.

With regard to planning, developing the ToC is helpful for testing the validity and soundness of the solution developed, for understanding what will be needed to make the solution happen in terms of activities and resources, to be specific about the impact and outputs desired, to reflect on the timeframes in which change is expected to happen, and to check the external variables that might support or hinder success and thus to identify potential barriers to address. In a way, developing a ToC encourages social entrepreneurial organisations to unpack the different elements that might enable them to achieve their mission, thus ensuring that what they are setting up is indeed aligned to their main purpose. It also supports a switch in focus from what an individual or organisation wants to do to the social or environmental impact that they want to have.

When used as starting point for developing a social business model (see Chapter 8) and/or the estimate of costs for activities, a ToC can help to evaluate, at least at a broad level, if the organisation is likely to create added value or, instead, might incur in excessive costs and resource-needs when weighed against the benefits it aims to provide. Similarly, a ToC can become a reference point, as the organisation starts to operate, to check whether the plans and expectations are being met or not and, if not, to either adjust the ToC or the plans to account for needed adjustments.

With regard to monitoring, the ToC is increasingly considered a fundamental first step of any impact measurement process (see Chapter 11), since it provides the targets and key metrics that an organisation needs to monitor if it wants to ensure it is achieving the desired impact. In particular, specifying the key outputs and outcomes and the timeframe in which they should be achieved in order to ultimately fulfil the organisation's mission is a helpful starting point for developing an impact measurement system that tracks not only end goals but also intermediate ones, establishes the frequency of data collection, and allows for goals rather than reporting tools to drive the impact measurement effort. Broadly speaking, a ToC provides an opportunity for organisations to monitor their performance in a transparent way and to explore what works and what does not, and why reality might differ from expectations.

With regard to learning, the development of a ToC might highlight additional, unexpected resources and activities needed and/or available, and a new awareness of knowledge gaps that need to be addressed to strengthen trust in the proposed solution. It also supports learning by encouraging the use of multiple sources of data and insights to develop causal links and assumptions, and by providing a benchmark against which to compare actual results. The comparison, in itself, can favour additional learning and discussions and, if it results in corrective action and in the adjustment of the ToC, keeping multiple versions of a ToC can help to keep track of what was learnt along the way. Learning can be further enhanced if the ToC is effectively developed by engaging multiple stakeholders, since they can quickly point out things that are not acceptable, unfeasible, or problematic, and by engaging them in negotiations to overcome obstacles. When shared after an organisation has operated long enough to test its validity and/or bring in some modifications, the ToC can also support learning in other organisations, who might be able to use it to create the causal links in their own ToC and/or to design their interventions.

With regard to stakeholders' support, the ToC helps to communicate the intentions of a social entrepreneurial organisation to others, shows its understanding of a social/environmental issue and how it can be addressed, and provides a well-articulated rationale for the request of resources, contributions, and funding. It can also help to translate into a more intuitive framework or narrative something that might actually be fairly complex, both in the initial phases and when reporting impact to funders and other stakeholders. Additionally, it creates external accountability for the social entrepreneurial organisation, because it is a detailed promise of what it wants to achieve and how, and thus a tool to set stakeholders' expectations and for them to make sure the promise is being kept. This supports the creation of credibility, trust, and also creates the opportunity for stakeholders to offer feedback during the planning, implementation, and measurement phases. In a way, developing a ToC can also support negotiations with stakeholders, since the ToC can represent a starting point for jointly establishing the outputs and outcomes with funders and other supporters, to align efforts and intentions, and to identify the key impact metrics and incentives that would satisfy everyone involved.

The main risk of a ToC is that it shows the generation of change and impact as a linear, logical process, which it is likely to be anything but so. This might push a social entrepreneurial organisation to focus too much on what they are doing, in lieu of checking what is already happening or joining forces with others. Similarly, it might end up excessively simplifying real-life complexity, limiting the solution proposed to a superficial level of effectiveness. There is indeed a fine line between developing a ToC that is clear and simple enough for communication purposes and one that is detailed enough for planning and monitoring purposes.

Another risk is to make assumptions about causal links without being aware of them, or to make assumptions that are wrong in an attempt to reconcile the views of different stakeholders or in the absence of clear proof or information. Relatedly, there is always the risk of creating false causal attributions, especially when linking outcomes and impact, when in reality the link might be non-existent or due to chance, and of claiming that the organisation has more power in creating the ultimate impact than it actually has. In general, developing a ToC can be expected to be a complex task, which might become especially complex for systems change projects or for organisations whose contribution to the realisation of impact is strongly dependent on the contribution of others as well, and, for this reason, might be very difficult to demonstrate. Similarly, the development of a ToC might become even trickier if the organisation comprises multiple activities, each delivering various outputs and outcomes, as it might be difficult to unpack their relative contributions to the ultimate impact.

A third risk is spending too much time and effort in building and monitoring a ToC, thus taking resources away from actually implementing a solution. Conversely, the risk might lie in investing into it at the start but then forgetting about it, thus losing its benefits in terms of monitoring and learning. This can also be the case for stakeholders' engagement, which might fade after the planning phase, preventing additional learning, feedback, and changes along the way.

Ways to manage these risks include the engagement of stakeholders on a regular basis, to ensuring that feedback continues to be received on what is going on and on the validity of the ToC, regular reality checks about the progress made towards the desired impact and about other external conditions that might have contributed to it, the maintenance of an open and curious mindset, and the analysis of the ToC of other organisations working in the same space, both before producing one and at regular points in time as the ToC gets implemented.

SUMMARY BOX

- Design Thinking is a human-centred process to support innovation and problem-solving that involves a mix of research, analysis, observation, visualisation of ideas, rapid ideation, and prototyping. The five main phases of the Design Thinking process described in this chapter are Empathise, Define, Ideate, Prototype, and Test.
- Design Thinking has a long tradition rooted in research in and on design and in design practices but, in relation to social entrepreneurship, its process mostly derives from the literature and practice of business management.
- Design Thinking can be helpful for social entrepreneurship because it is inclusive and favours focusing on target beneficiaries; it reduces the risk of failure by encouraging stakeholders' engagement and the evaluation of different alternative solutions; it helps to adopt a learning and flexible mindset; and it is conducive to human-centred innovation.
- The key issues associated with the use of Design Thinking for social entrepreneurship are the over-simplification of the process; the lack of skills to conduct it properly; its usage as a shortcut to learn more about target beneficiaries; the power dynamics between the social entrepreneurial organisation and its stakeholders and beneficiaries; and the impossibility to implement the solutions developed.
- Implementing solutions and gathering the necessary resources and support require the development of a narrative. This begins with the elaboration of a mission statement, which should comprise the purpose of the social entrepreneurial organisation, the philosophy that underpins its existence, and a clear definition of target beneficiaries.
- A ToC is the explanation of how an individual, organisation, project, investment, or intervention aims to generate (intended) social and/or

environmental impact. It is frequently represented as a logic model connecting inputs, activities, outputs, outcomes, and impact.

- Developing a ToC requires reverse engineering, starting from the desired impact and working backwards to understand what it takes to achieve it, and reflection on the assumptions made about causal links and the risks that the ToC might not work as expected in practice.
- A ToC is helpful for planning, monitoring, learning and communicating, and engaging with stakeholders. However, it sometimes introduces the risks of explaining change in a too linear form, making an organisation adopt an excessively inward focus and to mis-attribute causality and ownership.

Check box – Self-reflection and discussion questions

- How would you describe the process of Design Thinking?
- What are its key phases, principles, and the skills you need to enact it?
- If you are/were a social entrepreneur or social entrepreneurial organisation, would you use Design Thinking? Why or why not? And if you would use it, when/for what purpose would you engage with this process?
- What are the main benefits and limitations of Design Thinking, especially in relation to social entrepreneurship?
- Why is it helpful for social entrepreneurial organisations to write a mission statement?
- What are the main components of a mission statement?
- Can you think of any potential substitutes for a mission statement?
- What is a ToC and how can it be represented?
- What can a ToC tell you about an organisation?
- What are the main steps for developing a ToC?
- Why is it beneficial to build a ToC?
- What are the main risks associated with building and having a ToC?
- Do all social entrepreneurial organisations have a ToC? Think about specific examples to answer this question.

Check out the "Additional resources" related to this chapter to learn more about the concepts and tools presented and how they can be used: www.routledge.com/9780367640231.

Exercises

Exercise 7.1 – Developing empathy

Identify someone in your class or among your neighbours whom you do not really know. Organise a coffee chat with them and ask them about the most recent issue they had to deal with and that they feel still hasn't been resolved. The issue can be as "straightforward" as "not finding the time to call a friend" or "not hearing the alarm yesterday morning". Try to build their persona or to map their experience in relation to the issue they chose by talking to them during the coffee chat. Then share the persona or map with them and ask them if this reflects their feelings and emotions and how they have related to the issue. Make the necessary adjustments based on their feedback and then develop some questions starting with "How can I help/solve/address ..." and prototype in any form you like/with whatever you have at hand three possible solutions by the end of the following day. If you can, share those with the person you met to collect their feedback and see what they think and suggest. Reflect on what you learnt through this exercise and how you might apply this way of approaching an issue in your study/work/personal life.

Exercise 7.2 – Engaging in Design Thinking

Pick a social or environmental issue that is affecting your community or that you care about in groups of four or five people (meeting in person or remotely). Based on what you learnt in this chapter on Design Thinking and using IDEO's guidance or the *d.school* resources that you can find online, develop a small Design Thinking project to be conducted in a week or two, to learn more about target beneficiaries and to test a few potential solutions with them. Report the findings of this exercise and how you conducted it to the rest of the class group, explain what you learnt from it and how you would do it differently the next time round, and receive feedback.

Exercise 7.3 – Analysing mission statements

Compare the examples of mission statements presented in Section 7.2.1 and discuss in small groups whether they are effective or not and why so. In particular, try to answer the following questions:

1 Do they have the main components of a mission statement?
2 Are they effective mission statements? Why or why not?
3 What do they help you learn about the organisation?
4 Is there anything you would change?

Exercise 7.4 – Analysing a Theory of Change

Find a ToC by doing an online search among organisations you know about or by picking one of the ToCs signalled on the book's website in the section "Theory of change in practice" or in the "Additional resources" section connected to this chapter (www.routledge.com/9780367640231). Analyse its content and the way it is expressed and explain:

1 What you think the main purpose of that ToC is
2 If you believe in it or not
3 What you think works well
4 What does not convince you
5 What the main assumptions made are
6 What you would want more information on.

Share the ToC you chose and your insights with the rest of the class or in small groups and compare your analyses.

Exercise 7.5 – Developing a Theory of Change

Pick a social entrepreneurial organisation that you like and try to develop their ToC, either individually or in small groups. Share it either as a logic model or in any other form that you think appropriate, explaining why you picked that specific option. Then reflect on what you found easy and what you found difficult, and what this exercise taught you with regard to developing a ToC. Present the ToC you developed to the rest of the class and receive feedback from other students or groups, both on its different elements and on the way you decided to present it.

Notes

1 ECOALF. (2022). *DNA*. Retrieved from: https://ecoalf.com/en/p/purpose--88
2 Tiwale. (2022). *Tiwale. Home page*. Retrieved from: https://www.tiwale.org/
3 CREN. (2022). *About CREN*. Retrieved from: https://www.cren.org.br/en/about-us/
4 Hospitals Beyond Boundaries. (2022). *Our mission*. Retrieved from: https://hbb.org.my/about
5 Wā Cup. (2022). Our crew and supporters. Retrieved from: https://wacollective.org.nz/pages/our-crew-2
6 Pandey, S., Kim, M., & Pandey, S. K. (2017). Do mission statements matter for nonprofit performance? Insights from a study of US performing arts organizations. *Nonprofit Management and Leadership*, 27(3), 389–410.
7 Weiss, C. H. (1995). Nothing as practical as good theory: Exploring theory-based evaluation for comprehensive community initiatives for children and families. In Connell, J. P., Kubisch, A. C., Schorr, L. B., & Weiss, C. H. (Eds), *New approaches to evaluating community initiatives volume 1 concepts, methods and contexts*. Washington DC: The Aspen Institute, 66.
8 Connell, J. P., & Kubisch, A. C. (1998). Applying a theory of change approach to the evaluation of comprehensive community initiatives: progress, prospects, and problems. *New Approaches to Evaluating Community Initiatives*, 2(15–44), 3.

8 From developing to implementing a social entrepreneurial idea

Key content

This chapter explains how to build a social business model starting from the organisation's mission and Theory of Change, and introduces marketing insights that can help a social entrepreneurial organisation to access what it needs to put its social business model into practice.

8.1 From theory to practice – the importance of business models
8.2 The social business model canvas
8.3 Marketing fundamentals for social entrepreneurial organisations

Learning objectives

- Learn what a social business model is and why it matters.
- Understand how to build a social business model starting from the organisation's mission.
- Acquire basic knowledge of marketing insights and tools that can be useful to connect with target beneficiaries and gain resources and support from key stakeholders.
- Reflect on opportunities for social entrepreneurial organisations connected to digital marketing and on the importance of ethics when devising marketing strategies.

8.1 From theory to practice – the importance of business models

Developing a Theory of Change (ToC) (see Chapter 7) is probably the most challenging step when elaborating a social entrepreneurial idea in response to an opportunity. There are many unknown variables and links, the stakeholders involved in the process might disagree about key activities or desired outcomes, there might be ideas that work in theory but not in practice, and sudden changes in the environmental forces may put at risk the working of the logic flow. Nonetheless, once a ToC is ready, social entrepreneurial organisations are up for an equal challenge: its translation into a concrete plan of action.

According to the business management literature, elaborating plans entails a strategic decision-making process of varying formality and inclusivity, geared at formulating both a strategy and a medium- and long-term business plan. In most cases, however, social entrepreneurial organisations in their infancy are too small and

DOI: 10.4324/9781003121824-11

informal to devise a fully-formed strategic process. For this reason, a helpful alternative for them can be to organise their ideas and insights through a social business model, which, according to Casadesus-Masanell and Ricart (2010)[1] and Smith et al. (2010),[2] can be seen as the articulation of strategic choices and of what will end up being the "realised strategy". To understand what social business models are and how they work in more detail compared to their brief mention in Chapter 3, it is helpful to discuss first business models in a traditional business context.

8.1.1 Business models

In 2005, Osterwalder, Pigneur and Tucci[3] defined a business model as

> a conceptual tool containing a set of objects, concepts and their relationships with the objective to express the business logic of a specific firm. It is a description of the value a company offers to one or several segments of customers and of the architecture of the firm and its network of partners for creating, marketing, and delivering this value and relationship capital, to generate profitable and sustainable revenue streams.

Similarly, in 2010, Teece[4] explained that

> a business model articulates the logic, the data, and other evidence that support a value proposition for the customer, and a viable structure of revenues and costs for the enterprise delivering that value. In short, it's about the benefit the enterprise will deliver to customers, how it will organize to do so, and how it will capture a portion of the value that it delivers.

The goal of a business model is to visualise and communicate why and how a business operates to reach its strategic objectives, and to explain the expected consequences of the answers to those questions. For this reason, it should contain information about the product or service the business will produce and deliver and the target market for it, an explanation of how that will generate profits, the activities, processes, and costs involved in its production and delivery, what makes the product or service unique, and how the business is going to set up a value chain from suppliers to customers. These characteristics, in turn, will suggest strategies in terms of location, extent of vertical integration of operations (how much of the production process the business should own), organisational structure, resources, and capabilities that the business needs, pricing policies, etc.

For example, the baseline business model of *Google* involves the creation of value for individuals, by making it easy for them to identify what they are looking for on the web, and for organisations, by supporting a more effective reach of target customers. To create this value, *Google* developed and continues to improve two key products: a search engine and a consumer analytics' service, which it delivers with user-friendly interfaces that match its mission to "organise the world's information and make it universally accessible and useful".[5] The combination of these products enables *Google* to capture value, by charging organisations for consumer analytics' services and advertisement, while keeping its search engine free to use, which is fundamental for providing value to individuals. The choice to realise and capture value in the way described above implied that *Google* had to structure itself as an IT company developing software solutions, hiring experts in computer engineering and computation, fundraising from family and investors until the information generated through its search engine became valuable enough to attract revenues, and creating a global organisation matching the global nature of the web and of many companies' businesses and of people's interests.

As the example above shows, a successful business model is one that generates value for customers and other stakeholders such as shareholders, suppliers, or complementors in unique ways, and allows the business to capture a significant part of the value created through revenues and profits. Business models that work well should also generate virtuous cycles, whereby the initial choice on how to create value for customers leads the business to develop unique resources and capabilities that then result in additional opportunities or stronger ability to create the desired value, thus leading to a growing competitive advantage for the business. For example, *Google* has managed to leverage its excellence in online searches/algorithms' development and in consumer analytics to expand its business in various areas such as driverless cars, digital maps, online advertisement services, and software for products related to smart homes. For these reasons, in many industries, business models have been credited to be a key source of above normal profitability as well as a source of innovation.

Talking about business models in relation to social entrepreneurship, however, is not ideal because they are entirely geared towards profitability, while social entrepreneurial organisations need to realise first and foremost social or environmental value, not just economic value. Business models also do not include streams of funding other than revenues, which are instead needed for the financial sustainability of most social entrepreneurial organisations. For this reason, in recent years, many researchers have theorised about the adaptation of business models into social business models.

8.1.2 Social business models

While the word "social business model" might create the impression that this is something helpful only for social enterprises (see Chapter 3), in reality it can be useful for any social entrepreneurial organisation. All of them need to understand how to deliver the impact they have in mind, what resources that will require, how to build relationships with key stakeholders to obtain those resources, and how to pay for what they need to set up. Broadly speaking, a social business model describes how the ToC will be implemented and, through that, how the mission of the organisation is going to be achieved. This is something that any social entrepreneurial organisation needs to have established.

A social business model, like a traditional business model, is the description of what kind of value an organisation wants to realise and for whom, how it plans to create and deliver it, and how it plans to capture part of that value in order to make its operations financially sustainable. Compared to a traditional business model, however, social business models need to prioritise social or environmental value over economic value, and create value for multiple stakeholders. This is both due to what social entrepreneurship stands for (e.g. respect, inclusivity, cooperation, consideration of impact on multiple stakeholders), and to the need of social entrepreneurial organisations to survive financially while generating social and environmental impact.

Elaborating a social business model has many benefits for social entrepreneurial organisations. It can help to understand how the new organisation will position itself in relation to competing or complementary efforts, thus also highlighting opportunities to partner and collaborate. Internally, it can foster dialogue between employees, align individual and teams' efforts, generate shared vision and understandings, and help to identify what key resources and capabilities are going to be. It can also prompt reflections on the potential to achieve a double or triple bottom line, managing tensions, and finding synergies between different types of value. Externally, it can enhance the autonomy and legitimacy of the organisation, by helping it to strategise about how to effectively manage its dependency from different external stakeholders and how to meet their expectations, and by supporting communication.

8.1.2.1 Archetypes and characteristics of social business models

Existing research has identified many archetypes of social business models, depending on how the social or environmental value gets created. For example, value can be created by:

- protecting something (e.g. environment, rights);
- selling new technological solutions (e.g. that allow carbon capture);
- transforming waste into a new product or selling it;
- offering social, training, and welfare services;
- favouring the formation of partnerships and pooling of resources;
- eliminating barriers (e.g. income, psychological, physical);
- giving voice to marginalised groups;
- setting up a cooperative.

Ideally, in a social business model, beneficiaries (those the organisation wants to help) are also customers (those buying the product or service offered by the organisation), so a social entrepreneurial organisation can focus on creating value for beneficiaries and also achieve financial sustainability through that. However, frequently, either beneficiaries and customers are the same but cannot afford to pay (partially or in full) for the product or service they use, or they differ and beneficiaries cannot pay for the value received. In these instances, the social entrepreneurial organisation needs to generate value both for beneficiaries (to realise the intended impact) and for customers or other stakeholders (to survive financially). This makes the creation of the value proposition, and decisions of how to capture at least part of the value created, more fundamental and less straightforward than in a traditional business model.

For example, a social entrepreneurial organisation like *Back on Track Syria* (presented in Chapter 1) cannot ask refugee children or their families to pay for the education it provides. However, it can ask governments and international organisations to fund its activities if, through the value it creates for refugees, it creates value for them too, e.g. by favouring integration and easier inclusion of refugee children in schools, or contributing to defending the rights of children, such as the right to education. Similarly, a social enterprise like the *London Early Years Foundation* (presented in Chapter 1) generates value both for customers who can pay and for those who cannot, and captures value by asking those who can pay to pay also for those who cannot. For a social business model like this to work, the social entrepreneurial organisation needs to either make sure that the value it provides to paying customers is significantly greater than the value they would get from competing offers (or they will not pay a high-enough price to cover the costs of the value offered to non-paying customers), or produce the product or service at lower cost compared to competing offers (so it can use the higher profit margin to cover the costs of the value offered to non-paying customers). The *Aravind Eye Hospital* (presented in Chapters 1 and 3) is an example of a social enterprise that developed a social business model respecting both these criteria at the same time. Its social business model is based on the standardisation of procedures and training to lower costs, and on richer customers paying for the surgeries of those who cannot afford to pay, in exchange for add-on services they receive at the hospital.

8.1.2.2 Characteristics of strong social business models

Whatever archetype chosen, social business models should aim to leverage the resources that typically represent a competitive advantage for social entrepreneurial organisations, such as their commitment to positive social and environmental impact, superior understanding of a community when they are embedded within it, elaboration of innovative solutions that enable the reaching of a double or triple bottom line, social networks, and the reputation of either the organisation or its founder(s). By analysing the work of three very successful social enterprises (*Grameen Bank, Sekem*, and *Mondragón Corporacion Cooperativa*), operating in three different contexts, Mair and Schoen (2007)[6] discovered that their social business models shared three common characteristics:

- They involved the proactive creation and management of networks of suppliers and partners sharing their same values;
- They presented a procurement strategy where securing critical and scarce resources happened in a sustainable and innovative way, making it possible to generate impact through different parts of their value chain;
- They enabled target customers and beneficiaries to be actively involved in the value chain, thus making it possible for them to contribute to the realisation of the value proposition and to capture a portion of the value created.

A social business model should be both feasible and confer the necessary legitimacy to the social entrepreneurial organisation. Feasibility can be verified by: assessing the respect of policies and regulations, potential obstacles, negative impacts, and risks (such as changes in environmental forces, wrong assumptions, and sudden crises); comparing the model developed with that of competing solutions; researching evidence that the model can achieve the desired impact. Legitimacy requires the social business model to meet the expectations of different stakeholders and, thus, an in-depth knowledge of key stakeholders and of the context.

Once set and forming the basis for strategising, social business models tend to become harder to change, given the investment of time, resources, and efforts that the organisation might have already deployed. Therefore, it is important to spend sufficient time elaborating a social business model and collecting feedback from key stakeholders about its viability, attractiveness, and effectiveness. Especially before starting operations, however, social business models can be difficult to articulate and, as seen in Chapter 6 with mind maps, sometimes the best way to understand and explain complexity is to render it visually. A tool increasingly used by social entrepreneurial organisations to explain their social business model is the social business model canvas.

8.2 The social business model canvas

There are many variations of the social business model canvas and they can be used both when starting an organisation and when planning substantial change or the scaling of operations. The one presented in Figure 8.1 is an adaptation, inspired by the work of the *Social Innovation Lab*, of the business model canvas originally developed by *Strategyzer*.[7] It consists of four different sections, differentiated through different colours.

The centrepiece of the canvas is the value proposition, which is an explanation of the added social/environmental and economic value that the social entrepreneurial organisation is going to create and deliver in relation to its mission. In a way, it is the promise that the organisation makes to key stakeholders about the value it will generate for them by solving a problem they are facing or addressing one or more of their needs. As such, it is the point of reference for the strategic direction of the organisation and for the development of its structure, activities, systems, and processes.

The left side of the canvas focuses on the elements that are necessary to realise the value proposition – namely key activities, the inputs necessary to realise them and the partners/key stakeholders that will provide those inputs. The right side explains instead whom the value proposition is targeting, focusing in particular on customers and beneficiaries, and how relationships with all key stakeholders will be built and maintained. Finally, the bottom of the canvas describes how the organisation plans to remain financially viable, by providing a list of key costs and of the different sources of funding that will pay for them, and how it will track and understand if it is realising its value proposition.

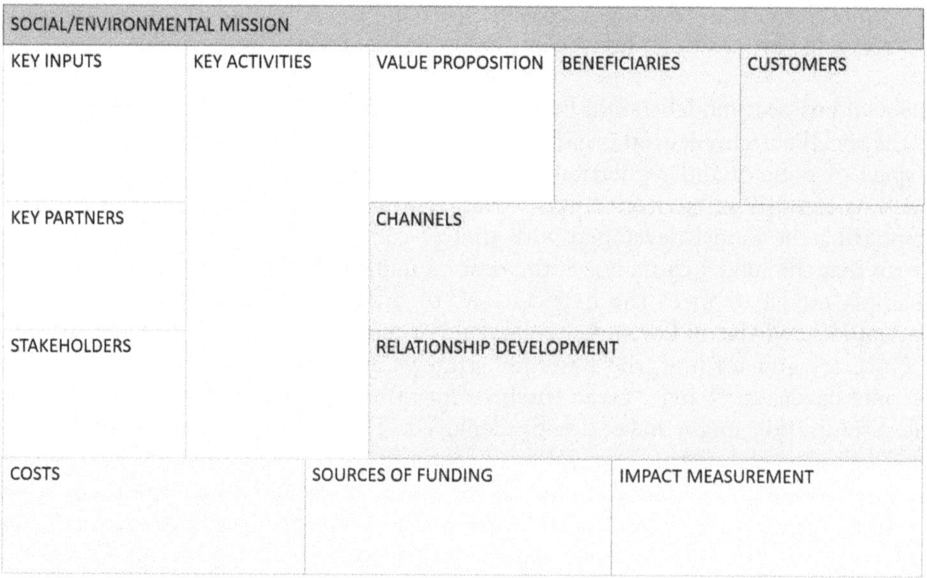

SOCIAL/ENVIRONMENTAL MISSION					
KEY INPUTS	KEY ACTIVITIES	VALUE PROPOSITION	BENEFICIARIES	CUSTOMERS
KEY PARTNERS		CHANNELS		
STAKEHOLDERS		RELATIONSHIP DEVELOPMENT		
COSTS		SOURCES OF FUNDING	IMPACT MEASUREMENT	

Figure 8.1 The social business model canvas (inspired by the work of the Social Innovation Lab, of the business model canvas originally developed by Strategyzer)

SOCIAL BUSINESS MODEL CANVAS IN PRACTICE

Watch how the social business models of four social entrepreneurial organisations are described in the videos that you can access at the links on the book's website (www.routledge.com/9780367640231), in the Chapter 8 section.

8.2.1 *How to build a social business model canvas*

Filling in a social business model canvas normally involves six steps. The first step consists of writing the social/environmental mission of the organisation at the top of the canvas. The mission should then be translated into the value proposition, by answering the following questions:

- How will the organisation realise its mission?
- What social, environmental, and economic added value will it create? What problems will it solve?
- How will the proposition stand out compared to existing ones?

The second step involves the explanation of who the target beneficiaries (those the organisation wants to help) and customers (those buying the product or service delivered by the organisation) are. Key questions to answer in this phase are whether customers and beneficiaries overlap or not, who they are, what they do and want or need, what barriers they might encounter in using the product or service offered, and why they would be willing to engage with the organisation. While social entrepreneurial organisations might be tempted to "help everyone" or "appeal to everyone", this is hardly ever possible. Thus, they must be clear about whom to prioritise and why, and there are several marketing practices they can use for that purpose (see Section 8.3).

The third step requires the specification of the channels (distribution channels, social media and media channels, promotion channels, etc.) that will be used to make a product or service available to beneficiaries and/or customers and to promote its existence, and of how relationships with key stakeholders will be built and maintained over time. The goal for this section is not to provide a detailed description of all the channels used or of all the tools and strategies for relationship management that will be deployed, but a summary of what the key channels are going to be, specifying which ones will be used for which target audience, and of the key approaches and activities to keep stakeholders on board over time, e.g. explaining what will help the organisation build trust and develop long-term relationships.

The fourth step involves retrieving information from the ToC and explaining what key activities are going to deliver the value proposition and, in turn, what key inputs (resources, assets, skills, facilities, intellectual property, etc.) and partners will be needed to make that happen. Wei-Skillern et al. (2007)[8] classified the activities that a social entrepreneurial organisation can undertake into four categories, based on their alignment with the mission and on their revenue-generation potential:

- **Integral** – Activities that are key to generating the desired social and environmental impact as well as profits. These are the activities that are fundamental for the survival of the organisation and should be given top priority.

- **Supplementary** – Activities that are key to generating the desired social and environmental impact but are not profitable and/or are unlikely to ever become so. Those are the activities that an organisation should focus on, finding ways to subsidise them/cover their costs even without the help of buyers/customers.
- **Sustaining** – Activities that are profitable but do not necessarily contribute much to the generation of social and environmental impact. These are activities that it might be worth starting or keeping, e.g. to subsidise those that generate impact but not profits, but ensuring that they do not take the precedence over other ones and cause a mission drift.
- **Disposable** – Activities that have both low impact and profitability potential and, therefore, can be avoided or discontinued.

When thinking about activities, it is also helpful to reflect on how social and environmental value could be created through each step of the value chain, i.e. the set of value-adding stakeholders and activities that jointly transform inputs such as raw materials into products and services and bring these to customers (and/or beneficiaries). According to Guo and Bielefeld (2014),[9] there are three main sections of the value chain that can help a social entrepreneurial organisation generate value, even beyond its value proposition. These are:

- **Procurement** – Sourcing inputs from suppliers that are social enterprises or non-profit organisations or from producers that aim for environmental sustainability.
- **Operations** – Minimising waste in the production process and employing people otherwise excluded from the job market.
- **Marketing** – Shifting public opinion or contributing towards lobbying for policy and behavioural changes, and making products and services more accessible, e.g. by removing barriers for target customers and beneficiaries.

When describing partners, it is important to explain what they are going to provide, when and how, and what their role is going to be (e.g. supplier, funder, supporter). In this section, it is also important to add a note on other stakeholders that might not be key partners but still important to realise the value proposition, and thus people or organisations to keep informed or engage with. Once established who the key partners and stakeholders are, it is necessary to go back to the channels and relationship sections, adding information on how they will be engaged over time.

Inputs/resources will depend based on the activities the organisation decides to implement and will likely fall in one of these typical categories:

- **Physical resources:** Any tangibles such as an office, a warehouse, a room where to hold workshops, equipment, raw materials needed for production processes, etc.
- **Reputational resources:** The image and perception of the social entrepreneurial organisation that stakeholders and the public have. This is prevalently affected by the mission, ethical, and sustainable behaviours, credibility, and track record of the team of people involved, potential partners, the quality of the product or service offered, etc.
- **Human resources:** The skills, know-how, personal traits, values, commitment, etc. of employees, managers, board members, and partners.
- **Financial resources:** Any type of funding.

- **Technological resources:** Social media profiles, mobile phones/smartphones, laptops, and any other IT equipment needed for the organisation's operations, broadband access, etc.

The fifth step entails the specification of how the organisation is going to verify whether it is delivering its value proposition and desired impact. As discussed in Chapter 11, this is fundamental to ensure the achievement of its mission and to gain and maintain the trust of stakeholders. While impact measures should already be implicitly or explicitly present in the ToC, it is important to include them in the social business model canvas, to check their fit with the overall plan and, in particular, with the value proposition.

The sixth and final step consists of specifying the expected costs of planned activities and operations and how they will be covered through various sources of funding. The funding mix (the different sources of funding an organisation needs or could access) should manage at least to balance the costs to guarantee the financial sustainability of the organisation. In this sense, it is also important to understand which costs are fixed and which ones are variable or semi-variable, which ones are project-specific and which ones are overhead costs – i.e. costs to support the entire organisation (as they might need to be funded through different funding streams), what their implications will be in terms of cash flows, and if there is any cyclicality. Cash flows are particularly key since no matter how good an organisation is, if it runs out of cash to pay what it needs to pay for in time, it is at significant risk of failure. Therefore, understanding how cash flows work and potential cyclicality in both funding and costs helps to make decisions regarding the funding mix by suggesting how much will be needed when. In this sense, even though these will not feature in the social business model, at this stage it is also helpful to reflect on sunk costs (costs that once incurred cannot be recovered – e.g. expensive equipment, acquisition of a building – and therefore constrain future choices and actions), and opportunity costs (cost due to the loss of other alternatives when one alternative is chosen).

In terms of sources of funding, the canvas should list both key sources and their relative expected contribution, for example specifying assumptions about the number of customers and the planned price per product/service in the presence of revenue-generating activities, or the donors and investors whose funds will cover costs, and the sums each of them will provide. This step will clarify if revenues will or won't be a source of income, and to what extent, and will thus also help to establish what incorporation options an organisation should consider (see Chapters 3 and 9). If the idea is for the social entrepreneurial organisation to incorporate as for-profit business, this section could also contain a note on plans related to potential profits – e.g. reinvest, distribute among stakeholders or distribute among shareholders and to what extent. There are social entrepreneurs like Muhammad Yunus, who believe that all profits should be reinvested in the pursuit of the social/environmental mission. Others, however, worry about the practical difficulties of adopting this approach, which might reduce the availability of buffer funds in case of a sudden crisis and dissuade investors from supporting social entrepreneurial organisations, given the impossibility for them to be appropriately rewarded for their capital.

Figure 8.2 shows the potential social business model canvas that could be built for the hypothetical social entrepreneurial organisation discussed in Chapter 7 (see Figure 7.4) by following the six steps explained above.

SOCIAL/ENVIRONMENTAL MISSION: Make sure that every member of our community has a place to call home				
KEY INPUTS • Trainers • Equipment for courses • Classrooms • Funds **KEY PARTNERS** • Mentors • Counsellors • Businesses • Homeless shelters • Other charities supporting the homeless **STAKEHOLDERS** • Local authorities • Healthcare providers • Potential donors	**KEY ACTIVITIES** • Training • Working with business partners to create placements • Delivery of CV clinics • Delivery of counselling sessions	**VALUE PROPOSITION** • Support homeless people in starting a new life through employment • Training and support to enhance employability **CHANNELS** • Beneficiaries: homeless shelters, other charities supporting the homeless • Customers: social media, traditional advertisement, universities' career services • Partners: connecting to local networks, LinkedIn • Stakeholders: organisation website and communications, local networks **RELATIONSHIP DEVELOPMENT** • Ability to place homeless trainees • Impact reporting to donors/funders • High quality training and services and their refinement based on feedback • Checking in with business partners how placements are going • Collaborating with other organisations to provide affordable housing	**BENEFICIARIES** • Homeless people of the town	**CUSTOMERS** • Potential funders • Potential paying non-homeless users of CV clinics, training and counselling
COSTS • Rental costs of classrooms and office • Equipment costs • Staff costs • Marketing costs	**SOURCES OF FUNDING** • Donations • Fees from businesses who find new employees thanks to the partnership • Subsidies or grants from local authorities • Sale of services		**IMPACT MEASUREMENT** • Training completed • Placements realised • Effects on trainees over time • Creation of support network for trainees	

Figure 8.2 Example of social business model canvas

Like the ToC, the canvas should be revised regularly, as plans, strategies, and operations change according to both internal and external factors. It is likely that elements of any canvas will be proven wrong as soon as an organisation starts operating. This is natural, since in any organisation, strategy is the result of a mix of planning and learning by doing. What matters is that the ultimate mission and value proposition remain an anchor of strategic direction and that the changes that are made have the goal of guaranteeing or enhancing their delivery.

Once a canvas or a social business model is finalised, the first step in starting to realise it is to acquire the necessary inputs – i.e. skills, resources, legitimacy, and funds. Some social entrepreneurs or founders of social entrepreneurial organisations might do that through informal networking, some through pitching during competitions or formal meetings with potential funders, and some through a mix of formal and informal strategies. Whatever the approach adopted, they will need to know their target audience well to develop communication, pitches or proposals that are effective at appealing to their emotions and minds or at connecting to their lived experience, knowledge, and goals. This implies the usage of marketing strategies and techniques, either intentionally or unintentionally, and an early elaboration of clear ideas about what the key message of the organisation is going to be, how it will be delivered, and how it will both inform stakeholders about the problem and solution, and inspire and energise them to attract attention and support.

8.3 Marketing fundamentals for social entrepreneurial organisations

While marketing is traditionally associated with business, it is extremely valuable for social entrepreneurial organisations too. Research established that marketing principles and practices can be leveraged to engage stakeholders, maximise the reach and

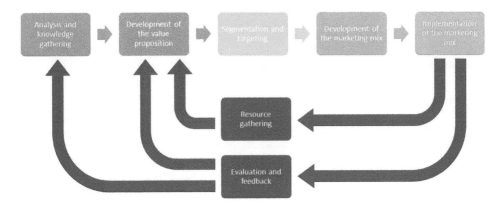

Figure 8.3 The role of marketing

enhance the satisfaction of beneficiaries and customers, fundraise, attract the attention of potential employees and volunteers, establish partnerships, and identify and leverage commercial opportunities. An in-depth discussion of marketing strategies and tools for social entrepreneurial organisations is well beyond the scope of this book. However, it is helpful at this stage to introduce some key concepts and frameworks that are relevant for social entrepreneurial organisations during the shift from ideas development to implementation. Figure 8.3 shows how marketing can support the transformation of initial insights into action.

In the context of social entrepreneurship, people talk about both marketing and social marketing. Marketing is "the activity, set of institutions, and processes for creating, communicating, delivering, and exchanging offerings that have value for customers, clients, partners, and society at large".[10] Social marketing was defined by Lazer and Kelley (1973)[11] as "the application of marketing knowledge, concepts and techniques to enhance social as well as economic ends. It is also concerned with analysis of the social consequence of marketing policies, decisions and activities". So both the definitions of marketing and social marketing encapsulate the idea that marketing activities should benefit many different stakeholders. What distinguishes them is their practical application, whereby marketing tends to be conducted to benefit the marketer's organisation and social marketing to benefit a community or society at large, and the stronger emphasis that social marketing puts on understanding the social consequences of marketing strategies and on changing behaviours. Additionally, while marketing tends to be focused on affecting individual or groups of customers, social marketing is used to persuade institutional decision-makers such as politicians, healthcare professionals, and corporations. Based on these definitions, not all the marketing of a social entrepreneurial organisation is going to be social, since the organisation might want to engage in some activities that actually support its own reputation, sales or attraction of resources. However, it is likely that it might aim for behavioural change or widespread social change through its marketing activities. Thus, it is possible to assume that most social entrepreneurial organisations will leverage a mix of marketing and social marketing to deliver their value proposition.

Whatever the type of marketing employed, according to the work of Facca-Miess and Santos (2014),[12] social entrepreneurial organisations need to engage in marketing strategies that: generate authentic engagement with consumers, particularly impoverished ones, with non-exploitive intent; co-create value with customers; invest in future rather than present consumption; represent the interests of all stakeholders, particularly of marginalised or voiceless ones; privilege a focus on long-term financial sustainability rather than short-term profit maximisation.

8.3.1 The practice of marketing

The first step of any marketing strategy is to establish who the target audience is. This can include one or more among customers, beneficiaries, funders, partners, people who influence any of these categories, policymakers, media, employees, volunteers, and even competitors. Once the target audience(s) is established, social entrepreneurial organisations need to gather more in-depth insights on them, ideally through a two-way dialogue. For this purpose, they can and might use some of the tools already discussed in Chapter 6, such as codebooks and mind maps, elements and tools of Design Thinking (e.g. the construction of personas), or marketing-specific techniques, such as segmentation and targeting.

8.3.1.1 Segmentation and targeting

Segmentation is the division of the target audience into groups of individuals or organisations that are relatively similar to one another in relation to characteristics of interest, and different from others in relation to those same characteristics. Typical characteristics for segmentation include demographics, geography, physical characteristics, psychographics traits, attitudes, and behaviours. Normally, organisations segment according to whatever the most relevant characteristics in relation to their value proposition are and use a combination of two or more such characteristics to segment their target audience in a useful way. A helpful example of how segmentation works was published by *Radio One* in collaboration with Yankelovich in 2008,[13] and can be accessed under the name of Link 8.1 in the book's website (www.routledge.com/9780367640231).

Segmentation is important because even within the same target audience there can be different behaviours and preferences. These might affect the target audience's response to the value proposition or organisation, and knowledge of them might also support the ability of the organisations' employees to develop empathy and effective solutions for the issue to be tackled and communication with external stakeholders.

Yankelovich and Meer (2006)[14] developed six questions that, with some adaptation to reflect the specificities of social entrepreneurship, can help a social entrepreneurial organisation to understand how to proceed with segmentation:

1   What are we trying to do?
2   Which segments of the target audience drive financial sustainability and which ones drive impact?
3   Which attitudes matter to the decision of the target audience of engaging with the organisation?
4   What are the key needs, requirements, and preferences of segments within the target audience?
5   What segmentation will be understood and accepted by the leaders of the social entrepreneurial organisation and/or by its key stakeholders?

6 Can segmentation register change?

The latest developments in information technology have almost rendered some of these questions obsolete since they enabled the development of micro-segmentation, which refers to the division of a target audience into individual profiles, based on big data from websites and social media. This helps the realisation of personalised marketing strategies and the maximisation of their effectiveness. However, while micro-segmentation is increasingly used and available, it might not be feasible for social entrepreneurial organisations, since they might not have the resources and skills to benefit from this opportunity, and it also may raise significant ethical concerns. Online data are often collected without the explicit or informed consent of individuals and are frequently used to manipulate rather than to help them. Unless micro-segmentation is conducted with utmost care and knowledge of potential negative consequences, this makes traditional segmentation probably a better fit for social entrepreneurship.

Segmentation logically leads to, and is almost indivisible from, targeting. Targeting is the strategic choice of which segments, among the target audience, to focus on. Target segments should be those that are most critical for the success of the value proposition and not merely those that are most convenient or easy to reach. For this reason, targeting should be informed by the knowledge gathered in the idea's evaluation and development phases and further refined through segmentation. Effective targeting helps to use resources and funds more efficiently and to cater the value proposition and marketing to well-known key segments within the target audience, and thus increases the chances to deliver the desired impact and attract the desired resources. Targeting can consider not only segments that represent direct stakeholders but also those who influence their choices.

If more than one segment needs targeting, then resources and attention could either be equally divided among relevant segments or differentiated and focused more on some segments over others based on:

- Segment size;
- Severity of the issue experienced by different segments of beneficiaries or relevance of the potential contribution for different segments;
- The chance to reach different segments/different segments being able to access the product or service;
- Resources required to reach a segment;
- Expected responsiveness to the marketing mix (see section below) of different segments;
- Organisational capacity to deliver multiple marketing mixes.

Once segmentation and targeting are complete, the next step for a social entrepreneurial organisation is to develop a strategy to reach each key target audience, to obtain the resources necessary to realise its social business model. A helpful framework to think about marketing strategies, especially in relation to customers and beneficiaries, is the Marketing 7Ps, often referred to as the marketing mix.

8.3.1.2 *The marketing 7Ps*

The marketing mix, comprising the set of tools that managers use to satisfy the target audience, emerged as a concept in the 1940s, and was refined by McCarthy in 1964[15] by grouping these tools into four categories, namely the 4Ps of marketing: Product, Price, Place, and Promotion. Ever since, these have become the cornerstone of marketing teaching and practice. However, over time, many researchers have proposed additions and changes and, presently, the most accepted description of what constitutes the marketing mix is the one proposed in 1981 by Booms and Bitner[16] involving 7Ps: Product, Price, Place, Promotion, Process, Physical evidence, and Participants.

Product refers to anything (e.g. product, idea, service) through which the social entrepreneurial organisation aims to deliver its value proposition/fulfil its mission. In social marketing, it is the tool to trigger the desired behavioural change or to introduce a new practice in/for the target audience. A product needs to be something that satisfies a specific need, creates well-defined benefits, or solves a key problem. Ideally, it should also be different from existing alternatives, have high quality and ease of use, and be designed to maximise the chance the target audience will use/experience it in the way that potentially generates maximum impact.

Price represents the cost of the product for the target audience. In commercial marketing, this is generally expressed in monetary terms. However, it can also be thought about in terms of time, effort, emotional, and psychological cost of doing/buying something, the stigma that might derive from using a product or engaging with an organisation, or the opportunity cost of not doing something else. It is important for social entrepreneurial organisations to establish the full economic, psychological, social and emotional cost of their product to make sure that the expected benefits will outweigh costs for the target audience.

When customers and beneficiaries overlap, it is especially important to assess the monetary price that they can afford to pay, finding the right balance between financial sustainability and making the product available and affordable to all those who need it. Similarly, in relation to price, it is important to reflect on the opportunity of giving a product "for free". On the one hand, this might increase reach, favour adoption, and reassure the board members about the prioritisation of social or environmental value. On the other hand, a free product might have a lower perceived value and quality in the eyes of target beneficiaries/customers, and create a less efficient use of resources, since it might encourage its use even when not necessarily needed, and discourage the report of negative feedback. Finally, it is important to consider whether subsidised prices might generate the wrong incentive, and whether using flexible payment terms and pricing might maximise reach and make the product affordable for different segments.

Place concerns where and how a product is made available to the target audience. It involves setting up distribution and communication channels, to maximise the accessibility of both product and relevant information about it. Place can be physical or virtual and should remove as many barriers as possible that may prevent the product and key information about its existence and usage from reaching the target audience. For example, a social entrepreneurial organisation might think about creative solutions to provide easy access to its product by engaging members of the local community in its distribution or using available technology, such as mobile phones, to reach remote areas where it might be difficult to have a physical presence. If distribution happens through third parties, there should also be mechanisms to ensure that these parties know how to approach the target audience, maintain the desired quality, message clarity, and deliver needed information and explanations.

Promotion is the communication of the existence and benefits of a product and, in the case of social marketing, of an opportunity for change. It involves educating, inspiring, convincing, and providing information. It is more crucial, the more innovative a product is since any innovation requires to be explained and legitimised to be adopted. Promotion can be done through many different means (e.g. traditional adverts, campaigns, social media, influencers connected or committed to the social or environmental issue tackled by the organisation, the realisation of events, design). Developing a promotion strategy requires establishing what the best communication channels might be, what message will be most effective, and what will help give credibility to the organisation and its product. Promotion should also help to deliver guidance to the target audience about how to use and access the product, and to nudge desired behaviours. Even when a product is in the best interest of the target audience, they might not perceive it as such, understand it or embrace it, due to many potential psychological barriers (e.g. inertia, loss aversion, optimism/pessimism, feeling of inadequacy or unworthiness), or to insufficient knowledge or familiarity. Promotion is fundamental to overcome these barriers and, in this sense, crafting messages and strategies that leverage relevant behavioural change theories could be particularly effective.

When marketing a social entrepreneurial organisation or its product, one of the main decisions to make is how much to stress its identity. If a social entrepreneurial organisation aims to operate as a for-profit business, stressing that it is a social enterprise or that its product aims to generate positive social or environmental impact might be detrimental if customers or stakeholders do not know or understand social entrepreneurship. It might encourage them to consider its product as of lower quality, or to assume it gets subsidies and donations and therefore can be paid less for the job done. Conversely, if a social entrepreneurial organisation operates as a non-profit, showing its entrepreneurial or business traits might discourage potential donors and grant-makers or generate confusion in beneficiaries. On the other hand, when bidding for contracts for public entities or businesses that have sustainability requirements or when trying to attract socially- and environmentally-conscious customers, showing that the organisation is pursuing impact before profits might yield an important competitive advantage. The choice on how much to stress social entrepreneurship in promotion should be dependent on the knowledge of the target audience, the level of development of the relevant social entrepreneurship ecosystem, and the awareness of what competitors are doing.

Process entails the flow of activities to deliver the product, choices about the level of involvement of the target audience in contributing to the value proposition, the adopted degree of standardisation versus personalisation, and the setting up of policies in relation to any of the other elements of the marketing mix.

Physical evidence refers to the environment in which the value proposition is delivered, including considerations on accessibility, tangible clues on how to use or experience the product, colours, décor, furniture, and any other element that supports the delivery and communication of the product. In virtual environments, it also refers to the layout of the website or app, their ease of use, compatibility with different types of hardware, etc. Physical evidence can play a fundamental role in helping target audiences unfamiliar with the product or organisation to understand what they stand for, to make them feel at ease, and to build trust in the organisation and in its understanding of their needs and barriers.

Participants includes any individual or organisation who takes part in the delivery of the product. In particular, as a category, it highlights the importance of employees who are in direct contact with the target audience and responsible for the delivery of a product, since they play a key role in making the product accessible, understood, and in influencing the target audience's perception of the organisation. It is important to ensure that employees have the right skillset and attitude for what needs to be delivered, and to guarantee quality of delivery. This can be achieved by creating training that standardises as much as possible the aspects of the product delivery that are essential for the value proposition to be realised, and by supporting employees to develop empathy and listening skills. Similarly, it is important to understand how the target audience interacts with the organisation and its product, since this also shapes its delivery and is important to maximise the chances that the audience's experience will match the intended one.

While the 7Ps framework, like any simplification, has its limitations, dividing the marketing mix into its different components can help social entrepreneurial organisations to reflect on all the key aspects that contribute to the successful delivery of their value proposition to different stakeholders. The marketing mix can be leveraged to not only reach customers and beneficiaries but also to develop partnerships with suppliers, distributors, and competitors, to convince potential funders and employees to support the organisation and, in the case of social marketing, to address policymakers and other decision-makers whose input is necessary for behavioural change at scale.

When thinking about the 7Ps, it is important to remember that the main goal of a social entrepreneurial organisation is to maximise impact and reach, rather than profitability, and to balance the development of details for a specific part of the mix with the generation of coherence and synergies between its different elements. Additionally, it is helpful not to take the elements of the mix too dogmatically, allowing ideas and adjustments to emerge from serendipity and interaction with different target audiences, and privileging the Ps that make most sense based on the goals and social business model of the organisation. In particular, since the mix risks being developed without consulting external stakeholders, it is key to use even this framework to solicit feedback from the target audience and, in particular, to check with target customers and beneficiaries as to whether they believe what is being planned is solving a problem and delivering value to them. Otherwise, the whole exercise risks to be useless or, even worse, detrimental.

Increasingly, as in any other sector, social entrepreneurial organisations can and do leverage the internet, and especially social media, for multiple elements of the marketing mix. Practices in this sense are normally grouped under the umbrella of digital marketing, which includes anything done through the web, apps, a computer, phone, smartphone, tablet, and the like. Digital marketing can be used as place (e.g. online channel to sell a product or service), promotion (e.g. online advertisement and social media posts), process (e.g. app that makes banking services easily accessible), and physical evidence (e.g. website promoting a certain image of the organisation and its culture). When used for promotion purposes, it can be used to educate, inspire, entertain, involve, engage, and giving a voice to individuals who might otherwise not be heard.

8.3.2 Basics of digital marketing

Digital marketing includes having: social media profiles on widely-used platforms such as *Instagram, YouTube, TikTok, Pinterest, Twitter, WeChat, Facebook*, etc.; blogging and v-logging; creating and paying for digital advertisements; developing an app to deliver a product or engaging with stakeholders; setting up online distribution and sales channels; having a website and using related analytics to gather insights about the target audience, the relationships built, new potential leads for business or partnerships opportunities, or the effectiveness of the content posted.

While the relatively low costs of digital marketing might make it very attractive for social entrepreneurial organisations, using it effectively is not straightforward and requires a strategic approach as with any other element of the marketing mix. Social entrepreneurial organisations need to be clear about why digital marketing might be helpful from the point of view of the target audience and what exactly they want to achieve with it, as well as reserving enough resources for it and being smart about where to invest these given the multiple opportunities available. Often it is better to use few tools well, rather than to divide attention between many tools and social media platforms. Any digital tool or social media profile requires constant updates, tailored approaches and content, attention to detail and consistency. It needs to match the expectations and habits of a target audience, engage it, and help it to interact with the organisation.

Increasingly, social media represent a key component of digital marketing and, for this reason, need to be managed with special care and strategic effort, given the growing competition for people's attention. Social media profiles should include helpful keywords, relevant information on the organisation, and posts of sufficient variety (e.g. how-tos, inspirational quotes, behind-the-scenes posts, customer stories, and different formats such as blogs, photos, infographics, videos)[17] to keep the profile active and interesting. They should be managed through a scheduling tool ensuring posts appear at regular intervals, and be leveraged to re-share relevant content generated by others and to comment on what they post. This can help to further expand visibility and networks, and to create a strong image of what the organisation cares about. In this sense, the organisation also needs to be strategic about whom to follow and to connect with and about the hashtags it uses, remain proactive at replying to questions and comments, and post with the goals of entertaining, informing, and inspiring, ideally simultaneously. Given the speed at which news and posts circulate on the web and the need for social entrepreneurial organisations to maintain an image of coherence, adherence to ethics and moral values, and care, for social entrepreneurial organisations that engage in digital marketing it is pivotal to be extremely careful about what they post. To do so, it is helpful to establish who has the authorisation to speak in the name of the organisation, and a protocol for checking any posts, blogs, web pages, etc. before they are published.

As with anything else in marketing, digital marketing should aim to build relationships with the target audience, rather than to just generate content, and should be discontinued if not effective or not worth the effort and costs. This implies planning whom to reach, why, and how, committing resources over the long term, monitoring whether they are delivering expected outputs and outcomes, generating content that feels authentic and relevant, and engaging in dialogue rather than just sharing content.

Digital marketing can be used not only as product, place, or promotion, but also for triggering systems change (see Chapter 5), e.g. to co-create content, facilitate conversations among others and broker connections to support change efforts by developing dialogue, incentives, and removing barriers. While the COVID-19 pandemic encouraged many social entrepreneurial organisations to become smarter in their usage of digital marketing, this remains an area where many of them still lack the acumen, strategies, and skills of businesses, since they consider it as a side activity rather than a potential key tool to deliver and increase their impact. This will likely need to change in the near future, as the metaverse takes increasing centrality in many countries and might open up even more opportunities to generate important impact and changes in countries that are only just starting to digitalise.

8.3.3 Using marketing in social entrepreneurship – the importance of ethics

When using marketing strategies, planning or frameworks, or focusing on traditional, social or digital marketing, social entrepreneurial organisations need to adopt an ethical approach. Murphy et al. (2007)[18] suggest that this means building relationships with their target audience(s) through commitment, diligence, fairness, empathy, integrity, and respect. According to Lefebvre (2013),[19] in addition to these characteristics, ethical marketing entails doing no harm, treating everyone equally, being truthful and transparent, respecting privacy, avoiding stereotyping and scapegoating, respecting people's dignity and free choice, using research-based evidence whenever possible when making decisions, seeking consensus from stakeholders, being inclusive when developing strategies, and conducting an ethical review of plans with the help of stakeholders before implementation.

Since marketing emerged as a strategic activity to increase sales, attract attention, and increase the profitability of companies, adopting it makes it very easy to cross the fine line between reaching more and better versus causing harm through deception, manipulation and excessive nudging, leveraging people's insecurities, desire for social acceptance or ignorance. Additionally, it might be very easy for social entrepreneurial organisations to over-leverage their social or environmental impact as a promotional and differentiation device, instead of focusing on actual value creation and on what is best for their target beneficiaries. For example, as seen in Chapter 1, *La Fageda* decided not to mention their mission and employment of disabled people in any element of their marketing mix, because they felt that would have been a form of exploitation of disability. Similarly, it is easy to see how offering something, e.g. food, in exchange for target beneficiaries attending a certain support service or programme, might potentially be an exploitation of their hunger to attain a different objective and, while this might reach its immediate goal, it might also generate negative, unintended effects in the medium to longer term.

The adherence to strong ethics can become a source of competitive advantage for social entrepreneurial organisations in relation to traditional businesses but this should not be the main reason to think about the ethical implications of marketing decisions. The adoption of ethics should be based on the desire to maximise positive while minimising negative impact, on the belief in the existence of moral standards and rights that can never be breached, and on the adoption a truly socially-minded strategic approach.

Several studies found that social entrepreneurial organisations often struggle due to a lack of commercial positioning, understanding, and market strategy. Therefore, thinking about the social business model and making sure that the value proposition is attractive for all target audiences, is well communicated and delivered through an appropriate marketing mix, can help an organisation to gain an edge from the get-go. Marketing strategies and frameworks like the 7Ps can then be helpful throughout the life cycle of the organisation and of its activities, especially if applied in ethical ways that create trust in the organisation and in its commitment to positive social and environmental impact. At the same time, social entrepreneurial organisations should be weary of just adopting business or traditional economics' concepts, thinking instead if their marketing activities could also be targeted at changing the narrative about how society and markets work, encouraging each individual and organisation to act responsibly, respecting both others and the environment.

Once resources, skills, and support start to flow towards the organisation, it is possible to translate the social business model into operations, activities, systems, and processes. The next chapter discusses key choices that social entrepreneurial organisations need to make as they start to deliver their value proposition.

SUMMARY BOX

- Social business models are helpful tools to strategise for any social entrepreneurial organisation. They express how the organisation will achieve its mission through the delivery of a value proposition, how it will organise the delivery of its value proposition, and how it will ensure its financial sustainability and the generation of its intended impact.
- Elaborating a social business model can help to position an organisation in relation to competing and complementary offers, foster internal dialogue and shared understandings, gain resources and legitimacy, and assess the potential to achieve a double or triple bottom line.
- A social business model can be represented through the social business model canvas. This consists of four sections explaining: the value proposition; for whom it is delivered (specifying who key customers and beneficiaries are, and how they will be reached and engaged over time); how it is delivered (specifying activities, inputs, and partners); how financial sustainability and impact will be achieved (specifying costs, sources of funding and impact metrics).
- The resources, skills, and support necessary for the realisation of a social business model can be gathered with the help of marketing activities, tools, and frameworks. In particular, social entrepreneurial organisations can benefit from techniques to segment and target their key audience(s) and from developing marketing strategies to reach them through the marketing mix (which includes the 7Ps: product, price, place, promotion, process, physical evidence, and participants).
- Social entrepreneurial organisations developing marketing strategies should reflect on the opportunities provided by digital marketing and on how to remain ethical and coherent through each element of the marketing mix.

Check box – Self-reflection and discussion questions

- What is a business model?
- What do you think should distinguish a social business model from a "traditional" business model?
- What are the benefits of elaborating a social business model? And what are the potential issues?
- What are examples of social business model archetypes?
- What are the characteristics of successful social business models?
- What are the components of a social business model canvas and what should be included in each of them?

- What are the advantages and disadvantages of relying on multiple funding streams?
- What are marketing, social marketing, and digital marketing?
- Do you think that all the marketing of a social entrepreneurial organisation should be social? Why or why not?
- What do segmentation and targeting mean? Why are these activities helpful?
- What are the marketing 7Ps and what are the benefits and risks of using this framework to develop the marketing mix?
- What is necessary for effective digital marketing? Do you know any social entrepreneurial organisation that is effective at digital marketing?
- What does it mean to apply ethics to marketing?

Check out the "Additional resources" related to this chapter to learn more about the concepts and tools presented and how they can be used: www.routledge.com/9780367640231.

Exercises

Exercise 8.1 – Analysing social business models

Check the links to examples of social business model canvas provided in the book's website (www.routledge.com/9780367640231), in the Section 8.1. Pick one of the canvas presented and analyse it either individually or in a small group (in person or remotely). Based on your analysis, answer the following questions:

1 What does the organisation do?
2 What is the main value it delivers to beneficiaries and/or customers? And to other stakeholders?
3 What are the main activities of the organisation and how does it sustain them?
4 How does the organisation achieve financial sustainability?
5 What convinces you in the social business model presented?
6 What does not convince you in the social business model presented?
7 What information is missing?
8 Do you believe this is a successful organisation based on its canvas?

Exercise 8.2 – Building a social business model

Case study – Right to Dream

Right to Dream is a foundation created in Ghana in 1999 that provides a full high school scholarship and training to promising boys and girls who are passionate about football. Its founder realised that he could leverage his status as a talent scout in West Africa for Manchester United to provide an opportunity for development for children of the community where he lived. He started a football academy to train talented youth from across West Africa, providing education and character-building opportunities, beyond football training. Students who showed talent and met or exceeded expectations in terms of academic achievement could apply for a full scholarship to study abroad in a partner university, or to join a student-athlete pathway in partner schools in the United Kingdom and in the United States. The initial academy was so successful, that now *Right to Dream* operates additional academies in Denmark and Egypt, and trains both male and female footballers.

Its operations are funded through a mix of individual donations, philanthropic and corporate donations, and revenues generated through the offer of training programmes. For example, *Right to Dream* provides leadership and employee engagement programmes for partners and other corporations through their academies, in exchange for a fee and/or financial support over a period of time.

Thanks to their academies and to the support received from their partners – important universities and football clubs from Europe and the United States – *Right to Dream* has enabled several teenagers to either pursue a career in professional football or to obtain scholarship for university studies abroad. Over the years *Right to Dream* has assessed over 25,000 children across West Africa and has unleashed over $40m in scholarships for its alumni. Thirty-four of these have even become professional footballers in top European and US clubs.

Based on this information and on what you can find on its website and on its YouTube channel (see links in the book's website: www.routledge.com/9780367640231 with book materials) construct the social business model canvas of *Right to Dream*.

Share and compare the social business models created and, by combining them, create a class-wide canvas that represents as well as possible the functioning and impact of *Right to Dream*.

Exercise 8.3 – Analysing the marketing mix

Either individually or in groups search information on a social entrepreneurial organisation you admire. Try to describe its marketing mix through the 7Ps framework and present it to the rest of the class, explaining what convinces you and what you think could be improved and why. In particular, spend some time thinking how you would leverage digital marketing further and whether you think the organisation is adopting an ethical approach to marketing and, if not, what would you do to help it improve on that front.

Exercise 8.4 – Creating a marketing strategy for a social entrepreneurial organisation

Imagine you want to set up a social entrepreneurial organisation to market the social innovation discussed in the video that you can access on the book's website (www.routledge.com/9780367640231). Alternatively, develop a marketing strategy for the social entrepreneurial organisation you would like to set up or that you work for. When developing a marketing strategy, make sure to cover the following elements:

1   Explain who your key target audiences are and why.
2   Pick one among the key target audiences and segment it.
3   Focus on a segment and develop a marketing mix covering all of the 7Ps, also reflecting on whether deploying digital marketing might be helpful or not and, if so, how.
4   Discuss which Ps will be most strategic and how they will work together, reinforcing one another.
5   Explain how you will ensure the respect of ethics.

Notes

1   Casadesus-Masanell, R., & Ricart, J. E. (2010). From strategy to business models and onto tactics. *Long Range Planning, 43*(2–3), 195–215.
2   Smith, W. K., Binns, A., & Tushman, M. L. (2010). Complex business models: Managing strategic paradoxes simultaneously. *Long Range Planning, 43*(2–3), 448–461.
3   Osterwalder, A., Pigneur, Y., & Tucci, C. L. (2005). Clarifying business models: Origins, present, and future of the concept. *Communications of the Association for Information Systems, 16*(1), 17.
4   Teece, D. J. (2010). Business models, business strategy and innovation. *Long range planning, 43*(2–3), 179.
5   Google. (2021). *Our approach to search*. Retrieved from: https://www.google.com/search/howsearchworks/mission/
6   Mair, J., & Schoen, O. (2007). Successful social entrepreneurial business models in the context of developing economies: An explorative study. *International Journal of Emerging Markets, 2*(1), 54–68.
7   Strategyzer. (2022). The business model canvas. Retrieved from: https://www.strategyzer.com/canvas/business-model-canvas
8   Wei-Skillern, J., Austin, J. E., Leonard, H., & Stevenson, H. (2007). *Entrepreneurship in the social sector* (Vol. 13). London: Sage.
9   Guo, C., & Bielefeld, W. (2014). *Social entrepreneurship: An evidence-based approach to creating social value* (First ed., Bryson Series in Public and Nonprofit Management), 76.
10 American Marketing Association. (2017). *Definition of marketing*. Retrieved from: https://www.ama.org/the-definition-of-marketing-what-is-marketing/
11 Lazer, W., & Kelley, E. (1973). *Social marketing: perspectives and viewpoints*. Homewood, IL: Irwin, 9.
12 Facca-Miess, T. M., & Santos, N. J. (2014). Fostering fair and sustainable marketing for social entrepreneurs in the context of subsistence marketplaces. *Journal of Marketing Management, 30*(5–6), 501–518.
13 Lefebvre, C. R. (2008). *Segmenting Black America*. Retrieved from: https://socialmarketing.blogs.com/r_craiig_lefebvres_social/2008/07/segmenting-black-america.html
14 Yankelovich, D., & Meer, D. (2006). Rediscovering market segmentation. *Harvard Business Review, 84*(2), 122–131.
15 McCarthy, E. J. (1964). *Basic marketing*. Homewood, IL: Richard D. Irwin.
16 Booms, B. H., & Bitner, M. J. (1981). Marketing strategies and organization structures for service firms. In Donnelly, J. H., & George, W. R. (Eds), *Marketing of Services, American Marketing Association*, Chicago, IL, 47–51.
17 Mincher, H. (2021). *Expert essays: An agony aunt's guide to social media*. Retrieved from: https://www.the-sse.org/news/expert-essays-an-agony-aunts-guide-to-social-media/
18 Murphy, P. E., Laczniak, G. R., & Wood, G. (2007). An ethical basis for relationship marketing: A virtue ethics perspective. *European Journal of Marketing, 41*(1/2), 37–57.
19 Lefebvre, R. C. (2013). *Social marketing and social change: Strategies and tools for improving health, well-being, and the environment*. Hoboken: John Wiley & Sons, 71.

9 Creating strong foundations for social entrepreneurial organisations

Key content

This chapter explores the key elements needed to translate a social business model into an organisation, focusing on the implications that being a social entrepreneurial organisation has on the decisions regarding each of these elements.

9.1 The birth of a social entrepreneurial organisation
9.2 Legal form and governance structures
9.3 Organisational structure
9.4 Leadership styles
9.5 Human Resource Management
9.6 Organisational culture
9.7 Organisational ethics

Learning objectives

- Be aware of key elements that founders of social entrepreneurial organisations need to consider when translating a social business model into an organisation.
- Understand key constraints and considerations that should shape the choice of legal form and governance structures.
- Learn about different organisational structures and workflows that social entrepreneurial organisations can adopt.
- Reflect on what it means to lead a social entrepreneurial organisation.
- Become aware of the ways to enhance Human Resource Management in social entrepreneurial organisations.
- Appreciate the importance of organisational culture and of adopting an ethical approach.

9.1 The birth of a social entrepreneurial organisation

According to the business literature, success and survival are only possible if there are alignment and synergy between the value proposition, and the strategic plans, structures and processes, resources and capabilities established to realise it. This is no different for a social entrepreneurial organisation, although in this case the value it tries to create is predominantly social or environmental rather than financial. As aspiring founders of social entrepreneurial organisations start to attract resources

DOI: 10.4324/9781003121824-12

to realise the value proposition, they need to create an organisation, its systems, and processes to deliver it.

Given the variety of social entrepreneurial organisations, choices on how to implement a social business model tend to be complex and based on an extensive number of options. Thus, for the sake of speed and simplicity, they are often made based on advice or on what is familiar rather than through strategising. This frequently results in social entrepreneurial organisations changing their legal form, structures, systems, and processes many times over their first few years, until they find through trial and error what enables them to deliver their value proposition effectively.

Each development process of a social entrepreneurial organisation is going to be very different, based on the time, knowledge, and resources available, the decision makers involved and their characteristics, pressures of key stakeholders such as funders, and the institutional and regulatory context. For this reason, discussing step by step how founders of social entrepreneurial organisations might go about setting up their organisation is beyond the scope of this book. Instead, the chapter focuses on key organisational characteristics any founder will have to make decisions about, and presents some insights on what could be the key elements to consider given the social entrepreneurial nature of what is being set up.

The creation of an organisation to implement a social business model requires decision-making on seven main areas:

- The legal form;
- The governance structures;
- The organisational structure (units of work, functions, workflows, etc.);
- The leadership style;
- Human Resource Management;
- Organisational culture;
- How to include ethical considerations in any decision and activity.

The social business model, especially if expressed through a canvas (see Chapter 8), already provides a starting point for decisions on the legal form, governance, and organisational structure.

9.2 Legal form and governance structures

Legal forms and governance structures were already discussed in Chapter 3, but it is important to add some practical considerations on them here, in relation to other organisational characteristics. To recap, legal forms are instruments regulated by law that provide organisations with a legal status and, thus, with the opportunity to act as an independent entity with specific rights, obligations, and responsibilities. Social entrepreneurial organisations can incorporate as non-profit organisations, for-profit companies, associations, cooperatives, and if they exist, through tailored-made legal forms for social enterprises, according to the local laws. Governance is the set of rules, principles, systems, relationships, and processes through which an organisation operates and is controlled, and through which its actions and directions are held to account. It creates the framework within which decisions are taken, goals and strategies are established and monitored, legal compliance is verified, and the financial sustainability of the organisation is protected. Governance also contributes to promoting the organisation and reinforcing its legitimacy, is the system to hire top managers and to approve major projects, is one of the key ways to integrate the interests and perspectives of different stakeholders and to engage them in decision-making, and to ensure transparency and accountability.

The legal form should be chosen based on the mission and social business model and reflecting on how different options will affect:

- funding options;
- the governance structures that need to be set up;
- who has the right to influence decision-making in critical situations;
- the possibility to generate and distribute profits;
- which stakeholders are going to be "legally" prioritised;
- the legitimacy of the organisation;
- the attraction of needed talent and skills, and in particular the opportunity to rely on volunteers.

For example, cooperatives are particularly well-suited to ensure the involvement of employees and suppliers in decision-making in sectors such as agricultural production, artisanal goods, or artistic endeavours. All producers/contributors that sell their products, talent or produce through the cooperative can obtain its shares in exchange for their contribution, and through these have a say on what and where the cooperative decides to sell, or on which opportunities it takes and refuses. At the same time, incorporating as a cooperative might constrain growth, making it harder to attract investors given the impossibility of rewarding them with shares, limit funding options to those available to for-profit businesses (see Chapter 10), and create the need to regulate how shares can be transferred and allocated to allow the easy entry and exit of employees/other stakeholders and the maintenance of fair representation.

In relation to the legal form, social entrepreneurial organisations also need to decide how to handle the existence of potential profits. Profit-distribution rules have a strong impact on the ability to attract investment and grants, on the credibility of the pursuit of a double or triple bottom line, and on the possibility to extend decision-making rights through the creation of different types of shares. Social entrepreneurial organisations that are set up as non-profit organisations are normally obliged to reinvest all profits in their impact-generating activities, while those set up as for-profit businesses can choose how much of their profits to reinvest in their mission versus to redistribute to shareholders or use otherwise (e.g. transfer to a non-profit entity through a donation). In countries where there are specific legal forms for social enterprises, these can come with restrictions on to what extent profits can be redistributed.

Often, the legal form is based on familiarity rather than on considerations about its various implications, due to the pressures of prospective or current funders, due to the business advice of mentors or professionals met at incubators and networking events, or due to the constraints imposed by local laws and governments, etc. If there is a mismatch between aspirations and the legal form, they are likely to emerge later and trigger re-incorporations (e.g. see Mayamiko case study in the Appendix), which take more effort and time than reflecting on what is the best choice when the organisation is created. That said, even once the legal form is set, there are still many subsequent choices that can shape how well it fits with the organisation's mission and social business model. For example, organisations incorporated as for-profit businesses still have the freedom to set up internal rules on who can be a member of the board, and thus to guarantee stakeholders' involvement in it, or can build an organisational culture and operational processes that support the pursuit of a double or triple bottom line. Choices on governance structures can be especially helpful in this sense.

Governance structures are the expression of both formal authority – i.e. who has legal authority and responsibility for decisions and who has the influence to affect key strategies and decisions. They vary depending on the type of social entrepreneurial organisation, its legal form, size, and stage of life cycle. The two key decisions that need to be made in relation to governance are who will be a member of governance structures and what will be the main function that the various structures will fulfil. When setting up governance structures it is important to seek the best balance between continuity – to support external credibility, long-term strategies, and adherence to the original mission – and the need to change and innovate.

In social entrepreneurial organisations, members of governance structures – board, committees, councils, etc. – can be hired on many different bases and, in non-profit organisations, are frequently engaged as volunteers/support the organisation pro-bono. They can be individuals whose value lies in, alternatively, representing stakeholders or main funders, matching the values of the organisation (e.g. if faith-based), having key technical or managerial skills, providing access to policy or business networks, or bringing knowledge of a sector of interest (e.g. academics or executives with a long-standing career). The choice of whom to engage and why should depend on which interests should be privileged, what the organisation is missing based on its existing team, and the synergy between individual membership and the set of governance structures established.

As seen in Chapter 3, governance structures of social entrepreneurial organisations normally privilege one of three functions: the support of stakeholders' inclusion in decision-making, the guarantee that leaders and managers will act in the best interest of the organisation as a whole, and the provision of legitimacy. While attention should be paid to pick the structures that perform at least one and, ideally, all of these functions well, it is also important to remember that governance is not the only tool to guarantee legitimacy or representation and that, rather, it is its combination with other organisational characteristics that can make a difference. For example, existing research has established that sometimes devolved decision-making and employee empowerment can be more effective than employee representation in the board as a way to ensure their involvement in decision-making, and that external stakeholders' involvement in the board might lead to long discussions and stagnation that end up frustrating their representatives and reduce their attendance to, and participation in, discussions. Similarly, what happens in practice is the result of individual and collective actions as much as of structure. There can be organisations giving voting rights to all employees but then not calling general meetings for most decisions and, conversely, organisations ensuring transparency and accountability not through legal and governance means but through regular and open communication and transparent impact reporting. It is important to design governance and other participatory structures in a strategic way, for example setting up multiple boards and committees with different operational and strategic functions and setting clear objectives for each, to promote meaningful engagement and to find the right balance between inclusion of multiple perspectives and the need to remain reactive and decisive when opportunities arise.

The other organisational elements that will support governance structures in ensuring stakeholders' engagement, transparency, accountability, and legitimacy are the organisational structure, leadership, Human Resource Management, and culture.

9.3 Organisational structure

Organisational structure is the framework through which organisational activities are divided and coordinated to ensure the achievement of an organisation's goals. Organisational structure establishes who has power and responsibility in relation to specific areas of operation and therefore who is going to perform the activities and take the decisions necessary to realise the social business model. There are many organisational structures that a social entrepreneurial organisation can adopt and, especially at the start, it is likely that the structure will be loose and informal, with each team member performing multiple roles and tasks to cover whatever needs to be covered both strategically and operationally. However, even when the organisation is in its initial phases, it is helpful to think about where it might head as it expands the original team, to guarantee the delivery of the value proposition.

Typical organisational structures are functional, divisional, or matrix. In functional structures, teams are organised based on functions (e.g. marketing, accounting, sales, operations). This promotes learning and standardisation, whenever functional expertise and/or economies of scale are key for performance and the organisation is small and undiversified enough that coordination does not represent an issue. In divisional organisations teams are grouped based on projects, products or geographical locations. Each division has employees with different functional expertise, all reporting to the manager responsible for the success of a given project, product or location. The advantages of divisional organisations are decentralised decision-making and the effectiveness in reaching the target audience of each division, since they all have autonomy in doing what makes most sense based on the project, product or location they are responsible for, relatively independently from what other divisions do. However, this structure makes it harder to maximise efficiency, knowledge sharing across projects, products or locations, and the development of functional-level competences. Matrix organisations are characterised by a dual reporting structure, whereby the same employee or team might report to both a function-based (e.g. marketing, accounting, operations), and a project-, product- or location-based manager. The matrix structure helps the sharing of information across individuals and teams and their gaining an overview of the different products, activities, and projects the organisation undertakes. However, it might also generate conflicts of interest and tensions, confusion about what objectives should take priority, and coordination costs. Social entrepreneurial organisations often adopt the matrix structure when they stabilise and grow, frequently organising both through functions and projects, but tend to be much more organic in their first years of operation or if they remain relatively small throughout their existence.

Whatever the structure adopted, the coordination of activities is also affected by the workflows (i.e. the sequence of processes, steps, and decisions through which a piece of work passes from initiation to completion), and by how much centralised or decentralised decision-making is. Based on the work of Serrano et al. (2006)[1] and on the literature on sustainable business, there are three main ways in which social entrepreneurial organisations can set up their workflows and distribute decision-making power:

1   **Hierarchical/centralised.** Decision-making and coordination happens at the top and teams or individuals who are not part of the leading team mostly execute and report back feedback from stakeholders to inform further decision-making.

This workflow is ideal for planning, sharing information, and coordination and, therefore, for organisations operating in relatively stable sectors and contexts, where fast decision-making is not key. However, it might generate resistance to change, excessive bureaucracy, and demotivation of employees, who might not feel sufficiently involved in strategic decisions.

2   **Team-based/decentralised.** Individuals or teams have significant autonomy in making decisions for the organisation, responding to what they hear and experience on the ground. What they jointly do ends up influencing what the value proposition turns out to be and the future strategic direction. Coordination mostly happens through values, shared goals, and culture. This supports flexibility, fast decision-making, adaptation, and employee engagement, but risks generating silos of expertise and lack of direction if values and culture are not sufficient in ensuring the convergence of efforts.

3   **Network organisation.** This is typical of cooperatives, hubs, Fair Trade Organisations, systems change coalitions, and partnerships. The organisation consists of either a group of self-employed or freelancing individuals, or of organisations of various sizes. Coordination is either centralised, if there is a leading organisation keeping everyone together, establishing contributions and directing efforts, or entirely decentralised, if each individual or organisation remains fully independent and contributes to the collective based on what they can and while pursuing their own goals. This structure minimises costs for everyone, enables flexibility in responding to local demands and conditions, and fosters creativity and innovation. However, it risks dispersing energies and resources, creating duplication of efforts, reducing the likelihood of sharing best practices, especially if there is no central coordination, and leading to members leaving if they disagree with what the organisation or other members are doing.

There is no single structure or workflow that works better than others in absolute terms, since their effectiveness depends on environmental factors (see Chapters 4 and 6), the people involved in the organisation and in its value chain, the requirements and expectations of external stakeholders and, most importantly, their fit with the other key organisational components such as governance, culture, and social business model. The choice of what structure and workflows to adopt depends on the founders' or leaders' beliefs about the environment in which the organisation operates, who is in the best position to make decisions and who benefits the most from working together, and their trust in others.

The more decentralised decision-making is, the more formal and informal coordinating mechanisms will be needed to ensure the collective pursuit of the organisation's mission. Common coordinating mechanisms include: governance structures; the organisation of cross-team meetings and committees; rules and directives; routines; the creation of shared objectives and culture through an initial agreement or ongoing negotiations; regular reporting and sharing of information; leadership and Human Resource Management practices.

9.4 Leadership styles

The identity and role of leaders in a social entrepreneurial organisation is likely to evolve as the organisation develops and grows. While in social entrepreneurship ecosystems attention historically tends to be on charismatic leaders and founders, all employees represent potential leaders.

In the founding stages, the leaders are normally the founders and are at the centre of all action, procuring support, resources, and funds through their networks, spotting opportunities, doing whatever needs to be done both at the strategic and operational level, and convincing others to get on board. In this phase, leaders play a key role in crafting the mission, values, and social business model of the organisation, as well as its governance, organisational structures, Human Resource Management practices, and culture. Their choices are based on their values, personal characteristics, beliefs about people's behaviours and trustworthiness, opinion on the importance of stakeholders' engagement, and required speed of decision-making. For example, if operating in a fast-changing environment or if being very attached to their own idea but believing in the need of including stakeholders' perspectives, leaders/founders might try to centralise decision-making, while setting up governance structures or coordinating mechanisms that favour stakeholders' and employees' engagement at specific points in time.

As the organisation starts to operate and evolves, founders need to become managers, remaining the formal leaders of the organisation and the point of reference for main strategic decisions and networking with key stakeholders, but delegating operational tasks, establishing processes for coordination, and accepting to let go of some ideas if outcomes and feedback suggest otherwise. They also need to focus on enlarging the original team, bringing in a mix of managerial skills and expertise on the issue to be tackled and, also through this, creating opportunities for new formal and informal leaders to emerge. The latter can bring new ideas and skills, and support the adaptation of the initial social business model to what is required by the context and key stakeholders.

As the organisation grows further, founders normally act as inspirational leaders through roles such as CEO or president of the board and the organisation has many formal leaders beyond them who reached the top of the hierarchy based on charisma, technical skills, or issue-based expertise. All formal leaders need to delegate some operational and strategic tasks, allowing them to focus prevalently on large projects, new partnerships, attracting the financial resources necessary for growth, coordinating others, and ensuring that the organisation remains aligned to its original mission. Informal leaders or formal leaders in lower hierarchical levels have room to shape motivation and efforts in their team, suggesting innovative approaches to higher hierarchical levels, and supporting opportunities to scale impact in different directions or locations (see Chapter 10).

Whatever style and role adopted by leaders depending on both their characteristics and those of the organisation, according to the work of Bacq and Eddleston (2018)[2] it is important that leaders of social entrepreneurial organisations

> carefully consider what capabilities are available to them and develop organizational processes that will best apply those capabilities so as to make progress toward their social objectives ... Without firm leaders who strongly identify with the enterprise's mission and gain a sense of accomplishment from its social achievements, these social enterprises may be easily swayed to alter their mission to appease the interests of others such as donors, volunteers, and government agencies, thereby jeopardizing their social impact.

All leaders of social entrepreneurial organisations are expected to lead by example, promoting through their actions and the way they relate to internal and external stakeholders, the organisational culture, and the attitudes and behaviours that they want in employees. The study of Pasricha and Rao (2018)[3] established the importance of ethical leadership in social entrepreneurial organisations and defined that as the combination of a moral person and a moral manager.

> As a moral person, the leader holds traits such as honesty, integrity, fairness, caring, and trustworthiness, exhibits ethical behaviour, and makes decisions based upon ethical principles. As a moral manager, the leader promotes ethics in the organization by serving as role model for ethical conduct, explicitly conveying ethical standards and values to employees, and using reward systems to hold employees accountable to the ethical standards.[4]

According to their work, ethical leadership supports social innovation and the perception of high social capital in the organisation (the benefits deriving from social relations) among employees. This, in turn, makes employees more likely to act based on expectations, trust leaders and one another, and be more prone to collaborate and share knowledge.

It is well established that organisations who empower and engage their employees, and create a loyal and committed workforce, are more likely to succeed. Employees and the way they work together represent the know-how, skills, and capabilities of a social entrepreneurial organisation. They are necessary to deliver its value proposition and are one of the key features that makes it unique. Thus, why Human Resource Management becomes critical from the very beginnings of a social entrepreneurial organisation.

LEADERSHIP STYLES IN PRACTICE

Read and listen to the testimonies from different leaders of social entrepreneurial organisations on the organisational challenges they had to handle and how they coped with them. To access the testimonies use the links on the book's website (www.routledge.com/9780367640231), in the Chapter 9 section.

9.5 Human Resource Management

In business contexts, employees are often perceived as an instrument to achieve profitability and, as such, treated as any other form of capital whose return needs to be maximised. However, in social entrepreneurial organisations, employees and volunteers need to be seen as people, and their well-being, development, and contribution to the success of the organisation should be an end in itself. For this reason, their talent should be nurtured, their contributions respected and rewarded, and they should be pushed to grow professionally, kept informed about what is going on with the organisation, involved in decision-making whenever feasible, paid at least the minimum wage, and treated fairly. Without careful and human-centred employee management, a social entrepreneurial organisation can risk to ruin its reputation, lose its social credentials, and lose some of the trust from both internal and external stakeholders. Decisions related to hiring, training, developing, engaging, rewarding, and retaining employees are therefore key throughout the existence of a social entrepreneurial organisation, and should be taken strategically, in alignment with the mission, Theory of Change (ToC) and social business model.

9.5.1 *Human Resource Management practices for employees*

Given their pursuit of both social/environmental impact and financial sustainability, social entrepreneurial organisations need to be clear about what skills they need and how to obtain a helpful mix of entrepreneurial/managerial competences and knowledge and skills relevant for the pursuit of their social/environmental mission. The hiring of new employees should reflect:

* The skills and expertise needed;
* The fit of the individual with the organisation, its mission, and values;
* The individual attitude and personal characteristics and how these match with the job requirements;
* Considerations about diversity and inclusion/equal opportunity.

Existing studies revealed several skills that are important in employees of social entrepreneurial organisations. These include: the ability to recognise and reconcile competing demands trying to find the synergies between different approaches; cultural sensitivity; understanding of both the social/environmental and economic/entrepreneurial sides; openness; listening skills; empathy; ability to turn problems into opportunities; creativity to make the best of limited resources. Based on these findings, both practitioners and researchers have stressed the importance of hiring based on attitude rather than skills because the latter can be gained and taught while the former is harder to shape and modify if it does not fit with the organisation or support the reaching of its mission.

Social entrepreneurial organisations frequently do not have the resources for formal training and development of employees. However, they should strive to do as best as they can in this regard, through creating opportunities for job rotations, informal and formal mentoring, shadowing of more senior colleagues, and career progression. For example, they can leverage partnerships strategically as learning opportunities, and, whenever possible, reserve some funds to subsidise or pay for externally-delivered training that employees might be interested in and that can enhance how they contribute to the organisation. Training (formal or informal) is also key in relation to hiring. It is one of the main ways to favour the integration of new hires in the company, give them a safe and structured space to interact with new colleagues and show them that the organisation values them and is investing time and resources to make sure they are put in the best possible situation to succeed.

Training can be especially important to help employees with a social/environmental background gain managerial skills and a good understanding of the economic aspects, and those with a managerial background to better understand the context in which the organisation operates and the issue it is trying to tackle. The lack of business-savviness often leads to mismanagement of resources and cash flows, which threatens the survival of the organisation, and to a poor exploitation of existing opportunities, e.g. for lack of appropriate marketing or market understanding. These problems can be compounded by the lack of governance and procedures guiding decisions, and by the fact that the beneficiaries served, while in need of help and support, might not actually represent a viable market from a commercial point of view. Conversely, as seen in previous chapters, a lack of understanding of the social or environmental issue at hand, of its causes, and of the constraints created by stakeholders and environmental forces, can lead to ineffective solutions, waste of resources, and loss of trust and reputation.

Salaries and rewards are one of the weak links in most social entrepreneurial organisations, since they often cannot afford to pay as much as their business or public sector counterparts, or hand out large bonuses based on performance. This negatively affects both their opportunity to hire and retain highly-skilled employees, and their ability to encourage outcome-based behaviours through forms of extrinsic motivation. Many social entrepreneurial organisations rely on volunteers and cheap labour, given their limited funds. While this is a potentially good practice for start-ups, as a way to overcome initial hurdles, as seen above, part of the mission of a social entrepreneurial organisation should be to guarantee the well-being of its employees and this is not compatible with low pay or excessive use of free labour. It is to be expected that social enterprises and innovative non-profits pay less than businesses. However, this should not mean paying employees a salary that does not sufficiently reward their competences and contributions and that does not allow them and their families a good quality of living.

Whenever possible, social entrepreneurial organisations should aim to pay their employees at least on par with organisations from other sectors (at the very least guaranteeing the minimum wage for all employees) and for internal fairness between pay levels (e.g. having a smaller difference between highest and lowest salaries than is the case in businesses). Investing in employees might be difficult at the beginning but fighting for the necessary funds to do so is worth it in the long run, since it might help the organisation to reduce turnover and to develop the competences that it needs internally. Additionally, organisations can compensate lower salary levels with alternative benefits such as flexible working hours and work from home opportunities (which are also helpful to encourage diversity and inclusion and a good work-life balance), and creating a feeling of involvement and care.

In order to support the realisation of the ToC (see Chapter 7) and value proposition, social entrepreneurial organisations might also consider the establishment of rewards based on the performance of the organisation, in particular with regard to its delivery of outcomes/social and environmental impact. Available levers in this regard are bonuses for employees who support the reaching of more beneficiaries or receive stellar reviews from beneficiaries using the company's products or services, or recognition through organisation-wide communications, internal awards, and the like for employees that suggest improvements or new ways of realising impact.

Ultimately, employee retention, which is one of the key goals of Human Resource Management, is the result of many policies and practices. Hiring people whose values and attitude align with those of the organisation, training them and rewarding them is just the beginning. A social entrepreneurial organisation should think about the different ways in which it can enhance job satisfaction. Common practices in this sense involve emphasising the impact generated and how employees contribute to that, creating challenging roles and opportunities for personal and professional development, establishing a positive and empowering work environment and organisational culture, and respecting all employees, their beliefs and opinions. An option for cooperatives, social enterprises, and organisations incorporated as limited shares companies (and the like) would also be to give shares to all employees, thinking about mechanisms through which they can cash them out when they leave. This way, if the organisation is successful, employees have an additional incentive to stay. At the same time, purely monetary incentives like this should be established after careful consideration, because they might clash with the prevailing culture and ethics and generate the motivation to privilege financial over social or environmental goals.

To ensure that what they provide is in line with employees' expectations and needs, social entrepreneurial organisations should regularly (ideally at least once a year) request feedback from employees on what they think of the Human Resource Management practices in place, how much they would like to be involved in decisions and in different projects/operations, or how they are affected by their work and by the way in which the organisation is managed.

EMPLOYEE MANAGEMENT IN PRACTICE

The case study on *Pactis Group*, a garment company based in Cambodia, written by Jack van Dokkum[5] is an excellent example of the many initiatives that social entrepreneurial organisations can set up for their employees. *Pactis Group* guarantees the minimum living wage plus a top-up dependent on contractual arrangements and productivity to all employees. It set up training on both work-related skills and knowledge, such as English or occupational health and safety, and on skills that valuable for the employees' life standards, such as health and household money management. Additionally, it provides subsidised lunches, helmets, and driving licenses; savings programmes; a company nurse and day care; a library and a set of regular company outings, parties, and traditional ceremonies.

9.5.2 *Human Resource Management practices for volunteers and interns*

In addition to employee management and engagement, social entrepreneurial organisations often need to think about how to manage potential interns and, in the case of organisations that operate as non-profits or social enterprises, volunteers. Volunteers are individuals who give their time and skills without pay to benefit others. They may be found among friends and family, the wider network of the founding team and employees, or through partnerships with businesses, which might allow employees to spend some days or months in a social entrepreneurial organisation as part of their Corporate Social Responsibility initiatives. A study by Salamon et al. (2011)[6] estimated that almost a million volunteers exist around the world in any given year, mostly operating in the Global South, thus representing an important resource to tap into. Interns are students or trainees who agree to work for an organisation for a short period of time, sometimes for free, as a way to gain skills, work experience, or to satisfy the requirements of their programme. They might be found by connecting to universities, professional training centres, and online training providers, which might be looking into internships and placements for their students.

Social entrepreneurial organisations might leverage their mission, impact, reputation, dynamic workplace, the creation of interesting roles, and the delivery of relational/networking benefits to attract both volunteers and interns. While the temptation for many organisations might be to accept any volunteer or intern, given they are an excellent way to obtain needed skills and time with limited resources, organisations should accept and manage volunteers and interns as strategically and carefully as they do employees. In particular, volunteers and interns are in a better position to bring added value if the organisation thinks about how their skills and experience can best be leveraged for the delivery of the value proposition, matches their interests with the tasks to be done, and attracts individuals whose competencies and knowledge are found neither in employees nor in members of governance structures.

Some successful non-profits and social enterprises have created directories of volunteers and call on those whose skills match their needs for a specific project or point in time, connect with academics to get their knowledge or expertise when it can support decision-making, and leverage volunteering as a way to engage the local community or establish stronger relationships with key partners. They also have in place formal training to introduce volunteers and interns to the organisation, assign them specific roles and tasks, reward their effort and contribution through non-financial means, and establish policies on volunteers' and interns' engagement to ensure that they have the opportunity to contribute and share feedback and ideas.

Broadly speaking, engagement of employees, volunteers and interns is strongly dependent on the presence of a culture that encourages trust and respect (which creates a safe space for exchanging ideas and voicing of different options), focuses more on outcomes rather than on activities or outputs, encourages cooperation and collaboration, and creates a sense of shared responsibility.

9.6 Organisational culture

Organisational culture is

> the pattern of basic assumptions that a given group has invented, discovered, and developed in learning to cope with its problems of external adaptation and internal integration, and that have worked well enough to be considered valid, and, therefore, to be taught to new members as the correct way to perceive, think, and feel in relation to these problems.[7]

This definition by Schein (1984) expresses well how culture guides behaviours, creates a collective identity, and influences all the components, processes, and workings of an organisation. Culture is visible both through tangible elements such as communications, shared stories, organisational structure, routines, behaviours, offices layouts, dress-codes, etc. and through asking employees what their beliefs and values are, who has power and why.

According to the business literature, culture complements strategy and governance and is a fundamental component for the realisation of the value proposition. If managed proactively, it helps to attract employees, volunteers, and contributors whose values and goals match those of the organisation. It also guides their actions, making their behaviours align "naturally" with expectations and desired ways of working and solving problems, and shapes how they relate to each other and to external stakeholders. At the same time, the behaviours and interactions of employees and how they decide to solve problems and perform their tasks shape organisational culture, creating a reinforcing loop.

Organisational culture depends both on the prevailing culture in the context where the organisation operates, and on the internal factors through which it is both enacted and shaped, such as:

- The founder(s)' beliefs, initial decisions, values, and leadership style.
- The training of both new hires and existing employees and their integration into the organisation, e.g. through team-bonding events, formal and informal training, mentorship arrangements, etc.
- The office layout or work from home routines, as well as in-person and virtual meetings, and how they shape interactions.
- Organisational practices – e.g. who is involved in office cleaning if needed, the existence of frequent all-staff coffee breaks for sharing information, the promotion of inclusion (e.g. celebration of festivities from different cultures and religions if members are from different states or ethnic groups), the realisation of special events and occasions to commemorate achievements or of "safe" systems for employees to share suggestions.
- The internal and external communications produced by the organisation, such as emails, websites, reports, social media profiles, and their degree of transparency and consistency.
- The other key organisational characteristics discussed in previous sections: organisational and governance structures, leadership, distribution of power and involvement in decision-making, workflows, rewards and recognition systems, etc.

The more the culture enables employees, volunteers, and interns to identify with the organisation and with its mission, the more likely they will have the motivation to go the extra mile to contribute to its success, solve problems, and work hard to deliver its value proposition. Additionally, the more the culture encourages respect, cooperation, and the consideration of employees' contributions, the more likely their well-being will be ensured through all Human Resource Management practices. Organisational culture can also be fundamental to encourage employees to engage with external stakeholders, thus helping the organisation to stay in tune with what is happening outside of its boundaries and to adjust to the expectations and needs of its environment.

The more leadership styles, Human Resource Management practices, and organisational culture are aligned with one another and with governance and organisational structures, and the more they are managed proactively, the more likely it is they will contribute to delivering the value proposition and to the harmonious functioning of the organisation. These, however, will also be strongly dependent on the adoption of ethics that reinforce the social orientation of the organisation and ensure as much as possible the fair treatment of both internal and external stakeholders.

9.7 Organisational ethics

For social entrepreneurial organisations it is paramount to ensure or at least encourage key leaders and decision-makers to take ethics into consideration when acting in its name and shaping its characteristics. As expressed by the Social Enterprise World Forum

> Social enterprises should not only do good, but… should aspire to the highest ethical business standards and corporate citizenship. This includes respecting suppliers

by paying them on time, developing a social enterprise supply chain, and valuing staff by treating them well and paying a living wage. Value-based organisations should aspire to low pay differentials (between highest and lowest paid), participation in decision making, and employee benefits that are family friendly. If social enterprise hopes to be a business model for a sustainable global economy, then treating people well is fundamental. Social enterprises should also be transparent and clear in the ways they report the use of their surpluses and how they measure their annual social impact. In the social enterprise sector, how social enterprises do business should be just as important as what business they do.[8]

As shown by the quote above, ethics can mean many things, but the bottom line is that adopting an ethical approach means remaining aware of the context of operation and the culture, beliefs and constraints of beneficiaries and other stakeholders. It means respecting people and avoiding any form of exploitation; paying, rewarding, and treating everyone (employees, partners, suppliers, etc.) fairly; being inclusive and honest. It implies reflecting on the social and environmental consequences of any choice and trying to maximise positive while minimising negative impact. It also requires trying to do "the right thing" beyond what is legally required, feeling a sense of responsibility and accountability in relation to all stakeholders, and striving to maintain satisfactory relationships with them. Finally, adopting an ethical approach involves enabling challenges to the status quo within and outside the organisation, to ensure it continues to pursue its mission and meet the expectations of its stakeholders and, especially, beneficiaries.

Moore (2005)[9] identified several characteristics that help corporations to be virtuous. Many of these can be applied to social entrepreneurial organisations as well. They include

- the pursuit of the original mission and of excellence;
- having processes and systems that encourage the organisation to weigh its own advantage with the one of its community and to only accumulate what is necessary for achieving its purpose;
- a power structure that ensures fair consideration of different views;
- exercising prudence when dealing with uncertainty;
- having the necessary fortitude to handle external influences and a culture that supports ethical and virtuous behaviours.

Given the small size of most social entrepreneurial organisations, the ethics of individual members and leaders might be even more important than those of the organisation. Thus, it is helpful to set up a system of checks and balances that limit the power of the founder or of key leaders, to attract employees that embrace the values of the organisation, and to instil in them a sense of responsibility towards others as well as the social/environmental mission.

While the perception of what is ethical varies based on the context in which a social entrepreneurial organisation operates, there are some universal ethical and moral standards that all social entrepreneurial organisations should apply, such as respecting basic human rights, protecting natural resources and reducing waste as much as possible, minimising damage if it is unavoidable, remaining responsive to the feedback of target beneficiaries and stakeholders, ensuring transparency in decisions and communications, providing equal opportunities, and taking into consideration distributive, compensatory, and retributive justice when handling stakeholders and issues.

Attention to ethics and the set-up of appropriate governance, organisational structure, and Human Resource Management systems and practices requires resources. Thus why, as an organisation comes to life, its founder(s) need to gather financial resources first to get going and then to keep operating and delivering their value proposition as planned.

CREATING STRONG FOUNDATIONS IN PRACTICE

Here below is an extract of the interview I did to Goya Gallagher, one of the co-founders of *Malaika* (see Chapter 3), where she discusses how *Malaika* started and is managed:

How did the idea to found *Malaika* come up?

Both Margarita and I had a passion for Egypt and were looking for an idea to justify going there frequently. We started with buying good Egyptian cotton bedding to sell it in Ecuador. While doing this we realised that working conditions in Egyptian manufacturing factories were quite harsh for workers and that therefore our initiative was probably contributing to an existing problem rather than providing a solution to unemployment. So we thought about a way to produce bed linens that would not be based on exploitation but would actually empower women.

Initially, we rented a room in Cairo and started to teach embroidery to women. We promoted our initiative through our contacts and soon word of mouth attracted so many women looking to learn a new skill that we had to turn them away for lack of space. We funded the rental of the room and the training through our personal funds and then set up a business because we thought it would be the only possibility to sustain the training over time. Women that we trained, once completed the training, would receive pieces of fabric they could work on, if they so wished, and get back to us with an embroidered product. We would then bring these to a factory we contracted, which would put all together and enable us to sell it as a complete set of bed linens under the brand *Malaika*.

At the time, we didn't know social enterprise existed as a word, so we never thought about our business in those terms. We just didn't like how things worked and wanted to do it better. What makes me proud is that *Malaika* became a well-known brand in Egypt.

How did this initial idea turn out into the business *Malaika* is today?

Egyptian cotton is really famous but when we started there was no Egyptian brand selling cotton-based products in the high-end household items sector. All cotton was exported and then developed countries would transform this raw material into high-end products and sell it. People in Egypt with high disposable impact were basically buying linens from abroad and importing it back. So we decided from the beginning to create a high-end product and were lucky and could grow operations quite fast because we had no local competition. We began selling our products at home, doing demonstrations with friends, while still maintaining our previous jobs to fund our initiative. We had to cold call people to keep getting new customers. Then sales started to pick up and we opened the shop. The retail experience helped us understand that to ensure the quality we needed for a high-end product we could not depend on others. So we decided to build our own factory and move the training there from the room we had rented. Women had worked from home at their own convenience, but when we opened the factory, we hired those who wanted to work full time. Thanks to the existence and success of the factory, we have now set up different forms of training so we can teach women also how to work in manufacturing and/or management. In the factory we employ both women and men and given the fast growth we had to hire some who were not initially trained by us. If women show interest in doing other work, we train them. For example, women can become part of *Malaika* by being hired at the factory and then move onto embroidery, or the other way round. It is very free-flowing. What we want is to be there for women and to empower them.

How did you set up the workflow to ensure that women could work from home and still guarantee the quality you expected?

It is white cotton. Women take public transport. They collect fabric and threads from downtown Cairo, embroider it at home and bring it back. Ninety per cent of it is impeccable. It always impressed us. I think it is down to the pride women have in their work and in how they set up our relationship with them. Many of them have never worked before in their life. It might be the atmosphere in training or something else, but they really like it. They always say they feel like it is the first time they are seen and respected and feel it is a safe environment. Many of them will also try to go back to work after training, instead of working from home. We always ask women what we can do to make their life better or easier and try to implement it, and I think this encourages them to do their best. We want to tap even more into the creativity of these women going forward. We are thinking about new workshops to teach them design and colouring. We also would like to do an exhibition, giving women a theme or topic, making embroidery a journey helping them to express themselves.

Is it difficult to balance ethical choices with business choices, e.g. in terms of suppliers, wages, etc.?

It is never a trade-off. Egypt cotton is more expensive than any cotton anywhere else and hand-made embroidery adds value. So we have to ensure that we deliver something of the highest quality and this then enables us to charge a premium price. It takes time and effort to produce our products so we want to only sell products with a long lifetime, which can be passed on to the next generation. The nature of the product makes it possible to do ethical choices while also pursuing the best business opportunities.

SUMMARY BOX

- In order to implement their social business model, social entrepreneurial organisations need to make decisions on the legal form, governance structures, organisational structure, leadership style, approach to Human Resource Management, and organisational culture that they want to adopt.
- Decisions on legal form and governance structures should take into consideration funding and growth opportunities, the involvement of stakeholders in decision-making, what best fits the mission of the organisation, and what can help it gain the necessary legitimacy with external stakeholders.
- There are three main organisational structures – functional, divisional, and matrix – and three types of workflows and distribution of decision-making – centralised, decentralised, and network – that a social entrepreneurial organisation can adopt as it grows. The choice should depend on who benefits the most from working together, on the social business model, and on the characteristics of the sector of operation and of the external environment.
- Leaders of social entrepreneurial organisations can adopt different leadership styles and should perform different roles based on the life cycle of the organisation but, whatever role adopted, need to lead by example, empower employees, and ideally show the key traits of ethical leadership.
- Human Resource Management is fundamental to make the most of the knowledge and skills of employees, volunteers and interns, and to guarantee their respect and well-being. Organisations should invest in their employees, volunteers, and interns, ensure that their contributions are rewarded fairly and sufficiently, engage them whenever possible, and deploy multiple approaches to enhance their job satisfaction.
- Organisational culture shapes behaviours and decision-making and can be shaped by Human Resource Management practices, communications, artefacts, training, and other ways of integrating new hires into the organisation. For social entrepreneurial organisations it is important to develop a culture that supports employees' identification with its mission, commitment, attention to the external environment, and a sense of shared responsibility.
- All social entrepreneurial organisations should adopt an ethical approach, meaning they should strive to remain aware of their context of operation, respect and not exploit internal and external stakeholders, treat everyone fairly, reflect on the social and environmental consequences of any choice they make, and do "the right thing" beyond what it is legally required.

Check box – Self-reflection and discussion questions

- What are the key elements that transform a social business model into a social entrepreneurial organisation?
- What are the key considerations that should shape the choice of legal form and governance structures?

- What are the three main organisational structures? And workflows?
- What are the benefits and limitations of different structures and workflows?
- What do you believe to be the key traits of a leader of a social entrepreneurial organisation?
- What is ethical leadership and why does it matter?
- What are the main activities involved in Human Resource Management?
- What can make the Human Resource Management practices of a social entrepreneurial organisation more effective?
- What is key in managing volunteers and interns?
- If you were the leader of a social entrepreneurial organisation, would you want to rely on volunteers and interns? Why or why not?
- What is organisational culture and why is it important? What should the key features of the culture of a social entrepreneurial organisation be?
- What constitutes an ethical approach?

Check out the "Additional resources" related to this chapter to learn more about the organisational elements presented and how to tailor them to social entrepreneurial organisations: www.routledge.com/9780367640231

Exercises

Exercise 9.1 – Describing a social entrepreneurial organisation

Pick any example of social entrepreneurial organisation presented so far in the book or in the "additional resources" sections of all chapters on the book's website (www.routledge.com/9780367640231 with book materials). In a small group (in person or remotely) find additional information on them through whatever means you can think of. Then try to build a presentation, in whatever format you prefer, about their:

- Legal form and governance
- Organisational structure
- Leadership and Human Resource Management practices
- Culture

Share your presentation with other groups and then jointly discuss recurring features that you discovered in the different social entrepreneurial organisations you analysed.

Exercise 9.2 – Consulting for a social entrepreneurial organisation

Go back to the marketing strategy you developed in Exercise 8.4 (individually or in groups) and pretend to have been hired also to develop recommendations on how to create an organisation that could deliver that marketing strategy. Create a presentation on the social entrepreneurial organisation you would advise to set up including details on its legal form, governance structures, organisational structure, culture, and Human Resource Management. Make sure to discuss the connections between the different organisational characteristics/how your choice in relation to one characteristic affects the others, and explain why you made each of the recommendations presented. Finally, provide some guidance on how the organisation can adopt an ethical approach.

Exercise 9.3 – Exploring existing approaches to governance, leadership, and Human Resource Management

Identify a social entrepreneurial organisation in your area and interview its founder or managers. Use the interview to discover their view on leadership, who makes what decisions in their organisation, how they include stakeholders' views in decision-making, and their approach to employee and (if applicable) volunteer management. Compare their answers to what you learnt in this chapter and see if you can discover anything new or what the key learning points from the interview are. Then share what you learnt with the rest of the class group and put together all of your insights to build a portrait of how leadership of social entrepreneurial organisations looks like in practice.

Notes

1 Serrano, L., Bose, M., Arenas, D., Berger, G., Márquez, P., Lozano, G., ..., & Fischer, R. M. (2006). *Effective management of social enterprises: Lessons from businesses and civil society organizations in Iberoamerica.* Washington, D.C.: Inter-American Development Bank.
2 Bacq, S., & Eddleston, K. A. (2018). A resource-based view of social entrepreneurship: How stewardship culture benefits scale of social impact. *Journal of Business Ethics, 152*(3), 598.
3 Pasricha, P., & Rao, M. K. (2018). The effect of ethical leadership on employee social innovation tendency in social enterprises: Mediating role of perceived social capital. *Creativity and Innovation Management, 27*(3), 270–280.
4 Pasricha, P., & Rao, M. K. (2018). The effect of ethical leadership on employee social innovation tendency in social enterprises: Mediating role of perceived social capital. *Creativity and Innovation Management, 27*(3), 272.
5 van Dokkum, J. (2018). Shared value creation: The inside story of Pactics in Cambodia. In van der Velden, F. (Ed.), *Towards a fair and just economy,* Voorhaven: LM Publishers.
6 Salamon, L. M., Sokolowski, S. W., & Haddock, M. A. (2011). Measuring the economic value of volunteer work globally: Concepts, estimates, and a roadmap to the future. *Annals of Public and Cooperative Economics, 82*(3), 217–252.
7 Schein, E. H. (1984). Coming to a new awareness of organisational culture. *Sloan Management Review, 25*(2), 3.
8 Social Enterprise World Forum. 2020. *Features – Ethical transparency and accountability.* Retrieved from: https://sewfonline.com/home/social-enterprise/
9 Moore, G. (2005). Corporate character: Modern virtue ethics and the virtuous corporation. *Business Ethics Quarterly, 15*(4), 659–685.

10 Funding and growing social entrepreneurial organisations

Key content

This chapter explores the main options to fund social entrepreneurial organisations and the factors that might make each of these options available or desirable, before providing some insights on how social entrepreneurial organisations can manage their networks, risks, and growth.

10.1   Funding social entrepreneurial organisations
10.2   Managing networks and risks
10.3   Managing growth and scaling impact

Learning objectives

* Appreciate the challenges of funding social entrepreneurial organisations
* Be familiar with the main funding opportunities available for social entrepreneurial organisations and their advantages and limitations
* Learn what affects the funding mix of a social entrepreneurial organisation
* Understand the importance of managing networks and risks
* Consider the challenges and risks associated with organisational growth
* Be aware of the many options available to scale social/environmental impact

10.1 Funding social entrepreneurial organisations

To understand what funding options to pursue, a social entrepreneurial organisation needs to start from its social business model and to reflect on what it implies in terms of resource needs and cash flows. Then it should identify all the potential sources of funding available and check both which ones fit best with its mission and desired impact, and whether they might provide support beyond funds (e.g. reputation, networks, in-kind support, strategic guidance). Options available will be strongly affected by several internal and external factors. Internal factors include the amount needed, the costs to be funded (e.g. overheads vs. project-related), the level of desired engagement of potential funders, networks and related knowledge of existing opportunities, the stage of development of the organisation, and its legal form. External factors include the existence and characteristics of local funders, the sector and country of operation, and the level of development of the relevant social entrepreneurship ecosystem.

DOI: 10.4324/9781003121824-13

10.1.1 *The challenges of funding social entrepreneurial organisations*

There are both demand and supply issues when it comes to funding. In relation to demand, the funding landscape is hard to navigate in both mature and developing ecosystems. There are many funding options but each funder has different requirements, criteria, and types of funding they provide. Additionally, in most contexts, there are no databases of funders and few intermediaries connecting social entrepreneurial organisations with suitable funders. For these reasons, many organisations lack the knowledge and understanding of available opportunities, and their suitability, and waste time and effort doing random, unsuccessful searches.

In relation to supply, existing funding opportunities might not benefit social entrepreneurial organisations. Their generally small scale makes it extremely difficult for funders to identify organisations worthy of support, and funders used to supporting traditional businesses and non-profits might struggle to effectively cater to the needs of social entrepreneurial organisations pursuing a double or triple bottom line. These might be under-competitive and too slow in achieving profitability compared to traditional businesses, and too innovative or profit-oriented for the liking and ethos of traditional donors and grant-makers. For example, according to a report of *Kordant Philanthropy Advisors*,[1] in Asia older donors are often too locally focused and attached to tradition to easily accept funding social entrepreneurship, preferring instead to fund infrastructure projects, such as the building of new schools. Only younger donors have appetite for a broader set of interventions and for innovative projects. On top of that, grants and donations tend to be project-based and thus have limited duration, which clashes with the longer timescales needed for impact, and do not cover overhead costs, which are necessary to attract the right talent and to develop high-quality initiatives that can survive over time. Finally, public authorities might not be able to involve social enterprises in public contracts, despite the willingness of many to do so. Contract sizes are often too large for a single social enterprise, payment terms are too long, and the cost and experience requirements of public tenders favour traditional businesses.

Combined, the barriers in both demand and supply create a missing link between people with resources and people who need them. Even in the United Kingdom, which is believed to have one of the most developed social entrepreneurship and social finance ecosystems in the world, social entrepreneurial organisations lament the lack of funding, and funders complain they do not manage to donate or invest what they have at their disposal. For example, grants tend to come as large bulk sums, so small or young social entrepreneurial organisations cannot apply for them, because they lack the capacity to put those sums to use in the agreed timeframes and/or the confidence and skills to apply for them. This means that while funds are more abundant for "winners", starters may rely only on their personal networks and on crowdfunding to support proof of the validity of their idea before they can access any substantial support. This causes the premature failure of many organisations that might have been successful given the chance.

Funding a social entrepreneurial organisation, especially in its start-up phase, is always one of the biggest challenges that founders face. Organisations that are most successful at attracting funds are those that have clear ideas about what they need and why and, based on that, search for funders extensively and carefully. They perform a due diligence on each potential funder, and focus on those whose values and interests align with theirs, and create targeted approaches for each of them.

10.1.2 *Funding options and their advantages and disadvantages*

Table 10.1 summarises the key forms of funding available for social entrepreneurial organisations. Each of the funding options presented has some advantages and disadvantages and, as the table shows, might be more relevant for certain organisations over others. Therefore, any social entrepreneurial organisation needs to reflect well

Table 10.1 Key funding options for social entrepreneurial organisations

Type of funding	Legal form for which it is available	Ecosystems in which it is available	Stage for which they are available
Awards from competitions	All, but would depend on award-making organisation	Mature and sometimes developing	Initial development
Corporate partnerships	All	All	Well-established organisations
Crowdfunding	All	Potentially all, but mostly mature and developing	Initial development, or projects of small organisations
Earned income/revenues	All	All	All, difficult for early stage
Government funding (grants, payments for supply contracts, subsidies)	All (payments for contracts and subsidies more likely for cooperatives and social enterprises)	Mature and sometimes developing	All. Contracts and subsidies mostly for well-established organisations
Grants from international organisations, foundations, and NGOs	All (but mostly non-profits)	All	All
Investments (impact investment, ESG investment, traditional investments, funds from angel investors)	For-profit and social enterprises	Mostly mature and developing	Well-established organisations (early-stage organisations for angel investment)
Loans (informal – from family, friends, and community – and formal – from financial institutions)	All	All	All, with different funders covering different stages
Microfinance	All, mostly for-profit	Mostly early stage and developing	All, mostly micro-enterprises in the Global South
Philanthropic donations (in cash, in kind, fellowships, grants)	Non-profits	All	All
Social Impact Bonds	All	Mature	Well-established organisations

on what it needs, what is possible, and what is available, before starting to approach funders or incurring in expenses and investments it might not be able to cover.

Awards are normally small sums of money, frequently ranging from USD1,000 to 10,000, that can be obtained through competitions and pitching events, either related to social entrepreneurship or to start-ups and sector-based initiatives. Awards are normally delivered by universities, public bodies, incubators, and intermediary organisations. This form of funding can be very helpful to top up personal funds or to create pilot projects, whose success can open more important and lasting doors, but are unlikely to cover costs for more than a handful of months, so they need to be used strategically with a specific follow-up option in mind.

Corporate partnerships (i.e. agreements between a business/corporation and a social entrepreneurial organisation where both parties remain independent but pool resources and efforts for a specific project) normally become a possibility after the organisation has proven its ability to deliver social or environmental impact and has established a good reputation in its field. They can deliver funds in the form of sponsorship (mostly in the case of non-profit), funding of joint social marketing initiatives or social and environmental programmes, royalties related to licensing agreements (e.g. the corporate pays for using the logo or name of the social entrepreneurial organisation on their products or communication), or the creation of a joint venture. In many cases, a partnership can also deliver access to expertise, know-how, visibility, and equipment, which are forms of indirect funding, especially when the partnership involves the shared development and distribution of new products and services. At the same time, corporate partnerships can represent a potential reputational risk and might create pressures, ultimately leading to mission drift.

Crowdfunding (see Chapter 4) can be an excellent way to raise funds beyond family and friends during the first stages of development of an organisation, when more traditional lenders, donors, and investors might not be available. Additionally, it can provide the organisation with the opportunity to experiment, attract the interest of potential volunteers and employees, and gain visibility and a repayment history that can help it access more significant funding opportunities in the future. When using a crowdfunding platform, founders of social entrepreneurial organisations need to reflect fully on the fit between the platform, its users, and their mission and social business model, on its terms and conditions, on its cost, and on the support it might provide. The main issues with crowdfunding relate to the difficulty of picking the right platform given the many available, the risk of not getting the money if the sum requested is not reached through individual donations/investments before the deadline, and the costs related to fundraising through the platform.

Earned income is probably the key source of funding for many social entrepreneurial organisations, and what distinguishes them from more traditional charities in most contexts. It can be obtained from:

- selling products and services to individual customers and beneficiaries
- becoming suppliers for charities, public bodies, or businesses
- membership or other fees, if the organisation is operating as an intermediary (e.g. helping members to access a market, information, support services) or has franchising and licensing agreements
- participating in large bids for public-service provision or private-led infrastructure projects and events

When revenue-generating activities lead to substantial profit this can enable organi-sational and impact growth that is entirely self-funded, and thus independent from the availability of external support and investments and, most importantly, from the related interference and demands of funders. However, revenues are unlikely to become income in the early stages of an organisation, when costs tend to be proportionally high compared to revenues, and they can also be very volatile and risky, since they depend on market trends, demand, and how much customers and beneficiaries can afford to pay.

Government funding can also take many different forms:

- Grants for social entrepreneurial organisations in their initial phases or that deliver important services of public relevance, disbursed directly or through third parties (e.g. intermediaries that they founded and fund to support social entrepreneurship);
- Payments for contracts, e.g. when social enterprises act as suppliers of public-sector organisations or deliver a public service in lieu of the state;
- Subsidies for the delivery of products and services that beneficiaries cannot afford to pay in full but that are for the public benefit;
- Provision of tax benefits and reduced tax rates.

Government funding can be helpful when private support is unavailable or insuf-ficient, and to establish a reputation that attracts private funds later on. In some European countries, government funding is actually the main funding source for many social enterprises. However, it normally comes with strings attached and, in many contexts, with high uncertainty about payment times.

Other grants available to social entrepreneurial organisations come from interna-tional organisations such as the UN, the European Union, the World Bank, interna-tional development organisations (e.g. USAID), and private foundations. These can normally be accessed by applying to calls for proposals and are a particularly impor-tant source of funding for micro-enterprises, small social enterprises, and non-profits operating in the Global South and in rural settings/hardest-to-reach communities. These grants are of significant variety and jointly cover most of the spectrum of social entrepreneurship activities. However, very large grants (USD1 million or more) might be unreachable for small organisations without the know-how and infrastructure to apply for them, and might be available only for collective bids/projects with many partners. Additionally, grants tend to fund specific projects, programmes, or out-comes and are therefore not enough to sustain the survival of a social entrepreneurial organisation in the long term.

Investments in social entrepreneurial organisations can take many forms, but are mainly delivered as traditional investment; impact investment; Environmental, Social, and Governance (ESG) investments; and angel investments (see Chapter 4). In recent years, another investment opportunity has arisen from Program-Related Investment (PRI) in the United States, where foundations loan money to or invest in social entrepre-neurial organisations instead of making a donation. This way, if all goes well, they get their funds back and can re-invest them in other programmes, and the social entrepre-neurial organisation can improve its credit rating and thus obtain access to more loans and investments also from traditional funding institutions. The type of investment available depends both on the financial returns that the social entrepreneurial organisa-tion can deliver and on the extent to which the investor is willing to sacrifice financial returns in order to support organisations that deliver social and environmental impact.

In any case, investments are available only to organisations incorporated as cooperatives or for-profits, and that can prove their realisation of social and environmental impact. Lengths of investment can vary significantly from a few years to a long-term support (e.g. patient capital, see Chapter 4) and, similarly, the range of interest rates applied or exit strategies varies based on the type of investor and on the type of incorporation adopted by the organisation, as well as on local laws, regulations, and functioning of financial markets. For these reasons, it is important for social entrepreneurial organisations to find and accept investors whose goals and approach are aligned to their mission, social business model, and related needs. The biggest risks related to accessing investments are the influence that investors might exercise on how the organisation is managed, and the consequent reduction of independence, and the risk of mission drift due to pressures related to profitability and growth. Also, as already discussed, social entrepreneurial organisations might find it difficult to access investment opportunities before they are well-established and successful.

Loans are rarely mentioned as a key source of funding but they can be important in the presence of a mismatch between incoming and outgoing cash flows, for the purchase of needed assets before operations start, for growth opportunities, or to start an organisation when earned income, donations, or investments might not be available yet. Social entrepreneurial organisations can obtain loans mostly from family, friends and community, microfinance providers, traditional banks, cooperative banks, credit unions, and banks specialised in impact investing (see Chapter 4). While loans can be helpful in emergencies or when everything else fails, they are obviously problematic because they represent a debt to be repaid, often with non-negligible interest on top. Additionally, they might be hard to get from banks because social entrepreneurial organisations frequently do not have much to offer as collateral, especially if grant-makers do not allow use of their grants in this regard.

Microfinance is a funding option mostly available to and helpful for micro-enterprises in the Global South but has been accessed increasingly by start-ups and micro-enterprises in the Global North. While initially it implied the undertaking of a small loan, now many microfinance providers also offer investment, patient capital, and accelerator programs to promising social enterprises with a clear double- or triple-bottom line. As discussed in Chapter 4, microfinance is fundamental for those without access to traditional credit lines and can represent an important starting point beyond family and friends for many start-ups and individual initiatives. However, it might require the payment of high interest rates, can generate issues with the community (see Chapter 5), and, like traditional loans, can represent a burden that might accelerate failure in times of crisis.

Philanthropic donations can be in cash (e.g. donations, grants, and fellowships) or in-kind (e.g. skills, time and support, equipment) and range from small, individual contributions to large donations from philanthropic organisations and venture philanthropists. Small and individual donations are normally unrestricted and without any specific expectations or constraints, whereas medium to large donations can be either tied to a specific project or funding both project-related and overhead costs, to help the organisation access growth opportunities. Donations have the general benefit of not having to be repaid and of not pushing the organisation towards maximising financial returns given their lack of interest rates, but can put the organisation at risk if they are the only source of funding (since they might disappear after each cycle), and when they do not incentivise the efficient and effective usage of resources. When donations are project- or programme-related they can both generate pressure towards mission drift, forcing the organisation to focus on what donors want rather than on what its own value proposition is, and can push the organisation to minimise over-head costs, given these are not covered, thus jeopardising its structure and future opportunities. Increasingly, philanthropists are being asked to match the need for and desire of social entrepreneurial organisations to generate long-term impact and engage in systems change initiatives (see Chapter 5). This requires providing funds and support over several years, paying for overheads and network-building activities as well as for projects' direct costs, and pooling funds with others to reach a common objective. However, this is still a relatively niche trend and most donations still tend to be tied to a specific organisation and, prevalently, to the realisation of specific projects and programmes.

Social Impact Bonds (SIB) are the financial instrument favouring the pooling of investments for the delivery of a specific socially-oriented outcome (see Chapter 4). They are now present in several countries all over the world (e.g. the United States, Canada, the United Kingdom, the Netherlands, France, Germany, Austria, Swit-zerland, Belgium, Finland, Sweden, Russia, Australia, New Zealand, Israel, South Korea, Japan, Argentina, Portugal, Colombia, and Peru). Given that SIB tie the fund-ing agreement to the realisation of a pre-set, normally quite ambitious outcome, they privilege service providers who are innovative and impact-driven and, in this sense, are ideal to sustain social entrepreneurial organisations such as social enterprises or innovative non-profits. They can be helpful to obtain enough funds to scale up, to find the incentives to focus on outcomes rather than activities, thus improving the impact realised, and to generate proof of the ability to deliver as a way to attract further investment, since the achievement of the agreed outcomes is normally verified and certified by an independent auditor. They are also a guarantee for the organisation winning the contract as service provider to receive substantial funding, normally for several years. At the same time, they are only available to organisations with a proven track record and enough resources to serve a high number of beneficiaries, might not be well advertised and thus known as an available opportunity, and, while already present in several countries, are still not available for the majority of contexts in which social entrepreneurship exists and for the issues it tackles.

10.1.3 Finding the right funding mix

In the early stages of any social entrepreneurial organisation, it is likely that most funds will come from the personal savings of the entrepreneur, loans from family and friends, crowdfunding, microfinance providers, awards/competitions, and, in most successful cases, from government or philanthropic grants. Crowdfunding, awards, and grants should be pursued not only for the money they might bring but also for their benefits in terms of reputation and related future opportunities. In some African countries, com-munities are also a frequently used source of funding. Groups of people contribute an agreed amount to a shared fund. This fund can be given as a lump sum to any member of the community who needs it, and, as such, can be used by entrepreneurial members of the community to set up a social entrepreneurial organisation. The loan is informal and normally requires its repayment to the community, without interest.

However, all of these funding options are generally not sustainable and, when used extensively in the first phases, require social entrepreneurial organisations to spend significant time and effort to transition as soon as possible to alternative sources. As the organisation starts to prove its value and impact, other opportunities such as large donations, investments (impact, traditional, and angel investment), participation into large bids, contracts and involvement in partnerships become available, depending on the legal form the organisation adopted (see Chapters 3 and 9). Table 10.2 summarises the most frequent funding options used by social entrepreneurial organisations based on their business model and legal form.

One important aspect to consider when choosing what type of funding to go for is how much the funder might end up shaping what the organisation is doing. Both investments and philanthropic donations can entitle the funder to exercise voting rights as board member or to have a say in how an organisation conducts operations, what projects it can undertake, how it can spend the funds, or how it should measure and report its impact. Grants and investments also risk coming with many conditions attached, which might limit the freedom and choices of the social entrepreneurial organisation the more they are dependent on that funding. In some cases related to social enterprises incorporated as limited shares companies or similar, private investment, e.g. in the form of stocks, might also complicate matters later on if the shares can be sold without constraints, since that might bring a change in ownership that might result in a higher risk of mission drift.

Table 10.2 Spectrum of most common funding options used by social entrepreneurial organisations

Social entrepreneurial organisation	*Innovative non-profit*	*Non-profit earning income*	*Social enterprise*	*For-profit business with social or environmental impact*
Legal form	Non-profit	Non-profit	Any	For-profit/cooperative
Funding mix	Highly dependent on grants and donations	Mostly dependent on grants and donations but with some earned income	Significant proportion of earned income (30–75% of mix)	Full financial sustainability through earned income
Common sources of funding	Donations, grants, partnerships, loans	Donations, grants, earned income (from sales, membership or programme fees, rent of assets), partnerships, loans	Depending on legal form, but frequently grants, earned income, investments. Additional options: loans, participation in large public bids, partnerships	Earned income (from sales, fees, and contracts, rent of assets, etc.), investments, loans, participation in large public bids, partnerships
Risks	Excessive dependence on donors and grants	Moderate dependence on donors and grants, loss of earned income due to market failure	Market failure, difficulty of finding appropriate funding sources beyond revenues due to double or triple bottom line, mission drift	Market failure, mission drift

According to the work of Boschee (1998),[2] financial sustainability can be achieved if there is a diversification of funding sources, a proactive search and attraction of new funds, and the creation of some slack funds. Having a funding mix is helpful mainly to reduce dependency on a specific funder or form of funding, and therefore the risk of failing if the funding disappears. For example, the products and services a social enterprise sells might suddenly be not in demand or profitable anymore due to sudden changes in markets or unexpected shocks like a pandemic, and this might cause its failure if earned income is its main source of funding. Similarly, grants and donations may be stopped or not renewed if decision-makers decide not to support the social entrepreneurial organisation and its activities any more, and this might cause its closure if that grant or donation was its main source of funding.

Having a mix of funding streams can also help to (a) address issues of cash flows, by ensuring that enough cash is available whenever needed, independently of funding cycles, (b) create more opportunities for future growth and for remaining connected to different networks, and (c) enable the accessing of information and feedback from diverse stakeholders.

Ideally, the funding mix should help to find the right balance between both:

a   reducing dependency on specific sources of funding and minimising transaction costs (e.g. cost of finding new funders and information about them, of negotiating support, of adhering to new reporting requests);
b   covering all costs (both overheads and project- or activity-related) and maintaining some independence to pursue opportunities as the organisation sees fit without external interference.

Additionally, the funding mix should allow the organisation's leaders to not spend most of their time looking for funds and should ideally reflect the added value that different stakeholders obtain from the organisation. For example, if a social entrepreneurial organisation delivers a service normally delivered by public authorities (e.g. schooling, care of the elderly), it should be supported, at least in part, by public grants or other forms of public funding. Similarly, if an organisation is improving agricultural productivity in rural Africa, it should receive donations and support from the World Food Programme or from international NGOs whose mission is to reduce hunger in the Global South. When this is not the case, there might be untapped opportunities for both funding and engagement. Whenever an organisation manages to get the right funding mix to realise and deliver its value proposition, it can survive and eventually encounter growth opportunities.

THE FUNDING MIX IN PRACTICE

Listen to the testimonies of different leaders of social entrepreneurial organisations on the funding mix they chose for their organisation. To access the testimonies use the links on the book's website (www.routledge.com/9780367640231), in the Chapter 10 section.

10.2 Managing networks and risks

Social entrepreneurial organisations that thrive typically manage two key areas on top of strategy, operations (see Chapters 8 and 9), and funding (see Section 10.1): networks and risks. A lot could be said about these and about the managerial and impact-related challenges that emerge once a social entrepreneurial organisation is established, as well as on key success factors. While a full in-depth discussion of these topics would be beyond the scope of this book, the next section presents some brief highlights about best practice in relation to networks and risk management.

10.2.1 Managing networks

Many studies have confirmed the importance of both formal and informal networks throughout the entire life cycle of a social entrepreneurial organisation. Networks provide necessary resources, knowledge, and skills, especially when the organisation cannot afford to own them, as well as reputation and legitimacy, which are fundamental for survival and growth. The contacts of the organisation can bring knowledge about new opportunities available, connect it with additional funders and supporters, and provide advice on how to proceed whenever the organisation does not have relevant experience or needs formal approvals. Additionally, as seen in Chapter 8, networks of partners and suppliers can be a fundamental component of the social business model and of the delivery of the value proposition. According to the study of Sharir and Lerner (2006),[3] four out of eight common success factors for social enterprises can be related to their networks, namely: their social network and related social capital; the capital and staff they have available to get established and grow; their long-term cooperation with other organisations; their acceptance in the public discourse.

Helpful ways to manage networks can be divided into two categories: activities that expand the network, and activities that strengthen relationships with existing contacts. Based on the work of Granovetter (1973),[4] both new or superficial relationships and strong relationships can support the creation of social capital. The expectation is that new or superficial relationships will be more helpful for a social entrepreneurial organisation to become aware of opportunities for change and growth, while established or strong relationships will be more helpful to feel a sense of belonging, mobilise joint efforts, and obtain the necessary resources and support.

Activities that expand the network include: joining the membership of intermediary organisations active in the social entrepreneurship ecosystem, of trade organisations, and of communities that share the same interest or involvement in a social or environmental issue; being proactive on social media; attending industry events or events related to social entrepreneurship; talking about the organisation and its impact at any informal networking opportunity. Activities that strengthen relationships include instead: creating within the organisation duties and roles associated with partnership management, establishing a culture supportive of stakeholders' engagement (see Chapter 9), communicating frequently and openly with all key partners and external stakeholders. In general, maintaining listening skills and attention to others, engaging stakeholders, and continuing to promote the organisation in different circles will support its survival and success. Even networks, however, are not always enough to manage the risks (i.e. the possibility of loss or other adverse or unwelcome circumstance) that will affect a social entrepreneurial organisation throughout its existence.

10.2.2 Managing risks

For any social entrepreneurial organisation, the main risk is that of failure both as an organisation and in realising its mission/the desired impact. According to Bornstein and Davis (2010),[5] there are four main reasons why social entrepreneurial organisations fail: poor talent cultivation, issues with resource acquisition, challenges in measuring impact, and inability to develop the necessary cross-sector collaborations. Additionally, there might be a mismatch between internal organisational components (e.g. culture, strategy, Human Resource Management) or between them and the social business model, as well as poor planning of governance, strategy, and operations, both at the start and in the growth phases of the organisation. As explained in previous chapters and sections, social entrepreneurial organisations can also suffer from the excessive ego of their founder(s), their dependency on a single source of funding, their poor knowledge or leverage of marketing, or might fail because they address the symptoms and not the causes of a social or environmental issue.

For organisations that operate in markets and earn income, failure can also arise from the inability to transform revenues into profits in the long term, to meet market demands or purchasing power, to the lack of slack resources and funds to deal with unexpected crises, or to a rise in competition. That said, paradoxically, in some cases, failing might actually be a form of "success" for social entrepreneurial organisations, whenever they have no more reason to exist because the social or environmental issue that they wanted to address ends up being tackled and solved. This, however, is relatively rare.

As seen in Chapter 3, another key risk is that of mission drift and of being seen as "making money off the poor and needy" or "ignoring those who cannot afford to pay or are too hard to reach". Social entrepreneurial organisations also face risks related to changes in any of the PESTEL components (see Chapter 6). These might reduce the effectiveness and appeal of the organisation's value proposition or the validity of its resources, systems, and processes given altered external requirements. Other risks involve the inability of the organisation to keep up with growth opportunities or demand, and to protect its reputation. As the organisation moves from being an informal entity to being fully structured, and when it attempts to scale its impact and operations, the required business and operational skills also change and the organisation might not recognise the need to adapt or adapt fast enough. Going back to the risk of failure, in some cases, it is the fear of failing that actually hampers the chances of success because it prevents an organisation from taking advantage of potential opportunities.

Risks evolve along with the organisation and its environment, so in order to manage and mitigate them, it is important for a social entrepreneurial organisation to assess periodically the issues that it might encounter, and the changes that are happening or likely to happen in its environment. Risk assessment is actually also an important opportunity for organisational learning. In addition to monitoring risks, an organisation should also always try to have some slack or buffer resources to mitigate risks that will inevitably occur.

There are two tools that are increasingly used to assess and manage risk: scenario planning and the risk register. Scenarios are "alternate futures in which today's decisions may play out".[6] Scenario planning therefore consists of estimating how the future might look like based on research, assumptions, and conversations with multiple stakeholders, and building three to five likely futures. The different futures should be constructed by combining possible states of key environmental and internal variables and reflecting on their possible interactions. Then the organisation should assess the consequences of these different combinations of variables (i.e. scenarios) on its activities and impact (for details on how to conduct scenario planning check out Links 10.1 in the book's website (www.routledge.com/9780367640231). Scenario planning draws attention to multiple future events that might happen and their individual and joint effects on the organisation, thus helping its successful delivery of the value proposition. However, building scenarios is a relatively complex process, which takes several months and iterations to be done properly and risks being used in a superficial, and thus not very helpful, way if the organisation does not have the skills and time to work on it.

The risk register, instead, is a relatively straightforward planning tool where the organisation records key risks, their nature, probability, expected impact, measures it might put in place to mitigate them, and who is responsible for monitoring their occurrence and prompting action when needed. It can be realised in table format or also as a matrix, where risks are assigned different colours based on their probability and impact (for details on how to create a risk register, check out Links 10.2 in the book's website: www.routledge.com/9780367640231). The risk register's main advantages are that it is intuitive, easy to build and update, and a tool that allows easy visualisation of what the main risks are and what to do if one of them passes from being a risk to being an actual negative occurrence. However, unlike scenario planning, it does not allow understanding of how risks might interact and generate compounded effects, and it might lose helpfulness and validity if it is not checked and updated regularly. This is highly possible unless the organisation assigns specific risk management tasks to one or more of its employees.

Beyond risks, social entrepreneurial organisations also need to manage growth opportunities with care. In most countries for which data exists, social entrepreneurial organisations tend to be micro-enterprises or small and medium organisations. This highlights the difficulties that social entrepreneurial organisations encounter in relation to growth. If anything starts going wrong, it is all too easy to quickly lose the trust of external stakeholders, which might not only bring the scaling project to a halt but also jeopardise the very survival of the organisation.

10.3 Managing growth and scaling impact

Most social entrepreneurial organisations that survive and succeed eventually feel pressure to grow. This is natural considering that one of their key characteristics is the pursuit of a social/environmental mission and that, therefore, any opportunity to grow represents an opportunity to help more. Growth opportunities may arise from the chance to better help existing beneficiaries/customers, from growing customer demand, from expansion in different locations, or from the opportunity to reach economies of scale (sharing costs between different activities). Some growth opportunities relate to the organisation and its operations, while others relate to the impact it generates. Either way, growth might not be desirable for all since some social entrepreneurial organisations might have originated from the need to help a specific community and a deep knowledge of and engagement with that community, and might be fulfilling their mission as they are.

Organisational growth can happen through various means:

1   Scaling up operations (reaching out to new customers/beneficiaries by expanding the size of the organisation and the amount of what it delivers);
2   Branching (creating new fully-owned organisations in other locations);
3   Franchising (allowing others to replicate the organisation and its delivery model in other locations, adhering to pre-determined standards and processes).

In either case, it presents many recurring issues and generates important risks, summarised in Table 10.3.

Additionally, there might be constraints to organisational growth due to the state of development of the local social entrepreneurship ecosystem (see Chapter 4). In mature ecosystems, extensive competition for the same kind of impact can render growth difficult, especially since funders might not be able to identify and support the best performer. In developing ecosystems, the recurring barriers to growth are many: lack of access to sufficient funding (especially in terms of commercial finance), networks, and business development support; regulatory barriers; lack of technical and

Table 10.3 Issues and risks associated with organisational growth

Main issues	*Main risks*
Understanding how costs will grow as operations and impact expand to avoid the risk of remaining without funds	Losing touch with the original beneficiaries and/or customers, which, in turn, might reduce the effectiveness of the organisation in achieving its mission
Identifying the key assets that will enable growth, (e.g. employees, infrastructure, digital tools, reputation) and nurturing or acquiring them	Worsening the existing value proposition or its delivery due to the need to combine ongoing operations with the activities necessary for growth
The need to create or expand: business support functions, such as accounting and finance; logistics; coherent branding across products or locations; processes	Not being able to replicate across beneficiaries, communities, geographical locations, etc. the original social business model, due to the different context
The need for leaders who can push for growth by motivating employees, promoting the organisation and its success to attract additional resources, and accepting the need to delegate as operations expand	Not having the right relationships or partners that can support and sustain growth. The more the organisation might have limited resources to scale, the more fundamental those of its network are going to be
Having or obtaining the right management and organisational skills (e.g. planning, having a good understanding of cash flows, ability to attract substantial funding and new talent) to handle the increasing complexity of operations and of coordinating efforts	The risk of mission drift due to the need of funds for growth, which might create pressures for the organisation to become more profitable, cut costs, or accept more demands from existing or new donors and investors
Handling the different views about growth plans of board members	

managerial skills in rural areas. In early stage ecosystems, growth might be hampered by the lack of access to funds beyond microfinance, little availability of information on and connection to new potential customers, and the fight for survival taking over any opportunity for thinking beyond the immediate. This does not imply that organisational growth is always going to be a problem or that it should not be attempted. It merely signals that it should be enacted in a more strategic way than many social entrepreneurial organisations have done up to now.

Many leaders of social entrepreneurial organisations also believe that in order to grow their impact, they have to pursue organisational growth. However, scaling impact can be achieved in many different ways. For example, social entrepreneurial organisations can enhance their impact on existing beneficiaries/customers, offering them more or better products, services, or benefits and generating deeper and more lasting change for them. In addition, they can scale impact through partnerships and strategic alliances with other organisations of any nature and sector. These can help to share costs, increase purchasing power in relation to suppliers, pool resources and expertise, and meet growing demand without the partners having to grow their operations proportionally. At the same time, partnerships are difficult to manage. To work well they require careful planning, the establishment of clear roles, contributions and expectations, sharing of the same goals and values, bringing complementary expertise and resources or additional funds, and the proactive management of the partnership as it unfolds. Alternatively, organisations can invest in research, communication, and social marketing, as ways to alter people's behaviours and beliefs at scale; disseminate knowledge on how they operate to allow others to replicate or adapt what they did to other contexts; or, most importantly, engage in lobbying and in collective action, through the generation or joining of social movements (see Chapter 2) and of systems change initiatives (see Chapter 5).

An organisation should also adopt a flexible approach to growth, accepting that sometimes it might be more helpful to stand still or even scale down if that represents the best course of action given the external environment, stakeholders' expectations and demands, and the resources available in terms of funds, time, and skills at that specific time. In some cases, scaling impact requires the organisation to specialise, focusing on what it does best and letting go of some of its impact-creating products or services where competing initiatives perform better.

To summarise, whenever taking a decision in relation to growth or scaling impact, any social entrepreneurial organisation should reflect on what course of action will maximise the impact it can deliver based on:

- what it has at disposal/can access through its networks;
- its mission, Theory of Change, and social business model;
- what helps it find the right balance between growing versus maintaining the quality and impact it already delivers;
- environmental factors.

Most importantly, no growth should be attempted without a clear understanding of the impact already created, since that would risk amplifying the negative impact that might be occurring or not leveraging existing strengths, putting the future of the organisation and of its main beneficiaries on shaky grounds. The final chapter will therefore discuss the many options available to measure impact.

MANAGING GROWTH AND SCALING IMPACT IN PRACTICE

Here below is an extract of the interview I did to Goya Gallagher, one of the co-founders of *Malaika* (see Chapter 3), where she discusses how *Malaika* has both grown its operations and its impact.

How are you keeping expanding your impact and operations?

Given our early success, in 2018 we realised we could aim higher. We rented two more apartments in Cairo to teach embroidery to even more Egyptian women and also to refugee women from all over Africa and the Middle East, left behind in Cairo from husbands that left for Europe or died. A lot of our trainees are now from Syria, Palestine, Sudan, and Ethiopia. We train women and guarantee them work. Training is free and on top of that we recently decided to support women by also offering them lunch and nursery services. The training lasts for two months and then they can work from home, as much or little as they want, and get paid accordingly. Demand was still well beyond what we could offer however. So we created *Threads of Hope*, a spin-off of *Malaika*. With *Threads of Hope* we can produce for other brands too, thus expanding training and work opportunities well beyond *Malaika*. And *Malaika* has been growing too.

Since 2020, we started selling online to reach foreign markets as well as Egypt. Someone that I met from an industry magazine that is very well respected in interior design community wanted to do an issue dedicated to Egypt, and someone told them about *Malaika*. I brought them to Egypt so they could work on the special issue and they suggested me to do a small collection for the magazine and that is how our international presence started. They gave us a window to the international market and forced us to re-organise to cater for it. Before this experience, we didn't even know some of the requirements of international customers. We have been learning all the time and had to frequently re-adjust to keep up with what has been happening and take advantage of opportunities. For example, *Instagram* has recently become a huge marketing and sales channel for the home accessory industry, because it gives easy, cheap access to customers from all over the world. So I took a five-day course on social media in London. Based on what I learnt, we deleted all the marketing materials we had and started from scratch to improve our branding and online presence. This experience forced us to write up who we are, what we are about, what we want, and how we want to portray ourselves. We just launched a new collection through *Instagram*, sending a message including our catalogue to all the shops that we liked and we had an incredibly good response. Basically, opportunities arose around us and we took them, doing our best to succeed.

Now we sell in the United States and in Europe, using various websites and also local shops. We started selling in five shops abroad and this had a snowball effect. We recently got contacted by a website in the US selling home-related products that has a section where they highlight products with sustainable characteristics. We made a partnership with them and have been launching our whole collection there. This opened a lot of doors that we are now exploring. The more we become known abroad, the more we get new leads.

How are you funding *Malaika* now that it is growing?

We still have no external funders. *Threads of Hope*, the company we just incorporated to be able to expand our training services, is a for-profit business like *Malaika*, because in Egypt it is not possible to open NGOs right now. This means both companies are cut off from grants. Luckily the brand has grown a lot in these years and, until now, we managed to sustain all operations and fund growth through revenues and profits. Having to rely on revenues is an important incentive to keep growing because no growth means no resources for training. This reliance on revenues is basically why we recently spun off the training arm through *Threads of Hope*. We hope that it can become a supplier for other companies, thus creating growth and revenues, and thus training opportunities, beyond the ones *Malaika* can offer. This was our way to fund something that normally would be funded through grants.

How do you keep the balance between the two elements of your double bottom line – the growth of both your business and your social impact?

Now we are recruiting other companies to become the customers of *Threads of Hope*. And we want to attract more customers globally for *Malaika*, leveraging the fact Egypt is close to Europe and cheaper. Expanding our business creates the foundations to expand our impact. This is why we are also interested in expanding in other places, maybe through replication or through organic scaling.

Thanks to our growth, we have literacy classes in our factory. All managers are women who started off learning embroidery. We always made efforts not to hire from the outside but to give people a career trajectory within the company. With *Threads of Hope* the best thing is that it has enabled us to help women refugees from many countries. Embroidery is therapeutic. Women can share experiences in a safe place around a table while doing embroidery. We now want to support them even more, bringing in therapists to offer a better mental health service and providing them with more guidance about where to go next in life.

What were the most difficult decisions you had to make in relation to *Malaika*?

Actually, the most difficult decision is the one we are facing now – how to move forward. It was difficult to create *Threads of Hope* as a separate company because training was very ingrained in what we did at *Malaika*. We knew we had to do this to expand our potential to generate social impact but, at the same time, we were worried about *Malaika* as a brand losing its social impact side. So now it is tough to make sure our brand doesn't lose identity while we pursue growth outside of its boundaries through *Threads of Hope*. We never made a business plan in our life. We never took a loan. It has been a slow learning process and I am not sure how replicable it all is. It took us seven years to make money. We could have a salary and pay for expenses but were not profitable. In the past eight years, we instead increased profits every year. So it works but we needed a lot of patience and it is hard to tell what will happen next.

SUMMARY BOX

- Funding a social entrepreneurial organisation is generally challenging, particularly in the early stages. In most ecosystems there are both demand-side and supply-side issues that hamper fruitful connections between social entrepreneurial organisations and funders. In particular, in most ecosystems the funding landscape is hard to navigate, funders do not always understand and appreciate the specificities of social entrepreneurial organisations, and there is a mismatch between needs and the type of funding available.
- To understand what funding options to pursue it is important to start from the social business model and to reflect what it implies in terms of resource needs and cash flows. Then it is necessary to identify all the potential sources of funding available, analyse which ones fit best with the organisation and its mission, and develop tailored funding requests for each funder that is considered desirable.
- Funding options available will be strongly affected by the amount needed, the costs to be funded (e.g. overheads vs. project-related), the level of desired engagement of potential funders, the knowledge of existing opportunities, the stage of development and legal form of the organisation, the sector and country of operation, and level of development of the relevant social entrepreneurship ecosystem.
- Typical funding options for social entrepreneurial organisations include: awards from competitions; corporate partnerships; crowdfunding; earned income; government funding; grants; investments; loans; microfinance; philanthropic donations; SIBs. In addition, in the early stages, any organisation is likely to get funded from family and friends or from the local community.
- The funding mix should help to find the right balance between (a) reducing dependency on specific sources of income and minimising transaction costs, and (b) covering all costs and maintaining some independence to pursue opportunities as the organisation sees fit without external interference. Additionally, the funding mix should reflect the value that different stakeholders receive, and reduce the likelihood that organisational leaders will spend most of their time fundraising.
- Managing networks effectively requires a combination of creating new contacts and nurturing existing ones. New contacts can help to spot opportunities while existing ones create a sense of belonging and are more likely to deliver needed resources and support.
- A social entrepreneurial organisation faces many risks as it operates and grows. Recurring ones are the risk of failure, that of mission drift, those related to changes in PESTEL conditions, and organisational growth. Helpful tools to manage risks are scenario planning and the risk register, while a way to mitigate the consequences of risks after they have occurred is to have some slack resources.
- Organisational growth creates several issues and risks, and thus should be pursued strategically, considering it is not the only way to scale impact. This can also happen by serving better existing beneficiaries; by sharing knowledge; and by engaging in partnerships, strategic alliances, and collective action.

Check box – Self-reflection and discussion questions

- Why is it difficult to fund a social entrepreneurial organisation?
- What are the main internal and external factors affecting the funding mix a social entrepreneurial organisation can access?
- What constitutes best practice in fundraising?
- What are the main funding options for social entrepreneurial organisations?
- What are the benefits and limitations of each of them?
- What are the characteristics of a good funding mix?
- Why is it important to manage networks and risks?
- What are common practices that social entrepreneurial organisations can undertake to manage their networks?
- What does "risk management" mean?
- What are the main challenges and risks related to organisational growth?
- What is the difference between scaling up and scaling impact?
- What are the different ways to scale impact and what are the benefits and limitations of each of them?

Check out the "Additional resources" related to this chapter to learn more about the funding options and tools presented: www.routledge.com/9780367640231 with book materials.

Exercises

Exercise 10.1 – Suggesting a funding mix

Continue (individually or as a group) your consulting work for the hypothetical organisation you supported in Exercises 8.4 and 9.2 and help it devise its funding mix, both for its early stages and for the next four to five years. In particular, make sure to cover:

1   What funding options you suggest in its first year and from the second or third year, and why
2   What funders are the more likely providers of the funding options you suggest (check out what funders/funding options are available in the context where the organisation would operate)
3   Potential amounts that you would encourage asking to each funder (use the social business model/marketing insights, etc. to develop some estimates of what costs the organisation might incur)
4   What to focus on when approaching different funders
5   How the overall initial fundraising campaign would look like

Share your consulting report with the rest of the class/group and ask for feedback.

Exercise 10.2 – Building a risk register

Use one of the case studies presented in the book and build a baseline risk register for them based on the information you have. Alternatively, think about a project you are working on right now and create a risk register for that.

Exercise 10.3 – Exploring the risks of growth

Find information about *Aspire Group* in the United Kingdom and their failed organisational growth (a good starting point is the paper of Tracey and Jarvis (2007, pp. 673–682)), which you can access through the link on the book's website in the Exercises section (www.routledge.com/9780367640231 with book materials). What happened? What worked and what did not? What can this teach to other entrepreneurial organisations in terms of managing their growth?

Exercise 10.4 – Scaling impact

Identify a social entrepreneurial organisation active in your own area or think about a social entrepreneurial organisation that you admire and that you analysed as part of the exercises in the first part of the book. Think about how you would scale its impact and prepare a short report describing your plan. In particular specify why you are suggesting something, the risks that you foresee, and how it would look like to implement your plan (e.g. what resources would be needed, how they could be obtained, what changes in organisation would be required).

Share your plan with the rest of the class and compare it with the other plans presented.

1   What are the most common proposals for scaling impact?
2   Why do you think that is the case?
3   Would you alter your plan after having heard or seen what others would do?
4   Is there something important you had not thought about?

Notes

1   Kordant Philanthropy Advisors. (2014). *Social enterprises in Asia: An introductory guide.* Research report, 110. Retrieved from: https://www.issuelab.org/resources/18117/18117.pdf
2   Boschee, J. (1998). *Merging mission and money: A board member's guide to social entrepreneurship*. Washington, DC: National Center for Nonprofit Council.
3   Sharir, M., & Lerner, M. (2006). Gauging the success of social ventures initiated by individual social entrepreneurs. *Journal of World Business*, 41(1), 6–20.
4   Granovetter, M. S. (1973). The strength of weak ties. *American Journal of Sociology*, 78(6), 1360–1380.
5   Bornstein, D., & Davis, S. (2010). *Social entrepreneurship: What everyone needs to know®*. Oxford: Oxford University Press.
6   Ogilvy, J. (2015). Scenario planning and strategic forecasting. *Forbes*. Retrieved from: https://www.forbes.com/sites/stratfor/2015/01/08/scenario-planning-and-strategic-forecasting/

11 Measuring impact

Key content

This chapter discusses the many reasons why social entrepreneurial organisations should measure their impact, as well as the main challenges that measuring impact entails. It also presents the most popular approaches for impact measurement and provides some guidance on how to set up an impact measurement system and to report impact.

11.1 The what and why of impact measurement
11.2 The challenges of impact measurement for social entrepreneurial organisations
11.3 The main approaches to measure impact
11.4 Understanding what to measure
11.5 Impact reporting

Learning objectives

- Understand the meaning and importance of impact measurement
- Become aware of the challenges of impact measurement
- Familiarise yourself with the most popular approaches for impact measurement
- Reflect on how to select the right metrics and to set up an impact measurement system
- Appreciate the complexities of impact reporting

11.1 The what and why of impact measurement

In Chapter 2, we defined social impact as the improvement of the livelihoods and prospects of individuals, organisations, or of entire communities through purposeful action. In the context of impact measurement, the definition of impact goes beyond just social impact. When considering their own impact, social entrepreneurial organisations need to account for different things:

1 Social, economic, and environmental impact
2 Both intended and unintended impact
3 Both positive and negative impact
4 Both short- and long-term impact

DOI: 10.4324/9781003121824-14

For this reason, starting from the definition of social impact assessment provided by Verner in 2003[1] and by Clark et al. in 2004,[2] in this chapter impact measurement is defined as the processes of analysing and monitoring the intended and unintended social, environmental, and economic consequences, both positive and negative, short- and long term, of an organisation and of any change process triggered by that organisation that would not have happened otherwise. Impact measurement, broadly speaking, is based on a retrospective evaluation of the various results achieved by an individual or organisation, starting from their original objectives.

Measuring impact helps an organisation to improve and learn in many different ways:

- It enables understanding how a social entrepreneurial organisation is performing, and assessing whether it is creating its intended impact. This allows the organisation to spot opportunities for growth and improvement, and to enhance its chances of survival through a deeper and timely understanding of its level of effectiveness, and thus through prompt adjustments in case results are not as expected.
- It helps an organisation to properly grasp what kind of changes are occurring in stakeholders' lives or in the environment due to the delivery of its value proposition.
- It enables the evaluation of the validity of the Theory of Change (ToC) and to update it as things evolve.
- It helps to reveal the unintended impact (both positive and negative) generated and thus additional opportunities to increase impact or minimise damage, while still delivering the desired impact.
- It encourages the commitment of an organisation to outcomes and results rather than to activities and procedures.
- It fosters an organisational culture of learning and improvement and, when affirming the realisation of positive impact, can be a strong motivator for employees, increasing their trust in the organisation and encouraging them to keep going the extra mile for it.

Additionally, measuring impact is also fundamental in relation to external stakeholders. Knowing what is going on and communicating it helps to attract the support of stakeholders and to develop strategies and future plans with them. Investors, public authorities, and, increasingly, philanthropists are rarely willing to fund organisations that cannot prove their effectiveness in reaching the outcomes and impact they promised. Many funders and public authorities are themselves required by their own stakeholders to prove the impact of what they decided to support. Therefore, they need to make sure that those they support have a way of confirming what they have achieved. Funders' reliance on impact measurement to assess the credibility of an organisation also means that the reception of funds and support frequently comes with an explicit request to measure impact, either through tailored metrics agreed between the organisation and its funder, or through a standardised approach that the funder has developed or adopted. Broadly speaking, measuring impact is helpful for marketing purposes, for legitimising an organisation and its work, and for confirming the identity of an organisation as a social entrepreneurial organisation by proving its social, environmental, and economic results.

11.2 The challenges of impact measurement for social entrepreneurial organisations

Despite all the benefits of impact measurement, it remains a relatively unestablished practice within social entrepreneurship ecosystems. This is explained by the numerous and significant challenges of conducting systematic, frequent, and meaningful impact measurement. These challenges can be grouped into four main categories: the lack of a universal approach, the intrinsic characteristics of outcomes and impact, the knowledge and technical skills needed, and the costs of measuring impact.

One of the recurring challenges with impact measurement is the lack of a standard approach by which to do it. While many organisations advocate for the need of a universal measurement system, this has not been established yet, for several reasons that are likely to hamper its creation for some more time to come:

1   Each social entrepreneurial organisation has specific ways of generating impact and different forms of impact, so it is difficult to establish a one-size-fits-all metric or impact measurement approach that different organisations can easily apply.
2   Many of the most popular approaches for measuring impact have been created by various funders for their own purposes. This makes some approaches inaccessible for those who are not funded by them and it also means that organisations with multiple funders end up combining multiple approaches.
3   Some EU countries, such as Belgium and Italy, have developed specific reporting requirements for social enterprises that incorporate as such through tailor-made legal forms (see Chapter 3) but, in most countries, reporting is voluntary or funder-driven and there are no fixed templates or benchmarks that social entrepreneurial organisations can use. This encourages organisations to either not measure impact or to develop their own approach.
4   Most approaches for measuring impact are relatively new and thus not well-established.

The lack of a standard approach for impact measurement not only makes it a complex task for social entrepreneurial organisations, but also creates issues for funders. It reduces the comparability between different organisations, and thus the possibility to easily establish which ones are most worthy of support, and makes it difficult to grasp at a glance how a social entrepreneurial organisation is actually performing and whether its methodology is robust and trustworthy, even when it reports its impact.

Outcomes and impact have several characteristics that make them difficult to measure: they are often intangible; they are subjective (i.e. each stakeholder perceives the value received by an organisation differently); sometimes they are unexpected; they happen over various time horizons. Moreover, measuring impact requires the ability to understand the causal link between inputs, outputs, and outcomes, as discussed in Chapter 7. This is hard to establish due to the number of internal and external factors that contribute to a certain outcome or impact and to the difficulty in understanding what exactly constitutes an output or outcome to be measured and how best to measure it. Given all of the above, measuring impact can require a relatively long time horizon with frequent data collection points, the cooperation of stakeholders in sharing information about the benefits (and potential damage) they are deriving from an organisation, the understanding of who key informants should be and of what needs to be measured at what level (e.g. individual, group, social, country, etc.). Each of these conditions is not always easy or possible to respect.

Impact measurement is difficult, and requires technical skills to be done properly. Thus, it is prone to errors and blind spots. Skills for measuring impact are skills that only sometimes overlap with those employees of social entrepreneurial organisations have. For example, listening skills, empathy, and ability to engage stakeholders might already be part of the organisation's capabilities, but the knowledge of techniques for quantitative and qualitative data analysis might not be as readily available, given this is normally not necessary for delivering a value proposition. Lacking the right skills might increase the probability that, even in the presence of impact data, the organisation might not know how best to interpret and act upon it. Sometimes the issue is even deeper, especially in the absence of a ToC, and relates to the non-understanding of what actually needs to be measured. Many social entrepreneurial organisations tend not to have a formal social mission statement, or have a very broad one – such as "protecting nature" or "delivering appropriate healthcare to those in need". This makes it difficult to think in concrete terms about what they are aiming to achieve and, thus, what they should keep track of.

Finally, due to the technical difficulties and the need to capture different forms of impact, across multiple stakeholders and time horizons, impact measurement is resource intensive and, for this reason, it can be costly and detract resources from the actual realisation of impact. Funders, while demanding proof of impact, rarely fund impact measurement and social entrepreneurial organisations rarely have excess resources and time to invest in this activity. For this reason, they tend to either skip impact measurement or carry it out in the easiest and cheapest way possible, rather than taking more effective and meaningful approaches.

11.3 The main approaches to measure impact

Ideally, measuring the impact of any organisation would require a Randomised Controlled Trial (RCT) – aka the comparison of two comparable groups, one benefiting from the work and presence of the organisation and one not, in order to isolate the effects produced by that organisation beyond other interventions and context-related events. This, however, is hardly ever possible, since it is a complex methodology that normally requires collaborating with a team of professional researchers to be conducted, and that it is long and costly to set up. Thus, it is unlikely to be an option for the vast majority of social entrepreneurial organisations. On top of this, RCTs are likely limited to measuring a set of pre-specified impact measures, which might not capture what is actually happening, and always carry the risk of being unethical. That is because, to have a control group, it is necessary to select a set of potential beneficiaries who will not be given support, at least for some time, purely to test the effectiveness of the intervention. As such, impact measurement is normally about finding the best proxies and narratives to capture the additional outcomes and impact triggered by an organisation.

A working paper on social impact assessment, published by the London School of Economics in 2016, mentioned the existence of over 150 approaches to measure impact,[3] all developed between 1995 and 2015. In addition, many social entrepreneurial organisations develop their own approaches to capture the impact they realise, based on their ability, resources, interests, and context. To simplify and manage this multitude of approaches, several researchers and organisations have tried to group them based on key characteristics.

Clark et al. (2004)[4] grouped the most popular approaches for impact measurement based on the information that they provide, whereby the same approach could have one or two main focal points:

- Process-focused methods – those that track measurable organisational processes and outputs.
- Impact-focused methods – those that connect outputs to outcomes and try to isolate the outcomes that would not have happened had the organisation not existed.
- Monetisation-focused methods – those that report outcomes or impact by translating them into a monetary value.

Olsen and Galimidi (2008)[5] instead divided the approaches for impact measurement into three categories, based on the function they fulfil:

- Rating systems – those that summarise impact through a standardised score and are therefore helpful for communication and comparison purposes.
- Assessment systems – those that summarise results.
- Management systems – those useful to monitor organisational activities and manage the organisation.

Additionally, they distinguished approaches based on what they report on: implied impact, because they focus on outputs and internal data; proven impact, because they are based on external or experimental data; optimised impact, because they relate the impact realised to the costs/investment necessary to realise it.

While there are many ways to measure impact, there are some that are more used and popular than others. This chapter focuses on these, while acknowledging that they are only a small fraction of the possible approaches by which impact can be measured. Since this field keeps evolving, it is possible that in the coming years new approaches will emerge and become prominent. Table 11.1 lists the main approaches discussed in this chapter, relating them to the classifications of Clark et al. (2004) and Olsen and Galimidi (2008).

11.3.1 Social Return on Investment

One of the most popular approaches to measure impact, as well as probably the first one ever to reach international recognition, is the Social Return on Investment (SROI). The SROI approach was originally developed by the *Roberts Enterprise Development Fund* in the United States in the 1990s, and further developed by the *New Economic Foundation* in the United Kingdom in the early 2000s. It is based on accounting principles and on cost–benefit analysis, since it aims to monetise all relevant metrics and compare the value created with the costs to realise it. Its main objective is to generate a quantitative/economic measure of the aggregate value realised by an organisation based on the perspectives of multiple stakeholders. The result of the SROI approach is a ratio that represents the monetary value of the total impact created for each monetary unit spent on creating it (SROI=Net Present Value of Benefits/Net Present Value of Investment). For this reason, it has been promoted as an approach that helps

Table 11.1 The main approaches for impact measurement

Approach	Focus	Function	Type of impact reported	Type of value considered
Social Return on Investment (SROI)	Monetisation	Assessment	Optimised	Economic, social, environmental
B Impact Assessment	Process	Rating and assessment	Mostly implied	Economic, social, environmental, governance
Balanced Scorecard (BSC)	Process	Management	Mostly implied	Economic and social
Social Cost–Benefit Analysis (SCBA)	Monetisation	Assessment	Optimised	Economic, social, environmental
Social Impact Accounting (SIA)	Impact	Assessment	Proven	Economic, social, environmental
IRIS/IRIS+	Impact	Assessment	Proven	Economic, social, environmental
Sustainability Accounting Standards Board (SASB) Standards	Process	Assessment and management	Mostly implied	Economic, social, environmental, governance
Global Reporting Initiative's Sustainability Reporting Standards (GRI SRS)	Process	Assessment and management	Mostly implied	Economic, social, environmental, governance

to understand the overall impact and effectiveness of an organisation and that makes the impact of different organisations comparable.

SROI combines the monetary metrics of impact and costs with narratives of how the organisation realised impact and of the characteristics of the impact realised. It requires stakeholders' engagement in all stages, often includes an evaluation of key risks, and can be used to measure the impact of a specific project or of the organisation as a whole. To generate the final ratio and accompanying narrative, the SROI approach consists of several steps:

1   Involvement of stakeholders to understand what should be included in the calculations
2   Collection of narratives about the positive and negative effects felt by internal and external stakeholders
3   Monetisation of the different forms of impact realised
4   Consideration and monetisation of the impact that would have happened independently from the existence of the organisation
5   Calculation of the cost of inputs and activities
6   Calculation of the SROI ratio
7   Description of the organisational activities, context, and of the change realised

The process should be repeated at least on a yearly basis, monitored and improved based on feedback.

The SROI approach has many advantages. It is intuitive and easy to interpret for potential and existing funders, who can immediately compare the value created by an organisation in relation to others and, therefore, evaluate whether to support it. In this sense, it can be especially helpful when participating in public tenders, since it gives social entrepreneurial organisations the opportunity to prove the value and savings they might generate compared to alternative approaches or suppliers. Most importantly, it is an approach that encourages stakeholders' engagement, thus supporting funders' involvement in the evaluation of impact (and their consequent trust in it), and the legitimation of the organisation in the context in which it operates. On top of that, it is an approach with wide, international recognition that therefore has intrinsic credibility, and which existing research has confirmed to be helpful for many social enterprises in the United States and Europe, in particular in relation to organisational learning, strategic improvement, and reinforcing management systems.[6]

At the same time, SROI has proven to have some limitations. The main one is connected to its complexity and consequent requirements in terms of time, resources, and skills. This makes it an approach that small organisations often cannot afford to adopt and one that easily takes away resources and funds from the actual generation of impact. Moreover, in order to calculate the SROI ratio, many assumptions need to be made to translate various forms of impact into monetary values, especially when they are intangible. This means certain outcomes like changes in behaviours, well-being, or self-esteem might not be considered or well represented, thus leading to an underestimation of the impact realised. It also means that the usage of SROI might actually not enable comparability across organisations, since it might be implemented inconsistently, and might not necessarily be trusted by all types of funders. The need to translate impact into monetary terms can also clash with the ethics and values of some social entrepreneurial organisations, which might therefore refuse to adopt this approach. Additional issues are the difficulty of understanding how much of the impact recorded would have happened anyway without the existence of the organisation in question in the absence of an RCT, and the lack of consideration for whether the impact generated will persist or not.

The overall success of the SROI approach compared to others has led to the creation of several related tools and versions, such as the SROI Framework, the SROI Calculator, the SROI Toolkit, the SROI Analysis, the SROI Lite, and Social Accounting and Auditing (SAA) practices. The SROI Lite, created by Eric Carlson of the *Global Social Benefit Incubator* at Santa Clara University, is probably the most helpful version of SROI for small organisations, which might struggle to find the time, skills, and resources to do the original SROI approach. In this version, managers of a social entrepreneurial organisation identify the most important impact they want to realise and only calculate the costs and benefits of achieving that specific impact. Similarly, SAA practices can be an easier alternative to SROI, since they involve only the creation of qualitative narratives of the impact generated on target beneficiaries. SAA normally consists of collecting data through different stakeholders, building narratives based on them, and having such narratives verified by a panel of external auditors, involving at least one professional auditor.

SROI IN PRACTICE

Check out how organisations implement the SROI approach through the link in the relevant section at www.routledge.com/9780367640231 with materials related to this book.

11.3.2 B Impact Assessment

The B Impact Assessment derives from the certification system created by the *B Lab Global* in 2006 to evaluate what businesses deserved the status of a *B Corp* (see Chapter 2), among those that applied for it. Its aim is to help businesses understand how well they are performing, both in isolation and in relation to their peers, in four areas: governance, workers, community, and environment. The B Impact Assessment consists of a set of standards for each of the four areas mentioned above, created and revised by the Standards Advisory Council (SAC), which is "a group of independent experts in business and academia",[7] and modified based on regular feedback received from users and from B Lab Regional Advisory Groups. For businesses aiming for the B Corp certification, the B Impact Assessment is just the first step of a relatively long process. However, as an impact measurement approach, the B Impact Assessment is available for free as a stand-alone digital tool to any for-profit business that wants it. The tool is interactive and the assessment process varies depending on the size, geographical location, and sector in which the business operates.

Given the success of the *B Corp* movement, its easiness of use and international recognition, and its applicability to different types of businesses, the B Impact Assessment is quickly becoming one of the most widely used impact measurement approaches in social entrepreneurship. By responding to the questions of the survey, businesses can measure their existing performance, via quantitative metrics, in relation to governance, impact on workers, community (all external stakeholders), and the environment. Once they have completed the survey, they receive a B Impact Report, reporting their scores for each area and contextualising it in relation to the average scores of other businesses. The company can then publish this report to prove its impact or just use it for benchmarking and learning purposes. *B Lab Group* supports businesses using its B Impact Assessment with customised improvement reports, best practice guides, and case studies showcasing companies that managed to improve their score over time.

The B Impact Assessment is very comprehensive since it includes economic, social, and environmental considerations and governance-related, process-related, and output-related standards. Additionally, it is free, intuitive, and provides resources offering guidance and support beyond guidelines on how to conduct the measurement process. Like SROI, it has international recognition and gives a business immediate credibility as a social enterprise or a business trying to deliver positive social and environmental impact. It is also particularly supportive of organisational learning, since it allows benchmarking and encourages change through bespoke support and success case studies, and can help in connecting with like-minded peers and to protect the social or environmental mission of the business. However, it does not encourage direct involvement of stakeholders in the evaluation process, and it just works for social enterprises and for-profit businesses, thus not covering the full spectrum of social entrepreneurial organisations.

B IMPACT ASSESSMENT IN PRACTICE

Check out how Certified B Corps score in the B Impact Assessment through the link in the relevant section at www.routledge.com/9780367640231 webpage with materials related to this book.

11.3.3 Balanced Scorecard

Another comprehensive approach to measuring impact, involving both internal and external perspectives, as well as both economic and social considerations, is the Balanced Scorecard (BSC) adapted for measuring social impact. This approach is based on the BSC developed by Robert Kaplan, and supports businesses with understanding their non-financial performance by helping them to keep track of Key Performance Metrics (KPIs) in multiple areas. The original BSC included KPIs in four areas: financial, customer, business processes, and learning and growth. Within each of these, a business is expected to include KPIs that it wants to monitor, based either on its specific strategy and practices, or on KPIs that are industry-wide.

The BSC adapted to measure social impact was developed by Kaplan himself together with *New Profit Inc*, a venture philanthropist, and places customers (which also includes beneficiaries) at the top of the scorecard, instead of financial performance, links all outcome metrics to the social mission of the organisation, making sure that the financial perspective contains metrics of both social and economic accountability, and encourages in each section the selection of KPIs that ensure the fulfilment of the social mission. This makes the scorecard a valuable tool not just for businesses but for any organisation. The specific metrics included in each area of the BSC are established by or negotiated between the social entrepreneurial organisation and its funders on a case-by-case basis, to reflect its social mission, ToC, and social business model. For example, studying the usage of the BSC among South African social enterprises, Mamabolo and Myres (2020)[8] proposed the metrics summarised in Table 11.2.

The BSC is helpful to track the same KPIs/impact metrics over time, to measure different processes and outputs, and to compare performance with other organisations, especially if most of the metrics used represent the sector standards/most common ones. At the same time, the BSC is an approach that can be easily tailored and adaptable to the specifics of each organisation. This makes it a valuable communication tool both internally and externally and, given its anchoring to the social mission of the organisation, a way to combine long-term and short-term perspectives. Additionally, since data for the BSC is normally gathered through surveys, this approach is generally cost- and time-effective compared to others. However, the BSC risks being uninformative if the wrong metrics are selected, and slightly reductionist since KPIs are normally numerical metrics not accompanied by narratives and explanations. Additionally, some of the KPIs that a BSC encourages tracking may not lead to actual impact and, like the B Impact Assessment, this approach does not encourage the direct involvement of stakeholders in impact measurement.

Table 11.2 Example of Balanced Scorecard metrics for social enterprises (adapted from Mamabolo & Myres, 2020, p. 80)

Customer perspective	Financial perspective	Learning and growth	Internal processes
Attracted new customers	Lowered costs	Increased number of full-time employees	Products/services regarded by beneficiaries/ customers as new and different
Served existing customers	Increased sales	Entered into a new and important partnership with another organisation	Delivered goods and services to beneficiaries/ customers in a new and different manner
Expanded to include more beneficiaries	Improved profitability	Increased market share relative to competitors	Offered better quality products/services than other similar organisations
Improved product/ service quality offered to beneficiaries and customers	Attracted equity investment from a new shareholder	Implemented a new technology or Prepared a business plan	Served more beneficiaries than other similar organisations

---

BALANCED SCORECARD IN PRACTICE

Check out the BSCs developed by different organisations through the link in the relevant section at www.routledge.com/9780367640231 with materials related to this book.

11.3.4 Impact measurement approaches derived from practices in economic development

Two approaches traditionally used in economic development and public interventions that have been adapted to measure impact in social entrepreneurship ecosystems are the Social Cost–Benefit Analysis (SCBA) and Social Impact Accounting (SIA). Both approaches are normally *ex ante* approaches to measure impact, i.e. they are traditionally used before an intervention takes place to evaluate whether to authorise it or implement it. In relation to social entrepreneurship, however, they can be used by organisations also to evaluate their impact *ex post*.

The SCBA, as the name suggests, is one of the inspirations for the SROI and has basically been superseded by it, so it will not be discussed in detail. It involves the calculation of the economic, environmental and social impact (direct and indirect) that an intervention is expected to generate, and its comparison with the amount to be spent on that intervention. SIA involves the definition of a process that can help organisations measure the economic, social, and environmental impact of their intervention through engaging systematically with all key stakeholders. According to a report from USAID,[9] one of the main public funders of economic development in the world, key steps for SIA involve:

1 Planning and developing the proposed project or activity to assess impact;
2 Understanding the context in which planned activities would be carried out;
3 Using screening tools and engagement with stakeholders to determine if possible adverse impacts exist and which populations are likely to be impacted;
4 Mapping key stakeholders;
5 Making a plan for engaging stakeholders, including considerations about how to safely engage affected communities, how to inform communities of potential activities without raising expectations, and how to conduct consultations and/or interpersonal interviews;
6 Conducting consultations with affected communities, key-informant interviews, and conversations;
7 Assessing the baseline condition before the planned intervention through gathering data on demographics, socio-economics, community organisation, socio-political structures, needs, values, etc.;
8 Evaluating the potential direct, indirect, and cumulative impacts on the overall communities and sub-groups who may experience differentiated impacts. If engagement and scoping exercises indicate that social impacts will be significant and the community indicates that they do not want the project, or there is a high likelihood of any human rights violation, then the activity or project should be sited elsewhere or an alternate activity should be designed in collaboration with stakeholders;
9 Collaborating with the community to jointly develop a plan for monitoring and mitigating social impacts;
10 Analysing data to identify opportunities for increasing social cohesion, addressing marginalisation, promoting resilience, and ensuring that the benefits of development programming are realised by all stakeholders;
11 Ongoing engagement and monitoring to understand evolving risks, evaluate opportunities, and adapt project design.

Both approaches – SCBA and SIA – are a helpful guidance to develop an impact measurement system but do not provide specific metrics or standards to follow. As such, they are very flexible and, as said, can be used both to plan what impact to measure and estimate whether it is worth setting up an organisation to realise it, and to track impact once it has happened. However, they might not be excessively helpful or applicable for small social entrepreneurial organisations, who need something easy and less resource-intensive to implement, and are not as widely adopted by social entrepreneurial organisations as the other three approaches described so far.

Given the lack of specific impact metrics in both SCBA and SIA, an interesting option is to combine them with the Impact Reporting and Investment Standards (IRIS). IRIS is a "set of standardised metrics that can be used to measure and describe the social, environmental, and financial performance of organizations and businesses receiving impact investment capital".[10] It was developed in 2009 by the Global Impact Investing Network (GIIN) and, for the past decade, impact investors have driven its wide usage in businesses, and social entrepreneurship ecosystems. IRIS metrics can be integrated in existing impact measurement approaches and provide a useful starting point for social entrepreneurial organisations trying to figure out what they might want to track. They are like a library of validated and widely used metrics, accompanied by standardised definitions and examples of how different organisations use them in practice, that social entrepreneurial organisations can pick and choose based on their specific needs and activities. Recently, the GIIN updated the IRIS metrics and created the IRIS+ Core Metrics Sets, which are grouped according to impact themes, containing instructions for calculation and the explanation of what various metrics allow to understand. The benefits of IRIS/IRIS+ are mostly connected to the flexibility they guarantee while allowing some standardisation and comparisons between organisations that adopt the same metrics. However, IRIS metrics are sometimes too complex to calculate for social entrepreneurial organisations and more appropriate for use by impact investors.

11.3.5 Impact measurement approaches derived from sustainable business

There are two additional approaches that have been used for impact measurement and reporting, which are tailored to sustainable businesses but can be used also by social enterprises. These are the Sustainability Accounting Standards Board (SASB) Standards and the Global Reporting Initiative's Sustainability Reporting Standards (GRI SRS). Recently both SASB and GRI SRS became part of an initiative of integrated financial and sustainability reporting for corporations. SASB comprises a set of industry-related sustainability standards that companies can use to disclose information about their environmental, social, and governance (ESG) profile. Those standards are presented together with disclosure topics, metrics, and technical protocols and are thus helpful to both calculate and disclose a business ESG performance and to make that comparable across the same industry. The GRI SRS comprises a set of two standards. The first set are universal standards on which any public or private company should disclose information to prove its ESG performance. The second set are topic-based standards, which relate to one or more among the environmental, social, or economic impact of an organisation. These allow an organisation to focus on the key activities and dimensions that have strategic relevance for it. Organisations can choose to either use the full standards or specific parts, in order to build a sustainability report to share with external stakeholders. GRI offers various levels of support to those willing to use its standard for sustainability reporting.

Similarly, there are two approaches currently aimed at corporations that might eventually lead to useful impact metrics and approaches for social enterprises: The Impact-Weighted Accounts Initiative and the Stakeholder Capitalism Metrics released by the *World Economic Forum's International Business Council* (IBC). The Impact-Weighted Accounts Initiative is led by *Harvard Business School* and is based on adding, to the financial statements of corporations, monetary metrics "that reflect the company's positive and negative impacts on employees, customers, the environment and the broader society",[11] so these can be included in the calculation of profits and losses. This approach aims to value the impact generated by a business both directly, through its products/services and operations, and indirectly, through its suppliers and customers. In terms of products and services, impact can be measured in relation to the materials they are made of and their recyclability, to the needs they serve, to their accessibility, and to their quality. For example, the impact of the products of food companies can be measured in terms of the nutrients they contain and how much they are estimated to improve or harm customers' health.

The Stakeholder Capitalism Metrics released by the IBC are a set of 21 ESG metrics and disclosures, based on existing standards and practices, which corporations can use to report on their impact on people and the planet. Examples of these metrics include board composition, stakeholder engagement, greenhouse emissions, water consumption, anti-corruption practices, and pay equality. Reporting using such metrics involves a mix of quantitative and qualitative measures and can be tailored to the activities and impacts of each business. The goal of these metrics is to increase the accountability of businesses towards their various stakeholders and to allow the latter to compare the performance of corporations with regard to ESG in a way that is sector and country agnostic.

11.3.6 *Simplified tools to measure impact and approaches used by funders of social entrepreneurial organisations*

As said above, in most cases social entrepreneurial organisations are too small to undertake one of the main approaches for measuring impact. A simple measurement approach that any organisation can use is the Outcomes Star. This involves the establishment of a set of target outcomes and then the surveying of stakeholders so they can rate how much they think that outcome was achieved on a scale from 1 to 10. This is a very simplistic way of measuring impact and does not capture unintended impact, but it helps with stakeholders' engagement and it is a good proxy for impact that can be obtained with minimal analytical skills and costs.

Alternatively, social enterprises that deliver welfare services or work as providers and suppliers for public authorities can calculate their impact by estimating how much cheaper it is for them to deliver that service and the related outcomes compared to what was the case when that service or outcome was delivered by a public body. This does not really capture the impact of the organisation but can be a helpful proxy to show efficiency and effectiveness in outputs and outcomes (see ToC). It can also support the attainment of new contracts for provision of public services. Estimates of existing costs are not always available but they may be found through conversations with existing service providers or through databases such as the Unit cost database managed by the *Government Outcomes Lab* at the University of Oxford.

Finally there are popular approaches for impact measurement, such as the United Nations' Principles for Responsible Investing, Social Rating (developed by Micro-Credit Ratings International), Pulse – a portfolio data management system, and the Best Available Charitable Option (BACO) ratio (developed by *Acumen*) that are used by funders rather than by social entrepreneurial organisations. There are many funders that have developed their own impact measurement systems to evaluate and compare potential and current grantees or investees. Normally, these are accessible from their websites and publications and are useful to understand what kind of information they might expect to receive from social entrepreneurial organisations regarding impact.

While no type of focus, function, or impact reported (see Table 11.1) is intrinsically better than another, the chosen approach should ideally deliver reliable and helpful information connecting activities, outcomes, and impact (i.e. be based on a ToC), be helpful for decision-making and communication purposes, and provide insights on both expected and unanticipated impact. Similarly, given the ethics underpinning social entrepreneurial organisations (see Chapter 9), the methodology chosen should include the perspectives of all the key stakeholders and be embedded in operations, to ensure the continuous consideration of impact in all decisions and activities.

None of the various impact measurement approaches presented in this section is perfectly accurate or all-encompassing but having proxies of impact is better than having nothing, as long as limitations are kept in mind and there are regular re-evaluations and improvements of the approach and metrics adopted, based on direct experience and feedback from stakeholders. Eventually, as happened for financial accounting, standards will emerge and will help to guide measurement choices. For example, several countries have begun to create organisations and standards related to impact measurement: Japan launched the Social Impact Measurement Initiative in 2016, France developed the MESIS tool to measure impact, and the European Union is requiring businesses with over 500 employees based in its member states to report on their social and environmental impact through a non-financial information statement. In the future, it is possible to envision a situation where impact will be measured both through standardised accounts and through a set of more targeted metrics that help an organisation ensure its ToC holds.

11.4 Understanding what to measure and how

The previous section presented different, relatively popular, approaches that social entrepreneurial organisations *can* use to measure their impact. However, realistically, most social entrepreneurial organisations are unlikely to follow one of the approaches discussed above, due to resource, time, and skills constraints, and might prefer to just make sure that they keep track of the key outcomes and impact that they realise based on their ToC. Similarly, with the exception of social enterprises using the B Impact Assessment, even social entrepreneurial organisations that adopt a specific approach normally need to establish what metrics to include in it, i.e. the specific impact(s) they want to measure. Therefore, this section shares some insights and best practices to understand what to measure independently of the approach adopted.

11.4.1 Selecting metrics

Any social entrepreneurial organisation creates impact through two different avenues: its operations and its value proposition (see Chapters 8 and 9). Operations generate impact because they create new employment opportunities, both directly and through suppliers; they affect the health, skills, and well-being of employees; and they require inputs, which implicitly means they have an impact on the environment. The value proposition generates impact for beneficiaries and various stakeholders, and on the environment, ideally according to the ToC. Therefore, any organisation should ideally consider both operations-driven and value proposition-driven impact (see Table 11.3 for examples).

The first step to understand what to measure is naturally represented by the ToC (see Chapter 7). Based on that, a social entrepreneurial organisation should already have a set of metrics (built with stakeholders' input or using standard lists) that it wants to track in relation to outputs, outcomes, and impact, and a relatively clear understanding of what it means with "impact". This list can then become a helpful starting point to ask stakeholders if it matches their needs and expectations or if something else is required, and to explore impact that might have not been initially considered, such as that deriving from operations or generated unintentionally. Once having a comprehensive list, the organisation needs to evaluate if it has the capacity to

Table 11.3 Examples of metrics of operations-driven and value proposition-driven impact

Area of impact creation	Social and economic	Environmental
Operations	People employed; quality and security of jobs created; level of wages (e.g. minimum living wage) paid; level of support of diversity and inclusion; opportunities offered for re-skilling; involvement of stakeholders in decision-making and re-distribution of added value; additional employment generated in suppliers	Resources used; carbon emissions; degree of circularity of business model; effectiveness of logistics
Value proposition	Affordability; reach of otherwise excluded groups; benefits provided; number of beneficiaries reached and their level of satisfaction; innovativeness; new connections created between stakeholders; amount of economic development generated	Amount of product features that are recyclable; types of materials used to deliver; customers/beneficiaries' efficient use and recycling of products

track all that it would like, or if it should focus just on the most critical metrics. These can be identified by reflecting on the main reason why the organisation is engaging in impact measurement (e.g. improvement, verification of the ToC, funders' requests, etc.). Additionally, Wei-Skillern et al. (2007)[12] suggest to select metrics that are reasonably objective, related to the main goals of the organisation, not too expensive to track and analyse, and observable within a reasonable time horizon, while Roetman and De Greve (2018) affirm that they should reflect a mix of both process and outcome measures.[13] The process to select metrics is summarised in Figure 11.1.

Any set of impact metrics derived from these steps should also be: affordable for the organisation; feasible given the skills and resources available (this criteria often requires the simplification of initial plans and the choice of metrics less complex than those that would be ideal); aligned as much as possible with those used by peers and with the social mission and social business model of the organisation; helpful to communicate with and attract the support of both external and internal stakeholders. Metrics should also be re-evaluated regularly and updated as the organisation keeps operating and grows or if there are changes in the external environment. Keeping planning and the selection of metrics separate from the actual measurement can help to ensure that the impact measure remains strongly tied to both the operations and the value proposition and that it reveals what an organisation really needs to know.

11.4.2 Establishing an impact measurement system and measuring impact

Selecting the most appropriate metrics is only part of planning how to measure impact. A fully formed impact measurement system also requires understanding how the necessary data will be collected and when, who will be responsible for collecting and analysing data, and creating an organisational culture that encourages and values measurement, as well as a constant process of learning and improvement. In particular, it is important to allocate resources and assign responsibilities, promote broad involvement in impact measurement, and establish measurement timeframes.

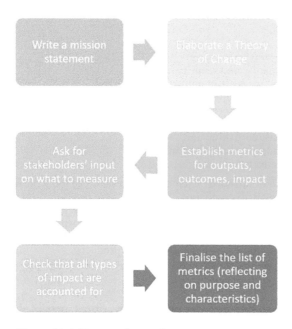

Figure 11.1 How to choose the metrics to measure impact

The measurement timeframe should match the assumptions made in the ToC about the time needed to generate impact and include intermediate points in time in which to measure outcomes, to verify whether the organisation is on track to achieve its ultimate impact by the end of the full impact measurement cycle.

Throughout the full process of measuring impact, it is important to engage stakeholders to check how they define impact and to verify whether they agree with the results of the impact analysis conducted. Sometimes even brief conversations with stakeholders, involving questions such as "Do you think we are reaching this kind of impact? Or do you think we are achieving something else?", "Did we change your life for the better or meet and surpassed your expectations in any way? Why or why not?", or "What evidence would you need to trust that we are doing a good job?" can already provide valuable and rich insights for testing assumptions, checking metrics, and learning about the intended and unintended impact generated. Similarly, learning from peers and gathering ideas from existing approaches can be good ways to improve an impact measurement system. Testing and piloting the chosen approach for impact measurement is fundamental to fine-tune it and ensure it provides the necessary insights for planning, decision-making, verifying the ToC, and communicating the impact realised to relevant stakeholders.

Impact can be captured through both quantitative and qualitative data. Traditional data collection methods include: surveys (distributed online or at events); experiments and RCTs; interviews; observations; and process tracing. Increasingly, however, social entrepreneurial organisations are leveraging Design Thinking (see Chapter 7), technology, and, in particular, mobile phones and social media to collect real-time data that helps them to be more responsive to stakeholders.

Quantitative data includes: financial data (e.g. amount of new funds raised for environmental projects, amount of money saved due to a different type of intervention); percentages (e.g. reduction in re-offending rates among prisoners, percentage improvement in university's completion rate); numbers (e.g. number of people reached through a training programme, number of surgeries performed); ratings/valuations (e.g. level of geographic reach compared to target, in a scale from 1 to 5). Quantitative data is practical and relatively easy to collect, but helpful only if there are pre-set targets or benchmarks for comparison. For example, saying that children attending school increased by 2% thanks to a social enterprise providing education programmes has limited value unless it is accompanied by information on the current rate of schooling for that group or comparable groups in the absence of such programmes, and more details about the age group and context in which the organisation operates.

Qualitative data includes: narratives of how an activity is experienced by beneficiaries and stakeholders or of how it affects their lives or the environment; interviews and testimonies collected among stakeholders; notes on observations from the field about what is happening to stakeholders or the environment. Qualitative data is particularly helpful to explore the depth and type of impact created, unintended consequences, and to understand the lived experience of beneficiaries and other stakeholders in relation to what the organisation is doing and delivering. The main challenges are finding the right balance between information richness and ease of understanding, comparability, and the higher cost and longer time of collection compared to quantitative data.

In most cases, a combination of quantitative and qualitative data is the ideal solution to convey a fair portrait of the impact created. Quantitative data facilitates comparisons and sharing/communication, and can help to visualise the added value of an organisation and to compare this to its costs, making it possible to assess the effectiveness of interventions. Meanwhile, qualitative data is needed to contextualise the information provided by quantitative data, to explain how and why impact happened, and to describe the actual experience of beneficiaries and other stakeholders, in order to give a meaning to whatever is assessed through quantitative data. Combined, quantitative and qualitative data compensate for one another's weaknesses and, when sustaining the same findings, reinforce the credibility of the impact reported. Ideally, the mix of data collected should provide information on the impact realised, on the extent of the change generated, and on its relevance for stakeholders and, especially, target beneficiaries.

It is widely acknowledged that social entrepreneurial initiatives need to be judged on the basis of the progress made towards the attainment of their social mission. However, it is also important to relate the impact created to the costs (economic and non-economic) of creating it, in order to fully assess the performance and effectiveness of a social entrepreneurial organisation and to plan how to move forward. If the impact generated does not justify the costs incurred, it is important to take a step back and revise the ToC or how the organisation operates. Similarly, impact measurement systems of social entrepreneurial organisations should be characterised by transparency and accountability, in line with the ethical approach discussed in Chapter 9.

A good measurement system should enable answering the following questions:

1   What impact is generated, for whom, and to what extent?
2   How does the impact generated relate to the social mission and ToC?

3　What impact is not sufficiently realised through the current activities of the organisation?
4　What outcomes and impact take place at different points in time?
5　How much of the impact is it possible to attribute to the organisation versus external factors or other interventions?
6　What might explain potential mismatches between results and goals/expectations?
7　What needs improving?

11.5　Reporting Impact

Measuring impact would not make sense if this impact was not communicated and used in some way. Given the multiple impacts to be measured, the various reasons for measuring them, and the different requirements that different stakeholders might have in relation to impact reporting, effective communication of the impact realised is complex.

Forms of reporting impact can and should vary based on their target audience. They include: annual and impact reports; internal communications to staff; bespoke reports for funders; fundraising and promotional materials such as leaflets and posters; videos, podcasts, or infographics to communicate to a wide audience through the organisation's website and social media. Often, reporting requirements are shaped by funders and other stakeholders, by reporting standards relevant for the context or sector in which the social entrepreneurial organisation operates, by its own culture and goals, and by the provisions related to the legal form it chose. For example, customers might be more interested in stories about the lives touched by a social entrepreneurial organisation, while funders might want numbers and statistics to verify that all intended beneficiaries were reached or that resources were deployed efficiently. Elaborating the different narratives and gathering the necessary information is an additional burden, generating complications and costs, especially when an organisation has multiple funders from different sectors having their own expectations and reporting standards.

General best practice, independently from the goal or the format chosen for reporting, is to explain the purpose of the organisation, the context in which it delivers its value proposition, and the nature and extent of the issue it tackles. On top of this, it is helpful to share some information on what an organisation does and to illustrate its ToC, so the target audience can understand the relevance of the impact being reported, and see for themselves what the organisation is achieving and why. It is also important to be fully transparent and disclose both positive and negative impact and both satisfactory and unsatisfactory results, and to provide some insights about the lessons learnt, since those might be as valuable as the results achieved.

In 2012, *New Philanthropy Capital*, with the help of other UK charities and intermediaries, developed a set of principles[14] for good impact reporting that can be used as a guide for any organisation approaching this task for the first time:

1　Clarity: the reader can quickly and easily understand the organisation through a coherent narrative that connects aims, plans, activities, and results.
2　Accessibility: relevant information can be found by anyone who looks for it, in a range of formats suitable for different stakeholders.
3　Transparency: reporting is full, open, and honest.

4 Accountability: reporting connects with stakeholders, partners, and beneficiaries to tell them what they need to know, and provide reassurance.

5 Verifiability: claims about impact are backed up appropriately, allowing others to review. This can range from informal stakeholder feedback to external audits.

6 Proportionality: the level and detail of reporting reflects the size and complexity of the organisation, and the complexity of the changes they're trying to bring about.

The more effective and believable a social entrepreneurial organisation is in reporting its impact, the higher its chances are to keep improving and growing, to attract the necessary funds and support, and to become a valued and trusted player in its social entrepreneurship ecosystem and sector of operation.

SUMMARY BOX

- Impact measurement is defined as the processes of analysing and monitoring the intended and unintended social, environmental, and economic consequences, both positive and negative, short and long term, of an organisation and of any change process triggered by that organisation that would not have happened anyway, even if the intervention did not exist.

- Measuring impact enables the understanding of how a social entrepreneurial organisation is performing, to assess whether it is creating its intended impact and how it is actually affecting stakeholders or the environment, to spot opportunities for growth and improvement, to validate its ToC, to foster organisational learning, and to attract support from stakeholders.

- Measuring impact, however, is also challenging. There is no single approach to measure impact, most approaches are funder- or organisation-driven, thus making comparisons and their understanding complex, it is difficult to establish what to measure and to measure it effectively, and impact measurement risks taking resources away from actually realising impact.

- There are over 150 different approaches to measure impact. The most popular ones in social entrepreneurship ecosystems are SROI, B Impact Assessment, the BSC, and approaches borrowed from economic development and sustainable businesses. This said, most social entrepreneurial organisations opt for tailor-made approaches, either based on their ToC and resource, time, and skills constraints, or on the requests of their funders.

- It is important for social entrepreneurial organisations to spend time planning what to measure, how, and to set up an impact measurement system. The goals are to find the right balance between capturing key impact and not using too much effort and resources to do so; to connect impact measurement with the social mission, ToC, and social business model of the organisation; to involve stakeholders in all the processes related to impact measurement; and to remain transparent and accountable.

- Reporting impact is necessary both for learning purposes and to maintain positive relationships with stakeholders. Reporting can take many different forms and should be tailored to the specific target audience. Whatever the form adopted, reporting should render impact clear, accessible, transparent, accountable, verifiable, and proportional to the size of the organisation and the extent of the change it generates.

Check box – Self-reflection and discussion questions

- What is impact measurement and what types of impact does it include?
- What are the benefits and main challenges of measuring impact?
- What are the main approaches used for measuring impact in social entrepreneurship ecosystems?
- What are the pros and cons of the different impact measurement systems mentioned in this chapter?
- Can you think of additional ways to measure the impact of a social entrepreneurial organisation?
- Is there any impact measurement system that you believe has the potential to become the industry standard in the near future?
- If you were the leader of a social entrepreneurial organisation, how would you approach impact measurement and identify the best metrics?
- What are the key characteristics of a good impact measurement system?
- What might be the challenges related to different types of data (quantitative versus qualitative) both in terms of measurement and of value for external stakeholders?
- What information should a good impact measurement system provide?
- Why is impact reporting important and how should it be done?

Check out the "Additional resources" related to this chapter to learn more about impact measurement: www.routledge.com/9780367640231 with book materials.

Exercises

Exercise 11.1 – Reporting impact

Look at the websites of social entrepreneurial organisations from all over the world using the links provided in the book's website (www.routledge.com/9780367640231 with book materials) in the relevant section connected to Chapter 11. First make up a list of what you think their main impacts are and how you would measure them. Then see whether or not they are reporting impact and note down:

1 If they are or they are not
2 If they are – how they do it and whether it matched your expectations in terms of what they would measure and report on
3 If they are not – why you think it is the case and what you would suggest them to report on

Exercise 11.2 – What to do with limited resources

Reflect on what impact a social entrepreneurial organisation with limited resources should make sure to measure. Is it just about the impact on beneficiaries or is there more? Shall the impact on employees be included? If so, how would you measure that? What are more intangible and long-term impacts that a social entrepreneurial organisation might generate?

Exercise 11.3 – Understanding the main approaches for impact measurement

Use the links in the book's website (www.routledge.com/9780367640231) that present examples of how the main approaches for impact measurement mentioned in Section 11.2 are used in practice. Analyse one of the reports provided and reflect on and write down in a short note (200–300 words) how effective that report is in showing the impact of the organisation in question. In particular, reflect on the following:

1   Was it easy for you to understand the impact of the organisation? Why or why not?
2   Is there unclear or unnecessary information?
3   Is there missing information that makes you doubt what is reported?
4   Is this approach respecting the characteristics of an ideal impact measurement approach? Why or why not?
5   Would you have used a different approach?

Exercise 11.4 – Measuring impact

Assume you wanted to measure the impact of one of the organisations you picked for the exercises in previous chapters or that was mentioned as one of the case studies in this book or in the "Additional resources" sections of the book's website (www.routledge.com/9780367640231 with book materials), and answer the following questions:

1   What stakeholders would you involve and how?
2   What activities, outputs, and outcomes would you measure?
3   What existing approach or set of metrics would you use and why?
4   How would you collect the necessary data?
5   How would you verify that your data and findings are correct or at least good and helpful estimates of the impact the organisation is generating?
6   What would be the best way of reporting your impact? With whom would you share the report(s) and how?

Notes

1 Vanclay, F. (2003). International principles for social impact assessment. *Impact Assessment and Project Appraisal*, 21(1), 2.
2 Clark, C., Rosenzweig, W., Long, D., & Olsen, S. (2004). *Double bottom line project report: Assessing social impact in double bottom line ventures*; methods catalog. Berkeley: University of California, 7.
3 Florman, M., Vidra, R. K., & Facada, M. J. (2016). *A critical evaluation of social impact assessment methodologies and a call to measure economic and social impact holistically through the external rate of return platform*, London School of Economics Enterprise Working Paper #1602, 4.

4 Clark, C., Rosenzweig, W., Long, D., & Olsen, S. (2004). *Double bottom line project report: Assessing social impact in double bottom line ventures*; methods catalog. Berkley: University of California, 11.

5 Olsen, S., & Galimidi, B. (2008). *Catalog of approaches to impact measurement: Assessing social impact in private ventures*. Social Venture Technology Group with the support of The Rockefeller Foundation.

6 Manetti, G. (2014). The role of blended value accounting in the evaluation of socio-economic impact of social enterprises. *Voluntas: International Journal of Voluntary and Nonprofit Organizations, 25*(2), 443–464.

7 B Impact Assessment. (2021). *Frequently asked questions: Top 10.* Retrieved from: https://bimpactassessment.net/how-it-works/frequently-asked-questions/top-10?_ga=2.241181762.1166761515.1643381127-382389521.1643381127#what-is-considered-a-%22good%22-score

8 Mamabolo, A., & Myres, K. (2020). Performance measurement in emerging market social enterprises using a balanced scorecard. *Journal of Social Entrepreneurship, 11*(1), 80.

9 USAID. (2019). *Optional social impact assessment framework.* Retrieved from: https://www.usaid.gov/sites/default/files/documents/1866/USAID-Social-Impact-Assessment-508.pdf, p. 7.

10 Gelfand, S. (2012). *Why IRIS? The second in a four-part series on impact investing and the role of metrics.* Stanford Social Innovation Review, Oct 10, 2012. Retrieved from: https://ssir.org/articles/entry/why_iris

11 Harvard Business School. (2022). Why impact-weighted accounts. Retrieved from: https://www.hbs.edu/impact-weighted-accounts/Pages/default.aspx

12 Wei-Skillern, J., Austin, J. E., Leonard, H., & Stevenson, H. (2007). *Entrepreneurship in the social sector* (Vol. 13). London: SAGE.

13 Roetman, E., & De Greve, P. (2018). Measuring performance and impact of a social business: Reflections from practice. In van der Velden, F. (Ed.), *Towards a fair and just economy*, Voorhaven: LM Publishers, 131.

14 New Philanthropy Capital (2012). *Principles of good impact reporting for charities and social enterprises.* Retrieved from: https://www.thinknpc.org/wp-content/uploads/2018/07/Principles-of-good-impact-reporting-final.pdf, slide 6.

Appendix – Case study
Mayamiko

Mayamiko is a social enterprise operating in the fashion industry. This case brings together many of the concepts learnt throughout the book and is meant to be an additional resource to explore the theoretical and practical foundations of social entrepreneurship. The goal for you is to read each section and, before going to the next, to spend some time reflecting on how it relates to what you learnt and to answer the questions.

Section 1 – The social entrepreneurial idea

Mayamiko was founded by Paola Masperi in 2008. It is "an ethical and sustainable woman's wear and lifestyle brand, producing clothes, accessories and homeware made in Malawi and other artisanal focused locations by teams of tailors, pattern cutters and seamstresses".[1] Before founding *Mayamiko*, Paola had spent four years as an employee of an IT company. She worked in several African countries on a project in partnership with local ministries of education that aimed to understand how digital tools could support primary education in rural Africa. During that period, she was in close contact with several children, teachers, families, and with the Ministry for Women and Child Development in Malawi, which had sponsored and supported the initiative. As she kept talking with local stakeholders, Paola realised that she wanted to do more to help local communities and that she had the useful skills, networks, and ideas to make a difference.

Together with the Malawi Minister for Women and Child Development, Paola developed a fashion-based project that could empower local women, while also having a strong education component. The idea was to leverage women's existing skills in sewing and weaving to train them to realise clothes inspired by the local textiles that could be sold on the international market, and to set up a structure that would enable the sale of the clothes they produced.

The first difficult choice was on how to set up an organisation that could fulfil these two objectives – providing training and helping women to sell the output of their work. There were three different options available and Paola was not sure about which one would be the most suitable.

One option was to set up *Mayamiko* – the name that Paola had chosen for the organisation – as a charity. This would enable the reception of donations and grants, the usage of all resources on training women independently from the end results, and to operate even at a loss. However, it would also make the charity difficult to sustain in the absence of donations and grants and, from a branding point of view, it would risk to reduce the perceived quality of the clothes and accessories realised and, thus, the channels and opportunities to sell them.

A second option was to set up *Mayamiko* as a business. This would enable the generation of revenues and profits through sales in international fashion markets, access to investments, and more aggressive risk-taking. However, it would also require the pursuit of profits to the potential detriment of the educational and empowerment sides of the project.

Finally, *Mayamiko* could be set up as a social enterprise. This would have combined both the advantages and disadvantages of the other two options, while creating new opportunities in terms of funding and branding. This option seemed ideal to pursue both charitable and business objectives (double bottom line) but presented increased bureaucratic burdens and a tough choice in terms of incorporation options.

QUESTIONS

1   *What makes Paola a social entrepreneur? What do you think might be her strengths and weaknesses in developing her idea, based on the information provided?*

2   *What type of knowledge would you want to gather to help Paola decide how to set up Mayamiko?*

3   *Who are the key stakeholders, customers, and beneficiaries of Mayamiko? What do they want and need?*

4   *How should Paola set up Mayamiko to maximise its chances of success and the fulfilment of its social mission (training and empowering Malawi women)?*

5   *Among the different options that exist to set up a social enterprise in your own country or in the country where Paola was based (the United Kingdom), which one would you choose for an organisation like Mayamiko?*

Section 2 – Incorporating a social enterprise

At the beginning, *Mayamiko* started as a charity providing training services to Malawi women. However, it soon ran into funding difficulties. The lack of funds was limiting the impact of the educational and training project that it was set up to deliver. To correct this worrying situation, Paola thought about transforming the charity into a business, able to sell products in specific outlets across the world and, thus, to self-fund its operations. Still, she worried about the risks of mission drift and of having to rely on market trends and preferences. What if products couldn't be sold? What if costs were higher than revenues? What if pursuing profits put at risk the ethics and beliefs underpinning the project? What if different/cheaper materials or cuts to training were needed to make ends meet? What would happen to the social impact if the start-up failed as many others did?

Paola had two certainties:

1   She wanted to separate the commercial risk from the charity, given the fashion industry is extremely risky and volatile.
2   She wanted to create safety mechanisms that would help *Mayamiko* stick to its values and social mission.

In the end, she opted to set up *Mayamiko* as a collection of three different organisations, connected through contracts:

1   *Mayamiko Ltd.* – a limited company registered in the United Kingdom that would sell fashion clothes prevalently relying on online marketing and distribution. The ways in which *Mayamiko Ltd.* could differentiate itself from competitors would include selling clothes inspired by Malawi textiles and created by Malawi women, and being a member of the World Fair Trade Organization (WFTO). Being a member of WFTO requires the respect of several principles meant to ensure "no harm" to stakeholders, and supports the realisation of active social impact. Thus, it could act as a guarantee of *Mayamiko Ltd.*'s pursuit of a double bottom line. The plan was to transfer most of the profits that the business might obtain to a connected charity employing them to fulfil *Mayamiko*'s original social mission – the empowerment of women in Malawi.
2   *Mayamiko Trust* – a charity registered in the United Kingdom, which would attract donations and grants and reinvest the profits eventually received from *Mayamiko Ltd.* to generate social impact projects in Malawi, such as training for women. The choice of where to spend the profits from *Mayamiko Ltd.* and additional donations would sit with its Board of Trustees. Projects that the *Mayamiko Trust* could fund would include training Malawi women, especially those affected by HIV or who are carers of HIV orphans, and offering them mentoring programs, access to micro-finance schemes, and education programmes in sanitation and nutrition.
3   *Mayamiko Fashion Lab* – a company limited by guarantee registered in Malawi with a board of guarantors composed by a mix of representatives of *Mayamiko Ltd.*, *Mayamiko Trust*, and local stakeholders. The *Fashion Lab* would produce the clothes sold by *Mayamiko Ltd.*, deliver the necessary expert-level training and infrastructure to the Malawi women responsible for the production, and deal with local suppliers of raw materials such as fabrics. All the managers and employees of this company would be from Malawi, thus preventing locals from having to work freelance, which would pose a risk to their income in periods where market conditions are tougher. At the same time, all the equipment used would be owned by *Mayamiko Ltd* and all the proceedings derived from producing the clothes for *Mayamiko Ltd.* would be reinvested in the *Fashion Lab*.

Once having re-incorporated *Mayamiko* through the plan described above, Paola focused on ways to make a difference not only within the boundaries of the organisation but also in the fashion industry and social entrepreneurship ecosystem. On top of its WFTO membership, *Mayamiko* became a member of the Ethical Fashion Forums *Fellowship 500* and the *Textile Exchange*. Being a member of the WFTO was not only beneficial to encourage *Mayamiko's* adherence to their membership criteria but, most importantly, enabled *Mayamiko* to support the development and rejuvenation of the Fair Trade movement through *Mayamiko's* experience and partners. Joining *Fellowship 500* and the *Textile Exchange* was instead helpful for lobbying for the adoption of more sustainable practices at industry level. Members of these organisations included large fashion conglomerates (e.g. *Kering* and PVH) and well-known high fashion brands such as *Stella McCartney* and *Vivienne Westwood*, which had the power to drive change at scale. In Paola's view, being part of these groups was also important to stay in tune with the direction of the industry and of Fair Trade, and to remain alert to key innovations and change projects initiated by others.

QUESTIONS

1   *What are the advantages and disadvantages of incorporating Mayamiko as three different entities?*
2   *Would you change anything in Mayamiko's structure, or do you think it works well this way? If you were to change anything, what would that be a why would you want to do it?*
3   *Why is this form of incorporation better in terms of financial sustainability compared to the original one?*
4   *What are the benefits and limitations of being a member of organisations such as the WFTO or the Textile Exchange?*
5   *What functions do the social entrepreneurship and fashion ecosystems perform in relation to Mayamiko based on the information in Sections 1 and 2? And what are the roles of Mayamiko in these ecosystems?*

Section 3 – Operating as a social enterprise

Both the division of *Mayamiko* into three different entities jointly pursuing a double bottom line and its being a member of the WFTO currently make *Mayamiko* a social enterprise, even if it is not incorporated as one. They allow higher risk-taking and diversification of income sources, while guaranteeing as much as possible the respect of its original values and social mission. Additionally, its hybrid structure gives *Mayamiko* the opportunity to decide how to market itself between three different options: as a traditional business paying attention to sustainability; as a social enterprise explicitly pursuing a double bottom line; or as a charity that uses the profits of a connected entity as one of its sources of income. Most importantly, the separation in different entities created the opportunity to eventually handing over the *Mayamiko Fashion Lab* to local owners in Malawi, which was one of Paola's long-term goals. At the same time, however, it presented some managerial and operational complexities. For example, it reduced the accountability and determination of the employees of *Mayamiko Fashion Lab*, since they saw *Mayamiko Ltd.* as the ultimate entity responsible for financial and operational success of the group, and as a funder that would end up covering any financial loss incurred.

To ensure that not only a double, but actually a triple bottom line is consistently achieved through all three organisations, *Mayamiko* has resisted the temptation to enter the fast-fashion industry – it does not do sales and its collections are cross-seasonal. It also uses recyclable or compostable materials for packaging, and its managerial team takes into consideration the effects on the Malawi women they want to help and who represent their key suppliers, whenever they make a new decision. As Paola puts it "We see those who make clothes as 'us'. They exist to help us and would not be able to operate and succeed if it was not for us". Additionally, *Mayamiko* has several initiatives to reduce waste – it maintains a lean and just-in-time approach to production, uses materials destined to the landfill, designs clothes to minimise the waste of fabric, and recycles some textiles to create sanitary pads to donate to schools.

Mayamiko also maximises opportunities for positive social impact throughout its supply chain. Its fabrics are sourced through local markets or ethical businesses whenever possible; and cooperatives, social enterprises, and FTOs constitute the core of its suppliers. The warehouse it uses in London is a WISE employing people with learning disabilities. *Mayamiko Fashion Lab* in Malawi

OUR ETHICAL PROMISE

- NO FORCED LABOUR
- FREEDOM OF ASSOCIATION AND THE RIGHT TO COLLECTIVE BARGAINING
- SAFE AND HYGIENIC WORKING CONDITIONS
- NO CHILD LABOUR
- LIVING WAGES
- NO DISCRIMINATION
- NO EXCESSIVE WORKING HOURS
- REGULAR EMPLOYMENT TO BE PROVIDED
- NO HARSH OR INHUMANE TREATMENT
- TRAINING AND PROFESSIONAL DEVELOPMENT FOR ALL EMPLOYEES
- A NUTRITIOUS MEAL EVERY DAY
- LIFE SKILL SENSITISATION AND INDIVIDUAL SUPPORT
- SUPPORT TO SET UP INDEPENDENT BUSINESSES AND COOPERATIVES WHEN DESIRED
- FINANCIAL EDUCATION AND ACCESS TO MICROFINANCE, LOANS AND GRANTS
- PENSION SCHEME AND GRATUITY

is solar-powered, collects rainwater, and sources organic cotton from Uganda, from suppliers who pay fairly and reinvest in their community, as *Mayamiko* does. On its website, *Mayamiko* also published its "Ethical promise",[2] which it strives to respect in all decisions and operations and which reflects the International Labour Organization (ILO)'s principles, as well as the ten principles of Fair Trade established by the WFTO (Figure A1).

QUESTIONS

1   Can you build a hypothetical Theory of Change and Social Business Model of Mayamiko?
2   Based on Mayamiko's story so far, how can a social enterprise risk to inadvertently deviate from its social mission and/or to become either too business-like or to charitable in its approach?
3   If a social enterprise doesn't proactively manage its supply chain, does it become less of a social enterprise? And if it does, what are the benefits and difficulties?
4   How would you market Mayamiko, given it has three different options to present its identity?

Section 4 – Marketing and managing success

Despite the choice of joining the WFTO and the commitment to the highest possible social and environmental values, ultimately Paola opted to market *Mayamiko* as a "traditional business". Product quality and originality, design and competitive price for its target segment are the main selling points of *Mayamiko Ltd.* The generation of social impact among Malawi women has always remained an integral part of *Mayamiko*'s identity but that is not the message through which *Mayamiko* wants to attract and retain customers. The social impact of *Mayamiko* is mentioned on its website for those who are interested, but never at the front. Its collections target global, independent, and fashion-aware women offering them unique designs realised with traditional locally sourced fabrics, referred to as Chitenje. The main marketing and retail channel for *Mayamiko*'s collections is its website (https://www.mayamiko.com/).

The considerations behind this choice were many, among which the realisation that now many companies brand themselves as sustainable even if they are not, and for customers it is very difficult to distinguish genuine from opportunistic claims. As the fashion industry woke up to the need for sustainable, ethical, and transparency credentials, it was hard to differentiate and compete on those values. It was more important to build a community of customers who love the products, as well as their stories, are satisfied with them, repeat-buy and are ambassadors with others.

This choice has worked out well and *Mayamiko* has consistently been a successful and profitable business since launching the label in 2015, gaining recognition from key players of the fashion industry. In 2017, it won the *"Brand to Watch"* industry awards, and in 2019 it was recognised as a sustainability leader from *Vogue, Vivienne Westwood*, and *Stella McCartney*. In the same year, *Mayamiko* was mentioned in several fashion blogs and magazines following the decision of Meghan Markle, back then Duchess of Sussex, to wear a dress from its collection to being the tour of Africa with the then Duke of Sussex Prince Harry.

However, also the choice on how to leverage this success hasn't been easy. The maintenance of such a complex structure, despite the support of volunteers in the United Kingdom, is very expensive and burdensome in terms of costs and bureaucratic duties. This makes further expansion difficult if profits need to remain for continuing the provision of social impact. The growth trajectory is also problematic, as it requires moving away from artisanal production to industrial scale production, and this is not aligned with the original vision and mission. As Paola reflected on where to go next, she kept wondering how to avoid mission drift or the dilution of resources and values that might lead to a smaller impact for Malawi women.

QUESTIONS

1   How could Mayamiko reduce its operational complexity without hampering its current success?
2   Do you think Mayamiko should scale up or just enjoy its momentum? What are the benefits and risks either way?
3   What options would you consider to scaling up the operations of Mayamiko?
4   And what options would you consider to scale up its impact?

Section 5 – Scaling up and measuring

Mayamiko has taken two key strategic decisions to scale its impact while also growing as a business:

1   In 2019, *Mayamiko Ltd.* handed over the ownership of *Mayamiko Fashion Lab* to a local manager previously employed by the same company, who established *Tatenda Clothing*. *Tatenda Clothing* employs around 30 people in Malawi as artisans, managers, and trainers and continues the close collaboration between the United Kingdom and Malawi entities as part of its joint venture with *Mayamiko Ltd.* In this joint venture, *Mayamiko Ltd.* oversees the overheads' management, while *Tatenda Clothing* looks after human resource management and the daily operations related to the production of fashion garments and the training of women. The full separation between *Mayamiko Ltd.* and *Mayamiko Fashion Lab* freed up resources to invest in other artisanal projects with similar ethos around the world, managed by *Mayamiko Trust*, and in the market growth strategy of *Mayamiko*

Ltd. Additionally, it gave *Tatenda Clothing* the freedom to supply other businesses. At the same time, it posed some branding challenges, as well as some auditing and relationship-building challenges, especially as travel was restricted in 2020 due to the COVID-19 pandemic.

2   Since 2019, *Mayamiko Ltd.* established partnerships with trusted suppliers and producers of garments and accessories based in Malawi, Sri Lanka, Peru, and Italy. *Mayamiko* shares its resources and designs with them and gives them access to its sales channels. In return, it has the opportunity to expand its sales and product range. On its website, customers can now buy not only clothes but also jewellery, hair accessories, shopping bags, products for the home, and gift ideas made across different geographies. According to its latest plans, *Mayamiko* is now trying to expand its sales to Africa, to create an even stronger connection between the production and consumption of its collections.

To ensure that scale doesn't go to the detriment of its triple bottom line, *Mayamiko* performs an in-depth due diligence on any new partner before confirming an agreement and ascertains that their values are aligned. As it continues to grow, *Mayamiko*'s vision remains to bring customers "a growing selection of carefully crafted pieces, made by handpicked artisans all over the globe".[3] Nonetheless, the more it expands its network, the higher are its chances of losing control over the supply chain and the quality of its offer. Expanding on a purely commercial basis might also risk to directly dilute its original training intent, since *Mayamiko Ltd* now does not directly control any of the training delivered to its trusted producers, neither in Malawi, nor in the countries where its new suppliers operate. To ensure its achievement of a triple bottom line remains strong across its supply chain and that it keeps realising its social mission of giving Malawi women "choice", it is more important than ever for *Mayamiko* to keep track of the social impact it creates. The key sources of social impact it identified are:

1   Profits generated by *Mayamiko Ltd.*, plus an additional £1 donation for every garment sold, are transferred to *Mayamiko Trust*. This keeps funding *Tatenda Clothing* to deliver training to an ever-increasing number of Malawi women as well as other social impact projects. Through *Tatenda Clothing* Malawi women are trained not only in sewing and tailoring but, now, also in business skills and financial literacy, and are encouraged to become solar light agents. At the end of their training with *Tatenda Clothing*, normally lasting six months, women receive a grant to buy a sewing machine and other necessary materials, and a completion certificate, which gives them additional business opportunities both in the fashion and solar light industries. Women are free to use this and the additional guidance, mentoring, training, and micro-finance schemes available through either *Tatenda Clothing* or the *Mayamiko Trust*, either to join *Mayamiko/Tatenda Clothing* as an employee or supplier, or to set up their own business/ workshop to supply or work for someone else.

2   In the last few years, *Mayamiko* started to commission *Tatenda Clothing* reusable sanitary kits produced using scrap fabric from the workshops, to provide Malawi women with safe and hygienic options to deal with their period. While being an additional source of impact, this project is also helping *Mayamiko* to further reduce the waste associated with the production of its collection. During the COVID-19 emergency, *Mayamiko* also adopted the model of buy-one – donate-one for face masks. It offered on its website face masks matching the fabrics of its clothes and for most of them it promised to donate one mask to communities in need for every mask bought by its international customers.

3   In 2020, *Mayamiko* enhanced its marketing and social impact with the new tagline "*Made For Joy*" and a more neutral branding that could shine a light on each individual product range and their makers. Through *Made for Joy Mayamiko*'s customers can learn more about the woman who made the product they bought and, in this way, connect with her and become aware of the impact they contributed to realise with their purchase.

4   In the same year, *Mayamiko* focused on migrating much of its training content online to be able to reach wider audiences and by-pass physical limitations.

5   Finally, *Mayamiko* empowers other organisations – its suppliers – to deliver social impact. Several of the social enterprises and Fair Trade Organisations that make up *Mayamiko*'s supply chain reinvest part of their profits through *Mayamiko* or independently into training and other opportunities for their own employees, and in community projects.

As Paola thought about new ways of growing, she kept wondering what the best ways could be to track the various social and environmental impacts of *Mayamiko* to keep scaling the impact realised.

QUESTIONS

1   *How can Mayamiko measure its impact?*
2   *What would be the benefits for Mayamiko to measure impact?*
3   *Based on what you read, are there sources of impact currently not under the radar of Paola? Or is there impact she should not be considering?*
4   *How would you keep in check Mayamiko's scaling initiatives, to ensure that its growth is not coming to the detriment of its social impact?*
5   *What could be additional ways to expand Mayamiko's impact?*

Notes

1 Mayamiko. (2021). *Our story.* Retrieved from: https://www.mayamiko.com/pages/mayamiko-the-label

2 Mayamiko. (2021). *Our promises.* Retrieved from: https://www.mayamiko.com/pages/mayamiko-and-the-planet

3 Mayamiko. (2021). *Our story.* Retrieved from: https://www.mayamiko.com/pages/mayamiko-the-label

Glossary

#MeToo: social movement against sexual abuse and sexual harassment, especially in relation to the workplace

Accelerator: organisation providing limited, cohort-based programmes that help social entrepreneurs to translate their ideas into a start-up or to identify and act on opportunities for growth

Accountability: the acceptance of responsibility for honest and ethical conduct towards others and for being evaluated based on the performance reported

Activity: what an individual or organisation does or will do

Angel investor: rich individual willing to bet part of their wealth on supporting social entrepreneurs and social entrepreneurial organisations through the provision of seed capital

Arab Spring: a series of anti-government protests, uprisings, and armed rebellions that spread across much of the Arab world in the early 2010s

Archetype: very typical example of something

Association: a group of people organised for a joint purpose

AVPN: Asian Venture Philanthropy Network

Award: small sum of money, frequently ranging from USD1,000 to USD10,000

B Corp: Certified B Corporation

B Impact Assessment: digital tool to measure the social and environmental performance of a business across four dimensions: governance, workers, community, and environment.

Beneficiary: a person the organisation wants to help

Black Lives Matter: political and social movement that seeks to highlight racism, discrimination, and inequality experienced by black people

Board of directors: governing body supervising the activities of a business composed by an elected group of individuals representing shareholders

Board of trustees: governing body supervising the activities of a charity composed by an elected group of individuals

BoP: Bottom of the Pyramid – people living below or just above the poverty

Bricolage: the assembling of existing resources in new ways and combinations

BSC: Balanced Scorecard – tool for measuring impact through key performance indicators related to four dimensions: customers perspective, financial perspective, learning and growth, and internal processes

Business model: a conceptual tool containing a set of objects, concepts, and their relationships with the objective to express the business logic of a specific firm. It is a description of the value a company offers to one or several segments of customers and of the architecture of the firm and its network of partners for creating, marketing, and delivering this value and relationship capital, to generate profitable and sustainable revenue streams

Business School of Thought: is the school of thought defining social enterprises as for-profit businesses whose main goal is to generate social and/or environmental impact

Carbon footprint: total greenhouse gas (GHG) emissions caused by an individual, event, organisation, service, place, or product

Cash flow: net amount of cash and cash equivalents being transferred in and out of a company, which therefore affect its liquidity

Channel: any channel (distribution channels, social media and media channels, promotion channels, etc.) that will be used to make a product or service available to beneficiaries and/or customers and to promote its existence

Charity: an organisation whose purpose is to give money, food, or help for free to those who need it or to carry out activities such as medical research that will help people in need, and not to make a profit

Civil rights movement: political movement and campaign from 1954 to 1968 in the United States to abolish institutional racial segregation, discrimination, and disenfranchisement throughout the United States

Climate activism: ways through which a collective of individuals and organisations is raising awareness about the issues related to climate change

Coalition government: this refers to the government formed by the Conservative and Liberal Democrat parties in the United Kingdom in 2010

Code: descriptive word, illustration, or short sentence that summarises the information contained within it

Codebook: way to synthesise and interpret large volumes of information derived from qualitative data

Collaborator: an individual or organisation who works jointly on an activity or project

Commonwealth: political association of 54 member states, almost all of which are former territories of the British Empire

Community Interest Company: legal form to incorporate social enterprises in the United Kingdom

Community School of Thought: it is the school of thought that interprets as social entrepreneurship any activity, whether pursued by an individual or organisation, which aims to benefit the local community and to generate local development

Company Limited by Guarantee: company that does not have shareholders but, instead, it is owned by a group of members known as guarantors who all agree to pay a certain amount of money when the company gets into any problems

Competitive analysis: analysis of potential and existing competitors

Competitor: rival organisation operating in the same sector or industry

Complementor: a company that sells a product or service that complements the products or services of another company

Cooperative: autonomous association of persons united voluntarily to meet their common economic, social, and cultural needs and aspirations through a jointly-owned enterprise

Corporate partnership: formal agreement between a business/corporation and a social entrepreneurial organisation where both parties remain independent but pool resources and efforts for a specific project

Crowdfunding: system through which a group of independent individuals lends or invests small sums of money to someone who is starting a project or organisation, in exchange for nothing, a token product, or a pre-determined interest rate or share

Corporate Social Responsibility (CSR):   the activities of a traditional business meant to generate positive social or environmental impact

Customer: person who buys a product or service

Cyclicality: occurrence of revenues and costs in cycles (e.g. with peaks always in the same month)

Design Thinking: a human-centred process to support innovation and problem-solving that involves a mix of rigorous research and creativity, which focuses on end users and their needs and experiences

Digital marketing: any marketing/part of the marketing mix done through the web, apps, a computer, phone, smartphone, tablet, and the like

Digital innovation: the creation of (and consequent change in) market offerings, business processes, or models that result from the use of digital technologies

Division: organisational team working on a specific project, product, or geographical location

Double bottom line: the simultaneous pursuit of social impact and profits

Due diligence: comprehensive appraisal of an organisation

Earned income: income generated by selling a product or service in a market

Earned Revenues School of Thought: it is the school of thought that defines social enterprises as the charities, NGOs, and non-profit organisations that start side activities to generate revenues as a way to become less dependent on donations and grants

Ecosystem: a community of interdependent stakeholders – individuals and organisations – their relationships and interactions, the physical environment surrounding them, and the environmental forces that shape their relationships

Empathy: the capacity to understand or feel what another person is experiencing

Empowerment: the process of becoming stronger and more confident, especially in controlling one's life and claiming one's rights

Entrepreneurship: identification, evaluation, and exploitation of opportunities or creation of a new firm in a for-profit market

Environmental sustainability: what is commonly known as sustainability

ESG: Environmental, Social, and Governance

Ethical approach: remaining aware of the context of operation and the culture, beliefs, and constraints of beneficiaries and other stakeholders

Externalities: effects on third parties that get inadvertently created

Fair Trade Organisations: organisations that have a clear commitment to Fair Trade as the principal core of their mission. They, backed by consumers, are engaged actively in supporting producers, awareness raising, and in campaigning for changes in the rules and practice of conventional international trade

Feedback loop: representation of how different elements in the system influence each other – whether in a positive or negative way

Fellowship: monetary award to an individual to sustain their pursuit of social entrepreneurship

Financial capital: money

Financial intermediary: organisation that facilitates and executes financial transactions

Financial sustainability: the ability of an organisation to maintain enough funds over time to survive

Franchising: method of distributing products or services involving a franchisor, who establishes the brand's trademark or trade name and a business system, and a franchisee, who pays a royalty and often an initial fee for the right to do business under the franchisor's name and system

Frugal innovation: the creation, under conditions of highly constrained resources, of new products and services that are "good enough" to meet a given need at a lower cost, with fewer resources and, sometimes, in a shorter time frame, than available alternatives

Foundation: type of non-profit organisation that uses an endowment to support or tackle a cause of interest

Function: marketing, accounting, sales, operations, etc.

Funder: a person or organisation that provides money for a particular purpose

Funding mix: the different sources of funds an organisation needs or has

Generation Z: demographic cohort succeeding Millennials and preceding Generation Alpha, composed of individuals born between 1995 and 2010

Global North: a grouping of countries that encompasses the rich and powerful regions such as North America, Europe, Australia, and New Zealand

Global South: a grouping of countries that encompasses low-income countries, in particular in the regions of Latin America, Asia, Africa, and Oceania

Governance: the set of rules, principles, systems, relationships, and processes through which an organisation operates and is controlled, and through which its actions and directions are held to account

Governance structures: the expression of both formal authority – i.e. who has legal authority and responsibility for decisions and who has the influence to affect key strategies and decisions

Grant: a sum of money given by a government or other public or private organisation for a particular purpose

GRI SRS: Global Reporting Initiative's Sustainability Reporting Standards – set of standards for any public or private company should disclose information to prove its sustainability performance

Hero-preneurship: approach that views social entrepreneurs as lonely heroes capable of leading teams and coalitions, overcoming any obstacle, and changing the status quo of entire systems

Human capital: people's attributes considered useful for delivering products and services (e.g. employee's knowledge, skills, know-how)

Human Resource Management: the strategic approach to manage people in an organisation (includes employees' recruitment, hiring, training, engagement, and rewarding)

Human-centred: focused on end users and their needs and experiences

IBC: International Business Council – organisation created by the World Economic Forum that developed 21 environmental, social, and governance (ESG) metrics and disclosures, based on existing standards and practices, that corporations can use to report on their impact on people and the planet

Iceberg model: visual representation of the forces influencing the stakeholders within a system

IDEO: innovation firm

Impact investor: individual or organisation that expects both a financial return and a social/environmental return for their investment

Impact measurement: the processes of analysing and monitoring the intended and unintended social, environmental, and economic consequences, both positive and negative, short- and long-term, of an organisation and of any change process triggered by that organisation that would not have happened anyway, even if the intervention did not exist

Impact-Weighted Accounts: initiative led by Harvard Business School based on adding, to the financial statements of corporations, monetary indicators that reflect the company's positive and negative impacts on employees, customers, the environment, and the broader society

Income: money that individuals and organisations receive in exchange for working, producing a product or service, or investing capital

Incorporation: the process of constituting a an organisation as a legal entity

Incubator: organisation that supports social entrepreneurial organisations for prolonged time periods, until they have acquired the resources and focus to become independent

Innovation School of Thought: the school of thought that defines social entrepreneurs as the founders of innovative non-profit organisations, empowering people, and challenging the status quo to end injustice, inequalities and entrenched social issues, thus ultimately catalysing social transformation

Input: all the human, technological, natural, physical and financial resources, information, contributions and support that an organisation needs

Institutions: formal and informal rules (e.g. laws, regulations, norms, routines, shared beliefs, and traditions) that organise social, political, and economic relations

Institutional change: the change to norms, habits, understandings and ways of operating

Institutional theory: theory that encourages the adoption of a governance structure that confers external legitimacy to the social enterprise

Institutional voids: lack of intermediaries and institutions that support market transactions such as banks giving access to credit, enforcement of property rights, or information on market participants

Intermediary: networks and organisations that support the work of social entrepreneurs and enterprises through promotion, connections, and provision of resources and advice

International development organisation: organisation dedicated to distributing aid, prevalently in low-income countries

Intervention: carefully planned process to solve a specific issue

Investor: individual or organisation that allocates capital with the expectation of a future financial return (profit) or to gain an advantage (interest)

IRIS: Impact Reporting and Investment Standards – set of standardised metrics that can be used to measure and describe the social, environmental, and financial performance of organisations and businesses receiving impact investment capital

Legal form: instrument regulated by law that provides organisations with a legal status and, thus, with the opportunity to act as an independent entity with specific rights, obligations, and responsibilities

Legitimacy: a value whereby something or someone is recognised and accepted as right and proper

Leverage point: the places within a complex system where a small shift in one thing can produce big changes in everything

Licensing: official permission or permit to do, use, or own something, normally in exchange for a fee

Limited shares company: company owned by shareholders who are liable to creditors only up to the amount they invested in the company

Logic model: model that openly and visually shows the pathway to change through unpacking the logical connections between inputs, activities, outputs, outcomes, and impact

Market economy: economic system in which the decisions regarding investment, production, and distribution are guided by the price signals created by the forces of supply and demand

Marketing: the activity, set of institutions, and processes for creating, communicating, delivering, and exchanging offerings that have value for customers, clients, partners, and society at large

Marketing mix: The set of the 7Ps of marketing: Product, Price, Place, Promotion, Process, Physical evidence, and Participants

Marshall Plan: a US-sponsored program designed to rehabilitate the economies of 17 western and southern European countries in order to create stable conditions in which democratic institutions could survive in the aftermath of World War II

Media: television, newspapers, magazines, cinema

Metaverse: a virtual-reality space mimicking the real world in which users can interact with a computer-generated environment and other users

Monetise: give monetary value

Micro-credit: the extension of very small loans to impoverished borrowers who typically lack collateral, steady employment, or a verifiable credit history

Micro-enterprise: enterprise with up to five employees

Micro-segmentation: division of a target audience into individual profiles, based on big data from websites and social media

Millennials: demographic cohort of anyone born between 1981 and 1996

Mind map: graphic tool that helps visualising thoughts and ideas and exploring the connections and relationships between them, by leveraging "radiant thinking", i.e. the spreading of thoughts out of a single idea

Minimum viable product: a functioning version of whatever they want to set up that will allow them to see if their idea works or not

Mission drift: the risk that there will be temptations and requests to slightly alter the initial mission of the organisation to get the necessary resources and support to make it grow and thrive further

Mission statement: statement that describes the fundamental purpose and philosophy of an organisation and thus provides an anchor and guiding principle for anything that it does

Neoliberalism: ideology and policy model that emphasises the value of free market competition

Necessity-driven enterprise: business that was started because there were no better options for work

Network: group of interconnected individuals and/or organisations

New Labour: a period in the history of the British Labour Party from the mid to late 1990s until 2010 under the leadership of Tony Blair and Gordon Brown

New Millennium: year 2000 onwards

Non-profit organisation: private organisation that furthers a social cause and provides a public benefit

Operations: activities that organisations engage in on a daily basis to create value

Opportunity cost: cost due to the loss of other alternatives when one alternative is chosen

Organisational culture: the pattern of basic assumptions that a given group has invented, discovered, and developed in learning to cope with its problems of external adaptation and internal integration, and that have worked well enough to be considered valid, and, therefore, to be taught to new members as the correct way to perceive, think, and feel in relation to these problems

Organisational structure: the framework through which organisational activities are divided and coordinated to ensure the achievement of its goals

Outcome: change in individuals, groups, or systems, as expressed by the altered functioning, opportunities, behaviours, knowledge, skills or capabilities, relationships, beliefs, attitudes, etc.

Outcomes Star: simplified measurement approach involving the establishment of a set of target outcomes and then the surveying of stakeholders so they can rate how much they think that outcome was achieved on a scale from one to ten

Output: direct/tangible results of activities

Overhead costs: ongoing costs to operate an organisation

Participant: any individual or organisation who takes part in the delivery of a service

Patient capital: capital provided by an investor for the long term to help the funded organisation combine the efficiency and scale of market approaches with the impact of philanthropy

Persona: fictional character representing a key stakeholder of the system, exploring and describing how they experience and relate to the system – e.g. their demographics, life standards, needs, hopes, fears, what drives or limit their actions, what influences their perceptions, what affects their power or desire to change

Personality: combination of a person's characteristics that form their distinctive character and shape their typical patterns of thoughts, feelings, and behaviours

PESTEL framework: framework to analyse the Political, Economic, Social, Technological, Environmental, and Legal forces potentially affecting an organisation

Philanthropy: the desire to promote the welfare of others, expressed especially by the generous donation of money to good causes

Physical evidence: environment in which the value proposition is delivered

Pilot: small-scale project that tests the viability, feasibility, and effectiveness of an idea without investing too much time and resources into it

Pitch: short presentation of a business or social entrepreneurial idea to another party

Place: where and how a product is made available to the target audience

Porter's Five Forces analysis: form of competitive analysis assessing the pressure on profitability exercised by five key forces affecting competition in any industry: competitors, suppliers, buyers/customers, substitutes, and the threat of new entrants

Price: the cost of the product for the target audience

Primary data: data collected first-hand, from original sources, for a specific purpose

Process: flow of activities

Procurement: the action of and choices related to obtaining or buying something for suppliers

Product: anything (e.g. product, idea, service) through which the social entrepreneurial organisation aims to deliver its value proposition/fulfil its mission

Profit: financial surplus generated by the difference between the price and the cost of producing and delivering something

Profitability: the degree to which an organisation or activity yields profit/financial surplus.

Profit margin: the amount by which revenue from sales exceeds costs

Promotion: communication of the existence and benefits of a product and, in the case of social marketing, of an opportunity for change

Prototype: a first or preliminary version of a product or service from which other forms are developed

Public authority: organisation that carries out activities in the public interest and is publicly funded through taxes at the local, regional, national, or international level. Examples include governments, ministries and government departments, the army, the police, and local administrations

Public tender: a contract which is published by a public sector organisation to invite competing offers from suppliers

Randomised Controlled Trial (RCT): the comparison of two comparable groups, one benefiting from the work and presence of the organisation and one not, in order to isolate the effects produced by that organisation beyond other context-related events or other interventions

Reformation: the start of Protestantism and the split of the Western Church into Protestantism and what is now the Roman Catholic Church

Return on investment: a ratio between net income and the investment to obtain it

Revenues: amount generated by the sale of goods or services

Risk: the possibility of loss or other adverse or unwelcome circumstance

SASB: Sustainability Accounting Standards Board – organisation that created a set of standards to enable companies to disclose information about their environmental, social, and governance (ESG) profile

Scaling up: organisational growth

SCBA: Social Cost-Benefit Analysis – impact measurement approach that involves the calculation of the economic, environmental, and social impact (direct and indirect) that an intervention is expected to generate, and its comparison with what will be spent on that intervention

Secondary data: data that has been already collected for other purposes but might contain relevant information

Segmentation: division of the target audience into groups of individuals or organisations that are relatively similar to one another in relation to characteristics of interest, and different from others in relation to those same characteristics

Share: one of the equal parts into which a company's capital is divided, entitling the holder to a proportion of the profits or to decision-making rights

Shared Ownership School of Thought: it is the school of thought that considers as social enterprises the organisations, such as cooperatives, that have a distributed ownership, i.e. that provide employees and/or stakeholders with shares, thus involving them in decision-making and enabling them to benefit economically from its activities

Shareholder: owner of a company's shares

SIA: Social Impact Accounting – impact measurement approach that involves the definition of a process that can help organisations measure the economic, social, and environmental impact of their intervention through engaging systematically with all key stakeholders

Social business model: description of how a social entrepreneurial organisation intends to generate value for key customers and/or beneficiaries, and how it ensures that its value-generation is going to be financially viable

Social business model canvas: template used for developing new social business models and documenting existing ones

Social capital: benefits deriving from social relations

Social change: the processes through which individuals, groups, and societies alter their structure and culture over both long and short timeframes

Social enterprise: social entrepreneurial organisations operating as businesses pursuing a double or triple bottom line, whose income is strongly dependent on revenue-generating activities

Social entrepreneur: individual who engages in social entrepreneurship or founds innovative non-profit organisations that aim to challenge the status quo and catalyse social transformation

Social entrepreneurship: an activity, pursued by an individual or organisation, that has as its main mission the pursuit of a social and/or environmental goal, that takes the interests of all stakeholders into consideration, and that presents entrepreneurial characteristics. These can take the form of a revenue-generating business model, a highly innovative approach and/or the employment of potential profits to benefit a given community of stakeholders

Social equality: a state of affairs in which all individuals within a specific society have equal rights, liberties, and status

Social impact: beneficial outcomes resulting from prosocial behaviour that are enjoyed by the intended targets of that behaviour and/or by the broader community of individuals, organisations, and/or environments (Note: In this book sometimes social impact is used to imply both social and environmental impact and both intended and unintended impact. When this is the case, it is explicitly mentioned)

Social Impact Bond: contract between a service provider (frequently a social enterprise), an outcome payer (normally a government or a private trust/foundation) and investors

Social innovation: a novel solution to a social problem that is more effective, efficient, sustainable, or just than existing solutions and for which the value created accrues primarily to society as a whole rather than private individuals

Social intrapreneurship: social entrepreneurship exercised within existing businesses, public authorities and non-profit organisations

Social marketing: the application of marketing knowledge, concepts, and techniques to enhance social as well as economic ends. It is also concerned with analysis of the social consequence of marketing policies, decisions, and activities

Social movement: a network of informal interactions between a plurality of individuals, groups, and/or organisations, engaged in a political or cultural conflict, on the basis of a shared collective identity

Social Purpose Company: a type of for-profit entity, a corporation, in some US states that enables, but does not require, considering social or environmental issues in decision-making

Solutions' landscape analysis: analysis of the solutions that exist to tackle a specific social or environmental issue

Spin off: independent company created through the sale or distribution of new shares of an existing business or division of a parent company

Spin out: synonym of spin off

SROI: Social Return on Investment – approach for impact measurement that consists of calculating the ratio between the additional economic, social, and environmental impact created by an organisation, and the costs it incurred in creating it

Stakeholder Capitalism Metrics: 21 environmental, social, and governance (ESG) metrics and disclosures developed by the IBC, based on existing standards and practices, that corporations can use to report on their impact on people and the planet

Stakeholders: parties that have an interest in the organisation and affect or are affected by it

Stakeholders theory: theory that encourages to establish governance structures in a way that guarantees the representation of the interests of different stakeholders

Stewardship theory: theory that encourages instead to establish governance structures in a way that guarantees that the leaders and managers of the social enterprise pursue its mission and best interests

Storytelling: the activity of telling or writing stories

Strategy: a plan of action designed to achieve a long term or overall aim

Subsidy: a form of financial aid or support consisting in granting a sum of money either to an organisation to keep the price of its product or service low, or to its customers, so they can better afford to purchase its product or service

Substitute: alternative product/service a customer can buy

Sunk cost: cost that once incurred cannot be recovered – e.g. expensive equipment, acquisition of a building – and therefore constrain future choices and actions

Supplier: a person or organisation that provides something needed to another organisation, such as a product, service, skills, or raw materials

Supporting infrastructure: set of basic services, support, and public infrastructure that make the activities of an individual or organisation possible

Sustainable Development Goals (SDGs): collection of 17 interlinked global goals designed to be a "blueprint to achieve a better and more sustainable future for all"

SWOT analysis: analysis of an organisation's Strengths, Weaknesses, Opportunities, and Threats

System: group of stakeholders that are linked to one other for a given purpose and whose actions and relationships are guided by power dynamics and environmental forces

Systems analysis: identifying which stakeholders are involved in a system, what role they play, how they relate to each other and where they stand in terms of supporting versus hindering the functioning of the system and of promoting/resisting change

Systems change: an intentional process designed to alter the status quo by shifting and realigning the form and function of a targeted system

Systems leader: individual or organisation who empowers others to bring about change, mobilising them and coordinating them to achieve more together than they could do alone

Systems thinking: the adoption of a perspective, which focuses on understanding the different elements of a system and the interconnections between them, with the goal of identifying ways to alter the system and the issues it creates or perpetuates

Target audience: the people who the organisation wants to affect

Targeting: strategic choice of which segments, among the target audience, to focus on

Theory of Change (ToC):   the explanation of how an individual, organisation, project, investment, or intervention aims to generate (intended) social and/or environmental impact

Think tank: research institute that performs research and advocacy concerning topics such as social policy, political strategy, economics, military, technology, and culture

Transaction costs: total costs of making a transaction, including the cost of planning, deciding, changing plans, resolving disputes, and after-sales

Triple bottom line: the simultaneous pursuit of social impact, financial sustainability, and the protection of the environment

Value: the importance, worth, or usefulness of something

Value chain: the set of value-adding stakeholders and activities that jointly transform inputs such as raw materials into products and services and bring these to customers (and/or beneficiaries)

Value proposition: explanation of the added social/environmental and economic value that the social entrepreneurial organisation is going to create and deliver in relation to its mission

Venture philanthropy: philanthropy by rich individuals, normally from technology-based sectors, or foundations, who want to support only innovative projects or initiatives with a potential to generate social or environmental impact at scale, characterised by a focus on impact measurement, strong involvement of the philanthropist in the funded organisation and their provision of support and connections as well as funds

Volunteers: individuals who give their time and skills without pay to benefit others

Welfare: type of government support intended to ensure that members of a society can meet basic human needs

Welfare state: form of government in which the state or a well-established network of social institutions play a key role in the protection and promotion of the economic and social well-being of citizens

Wicked problem: problem that is difficult or impossible to solve because of its multiple, interdependent causes, which are often difficult to recognise

WISE: Work Integration Social Enterprise. Social enterprise that employs vulnerable or marginalised people who would otherwise find it difficult to become integrated or re-integrated into the labour market

Women's suffrage movement: decades-long fight mostly active in the early 1900s to win the right to vote for women

Work from home (WFH):   practice of conduction someone's job from home instead of from the offices and premises of the organisation that employs them

Workflow: the sequence of processes, steps, and decisions through which a piece of work passes from initiation to completion

Bibliography

Abercrombie, R., Harries, E., & Wharton, R. (2015). *Systems change: A guide to what it is and how to do it*. New Philanthropy Capital Paper, June 2015.

Abila, R. O., Ojwang, W., Othina, A., Lwenya, C., Oketch, R., & Okeyo, R. (2013). Using ICT for fish marketing: The EFMIS model in Kenya. *Food Chain*, *3*(1–2), 48–63.

Abson, D. J., Fischer, J., Leventon, J., Newig, J., Schomerus, T., Vilsmaier, U., ... & Lang, D. J. (2017). Leverage points for sustainability transformation. *Ambio*, *46*(1), 30–39.

Acs, Z. J., Stam, E., Audretsch, D. B., & O'Connor, A. (2017). The lineages of the entrepreneurial ecosystem approach. *Small Business Economics*, *49*(1), 1–10.

ACT. (2019). *ACT. Aspire Coronation Trust Foundation Brochure*. Retrieved from: https://actrustfoundation.org/html_main/images/portfolio/pdf/2019_act_brochure.pdf [Last accessed on: 24 January 2022].

ACT. (2021). *About changemakers innovation challenge*. Retrieved from: http://changemakers.actrustfoundation.org/ [Last accessed on: 24 January 2022].

Acumen. (2021a). *Acumen's patient capital model is a new approach to solving poverty*. Retrieved from: https://acumen.org/about/patient-capital/ [Last accessed on: 04 April 2021].

Acumen. (2021b). *Impact measurement: We created lean data to listen to low-income customers and understand what impact means to them*. Retrieved from: https://acumen.org/lean-data/ [Last accessed on: 04 April 2021].

Acumen. (2021c). *Our approach: Patient capital that dares to go where markets have failed and aid has fallen short*. Retrieved from: https://acumen.org/approach/ [Last accessed on: 04 April 2021].

Acumen. (2021d). *Our story*. Retrieved from: https://acumen.org/about/ [Last accessed on: 04 April 2021].

Acumen Academy. (2021a). *Become a fellow: Join a committed cohort of leaders intent on building an inclusive, just and sustainable world*. Retrieved from: https://www.acumenacademy.org/fellowship [Last accessed on: 04 April 2021].

Acumen Academy. (2021b). *Learn: Choose your experience*. Retrieved from: https://www.acumenacademy.org/learn [Last accessed on: 04 April 2021].

Acumen Academy. (2021c). *Our story*. Retrieved from: https://www.acumenacademy.org/our-story [Last accessed on: 04 April 2021].

Acumen Fund Metrics Team. (2007). *Acumen fund concepts. The best available charitable option*. Retrieved from: https://acumen.org/wp-content/uploads/2013/03/BACO-Concept-Paper-final.pdf [Last accessed on: 8 October 2021].

Africapitalism Institute. (2015). *Unleashing Africa's entrepreneurs: Improving the enabling environment for start-ups*. Tony Elumulu Foundation.

Al Taji, F. N. A., & Bengo, I. (2019). The distinctive managerial challenges of hybrid organizations: Which skills are required? *Journal of Social Entrepreneurship*, *10*(3), 328–345.

All Answers Ltd. (2018). *Impact measurement tools for social enterprises: Use and efficiency.* Retrieved from https://ukdiss.com/examples/impact-measurement-tools-for-social-enterprises.php [Last accessed on: 8 October 2021].

Alter, K. (2007). Social enterprise typology. *Virtue Ventures LLC, 12*(1), 1–124.

American Marketing Association. (2017). *Definition of marketing.* Retrieved from: https://www.ama.org/the-definition-of-marketing-what-is-marketing/ [Last accessed on: 09 December 2021].

American Sociological Association. (2020). *Social change.* Retrieved from: https://www.asanet.org/topics/social-change [Last accessed on: 04 December 2020].

Anderson, V., & Johnson, L. (1997). *Systems thinking basics.* Cambridge, MA: Pegasus Communications, 1–14.

André, K., & Pache, A.C. (2016). From caring entrepreneur to caring enterprise: Addressing the ethical challenges of scaling up social enterprises. *Journal of Business Ethics, 133*(4), 659–675.

Anner, J. (2016). *Blended value accounting and social enterprise success* (Doctoral dissertation, Walden University).

Ariza-Montes, A., Sianes, A., Fernández-Rodríguez, V., López-Martín, C., Ruíz-Lozano, M., Tirado-Valencia, P. (2021). *Social Return on Investment (SROI) to assess the impacts of tourism: A case study.* SAGE Open.

Ashkenas, R., & Matta, N. (2021, January 8). *How to scale a successful pilot project.* Retrieved from: https://hbr.org/2021/01/how-to-scale-a-successful-pilot-project [Last accessed on: 10 October 2021].

Ashoka (2021). *Social entrepreneurship.* Retrieved from: https://www.ashoka.org/en-us/focus/social-entrepreneurship [Last accessed on: 14 October 2021].

AT&T (2021). *Sustainability Accounting Standards Board (SASB) index.* Retrieved from: https://about.att.com/csr/home/reporting/indexes/sasb.html [Last accessed on: 4 October 2021].

Austin, J., Stevenson, H., & Wei–Skillern, J. (2006). Social and commercial entrepreneurship: Same, different, or both? *Entrepreneurship Theory and Practice, 30*(1), 1–22.

B Impact Assessment. (2022a). *Frequently asked questions: The standards.* Retrieved from: https://bimpactassessment.net/how-it-works/frequently-asked-questions/the-standards [Last accessed on: 24 January 2022].

B Impact Assessment. (2022b). *Frequently asked questions: Top 10.* Retrieved from: https://bimpactassessment.net/how-it-works/frequently-asked-questions/top-10?_ga=2.241181762.1166761515.1643381127-382389521.1643381127#what-is-considered-a-%22good%22-score [Last accessed on: 24 January 2022].

B Impact Assessment. (2022a). *Step 1. Assess your impact.* Retrieved from: https://bimpactassessment.net/how-it-works/assess-your-impact [Last accessed on: 24 January 2022].

B Impact Assessment. (2022b). *Step 2. Compare your impact.* Retrieved from: https://bimpactassessment.net/how-it-works/compare-your-impact [Last accessed on: 24 January 2022].

B Impact Assessment. (2022c). *Step 3. Improve your impact.* Retrieved from: https://bimpactassessment.net/how-it-works/improve-your-impact [Last accessed on: 24 January 2022].

Back on Track. (2020). *Refugee children learn with back on track.* Retrieved from: https://backontracksyria.org/en/ [Last accessed on: 10 November 2020].

Bacq, S., & Eddleston, K. A. (2018). A resource-based view of social entrepreneurship: How stewardship culture benefits scale of social impact. *Journal of Business Ethics, 152*(3), 589–611.

Bacq, S., & Janssen, F. (2011). The multiple faces of social entrepreneurship: A review of definitional issues based on geographical and thematic criteria. *Entrepreneurship & Regional Development, 23*(5–6), 373–403.

Barby, C., & Gan, J. (2014). *Shifting the lens: A de-risking toolkit for impact investment.* London: Bridges Ventures LLP.

Barela, E. (2019). *Insights from Eric Barela.* In Theme 9: Limits of quantitative evidence. Impacting Responsibly Report.

Bell, B., & Haugh, H. (2014). Working for a social enterprise. An exploration of employee rewards and motivations. In Denny, S., & Seddon, F. (Ed.). *Social enterprise: Accountability and evaluation around the world*, New York: Routledge, Chapter 5, 67–84.

Bennett, S., & Muir, K. (2014). *The compass: Your guide to social impact measurement.* Centre for Social Impact, University of New South Wales.

Beugré, C. (2016). *Social entrepreneurship: Managing the creation of social value.* New York: Routledge

Bhatti, Y., & Prabhu, J. (2019). Chapter 20: Frugal innovation and social innovation: linked paths to achieving inclusion sustainably". In George, G., Baker, T., Tracey, P., & Joshi, H. (Ed.). Handbook of Inclusive Innovation. Cheltenham, UK: Edward Elgar Publishing, 354–376.

Black, S., Gardner, D. G., Pierce, J. L., & Steers, R. (2019). *Organizational Behavior.* Rice University: OpenStax.

Bloom, P. N., & Dees, G. (2008). Cultivate your ecosystem. *Stanford Social Innovation Review*, 6(1), 47–53.

Bloom, P. N., & Smith, B. R. (2010). Identifying the drivers of social entrepreneurial impact: Theoretical development and an exploratory empirical test of SCALERS. *Journal of Social Entrepreneurship*, 1(1), 126–145.

Bocken, N. M., Short, S. W., Rana, P., & Evans, S. (2014). A literature and practice review to develop sustainable business model archetypes. *Journal of Cleaner Production*, 65, 42–56.

Bonchek, M. (2016, March 25). *How to build a strategic narrative.* Retrieved from: https://hbr.org/2016/03/how-to-build-a-strategic-narrative [Last accessed on: 25 October 2021].

Bone, J., & Baeck, P. (2016, September 14). How to find the right crowdfunding platform for your good cause. *Nesta.* Retrieved from: https://www.nesta.org.uk/blog/how-to-find-the-right-crowdfunding-platform-for-your-good-cause/ [Last accessed on: 13 January 2022].

Booms, B.H., & Bitner, M.J. (1981). Marketing strategies and organization structures for service firms. In Donnelly, J. H., & George, W. R. (Eds), *Marketing of services,* Chicago: American Marketing Association, 47–51

Borges Ladeira, F. M., & Vier Machado, H. (2013). Social entrepreneurship: A reflection for adopting public policies that support the third sector in Brazil. *Journal of Technology Management & Innovation*, 8, 17.

Bornstein, D., & Davis, S. (2010). *Social Entrepreneurship : What Everyone Needs to Know®.* Oxford: Oxford University Press.

Borzaga, C., Galera, G., Franchini, B., Chiomento, S., Nogales, R., & Carini, C. (2020). *Social enterprises and their ecosystems in Europe. Comparative synthesis report.* Luxembourg, LU: Publications Office of the European Union.

Boschee, J. (1998). *Merging mission and money: A board member's guide to social entrepreneurship.* Washington, DC: National Center for Nonprofit Council.

Bosma, N., Schøtt, T., Terjesen, S., & Kew, P. (2015). *Special topic report – Social entrepreneurship.* Global Entrepreneurship Monitor.

Bosma, N., Schøtt, T., Terjesen, S. A., & Kew, P. (2016). *Global entrepreneurship monitor 2015 to 2016: special topic report on social entrepreneurship.* Lausanne: Global Entrepreneurship Research Association.

Boswell, K., & Handley, S. (2016). *Result! What good impact reporting looks like.* NPC Briefing, January, 2016.

Bounce Back. (2021). *About us.* Retrieved from: https://www.bouncebackproject.com/about-us/ [Last accessed on: 23 April 2021].

Bozhikin, I., Macke, J., & da Costa, L. F. (2019). The role of government and key non-state actors in social entrepreneurship: A systematic literature review. *Journal of Cleaner Production*, 226, 730–747.

British Council. (2017). *The state of social enterprise in Kenya.* The British Council report series. Retrieved from: https://www.britishcouncil.org/sites/default/files/state_of_social_enterprise_in_kenya_british_council_final.pdf [Last accessed on: 07 March 2021].

British Council. (2021). *Social enterprise*. Retrieved from: https://www.britishcouncil.org/society/social-enterprise [Last accessed on: 26 February 2021].

Brown, T., & Wyatt, J. (2010). Design thinking for social innovation. *Development Outreach*, 12(1), 29–43.

Buchanan, R. (1992). Wicked problems in design thinking. *Design Issues*, 8(2), 5–21.

Business Make Over (2021). *Competitor analysis*. Retrieved from: https://businessmakeover.eu/de/tools/competitor-analysis [Last accessed on: 14 August 2021].

Byronetics (2006). *Aravind Eye Hospital*. Retrieved from: https://www.youtube.com/watch?v=3cjnNPua7Ag&ab_channel=byronetics [Last accessed on: 04 February 2021].

Cambridge Judge Business School. (2017, June 12). *Reflecting on three years of Cambridge social ventures*. Retrieved from: https://www.jbs.cam.ac.uk/insight/2017/reflecting-three-years-of-cambridge-social-ventures/t - CJBS [Last accessed on: 04 January 2021].

Casadesus-Masanell, R., & Ricart, J. E. (2010). From strategy to business models and onto tactics. *Long Range Planning*, 43(2–3), 195–215.

Center for Theory of Change. (2021a). *TOC benefits*. Retrieved from: https://www.theoryofchange.org/what-is-theory-of-change/ToC-background/ToC-benefits/ [Last accessed on: 25 October 2021].

Center for Theory of Change. (2021b). *TOC origins*. Retrieved from: https://www.theoryofchange.org/what-is-theory-of-change/ToC-background/ToC-origins/ [Last accessed on: 25 October 2021].

Certified B Corporation. (2020a). *A global community of leaders*. Retrieved from: https://bcorporation.uk/ [Last accessed on: 18 December 2020].

Certified B Corporation. (2020b). *About B Corps*. Retrieved from: https://bcorporation.uk/about-b-corps [Last accessed on: 18 December 2020].

Checkland, P. (1999). Systems thinking. In Currie, W. L., & Galliers, B. (Eds). *Rethinking management information systems*. Oxford: Oxford University Press 45–56.

Cheney, C. (2017, September 22). *Social business: Muhammad Yunus on his new strategy for fighting poverty*. Retrieved from: https://www.devex.com/news/social-business-muhammad-yunus-on-his-new-strategy-for-fighting-poverty-91114 [Last accessed on: 28 October 2021].

Chilufya, R., & Kerlin, J. A. (2017). Zambia: Innate resource legacies and social enterprise development: The impact of human agency and socio-spatial context in a rural setting. In Kerlin, J. A. (Ed.). *Shaping social enterprise*. Bingley: Emerald Publishing Limited. Chapter 9, 217–252.

Choi, N., & Majumdar, S. (2014). Social entrepreneurship as an essentially contested concept: Opening a new avenue for systematic future research. *Journal of Business Venturing*, 29(3), 363–376.

Chou, D. C. (2018). Applying design thinking method to social entrepreneurship project. *Computer Standards & Interfaces*, 55, 73–79.

Clark, C., Rosenzweig, W., Long, D., & Olsen, S. (2004). *Double bottom line project report: Assessing social impact in double bottom line ventures*; Methods Catalog. Berkeley, CA: University of California, Berkley.

CNN (2019). *Their way of life in the Amazon rainforest may become extinct*. Retrieved from: https://www.youtube.com/watch?v=Srr3EDoHtqw&ab_channel=CNN [Last accessed on: 28 May 2021].

Cohen, R. (2014, March 31). *Design thinking: A unified framework for innovation*. Retrieved from: https://www.forbes.com/sites/reuvencohen/2014/03/31/design-thinking-a-unified-framework-for-innovation/#8109b3d56fca [Last accessed on: 22 October 2021].

Cohen, R. (2021). *Impact: Reshaping capitalism to drive real change*. New York: Morgan James Publishing.

Cohen, S. (2013). What do accelerators do? Insights from incubators and angels. *Innovations: Technology, Governance, Globalization*, 8(3–4), 19–25.

Collavo, T. (2018). Unpacking social entrepreneurship: Exploring the definition chaos and its consequences in England. *Journal of Entrepreneurship, Management and Innovation*, 14(2), 19–47.

Collavo, T., Nicholls, A., & Ventresca, M. (2018). *Brokerage as an institutional strategy in fragmented fields: The crafting of social entrepreneurship*. University of Oxford web repository.

Connell, J. P., & Kubisch, A. C. (1998). Applying a theory of change approach to the evaluation of comprehensive community initiatives: progress, prospects, and problems. *New approaches to evaluating community initiatives*, 2(15–44), 1–16.

Conservation International. (2013). *Constructing theories of change for Ecosystem-based Adaptation projects: A guidance document*. Arlington, VA: Conservation International.

Conservation International. (2021a). *About conservation international*. Retrieved from: https://www.conservation.org/about [Last accessed on: 31 May 2021].

Conservation International. (2021b). *Impact report 2020*. Retrieved from: https://www.conservation.org/about/annual-report [Last accessed on: 31 May 2021].

Conservation International (2021c). *Partnering with communities*. Retrieved from: https://www.conservation.org/priorities/partnering-with-communities [Last accessed on: 03 June 2021].

Conservation International. (2021d). *Protecting nature to halt climate catastrophe*. Retrieved from: https://www.conservation.org/priorities/protecting-nature-to-halt-climate-catastrophe [Last accessed on: 28 May 2021].

Coonaprosal. (2020). *History*. Retrieved from: https://coonaprosal.com/historia/ [Last accessed on: 9 September 2020].

Corporate Finance Institute. (2021). *PESTEL analysis*. Retrieved from: https://corporatefinanceinstitute.com/resources/knowledge/strategy/pestel-analysis/ [Last accessed on: 19 November 2021].

Corvo, L., Pastore, L., Manti, A., & Iannaci, D. (2021). Mapping social impact assessment models: A literature overview for a future research agenda. *Sustainability*, 13(9), 4750.

CREN. (2022). *About CREN*. Retrieved from: https://www.cren.org.br/en/about-us/ [Last accessed on: 02 February 2022].

Cross, J., & Street, A. (2009). Anthropology at the bottom of the pyramid. *Anthropology Today*, 25(4), 4–9.

Dacin, P. A., Dacin, M. T., & Matear, M. (2010). Social entrepreneurship: Why we don't need a new theory and how we move forward from here. *Academy of Management Perspectives*, 24(3), 37–57.

Dam, R. F., & Siang, T. Y. (2020). *What is design thinking and why is it so popular?* Retrieved from: https://www.interaction-design.org/literature/article/what-is-design-thinking-and-why-is-it-so-popular [Last accessed on: 18 October 2021].

Dam, R. F., & Siang, T. Y. (2021). *5 stages in the design thinking process*. Retrieved from: https://www.interaction-design.org/literature/article/5-stages-in-the-design-thinking-process [Last accessed on: 1 November 2021].

Datta, P. B., & Gailey, R. (2012). Empowering women through social entrepreneurship: Case study of a women's cooperative in India. *Entrepreneurship Theory and Practice*, 36(3), 569–587.

De Silva, M. J., Breuer, E., Lee, L., Asher, L., Chowdhary, N., Lund, C., & Patel, V. (2014). Theory of change: A theory-driven approach to enhance the Medical Research Council's framework for complex interventions. *Trials*, 15(1), 1–13.

Dees, G., Anderson, B. B., & Emerson, J. (2002). Developing viable earned income strategies. In Dees, J. G., Emerson, J., & Economy, P. (Eds). *Strategic tools for social entrepreneurs: Enhancing the performance of your enterprising nonprofit*, New York: Wiley.

Dees, J. G. (1998). The meaning of social entrepreneurship (unpublished).

Deetken Impact. (2019, May 28) *A look at social entrepreneurship in Peru*. Retrieved from: https://deetkenimpact.com/blog/a-look-at-social-entrepreneurs-in-peru/ [Last accessed on: 04 March 2021].

Defourny, J., & Nyssens, M. (2010). Conceptions of social enterprise and social entrepreneurship in Europe and the United States: Convergences and divergences. *Journal of Social Entrepreneurship*, *1*(1), 32–53.

Defourny, J., & Nyssens, M. (Eds). (2021). *Social enterprise in Central and Eastern Europe: Theory, models and practice*. New York: Routledge.

Della Porta, D., & Diani, M. (2006). *Social movements: An introduction* (2nd ed.). Malden, MA: Blackwell.

Dellinger, A. J. (2020, December 14). Meet the CEO selling boxes of "ugly" produce to help solve our food waste crisis. *Mic*. Retrieved from: https://www.mic.com/p/meet-the-ceo-selling-boxes-of-ugly-produce-to-help-solve-our-food-waste-crisis-49280642 [Last accessed on: 18 January 2021].

Deshpande, R., & Gatingon, H. (1994). Competitive analysis. *Marketing Letters*, *5*(3), 271–287.

Dey, P., & Steyaert, C. (Eds). (2018). *Social entrepreneurship: an affirmative critique.* Cheltenham: Edward Elgar Publishing.

Diani, M. (1992). The concept of social movement. *The Sociological Review*, *40*(1), 1–25.

DiStefano, J. N. (2020, July 22). Misfits Market, which distributes 'ugly' produce for cheap, raises $85 million and plans to double its work force. *The Philadelphia Inquirer*. Retrieved from: https://www.inquirer.com/news/misfits-market-abhi-ramesh-ugly-produce-20200722.html [Last accessed on: 18 January 2021].

Dogshun, J. (2018, June 22). *How change got global: The founding story of impact hub.* Retrieved from: https://impacthub.net/how-change-got-global-the-founding-story-of-impact-hub/ [Last accessed on: 28 March 2021].

Doherty, B. (2009). *Management for social enterprise.* Los Angeles; London: SAGE.

Doherty, B. (2014). Social enterprise management: How do social enterprises compete? In Denny, S., & Seddon, F. (Ed.). Social enterprise: Accountability and evaluation around the world, New York: Routledge, Chapter 3, 28–49.

Doherty, B., Haugh, H., Sahan, E., Wills, T., & Croft, S. (2020). *Creating the new economy: Business models that put people and planet first.* York: White Rose Research Online, Research Report.

Bitange Ndemo, E. (2006), Assessing sustainability of faith-based enterprises in Kenya, *International Journal of Social Economics*, *33*(5/6), 446–462.

Dollinger, M. (2008). *Entrepreneurship.* Norwood: Marsh Publications.

Donovan, R. J., Egger, G., & Francas, M. (1999). TARPARE: a method for selecting target audiences for public health interventions. *Australian and New Zealand Journal of Public Health*, *23*(3), 280–284.

Dorst, K. (2011). The core of 'design thinking' and its application. *Design Studies*, *32*(6), 521–532.

Dowla, A. (2006). In credit we trust: Building social capital by Grameen Bank in Bangladesh. *The Journal of Socio-Economics*, *35*(1), 102–122.

Doz, Y. L., & Kosonen, M. (2010). Embedding strategic agility: A leadership agenda for accelerating business model renewal. *Long Range Planning*, *43*(2–3), 370–382

Dushin, M., & Dodson, S. (2015). *Developing a social enterprise business plan.* Harvard Business School, February 11, 2015.

Ebrahim, A. (2019). *Measuring social change: Performance and accountability in a complex world.* Stanford, CA: Stanford University Press.

ECOALF. (2022). *DNA.* Retrieved from: https://ecoalf.com/en/p/purpose--88 [Last accessed on: 02 February 2022].

Ecochallenge.org (2021). *Iceberg model. Learn about the theory and practice of systems thinking.* Retrieved from: https://ecochallenge.org/iceberg-model/ [Last accessed on: 30 April 2021].

Edward Lowe Foundation. (2021). *How to conduct and prepare a competitive analysis.* Retrieved from: https://edwardlowe.org/how-to-conduct-and-prepare-a-competitive-analysis/ [Last accessed on: 14 August 2021].

Emerald Publishing. (2021). *How to...Mind map*. Retrieved from: https://www.emeraldgrouppublishing.com/how-to/study-skills/mind-map [Last accessed on: 24 July 2021].

Epstein, M. J., & Yuthas, K. (2014). *Measuring and improving social impacts: A guide for non-profits, companies, and impact investors*. New York: Routledge.

Esmée Fairbairn Foundation. (2022a). *Our support. Funding plus*. Retrieved from: https://esmeefairbairn.org.uk/our-support/funding-plus/ [Last accessed on: 24 January 2022].

Esmée Fairbairn Foundation. (2022b). *Our support: Using all the tools in our toolbox*. Retrieved from: https://esmeefairbairn.org.uk/our-support/ [Last accessed on: 24 January 2022].

Ethical Rebel. (2022). *Thrædable*. Retrieved from: https://ethicalrebel.co.uk/ethical_brands/thr%C7%A3dable/ [Last accessed on: 24 January 2022].

European Commission. (2015). *A map of social enterprises and their eco-systems in Europe*. Directorate-General for Employment, Social Affairs and Inclusion report.

European Investment Fund. (2020). *Connecting impact investors with social enterprises: The European Social Innovation and Impact Fund launches after a successful first closing*. Retrieved from: https://www.eif.org/what_we_do/guarantees/news/2020/european-social-innovation-and-impact-fund-launches-after-successful-first-closing.htm?lang=-en [Last accessed on: 23 March 2021].

Facca-Miess, T. M., & Santos, N. J. (2014). Fostering fair and sustainable marketing for social entrepreneurs in the context of subsistence marketplaces. *Journal of Marketing Management, 30*(5–6), 501–518.

Farnham, L. (2021, April). *Field catalysts: How system change happens*. Panel discussion at the Skoll World Forum 2021, which can be accessed at https://skoll.org/session/skoll-world-forum-2021/field-catalysts-how-systems-change-happens/ [Last accessed on: 30 April 2021].

Fast Company. (2008, December 1). *The Acumen fund: Pulse*. Retrieved from: https://www.fastcompany.com/1094927/acumen-fund-pulse-2 [Last accessed on: 4 October 2021].

Financial Services Compensation Scheme. (2020, November 16). *What's crowdfunding? What are the risks?* Retrieved from: https://www.fscs.org.uk/news/investing/crowdfunding/ [Last accessed on: 13 January 2022].

FINCA. (2021a). *Investing in bold ideas and partnering with enterprising founders intent on eradicating global poverty in this generation*. Retrieved from: https://fincaventures.com/ [Last accessed on: 14 March 2021].

FINCA. (2021b). *Our impact*. Retrieved from: https://finca.org/our-impact/ [Last accessed on: 14 March 2021].

Fisher, H. L. (2019, December 18). Make an impact podcast: Shattering illusions and accelerating impact: Heidi on the Social Enterprise World Forum. Retrieved from: https://makeanimpact.buzzsprout.com/507019/2307701-shattering-illusions-and-accelerating-impact-heidi-on-the-social-enterprise-world-forum [Last accessed on: 7 December 2020].

Fisher, H. L. (2019, September 6). *Make an impact podcast - Why social enterprises must nurture their talent and how to do it with Craig Carey*. Retrieved from: https://makeanimpact.buzzsprout.com/507019/1661419-why-social-enterprises-must-nurture-their-talent-and-how-to-do-it-with-craig-carey?play=true [Last accessed on: 12 April 2021].

Fitzhugh, H., & Stevenson, N. (2015). *Inside social enterprise: Looking to the future*. Bristol: Policy Press.

Fleisher, C. S., & Bensoussan, B. E. (2003). *Strategic and competitive analysis: Methods and techniques for analyzing business competition*. Upper Saddle River, NJ: Prentice Hall.

Florman, M., Vidra, R. K., & Facada, M. J. (2016). *A critical evaluation of social impact assessment methodologies and a call to measure economic and social impact holistically through the External Rate of Return platform*, London School of Economics Enterprise Working Paper #1602.

Forbes. (2018). *Liberty & justice: A social enterprise impact story*. Retrieved from: https://www.youtube.com/watch?v=5J9i5qUgqw4 [Last accessed on: 8 December 2020].

Forbes. (2020). *The 2020 30 Under 30: Social entrepreneurs.* Retrieved from: https://www.forbes.com/30-under-30/2020/social-entrepreneurs/#486df01a4330 [Last accessed on: 18 January 2021].

Foster-Fishman, P. G., Nowell, B., & Yang, H. (2007). Putting the system back into systems change: A framework for understanding and changing organizational and community systems. *American Journal of Community Psychology, 39*(3–4), 197–215.

Fowler, A. (2000). NGDOs as a moment in history: Beyond aid to social entrepreneurship or civic innovation? *Third World Quarterly, 21*(4), 637–654.

Frontier Markets. (2020a). *Frontier markets: About.* Retrieved from: https://frontiermkts.com/about/ [Last accessed on: 15 November 2020].

Frontier Markets. (2020b). *Frontier markets: General information.* Retrieved from: https://frontiermkts.com/ [Last accessed on: 15 November 2020].

Fundacion Escuela Nueva. (2021). *About us.* Retrieved from: https://escuelanueva.org/en/mision-vision/ [Last accessed on: 22 April 2021].

Gao, C., Zuzul, T., Jones, G., & Khanna, T. (2017). Overcoming institutional voids: A reputation-based view of long-run survival. *Strategic Management Journal, 38*(11), 2147–2167.

Garmilla, A. (2017, March 20). *#WOWWOMEN! An interview with pioneering social entrepreneur Chiara Condi, founder of Led by HER.* W4. Retrieved from: https://www.w4.org/en/wowwire/social-entrepreneur-chiara-condi/ [Last accessed on: 4 July 2021].

Gasca, L. (2017, June 8). *3 reasons why social enterprises fail – And what we can learn from them.* World Economic Forum. Retrieved from: https://www.weforum.org/agenda/2017/06/3-reasons-why-social-enterprises-fail-and-what-we-can-learn-from-them/ [Last accessed on: 3 July 2021].

Gauteng. (2020). *Imbali visual literacy project.* Retrieved from: https://www.gauteng.net/attractions/imbali_visual_literacy_project [Last accessed on: 12 August 2020].

Gelfand, S. (2012, October 10). *Why IRIS? The second in a four-part series on impact investing and the role of metrics.* Stanford Social Innovation Review. Retrieved from: https://ssir.org/articles/entry/why_iris. [Last accessed on: 4 October 2021].

George, C., & Reed, M. G. (2016). Building institutional capacity for environmental governance through social entrepreneurship: Lessons from Canadian biosphere reserves. *Ecology and Society, 21*(1), 18.

Global Impact Investing Network. (2021). *What you need to know about impact investing.* Retrieved from: https://thegiin.org/impact-investing/need-to-know/#who-is-making-impact-investments [Last accessed on: 04 March 2021].

Global Reporting Initiative. (2021a). *The global standards for sustainability reporting.* Retrieved from: https://www.globalreporting.org/standards/ [Last accessed on: 4 October 2021].

Global Reporting Initiative. (2021b). *Why report?* Retrieved from: https://www.globalreporting.org/how-to-use-the-gri-standards/ [Last accessed on: 4 October 2021].

Goi, C. L. (2009). A review of marketing mix: 4Ps or more. *International Journal of Marketing Studies, 1*(1), 2–15.

González Vega, C. (1998). *Microfinance: Broader achievements and new challenges.* Economics and Sociology

Occasional Paper No. 2518. Ohio: Rural Finance Program Department of Agricultural, Environmental, and Development Economics.

Good finance. (2021). *Types of social investment.* Retrieved from: https://www.goodfinance.org.uk/understanding-social-investment/types-social-investment [Last accessed on: 13 March 2021].

Governance Institute of Australia. (2021). *What is governance?* Retrieved from: https://www.governanceinstitute.com.au/resources/what-is-governance/ [Last accessed on: 07 February 2021].

Government Outcomes Lab. (2015). *Unit cost database.* Retrieved from: https://golab.bsg.ox.ac.uk/knowledge-bank/resources/unit-cost-database/ [Last accessed on: 24 January 2022].

Graham, F. (2010, November 22). *M-Pesa: Kenya's mobile wallet revolution.* Retrieved from: https://www.bbc.co.uk/news/business-11793290 [Last accessed on: 22 April 2021].

Grameen Bank. (2020). *History.* Retrieved from: http://www.grameen.com/history/ [Last accessed on: 7 October 2020].

Granovetter, M. S. (1973). The strength of weak ties. *American Journal of Sociology, 78*(6), 1360–1380.

Grant, R. M. (2012). *Contemporary strategy analysis: Text and cases* (8th ed.). Hoboken: John Wiley & Sons.

Gray, I. (2017). *A quick guide to theory of change.* NIDOS - Scotland's International Development Alliance, April 2017.

Green, D. (2016). *How change happens.* Oxford: Oxford University Press.

Grieco, C. (2015). *Assessing social impact of social enterprises: Does one size really fit all?* Heidelberg: Springer.

Guo, C., & Bielefeld, W. (2014). *Social entrepreneurship: An evidence-based approach to creating social value.* Hoboken: John Wiley & Sons.

Hall, K., & Arvidson, M. (2014). How do we know if social enterprise works? Tools for assessing social enterprise performance. In Denny, S., & Seddon, F. (Ed.). *Social enterprise: Accountability and evaluation around the world,* New York: Routledge, Chapter 9, 141–157.

Hannam, M. (2008, April 27). *Muhammad Yunus: The Bangladeshi economist has helped millions by pioneering microcredit. Now he has a new idea—social business—which he believes can eliminate world poverty.* Retrieved from: https://www.prospectmagazine.co.uk/magazine/muhammadyunus [Last accessed on: 22 October 2021].

Harvard Business School. (2022). *Why impact-weighted accounts.* Retrieved from: https://www.hbs.edu/impact-weighted-accounts/Pages/default.aspx [Last accessed on: 24 January 2022].

Haugh, H. M., & Talwar, A. (2016). Linking social entrepreneurship and social change: The mediating role of empowerment. *Journal of Business Ethics, 133*(4), 643–658.

Hazenberg, R., Bajwa-Patel, M., Mazzei, M., Roy, M. J., & Baglioni, S. (2016). The role of institutional and stakeholder networks in shaping social enterprise ecosystems in Europe. *Social Enterprise Journal* 12(3), 302–321.

Henderson, S. (2019, July 30). *Design DNA: The perils of design thinking.* Retrieved from: https://www.idsa.org/news/innovation/design-dna [Last accessed on: 1 November 2021].

Hillyer, M. (2021, January 26). *Global business leaders support ESG convergence by committing to stakeholder capitalism metrics.* World Economic Forum. Retrieved from: https://www.weforum.org/press/2021/01/global-business-leaders-support-esg-convergence-by-committing-to-stakeholder-capitalism-metrics-73b5e9f13d/ [Last accessed on: 4 October 2021].

Hoogendoorn, B., Pennings, E., & Thurik, R. (2010). *What do we know about social entrepreneurship: An analysis of empirical research.* Report series: Research in management. Rotterdam.

Horoszowski, M. (2020, September 1). *Using the business model canvas as a social enterprise.* Retrieved from: https://blog.movingworlds.org/business-model-canvas-for-social-enterprise/ [Last accessed on: 29 October 2021].

Hospitals Beyond Boundaries. (2022). *Our mission.* Retrieved from: https://hbb.org.my/about [Last accessed on: 02 February 2022].

Huang, C. C., & Donner, B. (2018). *The development of social enterprise: Evidence from Europe, North America, and Asia.* Huamin Research Centre. Research Report 40, 1–14.

Huybrechts, B., & Nicholls, A. (2012). Social entrepreneurship: Definitions, drivers and challenges. In *Social entrepreneurship and social business.* Wiesbaden: Gabler Verlag, 31–48.

Huysentruyt, M., Le Coq, C., Mair, J., Rimac, T., & Stephan, U. (2016). *Social entrepreneurship as a force for more inclusive and innovative societies: Cross-country report.* SEFORÏS Report.

IDEO. (2021). *What is design thinking?* Retrieved from: https://www.ideou.com/blogs/ inspiration/what-is-design-thinking [Last accessed on: 22 October 2021].

IDEO.org. (2021). *Human-centered design sits at the intersection of empathy and creativity.* Retrieved from: https://www.ideo.org/tools [Last accessed on: 22 October 2021].

IESE. (2009). *La Fageda: Social integration through manufacturing.* Retrieved from: https://www.ieseinsight.com/doc.aspx?id=984&ar=3 [Last accessed on: 16 September 2020].

Imbali Visual Literacy Project. (2020). *Imbali visual literacy project: General information.* Retrieved from: https://www.facebook.com/pg/Imbali-Visual-Literacy-Project-153237654745539/about/?ref=page_internal [Last accessed on: 12 August 2020].

Impact Amplifier. (2021). *Accelerating social enterprises.* Retrieved from: https://www.impactamplifier.co.za/what-we-do/accelerating-social-enterprises [Last accessed on: 04 April 2021].

Impact Hub. (2021). *Get to know us: Frequently asked questions.* Retrieved from: https://impacthub.net/get-to-know-us/#frequent [Last accessed on: 04 April 2021].

Impact Management Project. (2021). *How much.* Retrieved from: https://impactmanagement-project.com/impact-management/impact-management-norms/how-much/ [Last accessed on: 1 October 2021].

Inter-American Development Bank. (2021). *Grants.* Retrieved from: https://www.iadb.org/en/about-us/grants [Last accessed on: 12 March 2021].

International Cooperative Alliance. (2021). *Our history: The Rochdale pioneers.* Retrieved from: https://www.ica.coop/en/cooperatives/history-cooperative-movement [Last accessed on: 22 October 2021].

International Finance Corporation. (2019). *Creating impact: The promise of impact investing.* World Bank Document.

Ireland, R. D., & Hirc, M. A. (1992). Mission statements: Importance, challenge, and recommendations for development. *Business Horizons, 35*(3), 34–42.

Izuka, U. (2020). *Funding Wiki reflections - Funding forms.* Course on social entrepreneurship, Oxford Department for Continuing Education.

Janelidze, N. (2020). Regional features of social entrepreneurship development and Georgia. *European Journal of Marketing and Economics, 3*(1), 106–121.

Jeong, B. (2017). South Korea: Government directed social enterprise development: Toward a new Asian social enterprise country model☆. In Kerlin, J. A. (Ed.). *Shaping social enterprise.* Bingley: Emerald Publishing Limited., Chapter 3, 49–77.

Johansson-Sköldberg, U., Woodilla, J., & Çetinkaya, M. (2013). Design thinking: Past, present and possible futures. *Creativity and Innovation Management, 22*(2), 121–146.

Kalafatas, J. (2006). *Approaches to scaling social impact.* Retrieved from https://centers.fuqua.duke.edu/case/wp-content/uploads/sites/7/2015/02/Presentation_Kalafatas_ApproachesToScalingSocialImpact_2006.pdf [Last accessed on: 13 January 2022].

Kelley, B. (2019, February 1). *8 Design thinking flaws and how to fix them.* Retrieved from: https://customerthink.com/8-design-thinking-flaws-and-how-to-fix-them/ [Last accessed on: 1 November 2021].

Kerlin, J. A. (2012). Defining social enterprise across different contexts: A conceptual framework based on institutional factors. In *Social enterprises.* London: Palgrave Macmillan, 91–117.

Kerlin, J. A. (Ed). (2017). *Shaping social enterprise: Understanding institutional context and influence.* Bingley: Emerald Publishing Limited.

Ketterman, S. (2018). *Exploring the reasons for design thinking criticism.* Retrieved from: https://www.toptal.com/designers/product-design/design-thinking-criticism [Last accessed on: 1 November 2021].

Keup, M. (2020, February 11). *Pilot Study – How to make it work.* Retrieved from: https://www.projectmanager.com/blog/pilot-study [Last accessed on: 11 October 2021].

Kickul, J., & Lyons, T. S. (2020). *Understanding social entrepreneurship: The relentless pursuit of mission in an ever changing world*. New York: Routledge.

Kimbell, L. (2011). Rethinking design thinking: Part I. *Design and Culture, 3*(3), 285–306.

Kleemann, L. (2014). *Business models in social entrepreneurship and social business*. Heldenrat, 27/01/2014. Retrieved from: https://www.researchgate.net/publication/260917398_Business_models_in_Social_Entrepreneurship_and_Social_Business [Last accessed on: 10 December 2021].

Kolko, J. (2015, September). *Design thinking comes of age*. Retrieved from: https://hbr.org/2015/09/design-thinking-comes-of-age [Last accessed on: 18 October 2021].

Kordant Philanthropy Advisors. (2014). *Social enterprises in Asia: An introductory guide*. Research report, 1–10. Retrieved from: https://www.issuelab.org/resources/18117/18117.pdf [Last accessed on: 12 May 2021].

Korea Social Enterprise Promotion Agency. (2021). *The driving force for inclusive growth, a trusted companion for social economy enterprises*. Retrieved from: https://www.socialenterprise.or.kr/_engsocial/?m_cd=0101 [Last accessed on: 12 September 2021].

Korhan, J. (2013). *Built in social essential social marketing practices for every small business* (1st ed.). Hoboken: Wiley.

Kotter, J. P. (2012). *Leading change*. Boston, MA: Harvard Business Press.

Kotter. J. P. (2021). *The 8-step process for leading change*. Retrieved from: https://www.kotterinc.com/8-steps-process-for-leading-change/ [Last accessed on: 22 November 2021].

Kummitha, R. K. R. (2018). Institutionalising design thinking in social entrepreneurship: A contextual analysis into social and organizational processes, *Social Enterprise Journal, 14*(1), 92–107.

Lanteri, A. (2015). The creation of social enterprises: Some lessons from Lebanon. *Journal of Social Entrepreneurship, 6*(1), 42–69.

Lazer, W., & Kelley, E. (1973). *Social marketing: Perspectives and viewpoints*. Homewood, IL: Irwin.

Leadbeater, C. (1997). *The rise of the social entrepreneur*. London: Demos.

Lefebvre, C. R. (2008). *Segmenting Black America*. Retrieved from: https://socialmarketing.blogs.com/r_craiig_lefebvres_social/2008/07/segmenting-black-america.html [Last accessed on: 09 January 2022].

Lefebvre, R. C. (2013). *Social marketing and social change: Strategies and tools for improving health, well-being, and the environment*. Hoboken: John Wiley & Sons.

LendingCrowd. (2015, December 29). *A brief history of crowdfunding*. Retrieved from: https://www.lendingcrowd.com/blog/a-brief-history-of-crowdfunding#:~:text=So%20where%20did%20crowdfunding%20start,low%2Dincome%20families%20in%20Ireland. [Last accessed on: 13 January 2022].

Lester, J. N., Cho, Y., & Lochmiller, C. R. (2020). Learning to do qualitative data analysis: A starting point. *Human Resource Development Review, 19*(1), 94–106.

Liberty & Justice. (2020). Liberty & Justice: About. Retrieved from: https://libertyandjustice.com/#about [Last accessed on: 8 December 2020].

London Early Years Foundation. (2020). *39 nursery and pre-schools across London. Welcome to London Early Years Foundation*. Retrieved from: https://www.leyf.org.uk/about/ [Last accessed on: 7 October 2020].

Luke, B., Barraket, J., & Eversole, R. (2013). Measurement as legitimacy versus legitimacy of measures: Performance evaluation of social enterprise. *Qualitative Research in Accounting & Management 10*(3/4), 234–258.

Lukjanska, R., Kuznecova, J., & Cirule, I. (2017). The development of social entrepreneurship in Latvia: The role of municipalities. *International Journal of Business and Globalisation, 18*(3), 318–336.

Luminary Bakery. (2021). *About us*. Retrieved from: https://luminarybakery.com/pages/about-us [Last accessed on: 23 April 2021].

Maas, K., & Liket, K. (2011). Social impact measurement: Classification of methods. In *Environmental management accounting and supply chain management*. Dordrecht: Springer, 171–202.

Mair, J., & Martí, I. (2006). Social entrepreneurship research: A source of explanation, prediction, and delight. *Journal of World Business*, 41(1), 36–44.

Mair, J., & Noboa, E. (2006). Social entrepreneurship: How intentions to create a social venture are formed. In *Social entrepreneurship*). London: Palgrave Macmillan, 121–135.

Mair, J., & Schoen, O. (2007). Successful social entrepreneurial business models in the context of developing economies: An explorative study. *International Journal of Emerging Markets*, 2(1), 54–68.

Mair, J., Wolf, M., Rathert, N., & Ioan, A. (2017). *Policy brief on governance of social enterprises*. SEFORÏS European Policy Brief, 10 April 2017. Retrieved from: https://www.hiig.de/en/publication/policy-brief-on-governance-of-social-enterprises/ [Last accessed on: 04 February 2021].

Malaika. (2020a). *Handcrafted luxury*. Retrieved from: https://malaikalinens.com/pages/handmade-luxury [Last accessed on: 12 February 2021].

Malaika. (2020b). *Our story*. Retrieved from: https://malaikalinens.com/pages/luxury-social-responsibility [Last accessed on: 12 February 2021].

Mamabolo, A., & Myres, K. (2020). Performance measurement in emerging market social enterprises using a balanced scorecard. *Journal of Social Entrepreneurship*, 11(1), 65–87.

Manetti, G. (2014). The role of blended value accounting in the evaluation of socio-economic impact of social enterprises. *Voluntas: International Journal of Voluntary and Nonprofit Organizations*, 25(2), 443–464.

Marchington, M. (1995). Fairy tales and magic wands: new employment practices in perspective. *Employee Relations*, 17(1), 51–66.

Margiono, A., Zolin, R., & Chang, A. (2018). A typology of social venture business model configurations. *International Journal of Entrepreneurial Behavior and Research*, 24(3), 626–650.

Martin, R. L., & Osberg, S. (2007). Social entrepreneurship: The case for definition. *Stanford Social Innovation Review*. Spring 2007, 28–39.

Mason, C., Kirkbride, J., & Bryde, D. (2007). From stakeholders to institutions: the changing face of social enterprise governance theory. *Management Decision*, 45(2), 284–301.

Massa, L., Tucci, C. L., & Afuah, A. (2017). A critical assessment of business model research. *Academy of Management Annals*, 11(1), 73–104.

Mayamiko. (2021a). *Our promises*. Retrieved from: https://www.mayamiko.com/pages/mayamiko-and-the-planet [Last accessed: 20/01/2022]

Mayamiko. (2021b). *Our story*. Retrieved from: https://www.mayamiko.com/pages/mayamiko-the-label [Last accessed: 20/01/2022]

McCarthy, E. J. (1964), *Basic marketing*. Homewood, IL: Richard D. Irwin.

McCarthy, K., Emme, L., & Glasgo, L. (2019). *IRIS+ CORE METRICS SETS*. Retrieved from: https://s3.amazonaws.com/giin-web-assets/iris/assets/files/guidance/20190507-IRIS-FND-Core%20Metrics%20Sets_r8.pdf [Last accessed on: 4 October 2021].

Meadows, D. (1999, December). *Leverage points: Places to intervene in a system*. Hartland, VT: The Sustainability Institute.

Medic. (2021). *Building tools for people who care*. Retrieved from: https://medic.org/?ref=-remoteindex [Last accessed on: 22 April 2021].

Merrett, C. D., & Walzer, N. (2016). History of cooperatives Brett Fairbaim. In *Cooperatives and local development: Theory and applications for the 21st century*. New York: Routledge.

Mincher, H. (2021, May 4). *Expert essays: An agony aunt's guide to social media*. Retrieved from: https://www.the-sse.org/news/expert-essays-an-agony-aunts-guide-to-social-media/ [Last accessed on: 30 December 2021].

Mintzberg, H., & Waters, J. A. (1985). Of strategies, deliberate and emergent. *Strategic Management Journal, 6*(3), 257–272.

Mirvis, P., & Googins, B. (2018). Catalyzing social entrepreneurship in Africa: Roles for western universities, NGOs and corporations. *Africa Journal of Management, 4*(1), 57–83.

Mitticool. (2020). *About us.* Retrieved from: https://mitticool.com/about-us/ Last accessed on: 16 December 2020].

Monroe-White, T., & Coskun, M. E. (2017). An updated quantitative assessment of Kerlin's macro-institutional social enterprise framework. In Kerlin, J. A. (Ed.). *Shaping social enterprise.* Bingley: Emerald Publishing Limited, Chapter 2, 27–48.

Montgomery, M. (2015). *What entrepreneurs can learn from the philanthropic struggles of TOMS shoes.* Retrieved from: https://www.forbes.com/sites/mikemontgomery/2015/04/28/how-entrepreneurs-can-avoid-the-philanthropy-pitfalls/?sh=6c49f1291c38 [Last accessed on: 14 December 2020].

Moore, G. (2005). Corporate character: Modern virtue ethics and the virtuous corporation. *Business Ethics Quarterly, 15*(4), 659–685.

Mulgan, G. (2006). The process of social innovation. *Innovations: Technology, Governance, Globalization, 1*(2), 145–162.

Murphy, P. E., Laczniak, G. R., & Wood, G. (2007). An ethical basis for relationship marketing: A virtue ethics perspective. *European Journal of Marketing, 41*(1/2), 37–57.

Nee, E. (2015, February 18). Learning from failure. *Stanford Social Innovation Review.* Retrieved from: https://ssir.org/articles/entry/learning_from_failure [Last accessed on: 22 November 2021].

Nega, B., & Schneider, G. (2014). Social entrepreneurship, microfinance, and economic development in Africa. *Journal of Economic Issues, 48*(2), 367–376.

NESsT. (2020). *Annual report 2018–2019. Dignified employment and the metrics behind it.* Retrieved from: https://www.nesst.org/annual-report-2018-2019-presenting-dignified-employment-metrics [Last accessed on: 23 March 2021].

New Economics Foundation (2013). *Economics in policy-making 4. Social CBA and SROI.* Retrieved from: https://www.nefconsulting.com/wp-content/uploads/2014/10/Briefing-on-SROI-and-CBA.pdf [Last accessed on: 7 October 2021].

New Philanthropy Capital. (2010). *Social return on investment. Position paper.* London: New Philanthropy Capital.

New Philanthropy Capital. (2012). *Principles of Good Impact Reporting for Charities and Social Enterprises.* London: New Philanthropy Capital. Retrieved from: https://www.thinknpc.org/wp-content/uploads/2018/07/Principles-of-good-impact-reporting-final.pdf [Last accessed on: 28 January 2022].

Nicholls, J. (2019). *Insights from Jeremy Nicholls.* In Theme 2: Impact frameworks & standards. Impacting Responsibly Report.

O'Connell, H. (2009). *Costa Rican farmers' cooperative diversify and succeed.* Retrieved from: http://stories.coop/stories/costa-rican-farmers%C2%92-cooperative-diversify-and-succeed/ [Last accessed on: 9 September 2020].

OECD, & European Commission: Directorate-General for Employment, Social Affairs and Inclusion. (2017). *Boosting social enterprise development: Good practice compendium.* OECD Publishing.

OECD. (2013). *Policy brief on social entrepreneurship.* Retrieved from: https://www.oecd.org/cfe/leed/Social%20entrepreneurship%20policy%20brief%20EN_FINAL.pdf [Last accessed on: 28 November 2020].

Office for Civil Society. (2021) *About us.* Retrieved from: https://www.gov.uk/government/organisations/office-for-civil-society/about [Last accessed on: 26 February 2021].

Ogilvy, J. (2015). Scenario planning and strategic forecasting. *Forbes.* Retrieved from: https://www.forbes.com/sites/stratfor/2015/01/08/scenario-planning-and-strategic-forecasting/ [Last accessed: 25 January 2022]

Olsen, S., & Galimidi, B. (2008). *Catalog of approaches to impact measurement: Assessing social impact in private ventures.* Social Venture Technology Group with the support of The Rockfeller Foundation.

One Acre Fund. (2021). *What we do.* Retrieved from: https://oneacrefund.org/what-we-do/ [Last accessed on: 22 April 2021].

Onkka, A. (2017). *Theory of change explainer.* Retrieved from: https://www.youtube.com/watch?v=BJDN0cpxJv4&ab_channel=AlOnkka [Last accessed on: 25 October 2021].

Orejas, R., Buckland, H., & Castizo, R. (2016). *Study of social entrepreneurship and innovation ecosystems in the Latin American Pacific Alliance Countries.* Inter-American Development Bank, Office of the Multilateral Investment Fund Technical Note IDB-TN-1148

Osterwalder, A., Pigneur, Y., & Tucci, C. L. (2005). Clarifying business models: Origins, present, and future of the concept. *Communications of the Association for Information Systems, 16*(1), 1.

Ovans, A. (2015, January 23). What is a business model? *Harvard Business Review.* Retrieved from: https://hbr.org/2015/01/what-is-a-business-model [Last accessed on: 08 February 2021].

Oxfam, G. B. (2017). *History of Oxfam: Over 75 years. One amazing movement to end poverty.* Retrieved from: https://www.oxfam.org.uk/what-we-do/about-us/history-of-oxfam [Last accessed on: 20 October 2020].

Oxford College of Marketing. (2016). *What is a PESTEL analysis.* Retrieved from: https://blog.oxfordcollegeofmarketing.com/2016/06/30/pestel-analysis/ [Last accessed on: 11 November 2021].

Pandey, S., Kim, M., & Pandey, S. K. (2017). Do mission statements matter for nonprofit performance? Insights from a study of US performing arts organizations. *Nonprofit Management and Leadership, 27*(3), 389–410.

Pannozzo, A. (2015, September 9). *Why design thinking initiatives fail.* Retrieved from: https://www.continuuminnovation.com/en/how-we-think/blog/why-design-thinking-initiatives-fail [Last accessed on: 3 November 2021].

Parkinson, C., & Howorth, C. (2008). The language of social entrepreneurs. *Entrepreneurship and regional development, 20*(3), 285–309.

Partners in Health (2020). *Organisation general information.* Retrieved from https://www.pih.org/ [Last accessed on: 1 October 2020].

Parzefall, M., & Kuppelwieser, V. G. (2012). Understanding the antecedents, the outcomes and the mediating role of social capital: An employee perspective. *Human Relations, 65,* 447–472.

Pasricha, P., & Rao, M. K. (2018). The effect of ethical leadership on employee social innovation tendency in social enterprises: Mediating role of perceived social capital. *Creativity and Innovation Management, 27*(3), 270–280.

Pastorek, W. (2013). Africa's first fair-trade garment manufacturer is a model for women's empowerment. *Fast Company,* 05/11/2013. Retrieved from: https://www.fastcompany.com/3021131/africas-first-fair-trade-garment-manufacturer-is-a-model-for-womens-empowe#5 [Last accessed on: 8 December 2020].

Pearce, J. A., & David, F. (1987). Corporate mission statements: The bottom line. *Academy of Management Perspectives, 1*(2), 109–115.

Peattie, K., & Morley, A. S. (2008). *Social enterprises: Diversity and dynamics, contexts and contributions.* Social Enterprise Coalition and Economic and Social Research Council.

Peersman, G. (2014). *Overview: Data collection and analysis methods in impact evaluation.* UNICEF Office of Research-Innocenti.

Peredo, A. M., & McLean, M. (2006). Social entrepreneurship: A critical review of the concept. *Journal of World Business, 41*(1), 56–65.

Pereira, D. (2021, July 18). *Google business model.* Retrieved from: https://businessmodelanalyst.com/google-business-model/ [Last accessed on: 19 December 2021].

Persaud, R., Dixon, J., & Thorlby, K. (2017). *Exploring: Social entrepreneurs and failure.* UnLtd's Explore papers.

Phaal, R. (2020). *Engineering the future by design: Anticipating and responding to disruption and transformative change through collaboration.* The Fifth Cambridge-UTokyo Joint Symposium "UTokyo-Cambridge Voices"

Phillips W, Lee H, Ghobadian A, O'Regan N, James P. (2015). Social innovation and social entrepreneurship: A systematic review. *Group & Organization Management, 40*(3), 428–461.

Phills, J. A., Deiglmeier, K., & Miller, D. T. (2008). Rediscovering social innovation. *Stanford Social Innovation Review, 6*(4), 34–43.

Pono, M. (2018, August 15). *Competitive analysis: How to conduct a comprehensive competitive analysis.* Retrieved from: https://www.mykpono.com/how-to-conduct-competitive-analysis/ [Last accessed on: 14 August 2021].

Porter, L. W., & Lawler, E. E. (1968). Managerial attitudes and performance. In Rollinson, D. (2002). *Organisational behaviour and analysis.* New York: Pearson.

Porter, M. E. (1979). How competitive forces shape strategy. *Harvard Business Review, 57*(2), 137–145.

Prabhu, G. N. (1999). Social entrepreneurship leadership. *Career Development International, 4*(3), 140–145.

Prabhu, J. (2017). Frugal innovation: Doing more with less for more. *Philosophical Transactions of the Royal Society Series A, 375*(2095), 1–22.PricewaterhouseCoopers NL. (2018). *Early opportunities: Cooperation between social enterprises and municipalities in the Netherlands.* PwC report.

Radjou, N., Prabhu, J., & Ahuja, S. (2012). *Jugaad innovation: Think frugal, be flexible, generate breakthrough growth.* Hoboken: John Wiley & Sons.

Rafiq, M., & Ahmed, P. K. (1995). Using the 7Ps as a generic marketing mix: An exploratory survey of UK and European marketing academics. *Marketing intelligence & planning, 13*(9), 4–15.

Rapson, C. (2021, December 1). *Don't fear the P-word! Why social enterprises should be proud of profit.* Retrieved from: https://www.the-sse.org/news/dont-fear-the-p-word-why-social-enterprises-should-be-proud-of-profit/?utm_source=SSE+newsletter&utm_campaign=308ed486ce-EMAIL_CAMPAIGN_2021_12_02_09_46&utm_medium=email&utm_term=0_37ebc0341a-308ed486ce-325498965 [Last accessed on: 3 December 2021].

Rasmussen, B. (2007). *Business models and the theory of the firm.* Working Paper No. 32, Pharmaceutical Industry Project Working Paper Series.

Rawhouser, H., Cummings, M., & Newbert, S. L. (2019). Social impact measurement: Current approaches and future directions for social entrepreneurship research. *Entrepreneurship Theory and Practice, 43*(1), 82–115.

Reason Digital (2020). *Reason Digital: general information.* Retrieved from: https://reasondigital.com/ [Last accessed on: 7 December 2020].

Riders for Health. (2017). *Our history: Access of healthcare to the last mile.* Retrieved from: https://ridersintl.org/our-history/# [Last accessed on: 5 October 2020].

Ridley-Duff, R. (2009). Co-operative social enterprises: Company rules, access to finance and management practice. *Social Enterprise Journal, 5*(1), 50–68.

Ridley-Duff, R., & Bull, M. (2011). *Understanding social enterprise: Theory and practice.* London: SAGE.

Right to Dream. (2022). *How we work.* Retrieved from: https://www.righttodream.com/howwework [Last accessed on: 23 January 2022].

Roberts Enterprise Development Fund. (2018). *20+ years of impact.* Retrieved from: https://redf.org/about/our-story/ [Last accessed on: 10 November 2020]

Robinson, J. A., & Acemoglu, D. (2012). *Why nations fail: The origins of power, prosperity and poverty.* London: Profile.

Roetman, E., & De Greve, P. (2018). Measuring performance and impact of a social business: Reflections from practice. In van der Velden, F. (Ed.), *Towards a fair and just economy*, Voorhaven: LM Publishers.

Roy, K., & Karna, A. (2015). Doing social good on a sustainable basis: Competitive advantage of social businesses. *Management Decision*, *53*(6), 1355–1374.

Saebi, T., Foss, N. J., & Linder, S. (2019). Social entrepreneurship research: Past achievements and future promises. *Journal of Management*, *45*(1), 70–95.

Santos, F. M. (2012). A positive theory of social entrepreneurship. *Journal of Business Ethics*, *111*(3), 335–351.

SAP. (2018, October 29). *Why social entrepreneurs and big business need each other more than ever*. Retrieved from: https://news.sap.com/2018/10/sap-social-enterprises-big-business-need-each-other/ [Last accessed on: 04 March 2021].

Schein, E. H. (1984). Coming to a new awareness of organisational culture. *Sloan Management Review*, *25*(2), 3–16.

Schmarzo, B. (2017). *Can design thinking unleash organizational innovation?* Vienna: Kyklos.

Schumpeter, J. A. (1911). *Theorie der wirtschaftlichen Entwicklung* (transl. 1934, The Theory of Economic Development: An inquiry into profits, capital, credit, interest and the business cycle). Vienna: Kyklos.

Schumpeter, J. A. (1942). *Socialism, capitalism and democracy*. New York: Harper and Brothers.

Schwab Foundation. (2021a). *Awards – All awardees. Our global community*. Retrieved from: https://www.schwabfound.org/awardees?award=Social+Entrepreneur&page=16&q=&region_of_impact=&sector=&year_awarded= [Last accessed on: 12 April 2021].

Schwab Foundation. (2021b). *About: Our story*. Retrieved from: https://www.schwabfound.org/about [Last accessed on: 10 November 2020].

Seelos, C., & Mair, J. (2005). Social entrepreneurship: Creating new business models to serve the poor. *Business Horizons*, *48*(3), 241–246.

Seelos, C., & Mair, J. (2017). *Innovation and scaling for impact: How effective social enterprises do it*. Stanford, CA: Stanford University Press.

Semwal, L. P. (2018). A case of apples in the Himalayas: The story of a successful social business. In van der Velden (Ed.), *Towards a fair and just economy*, Voorhaven: LM Publishers, 19–39.

Senge, P., Hamilton, H., & Kania, J. (2015). The dawn of system leadership. *Stanford Social Innovation Review*, *13*(1), 27–33.

Sengupta, S., Sahay, A., & Croce, F. (2018). Conceptualizing social entrepreneurship in the context of emerging economies: an integrative review of past research from BRIICS. *International Entrepreneurship and Management Journal*, *14*(4), 771–803.

Serrano, L., Bose, M., Arenas, D., Berger, G., Márquez, P., Lozano, G.,..., & Fischer, R. M. (2006). *Effective management of social enterprises: Lessons from businesses and civil society organizations in Iberoamerica*. Washington, D.C.: Inter-American Development Bank.

Shane, S. (2012). Reflections on the 2010 AMR decade award: Delivering on the promise of entrepreneurship as a field of research. *Academy of Management Review*, *37*(1), 10–20.

Shane, S., & Venkataraman, S. (2000). The promise of entrepreneurship as a field of research. *Academy of Management Review*, *25*, 217–226.

Sharir, M., & Lerner, M. (2006). Gauging the success of social ventures initiated by individual social entrepreneurs. *Journal of World Business*, *41*(1), 6–20.

Sharra, R., & Nyssens, M. (2010). Social innovation: An interdisciplinary and critical review of the concept. *Université Catholique de Louvain Belgium*, 1–15.

SHRM. (2021). *Understanding organizational structures*. Retrieved from: https://www.shrm.org/resourcesandtools/tools-and-samples/toolkits/pages/understandingorganizationalstructures.aspx [Last accessed on: 02 January 2022].

Simms, S. V. K., & Robinson, J. A. (2008). Activist or entrepreneur?: An identity-based model of social entrepreneurship. In *International perspectives on social entrepreneurship*. Basingstoke and New York: Palgrave Macmillan, 9–26.

Skoll Foundation. (2006). *Riders for health*. Retrieved from: https://skoll.org/organization/riders-for-health/ [Last accessed on: 5 October 2020].

Skoll Foundation. (2013). *Crisis action*. Retrieved from: https://skoll.org/organization/crisis-action/ [Last accessed on: 25 November 2020].

Smiles, A. (2019, October 11). *Should you get B Corp certified?*. Retrieved from: https://gusto.com/blog/growth/b-corp-certification [Last accessed on: 24 January 2022].

Smith, W. K., Binns, A., & Tushman, M. L. (2010). Complex business models: Managing strategic paradoxes simultaneously. *Long Range Planning, 43*(2–3), 448–461.

Smith, W., & Darko, E. (2014). *Social enterprise: Constraints and opportunities–evidence from Vietnam and Kenya*. Overseas Development Institute report series.

So, I., Staskevicius, A., & Ebrahim, A. (2015). *Measuring the "impact" in impact investing*. Harvard Business School Social Enterprise Initiative.

Social Business Design. (2021). *Social business model canvas. What it is and how to use it*. Retrieved from: https://socialbusinessdesign.org/what-is-a-social-business-model-canvas/ [Last accessed on: 30 October 2021].

Social Enterprise Academy Africa. (2021). *Prospectus*. Retrieved from: https://www.socialenterprise.academy/za/programmes-prospectus [Last accessed on: 04 April 2021].

Social Enterprise Institute. (2021). *Social business model canvas. A tool to help plan, communicate and refine your business model in a simple, visual way*. Retrieved from: https://socialenterpriseinstitute.co/wp-content/uploads/2018/12/Social-Business-Model-Canvas.pdf [Last accessed on: 30 October 2021].

Social Enterprise UK. (2019). *Capitalism in crisis? Transforming our economy for people and planet -SOSE 2019*.

Social Enterprise UK. (2020). *The London early years foundation*. Retrieved from: https://www.socialenterprise.org.uk/media-centre/case-studies/public-services/the-london-early-years-foundation/ [Last accessed on: 7 October 2020].

Social Enterprise World Forum. (2021). *What is a social enterprise?* Retrieved from: https://sewfonline.com/about/about-social-enterprise/ [Last accessed on: 7 November 2021].

Social Enterprise World Forum. (2020). *Features – Ethical transparency and accountability*. Retrieved from: https://sewfonline.com/home/social-enterprise/ [Last accessed on: 04 December 2020].

Social Finance. (2021). *Social impact bonds*. Retrieved from: https://www.socialfinance.org.uk/what-we-do/social-impact-bonds [Last accessed on: 02 April 2021].

Social Sector Network. (2018, November 1). *Broke and idealistic: Why do social enterprises fail?* Retrieved from: https://socialsectornetwork.com/broke-and-idealistic-why-do-social-enterprises-fail/ [Last accessed on: 3 July 2021].

SocialUP. (2017). Design thinking for sustainability of social enterprises – Innovative and high impact solutions for social problems.

SoPact. (2020). *Effective Theory Of Change * Social change theory*. Retrieved from: https://www.youtube.com/watch?v=279Bf4Gb6lk&ab_channel=SoPact [Last accessed on: 25 October 2021].

Soule, S. A. (2013, October 30). *Sarah Soule: How design thinking can help social entrepreneurs*. Retrieved from: https://www.gsb.stanford.edu/insights/sarah-soule-how-design-thinking-can-help-social-entrepreneurs [Last accessed on: 28 October 2021].

Spicer, J., Kay, T., & Ganz, M. (2019). Social entrepreneurship as field encroachment: How a neoliberal social movement constructed a new field. *Socio-Economic Review, 17*(1), 195–227.

Stam, F. C., & Spigel, B. (2016). Entrepreneurial ecosystems. *USE Discussion paper series, 16*(13).

Stanford d.school. (2019). *Navigating Ambiguity | feat. Sarah Stein Greenberg and Scott Doorley.* Retrieved from: https://www.youtube.com/watch?v=4BjQlHDkZ1A&ab_channel=Stanfordd.school [Last accessed on: 25 October 2021].

Stanford d.school. (2020). *d.school Starter Kit.* Retrieved from: https://docs.google.com/presentation/d/1kMROhf-S6z0hLKb7Km0PddUff-wiYkuD5QCNeD8t-Ns/edit#slide=id.g82e1165b32_2_25 [Last accessed on: 25 October 2021].

Stefdr. (2012, January 18). *A brief history of design thinking: The theory [P1].* Retrieved from: https://ithinkidesign.wordpress.com/2012/01/18/a-brief-history-of-design-thinking-the-theory-p1/ [Last accessed on: 22 October 2021].

Stephan, U., & Folmer, E. (2017). *Context and social enterprises: Which environments enable social entrepreneurship?* SEFORÏS European Policy Brief, 15/06/2017.

Strategyzer. (2022). The business model canvas. Retrieved from: https://www.strategyzer.com/canvas/business-model-canvas [Last accessed on: 02 February 2022].

Stroh, D. P. (2015). *Systems thinking for social change: A practical guide to solving complex problems, avoiding unintended consequences, and achieving lasting results.* Hartford (VE): Chelsea Green Publishing.

Szczepanska, J. (2017, January 4). *Design thinking origin story plus some of the people who made it all happen.* Retrieved from: https://szczpanks.medium.com/design-thinking-where-it-came-from-and-the-type-of-people-who-made-it-all-happen-dc3a05411e53 [Last accessed on: 18 October 2021].

Taub, A. (2015, June 23). *Buying TOMS shoes is a terrible way to help poor people.* Retrieved from: https://www.vox.com/2015/7/23/9025975/toms-shoes-poverty-giving [Last accessed on: 14 December 2020].

Teach For All. (2021). *What we do.* Retrieved from: https://teachforall.org/what-we-do#27531 [Last accessed on: 22 April 2021].

TechTycoons. (2020). *Abhi Ramesh.* Retrieved from: https://techtycoons.com/abhi-ramesh/ [Last accessed on: 18 January 2021].

Teece, D. J. (2010). Business models, business strategy and innovation. *Long Range Planning,* 43(2–3), 172–194.

The Business Channel. (2017). *The business model canvas – 9 steps to creating a successful business model – Startup tips.* Retrieved from: https://www.youtube.com/watch?v=IP0cUB-WTgpY&ab_channel=TheBusinessChannel [Last accessed on: 30 October 2021].

The Japan Research Institute. (2016). *Study of social entrepreneurship and innovation ecosystems in South East and East Asian Countries country analysis: Japan.* Inter-American Development Bank, Office of the Multilateral Investment Fund Technical Note IDB-TN-1211, 1–30.

The Korea Bizwire. (2018, April 4). *Gov't to boost policy support for social impact investments.* Retrieved from: http://koreabizwire.com/govt-to-boost-policy-support-for-social-impact-investments/116052 [Last accessed on: 08 September 2021].

The Social Investment Business Group. (2014). *How to measure and report social impact. A guide for investees.* Investing for Good, January 2014.

The Story of Stuff Project (2013). *The story of solutions.* Retrieved from: https://www.youtube.com/watch?v=cpkRvc-sOKk&ab_channel=TheStoryofStuffProject [Last accessed on: 22 November 2021].

The Unilever Foundry. (2021). *Highlights: Explore the latest partnership case studies, upcoming events and news from the tech & innovation world.* Retrieved from: https://www.theunileverfoundry.com/highlights.html [Last accessed on: 08 April 2021].

Third Sector. (2018, September 12). *British Asian Trust announces 'world's largest impact bond for education'.* Retrieved from: https://www.thirdsector.co.uk/british-asian-trust-announces-worlds-largest-impact-bond-education/finance/article/1492576 [Last accessed on: 02 April 2021].

Thompson, J. L. (2002). The world of the social entrepreneur. *The International Journal of Public Sector Management, 15*, 412– 431.

Tiwale. (2022). *Tiwale. Home page*. Retrieved from: https://www.tiwale.org/ [Last accessed on: 02 February 2022].

TOMS Shoes. (2020a). *About TOMS – We are in business to improve lives*. Retrieved from: https://www.toms.com/uk/about-toms.html [Last accessed on: 14 December 2020].

TOMS Shoes. (2020b). *Your impact – 13 years of giving*. Retrieved from: https://www.toms.com/uk/impact-report-emea.html [Last accessed on: 14 December 2020].

Tracey, P., & Jarvis, O. (2007). Toward a theory of social venture franchising. *Entrepreneurship theory and practice, 31*(5), 667–685.

Tracey, P., Phillips, N. and Jarvis, O. (2011). Bridging institutional entrepreneurship and the creation of new organizational forms: A multilevel model. *Organization Science, 22*(1), 60–80.

Triggle, N. (2018, June 24). *The history of the NHS in charts*. Retrieved from: https://www.bbc.co.uk/news/health-44560590 [Last accessed on: 20 November 2020].

Trivedi C. (2010). A social entrepreneurship bibliography. *The Journal of Entrepreneurship, 19*(1), 81–85.

Turner, D., & Martin, S. (2005). Social entrepreneurs and social inclusion: Building local capacity or delivering national priorities? *International Journal of Public Administration, 28*(9–10), 797–806.

Unilever. (2015). *Enhancing livelihoods through partnerships across the value chain*. Retrieved from: https://www.unilever.co.uk/sustainable-living/global-partnerships/enhancing-livelihoods-through-partnerships-across-the-value-chain/ [Last accessed on: 08 April 2021].

Unilever. (2018). *Unilever partnership pledges £40 million to support social enterprises*. Retrieved from: https://www.unilever.com/news/news-and-features/Feature-article/2018/unilever-partnership-pledges-40-million-pounds-to-support-social-enterprises.html [Last accessed on: 08 April 2021].

United Nations Development Programme. (2015). *Impact investment in Africa – Trends, constraints & opportunities*. November 2015, New York: UNDP, One United Nations Plaza.

UpEffect. (2022). *Case study – Threadable*. Retrieved from: https://www.theupeffect.com/ [Last accessed: 24 January 2022]

USAID (2019). *Optional social impact assessment framework*. Retrieved from: https://www.usaid.gov/sites/default/files/documents/1866/USAID-Social-Impact-Assessment-508.pdf [Last accessed on: 24 January 2022].

Value Reporting Foundation. (2021a). *SASB standards & other ESG frameworks*. Retrieved from: https://www.sasb.org/about/sasb-and-other-esg-frameworks/ [Last accessed on: 4 October 2021].

Value Reporting Foundation. (2021b). *Standards overview*. Retrieved from: https://www.sasb.org/standards/ [Last accessed on: 4 October 2021].

van der Velden, F. (2018a). Introduction: Take back the economy. In van der Velden, F. (Ed.), *Towards a fair and just economy*, Voorhaven: LM Publishers, 11–18.

van der Velden, F. (2018b). Social business as an approach to transformational change. In van der Velden, F. (Ed.), *Towards a fair and just economy*, Voorhaven: LM Publishers.

van Dokkum, J. (2018). Shared value creation: The inside story of Pactics in Cambodia. In van der Velden, F. (Ed.), *Towards a fair and just economy*, Voorhaven: LM Publishers

Vanclay, F. (2003). *International principles for social impact assessment. Impact Assessment and Project Appraisal*, 21(1).

Vasi, I. B. (2009). New heroes, old theories? Toward a sociological perspective on social entrepreneurship. In *An introduction to social entrepreneurship: Voices, preconditions, contexts*. Cheltenham and Northampton: Edward Elgar, 155–173.

Vetiver Solutions. (2021). *About us*. Retrieved from: https://www.vetiversolutions.org/about-us/ [Last accessed on: 22 April 2021].

Wā Cup. (2022). *Our crew and supporters.* Retrieved from: https://wacollective.org.nz/pages/our-crew-2 [Last accessed on: 02 February 2022].

Weinreich, N. K. (2010). *Hands-on social marketing: A step-by-step guide to designing change for good.* London: SAGE.

Wei-Skillern, J., Austin, J. E., Leonard, H., & Stevenson, H. (2007). *Entrepreneurship in the social sector* (Vol. 13). London: SAGE.

Weiss C. H. (1995). Nothing as practical as good theory: Exploring theory-based evaluation for comprehensive community initiatives for children and families. In Connell, J. P, Kubisch, A. C., Schorr, L. B., & Weiss, C. H. (Eds) *New approaches to evaluating community initiatives volume 1 concepts, methods and contexts,* Washington DC: The Aspen Institute; 65–92.

Wharton, R., Evans, A. (2020). *Systems change: What it is and how to do it.* Retrieved from: https://londonfunders.org.uk/systems-change-what-it-and-how-do-it#:~:text=-Systems%20change%20is%20about%20addressing,behave%20in%20a%20certain%20 way. [Last accessed on: 28 December 2020].

World Economic Forum. (2020). *Measuring stakeholder capitalism: Towards common metrics and consistent reporting of sustainable value creation.* White paper, September 2020.

World Fair Trade Organisation. (2020). *Definition of Fair Trade.* Retrieved from: https://wfto.com/who-we-are [Last accessed on: 16 December 2020].

World Wildlife Fund (2021). *Deforestation causes.* Retrieved from: https://wwf.panda.org/discover/our_focus/forests_practice/deforestation_causes2/ [Last accessed on: 28 May 2021].

Yankelovich, D., & Meer, D. (2006). Rediscovering market segmentation. *Harvard Business Review, 84*(2), 122–131.

Young, D. R. (2013). *If not for profit, for what?* Washington DC: Lexington Books.

Yu, L. (2020). The emergence of social entrepreneurs in China. *Journal of the International Council for Small Business, 1*(1), 32–35.

Yüksel, I. (2012). Developing a multi-criteria decision making model for PESTEL analysis. *International Journal of Business and Management, 7*(24), 52.

Yunus, M. (2008). *Creating a world without poverty: Social business and the future of capitalism.* New York: Public Affairs Books.

Zahra, S. A., Gedajlovic, E., Neubaum, D. O., & Shulman, J. M. (2009). A typology of social entrepreneurs: Motives, search processes and ethical challenges. *Journal of Business Venturing, 24*(5), 519–532.

Zaman, H. (2004). Microfinance in Bangladesh: Growth, achievements, and lessons. *Scaling Up Poverty Reduction,* Washington DC: Consultative Group to Assist the Poor World Bank Financial Sector Network, 47.

Zbrodoff, S. (2012). *Pilot projects—making innovations and new concepts fly.* Paper presented at PMI® Global Congress 2012—North America, Vancouver, British Columbia, Canada. Newtown Square, PA: Project Management Institute.

Zeschky, M., Widenmayer, B., & Gassmann, O. (2011). Frugal innovation in emerging markets. *Research-Technology Management, 54*(4), 38–45.

Index

Note: **Bold** page numbers refer to tables, *Italic* page numbers refer to figures.

For Product Safety Concerns and Information please contact our EU
representative GPSR@taylorandfrancis.com
Taylor & Francis Verlag GmbH, Kaufingerstraße 24, 80331 München, Germany

www.ingramcontent.com/pod-product-compliance
Ingram Content Group UK Ltd.
Pitfield, Milton Keynes, MK11 3LW, UK
UKHW050930180425
457613UK00015B/352